A WELCOME HOME

A WELCOME HOME
ALEXANDRA KAEHLER

Inviting Interiors

With Hadley Keller
Photographs by Aimée Mazzenga
Styled by Cate Ragan

For my babies, Sadie, Jack, and Finn.
I wanted something that you could see and touch,
to understand what I do at work each day.
And for Spence. None of it would be
possible without you.

Introduction
6

DOUBLE DUTY
10

SHOW AND STEADY
40

BALANCING ACT
66

FRESH TRADITION
98

NEW OLD HOUSE
134

HOUSE PEOPLE
158

GREAT ESCAPE
192

OUR GARDEN HOUSE
222

Acknowledgments
252

About the Author
254

INTRODUCTION

Maybe it's because I'm the daughter of a therapist, but I have always been interested in the psychology of places and things. Growing up, I learned the language and significance of feelings through years of therapy. Once I became a designer, the importance of creating spaces that people feel good in became foremost in my mind. We can think a space is beautiful, but that doesn't mean we want to live in it. Understanding my clients, both how they feel about colors, patterns, textures, and scale, and how they want to live in each space, is my first step in every project.

In some ways, my job as an interior designer could be seen as superficial—glorified shopping—and it is fun to choose fabrics and furniture and accessories. But far more gratifyingly, my job lets me adopt a psychological approach to a practice that could be thought of as purely visual. Designing a home is a deeply personal and collaborative process. The part I love most about what I do is something I never expected: that I can enter people's lives, learn so much about

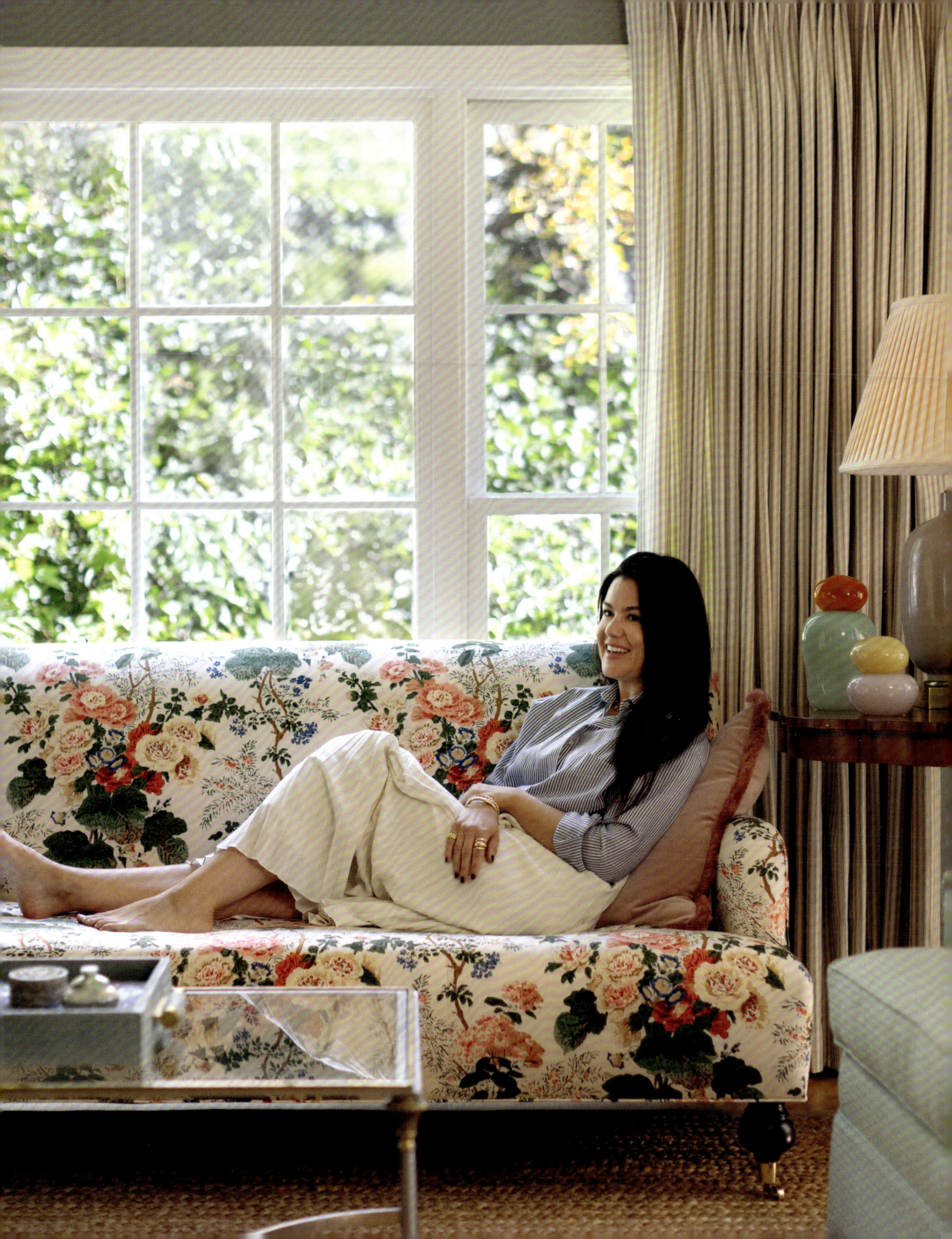

8

them, discover how they want to live, and then design a home that reflects that. The home we make together is not just a collection of pretty rooms; it's the place that best embodies who the homeowners are as people.

With this book, I want readers to discover through our work what their own hopes and dreams and needs are when it comes to their spaces. To state the obvious, your home is where you live your life. It is where exciting things happen and also where mundane things happen. Often, those mundane things are the most meaningful of all. Life happens in the everyday. There is something so special in creating a space that truly feels like home, that personifies you and your family, and then in appreciating that stage it provides for daily life. As I completed the installation of my sister's home ("House People," page 158) just before she gave birth to her first child, she put it so beautifully; she said that we had created a nest in which she would raise her chicks. That really moved me. There is no greater honor than to help create the meaning within the walls of someone's home.

When I begin working with people, I have exercises I use to get to know them. Through our initial meeting I try to find out who they are and how they see themselves. I ask what they want their life to look like in their space. What is the fantasy, and what does that look like in reality? (We know those can differ.) If you want a home to start a family, where will you be changing diapers? If you love to entertain, where will you hide the dirty dishes after you've finished dinner and before your guests have left? If you're looking for your post-retirement, rest-of-your-life home, does that look like comfy couches to envelop you as you read and watch movies, or big closets to store your suitcases for all the travel you plan to do? Perhaps most importantly, how do you want to feel in your space? What I learn about people in those initial conversations informs the way I design their space much more than their preferences when it comes to, say, color and pattern (although those are also important).

For example, a couple I worked with recently was moving from the city to the suburbs. They loved the historic feel and old-world charm of so many of the older homes in their new neighborhood, but they ended up buying a new-build in the middle of its construction ("New Old House," page 134). Central to my work was to make this brand-new home feel like it had history, warmth, and character, which we achieved by adding moldings, herringbone floors, and vintage lighting. But the couple also wanted modern conveniences, so behind those more traditional details, there is an open-plan kitchen and family room, an oversized mudroom, and a large walk-in pantry.

My husband and I both come from large families who live in our town. Several times a month, we have fifteen or more people over for casual dinners. So for my own house ("Our Garden House," page 222), I knew we needed to accommodate big gatherings. I wanted dining spaces that could seat everyone comfortably, while still allowing us to be close together. I wanted a place to easily hide our three young children's toys so our guests—family or otherwise—didn't feel like they were having a dinner party in a playroom. Each design decision was made with quite a bit of thought about how our lives would play out within these walls.

I am a proponent of wabi-sabi, the Japanese aesthetic philosophy of accepting imperfection and impermanence. I firmly believe that beauty lies in the imperfections. We all want our spaces to be beautiful, but we have to actually live in them, too. Marble countertops in a kitchen are lovely, but if you're going to be distraught if they get scratched, then let's use a different material. Let's create a space that you love and that you can truly, happily, and comfortably live in.

In the pages of this book, I will share eight projects that my team and I have designed over the last few years. Yes, I love color and pattern and bold artwork, but I don't have a defined look. Each project I create is reflective of the people who live in that house. In these projects, you'll see my interpretation of each person's vision for their home through my design for them. My wish is that by sharing these projects with you, reader, you will discover how you, too, can create a beautiful home to live in fully and meaningfully.

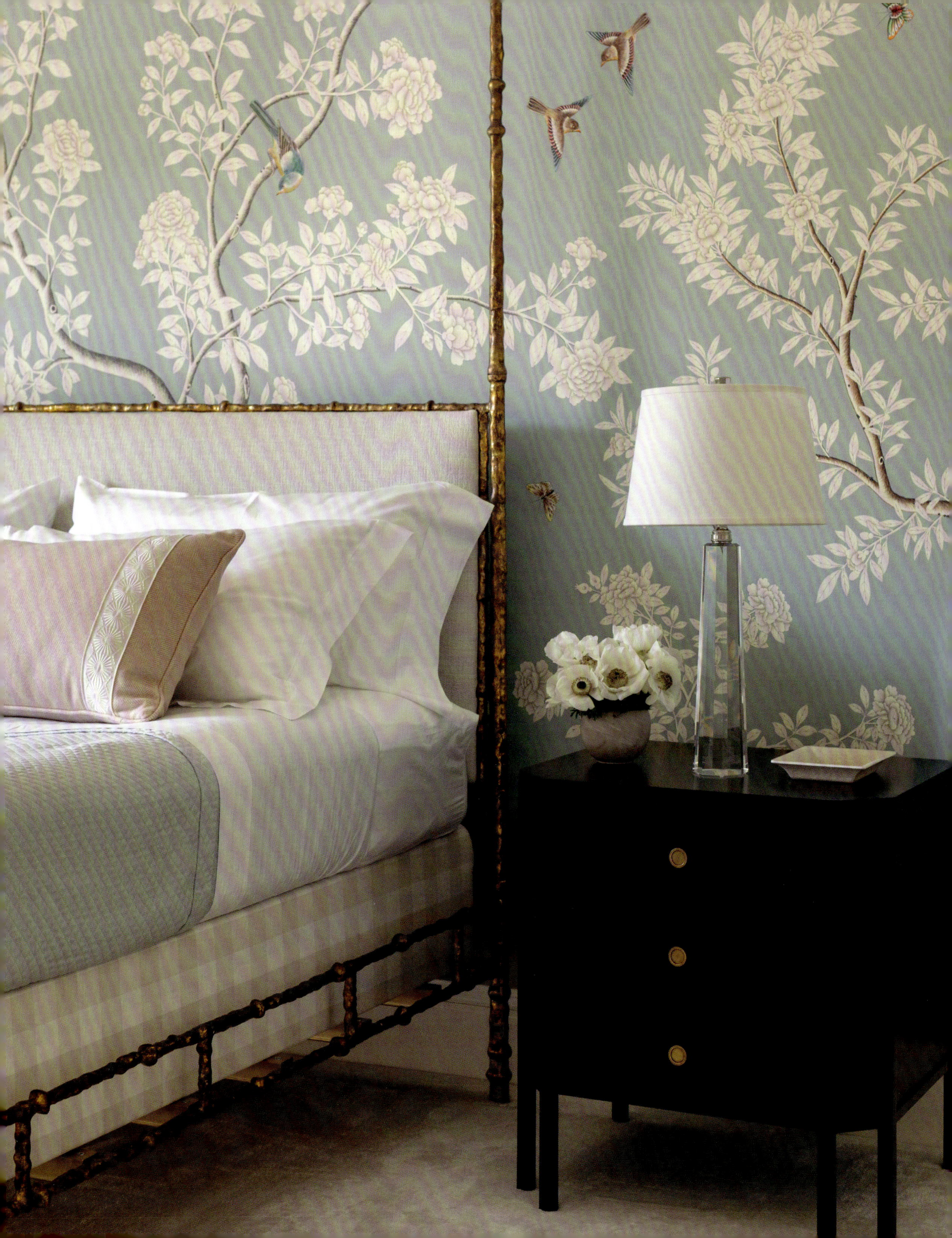

DOUBLE DUTY

An elegant townhouse with an unexpected rooftop oasis

For the bar, which links the kitchen and the dining room, we picked up a powdery blue from the dining room wallpaper and amped it up in high gloss, adding an antiqued mirror backsplash to make the small space feel larger.

When my clients began their house search, they wanted a historic home—but they soon realized that most old homes wouldn't offer the space they needed for their young family. So the direction shifted: Build new but tap a designer who could make the house feel as if it had stood for decades. That's where I came in.

In keeping with their vision, we looked to elegant historic townhomes for inspiration for this house, which is set in the bustling Lincoln Park neighborhood of Chicago. Bunny Mellon's townhouse on the Upper East Side of Manhattan might be the epitome of elegant, but it is also welcoming; I love that the building doesn't feel quintessentially New York—there's something a bit more pastoral about it. We also looked to historic buildings in Chicago, focusing on things like the ironwork and other details that lent personality. One thing the couple hated about most of the new-builds they saw was that many look the same: They all have the same big, white kitchen. The same coffered ceiling. The same moldings, and other heavy-handed details. We wanted to give the house its own identity

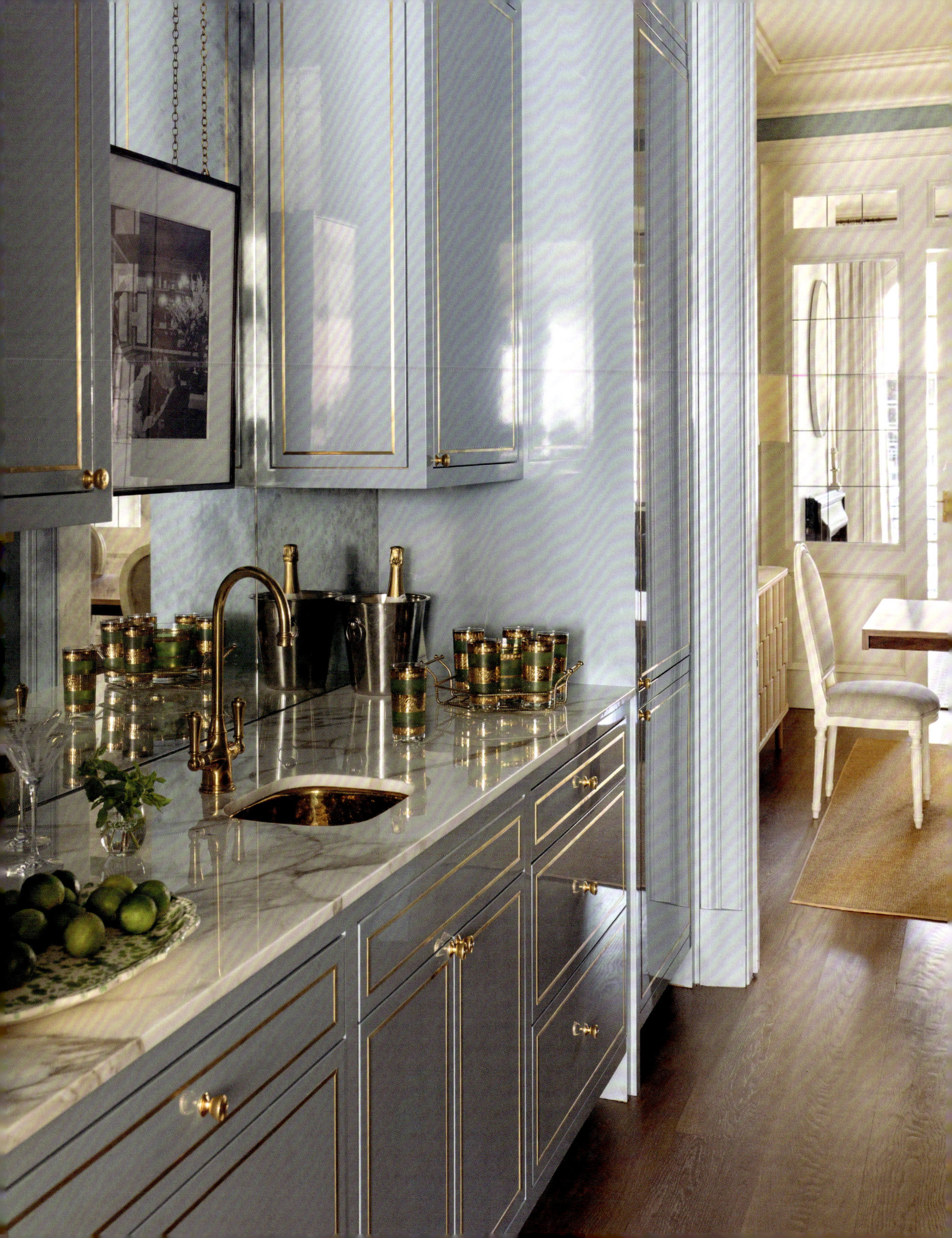

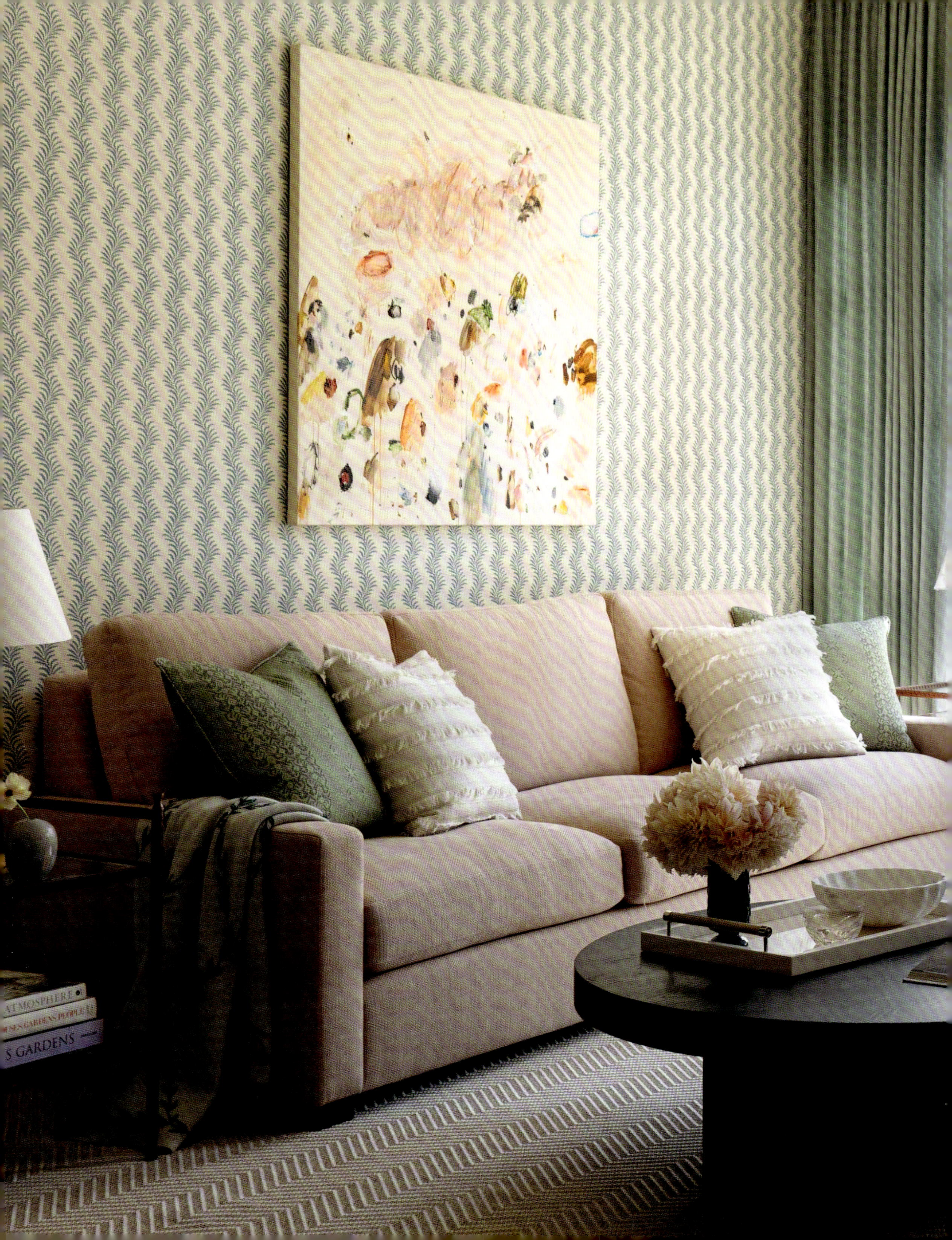
ATMOSPHERE
S GARDENS

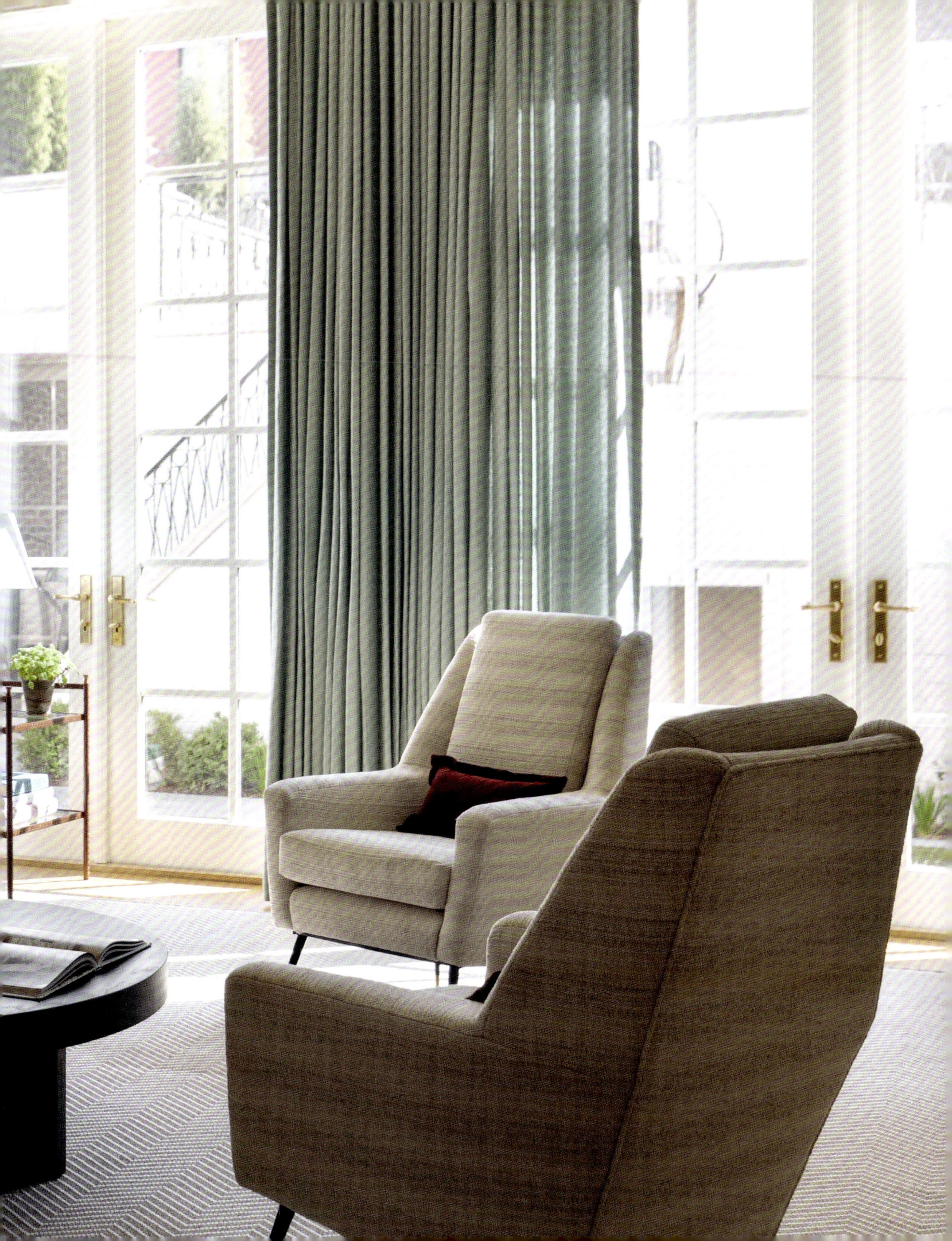

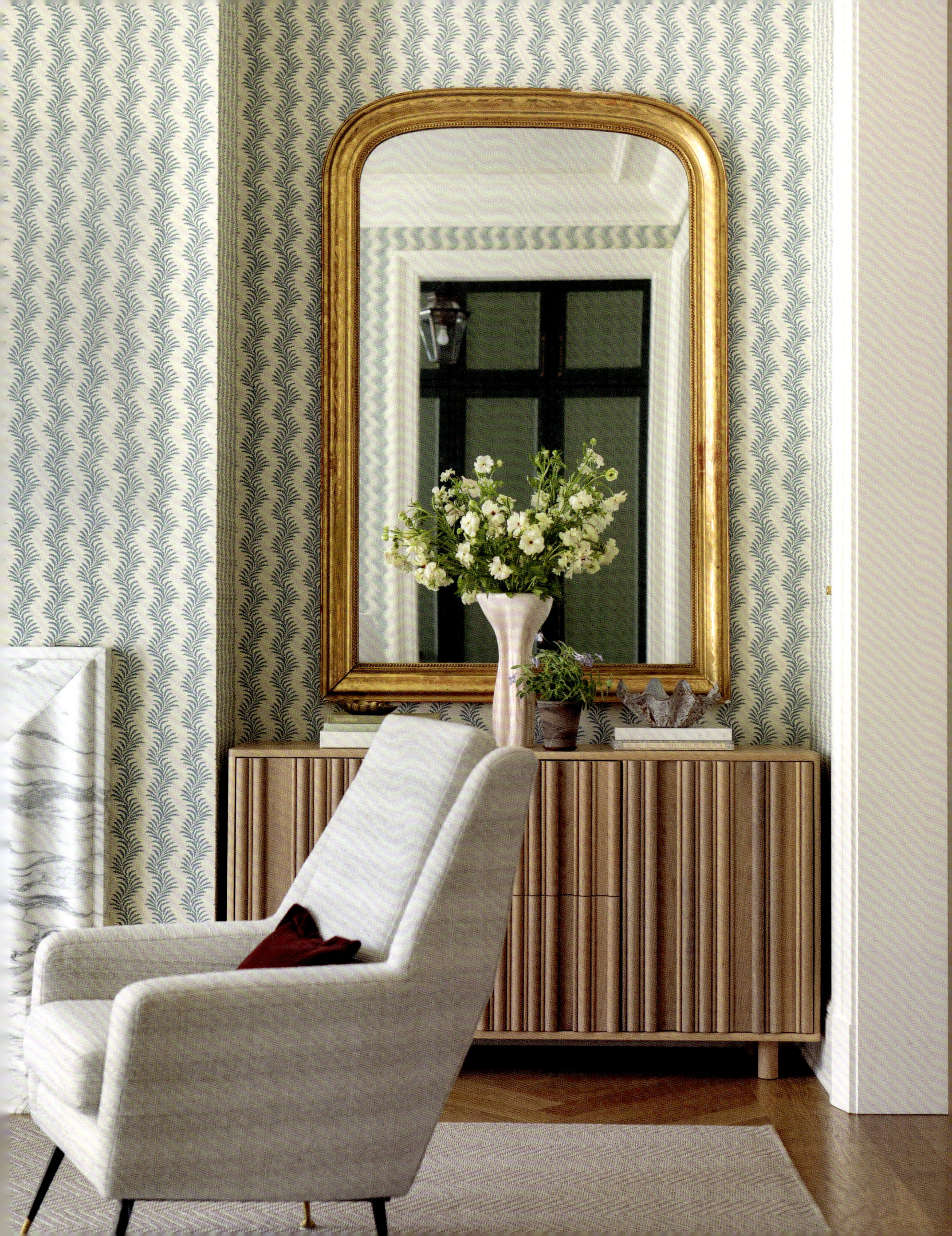

Previous: Since the family room is right off the kitchen, I wanted to ensure that it felt like its own space; the wallpaper delineates the area and gives it a character distinct from the white kitchen.

Opposite: Though I love built-ins, they would have felt too much like an extension of the kitchen cabinetry here, so we designed custom oak cabinets instead.

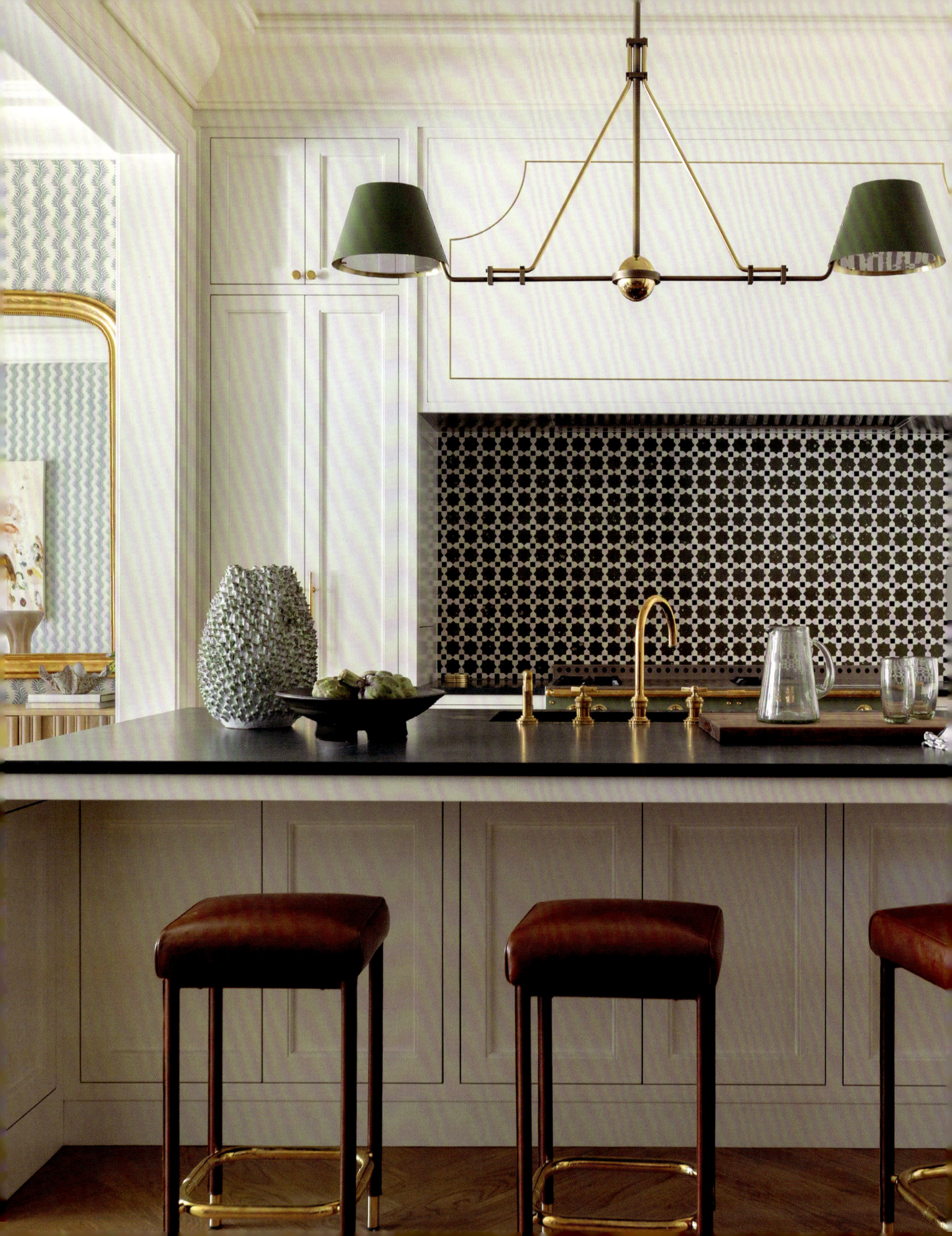

and a sense of history. In this case, we accomplished both through the details, which became the foundation of the interior design. Decisions such as arching the doorways, using brass hardware, and installing a leaded-glass room divider not only made the home feel older but also gave it so much personality. Of course, while the home has this sort of urban sophistication, we wanted it to still feel cozy for the couple and their two young kids. The key was making sure that we added warmth, whether that meant picking up the wood grain in the white oak floors, incorporating small-scale prints, or going big on super lush drapery.

When we did land on doing a (mostly) white kitchen, we were purposeful about finding ways to make it feel warm, organic, and not generic. A chocolate brown banquette, small-scale pattern on the drapery, and an intricate mosaic backsplash over the statement green range did the trick.

The home's most unexpected element may be the one that almost didn't happen: the rooftop garden room wasn't in the initial architectural plans; the space was going to be part of the roof deck or a kind of generic "bonus room." So many of my clients have created rooms like that for entertaining and not used them, so I challenged this couple to think of an extra space they would really want to spend time in. They both love gardening and plants, so we devised this idea of a conservatory to incorporate sunlight and nature, even in the heart of the city.

The ceilings in this home are so tall that significant crown moldings make sense—and align with what you would find in a more historic home.

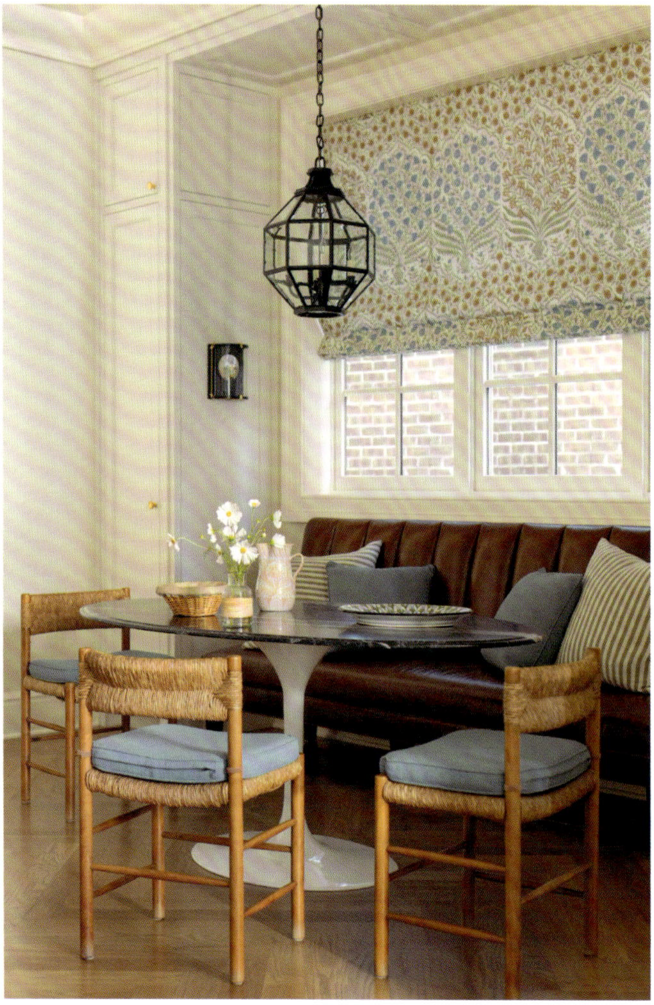

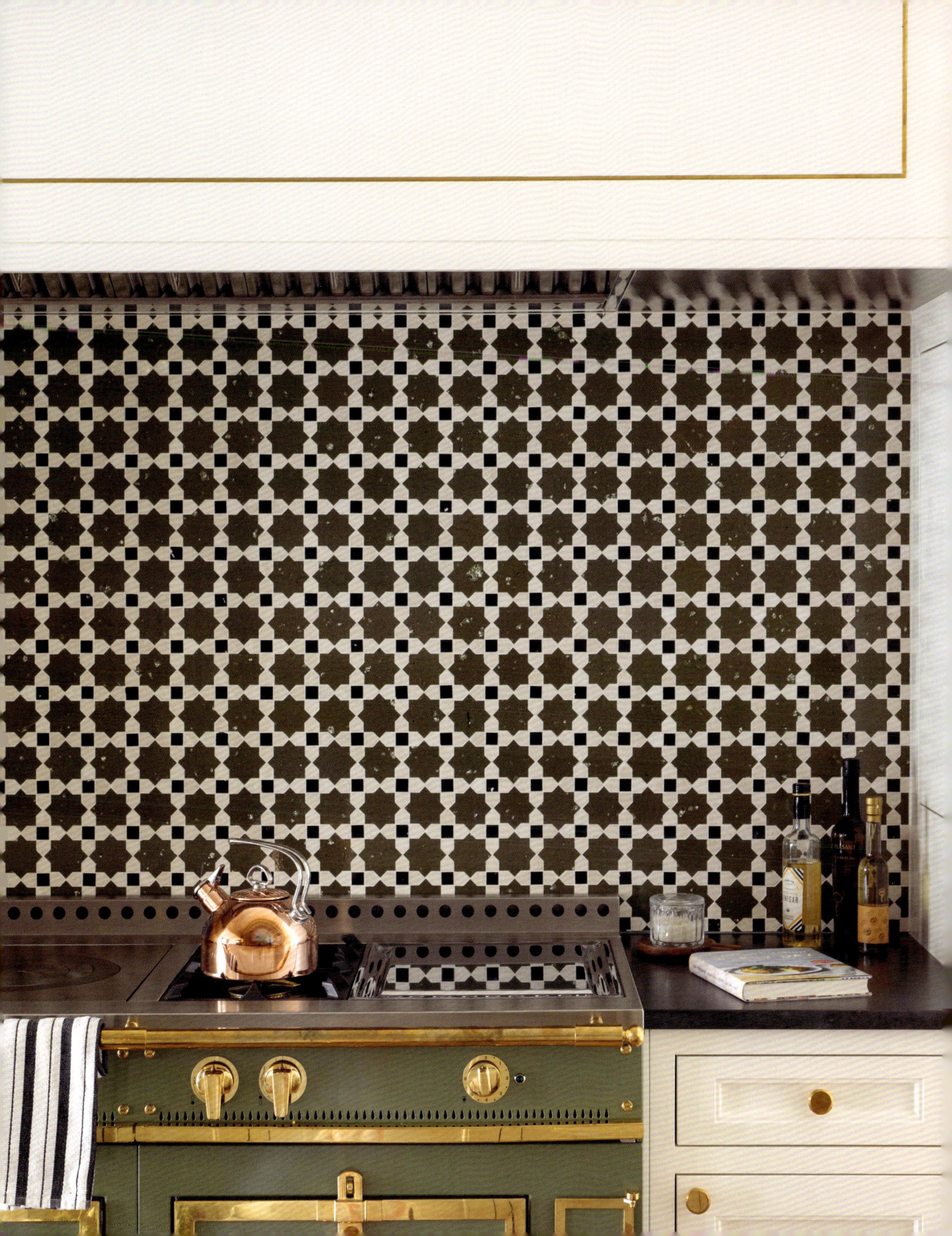

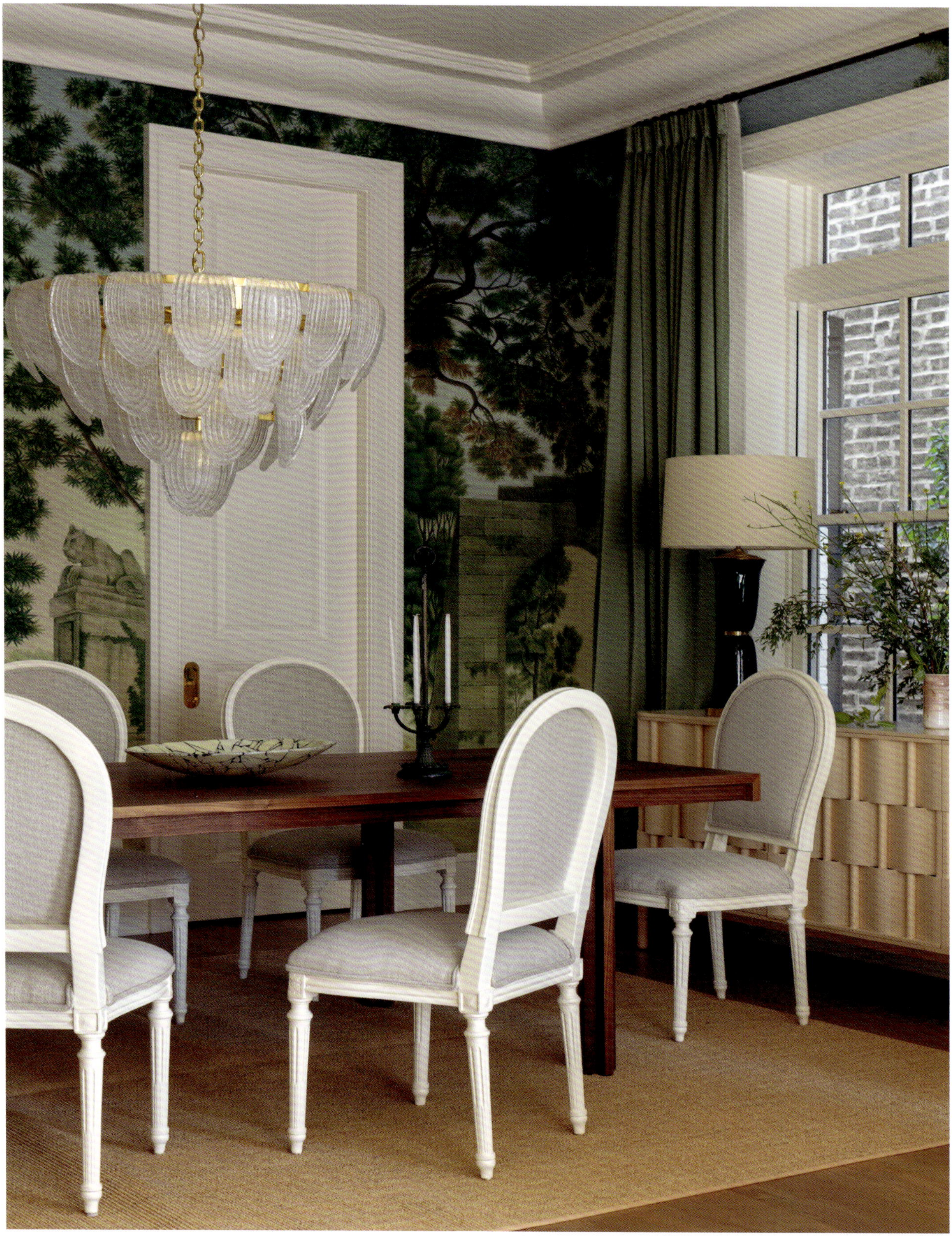

Opposite: The lack of one expansive wall in the dining room didn't stop us from installing a gorgeous scenic paper. We just made sure that the placement was such that even smaller parts of the mural were really impactful.

Right: I found an antique French door that I was absolutely in love with, and it became the inspiration for all of the interior doors in this house, creating a connection to history.

The family moved to this house from New York, where they had residences in the Tribeca neighborhood and the Hamptons, so they were used to life both in a small apartment and in a bigger house; our task became about combining their city and country lives and translating them into this new home. We talked a lot about making sure that the rooms were comfortable for everybody, but also that they could serve the dual purposes of cozy family spaces and backdrops for entertaining. To that end, we designed the living room to feel more formal than the family room; while the family room has a fantastically deep, comfortable sofa; soft carpet; and a television, the living room's sculptural, tailored furniture and fine art sets it up as a high-design salon (though I love that the denim we used on the armchairs keeps it from feeling too stuffy).

Similarly, though the kitchen banquette is a no-brainer for casual family meals, the couple also wanted a dining room where they could host dinner parties. The scenic Iksel wallpaper was one of our first selections; since we're in the middle of the city and don't have a lot of greenery outside, it felt important to bring that element into this central room of the house. Floor-to-ceiling cabinets in two corners house all their entertaining items without eating into the room's square footage. The brass cremone bolts on the cabinet doors are another example of a small detail that adds such a sense of history and so much personality.

The living room color and materials palettes speak to the whole concept of the home: The fringed, chocolate brown sofa and inlaid side tables inject a sense of formality, with a pair of blue denim–upholstered armchairs acting as a casual and comfy counterpoint.

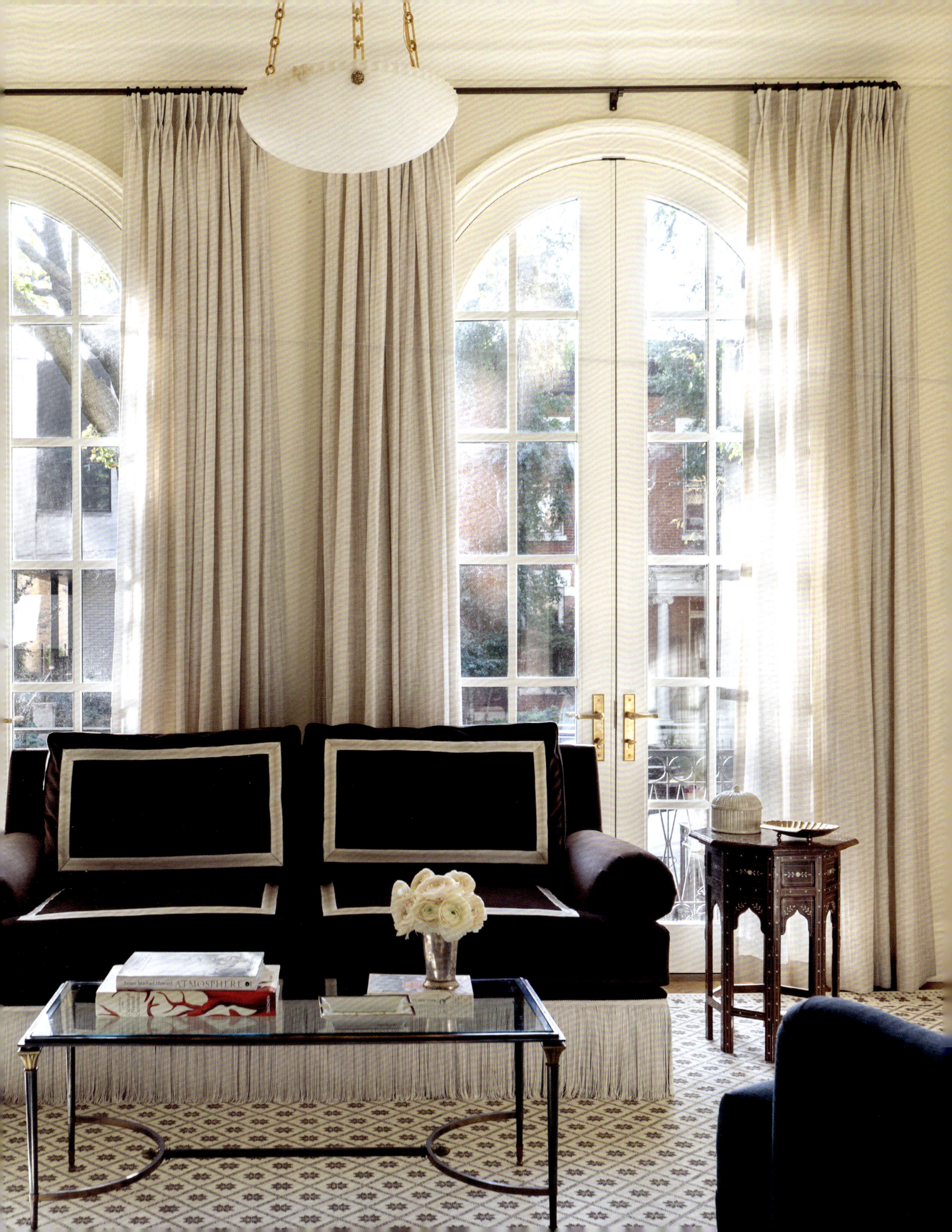
ATMOSPHERE

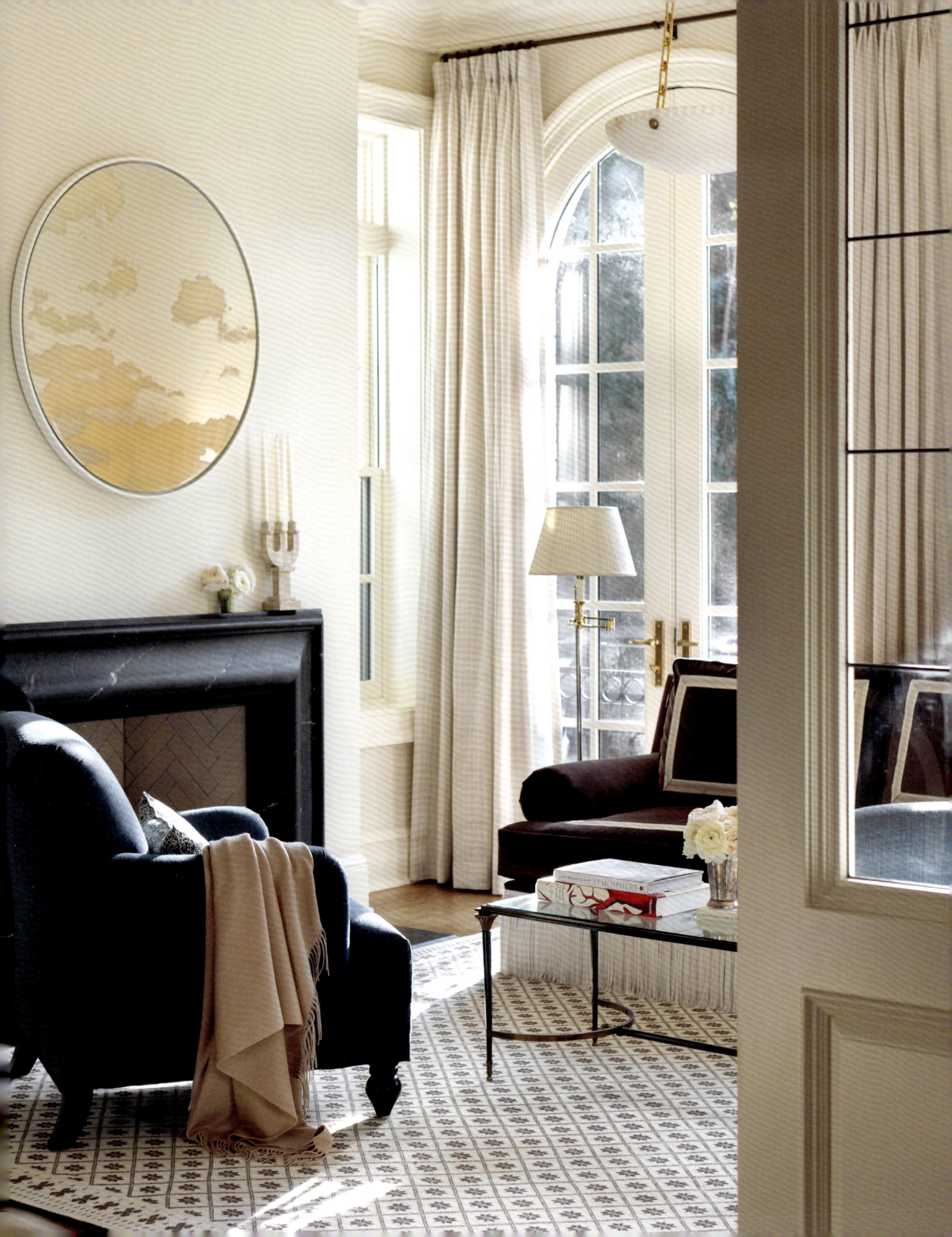
ATMOSPHERE

We faced the same challenge of creating character in the bedrooms, which were really just white boxes. With no real architectural significance, we relied on hand-painted wallpaper to inject that really special, inspiring element to the primary bedroom. And although it's undeniably elegant, the wallpaper also cocoons the room in a way that makes the space feel as cozy as the living spaces.

With the wallpaper as the showstopper, we wanted the primary bath to feel spa-like and utterly relaxing —but, of course, that couldn't mean boring. While we landed on traditional white marble, we went all in on the details, creating a reeded texture on the cabinetry and marble molding around the mirrors and into the shower, which is so transformative.

Ultimately, that's very much the sensibility of the house: there is a quiet elegance to it. Nothing we did is in-your-face, but there's a thoughtful sophistication to every single detail.

> "Nothing we did is in-your-face; there's a thoughtful sophistication to every single detail."

Most new-builds have combined living and dining spaces, but here it felt important to separate the rooms. The leaded-glass partition allowed us to do that without taking up too much visual space.

Overleaf: With its beautiful Gracie chinoiserie wallpaper and elegant, sculptural, four-poster bed, this is a dream bedroom.

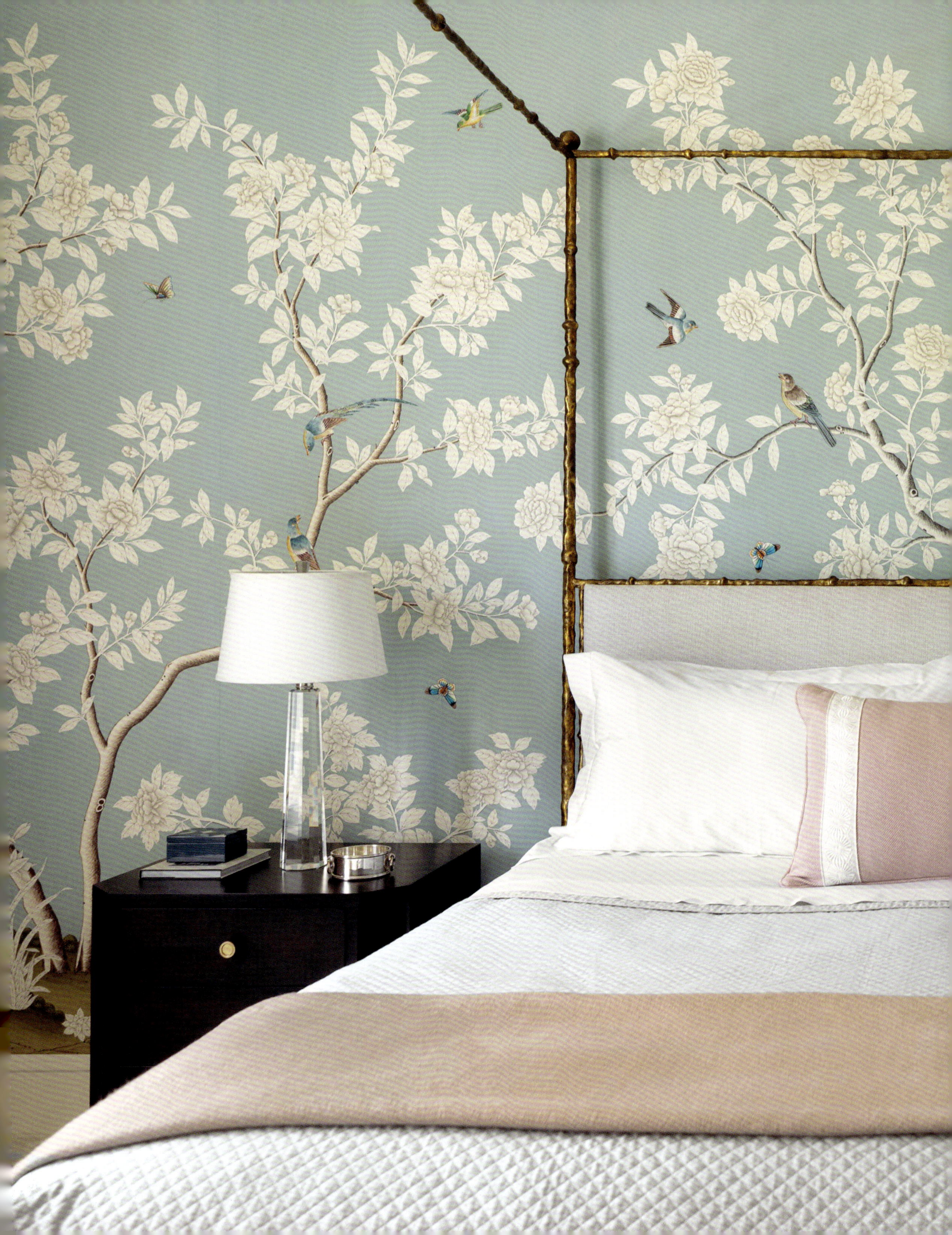

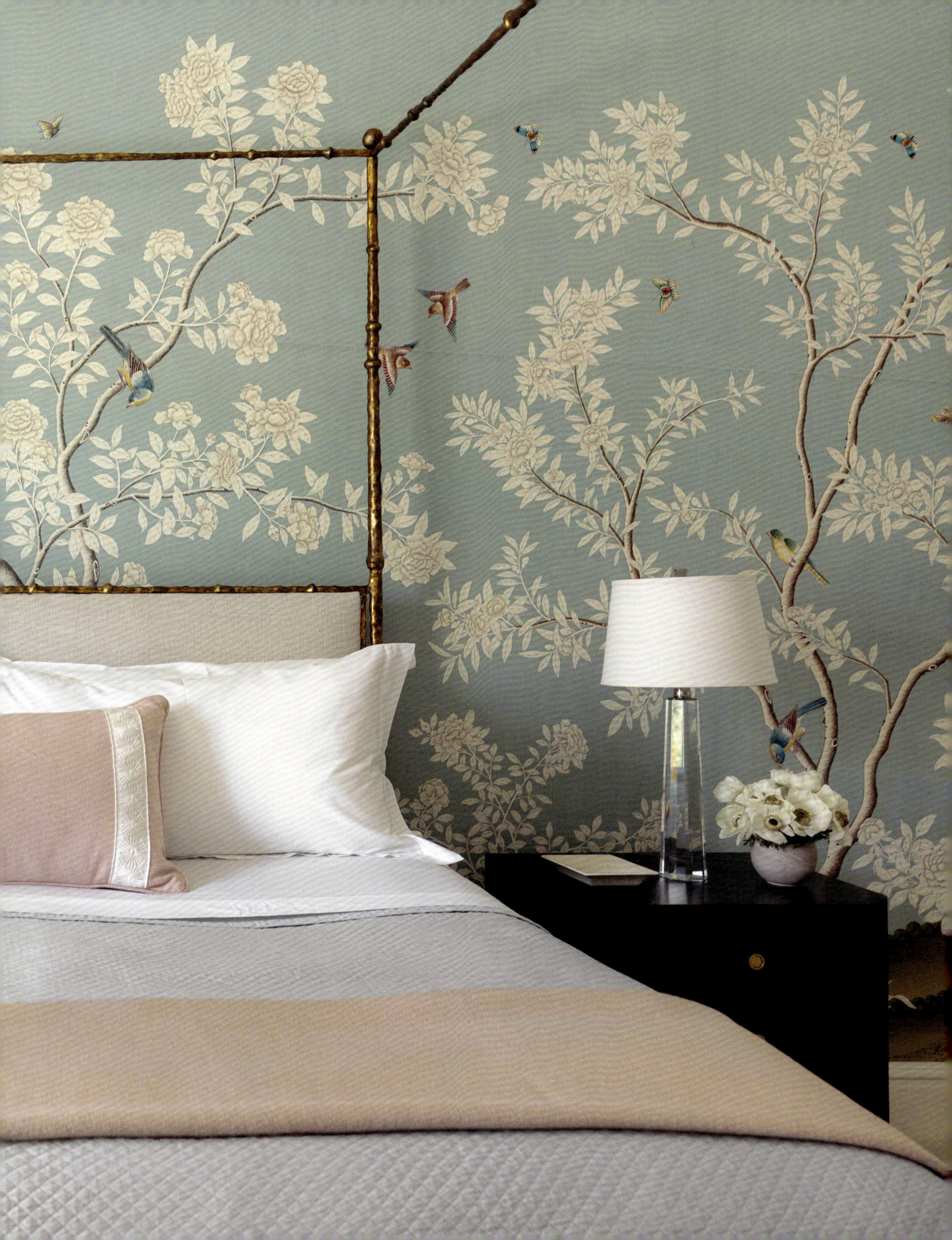

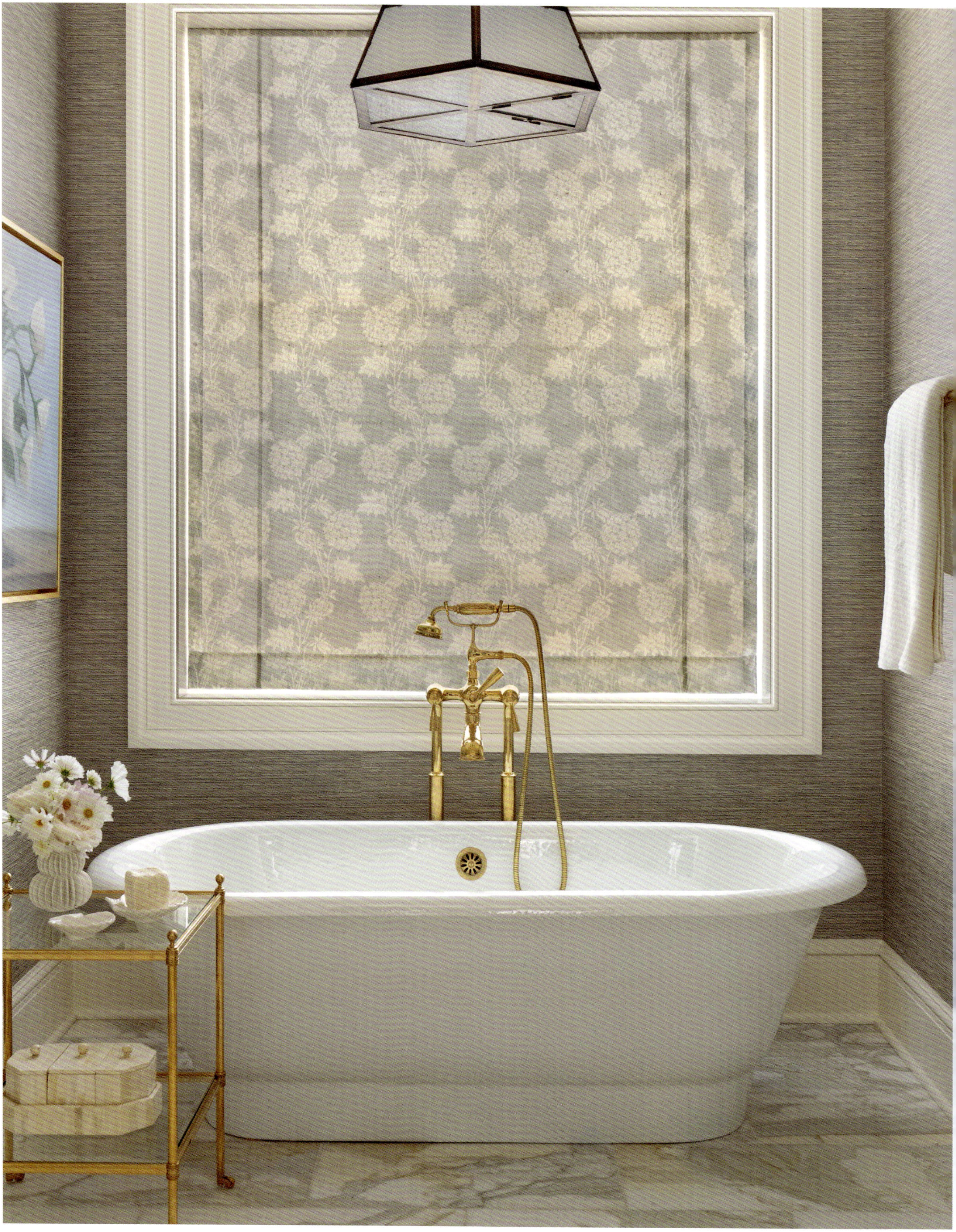

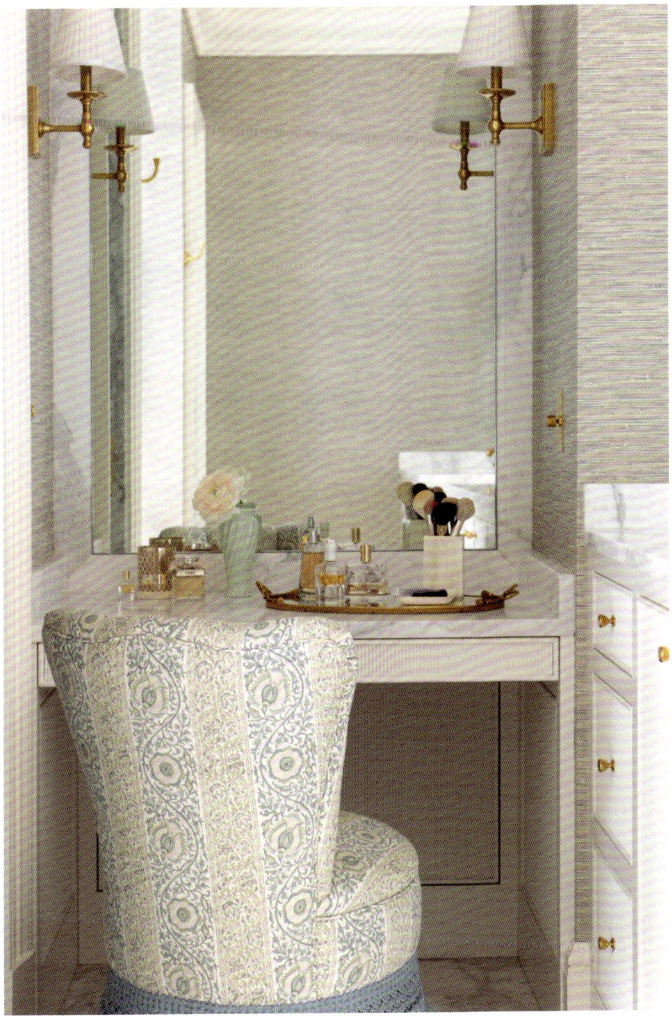

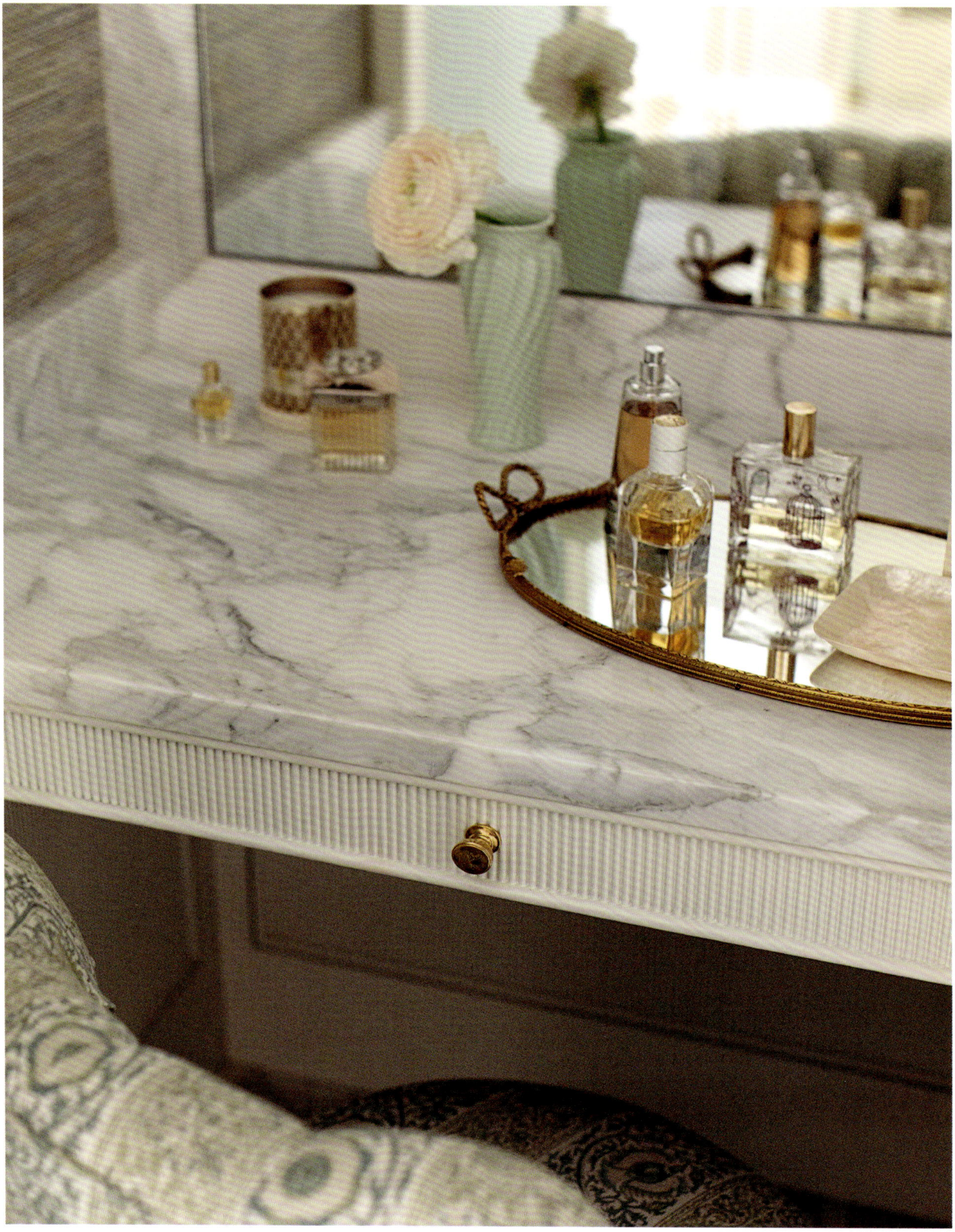

We tried to carry the house's
beautiful architectural details into
the bathroom in the form of reeded
cabinetry, paneled marble, and
grass cloth walls.

Overleaf left and right: In the kids'
rooms, which are mirror images of
each other, we kept things simple
to create spaces they could grow
into. The daughter's floral wallpaper
can read as both pretty and elegant,
and the painted trim in the son's
room is an unexpected way to add
a jolt of color.

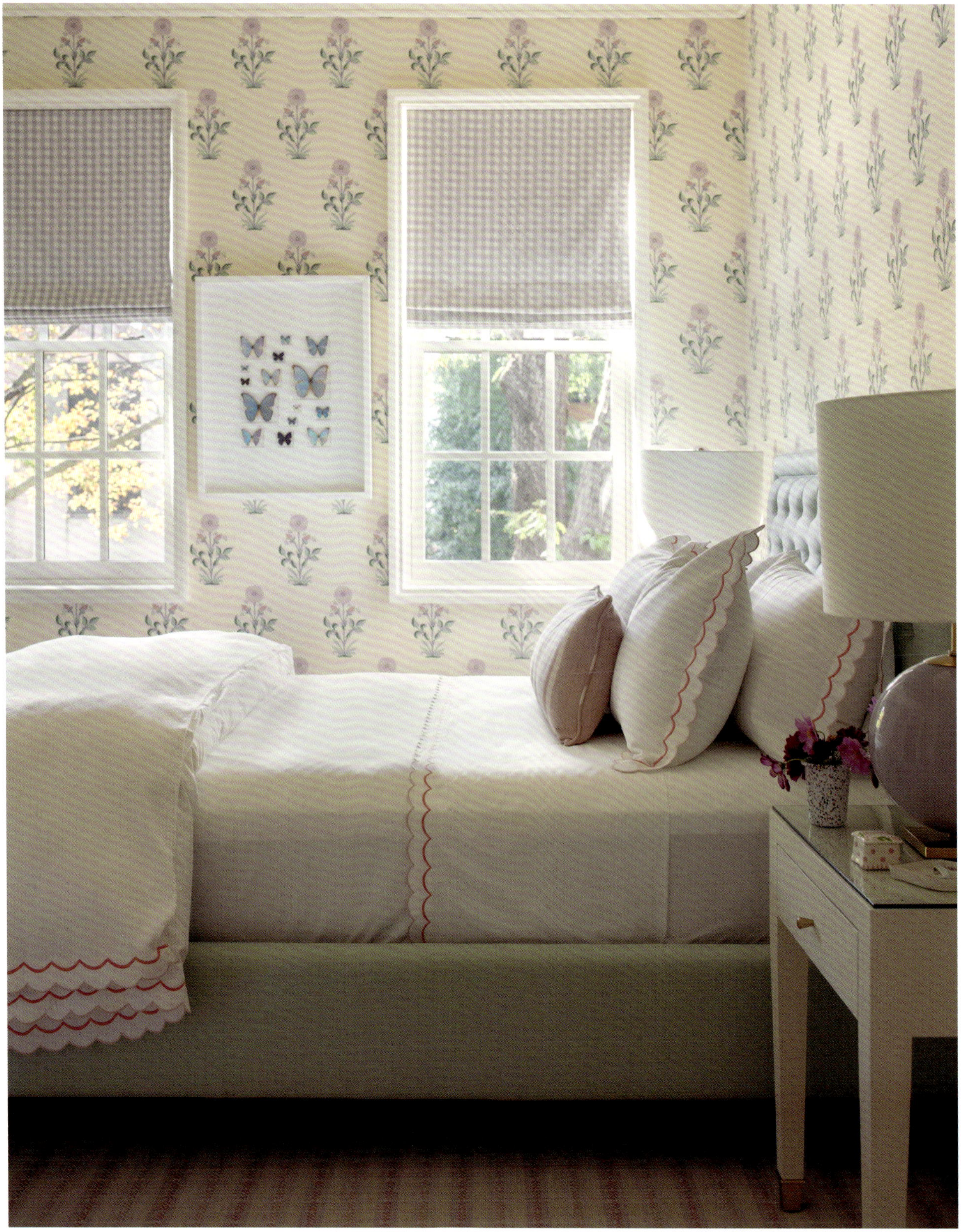

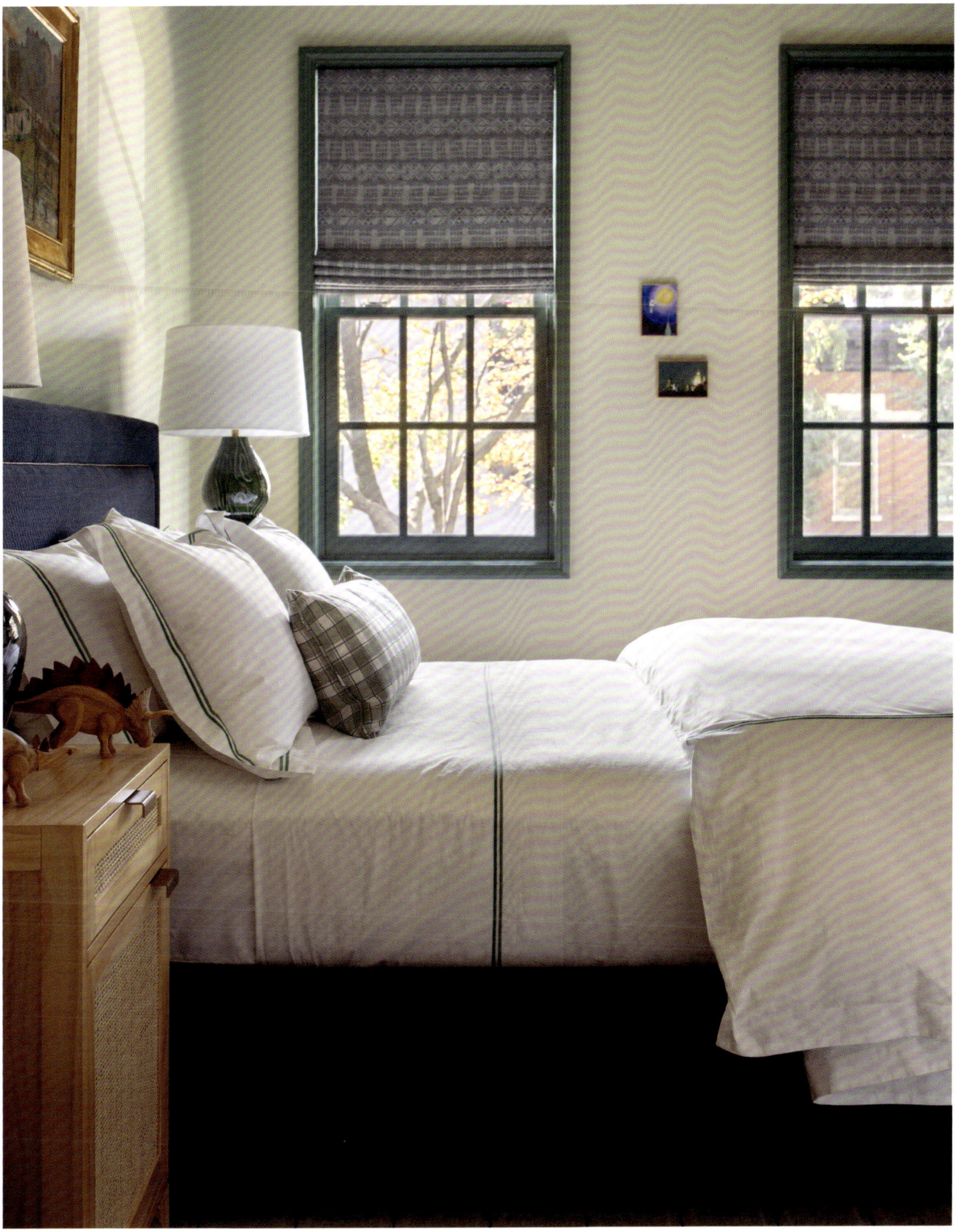

The light-filled rooftop conservatory includes a dishwasher and a sink, making it highly functional for entertaining.

Overleaf: Since the office is quite small, we kept the space very edited and leaned into materiality, going for high impact with wood paneling, sculptural furniture, and a geometric wool-and-silk rug.

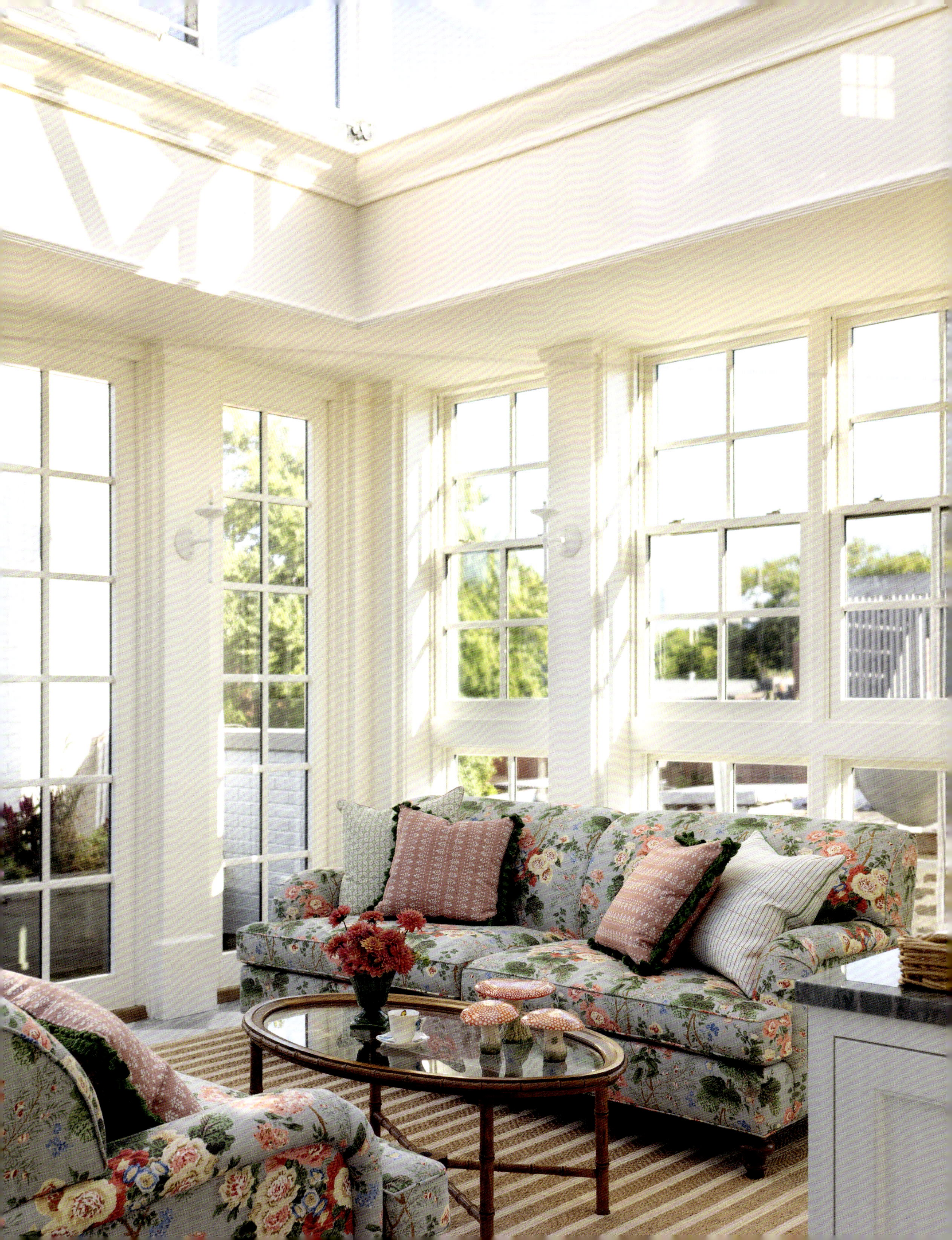

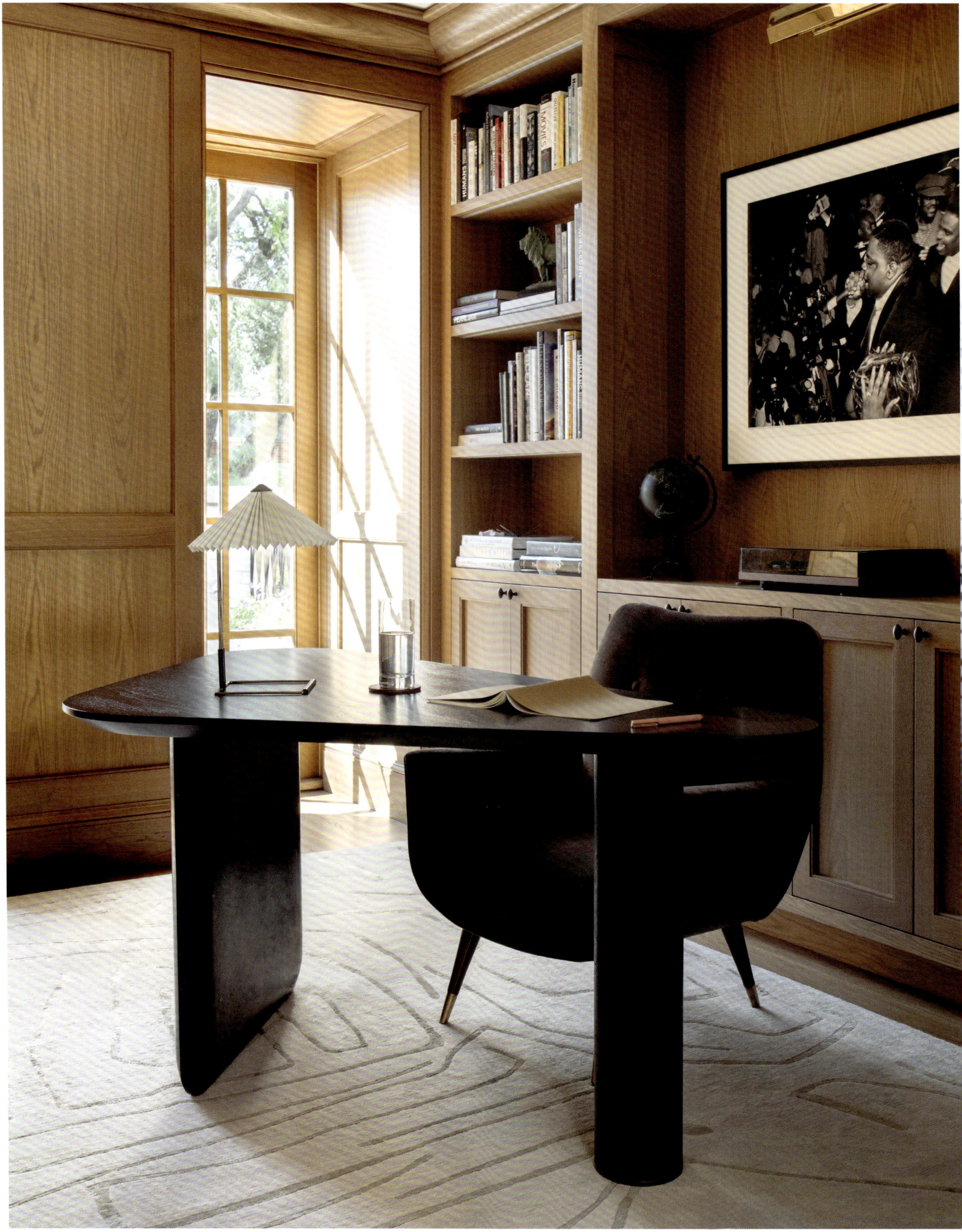

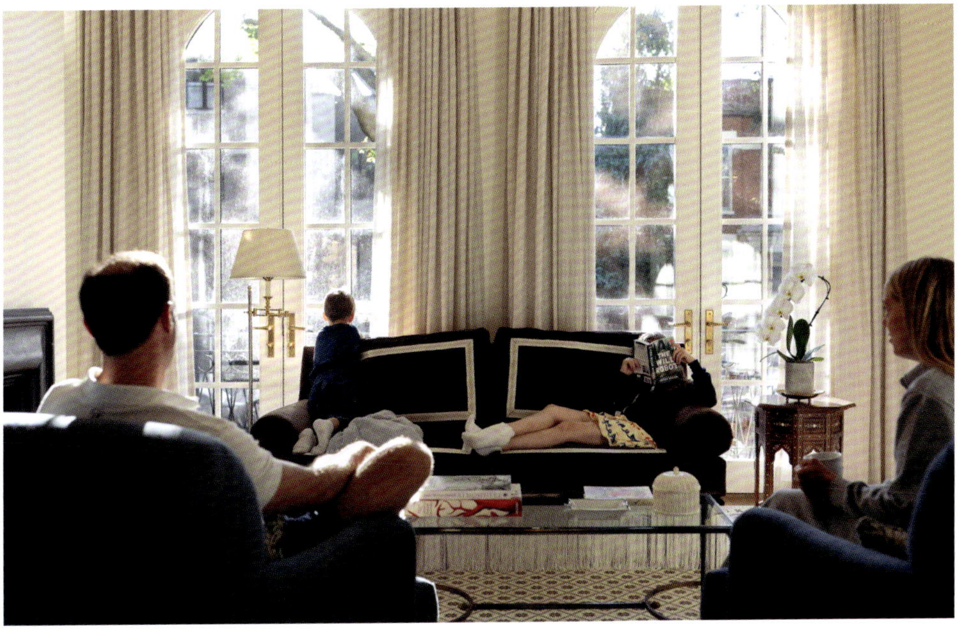

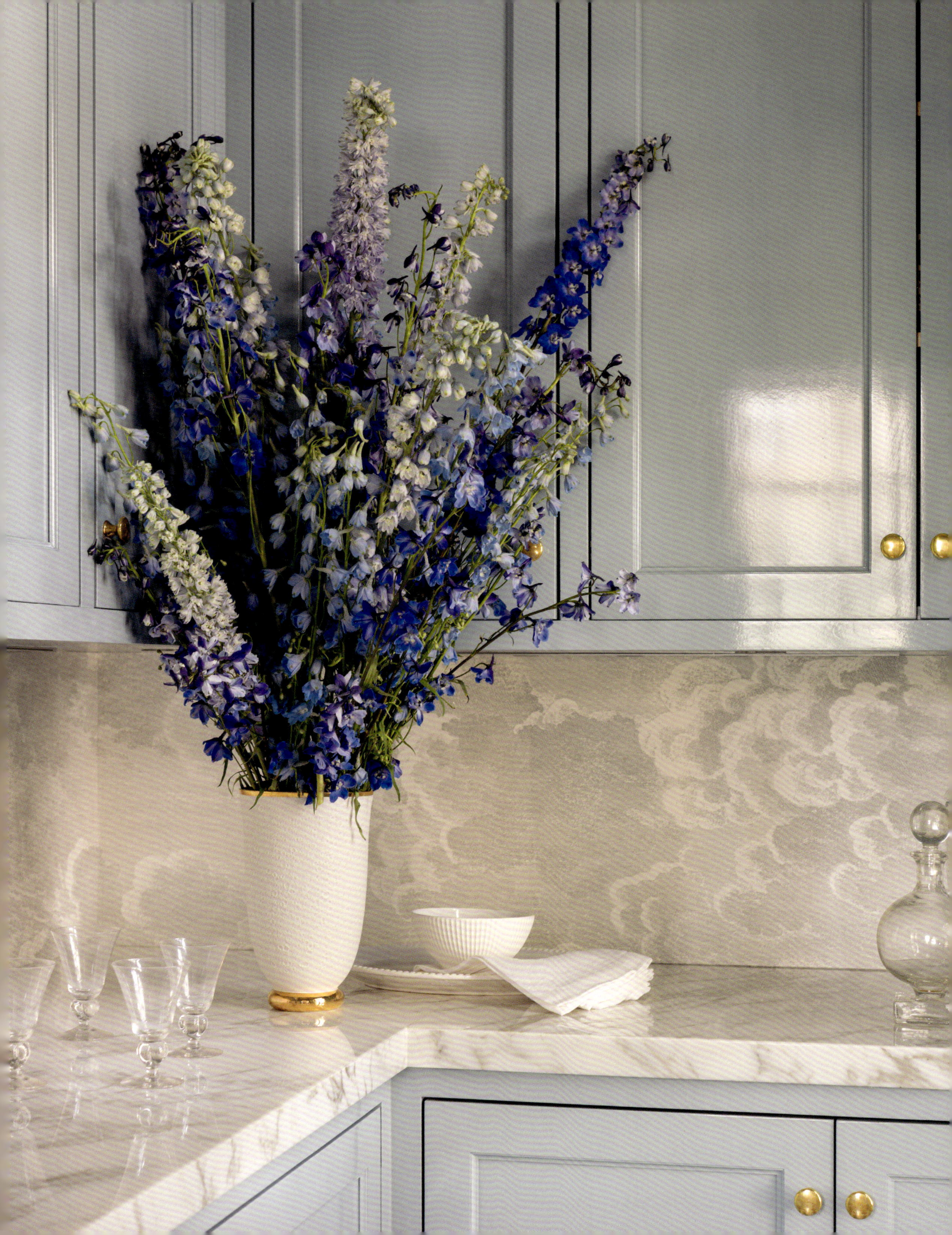

SHOW AND STEADY

A chic home that's decidedly not the party house

This passage between the dining and family rooms used to house a floating desk; we converted it to a much more functional (and prettier!) bar, with a backsplash of antiqued mirror to lighten up the space.

It is so fun designing for people who use their houses in many different ways—and this family is a great example. The parents are both partners at large law firms and their work is intense, so home is truly a place of respite for them. Our question from the outset was, How can we create spaces that help them feel relaxed and at ease during the few hours a day that they aren't working?

This is the third house that I've designed for this family. It's kind of a fun story: The wife and I grew up across the street from each other and her older sister used to babysit me, so I have known her my entire life. Several years ago, she and her husband hired me to decorate their home in Chicago. Once they had children and moved to a second home in the city, I designed that, too. Eventually, they moved back to the suburb where the wife and I grew up, and I was honored to design what might end up being their forever home (or not!). Because we've seen each other at so many stages in life, I feel I know them quite well, which made the design process even more fun.

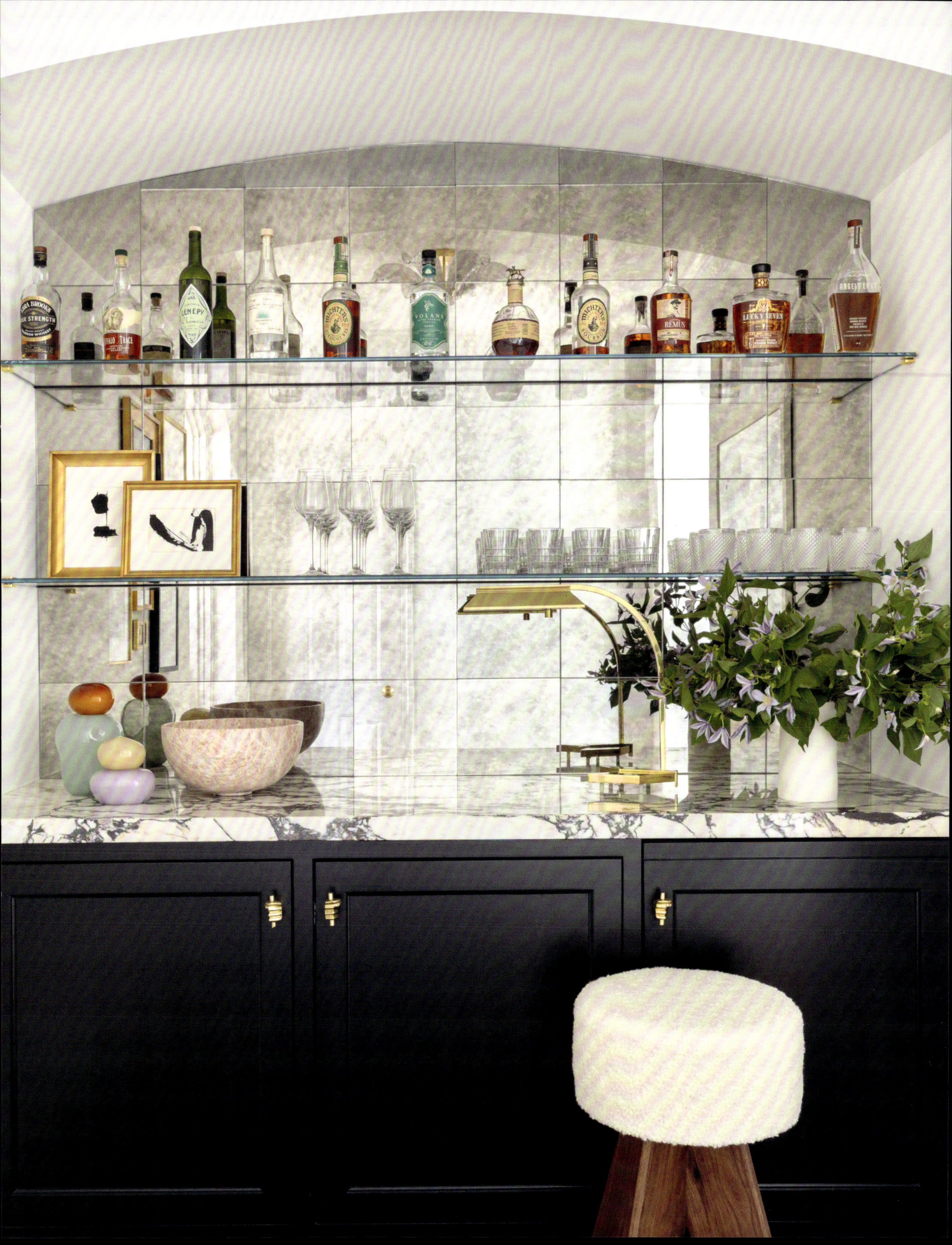
GENEPY
VOLANS
REMUS
LUCKY SEVEN

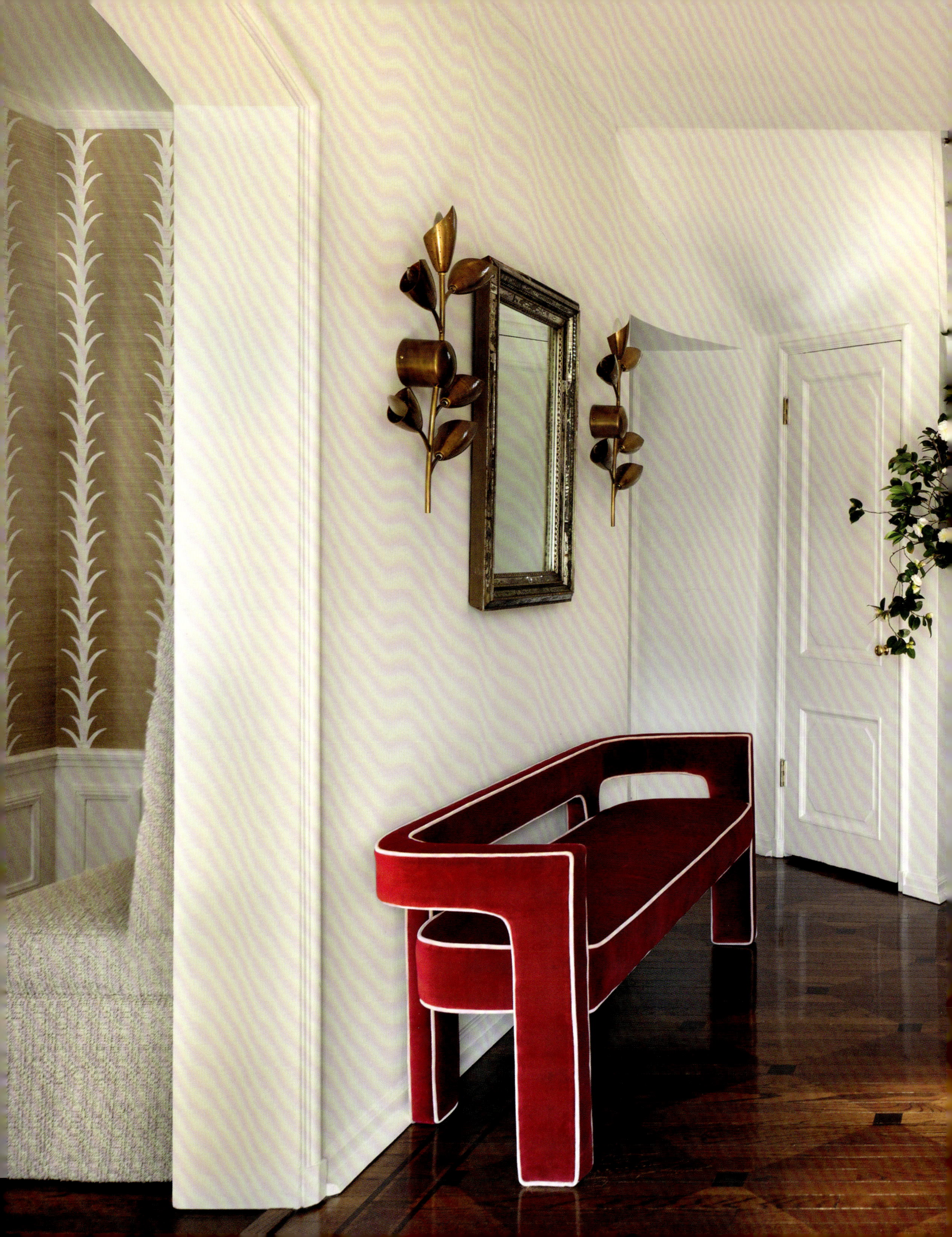

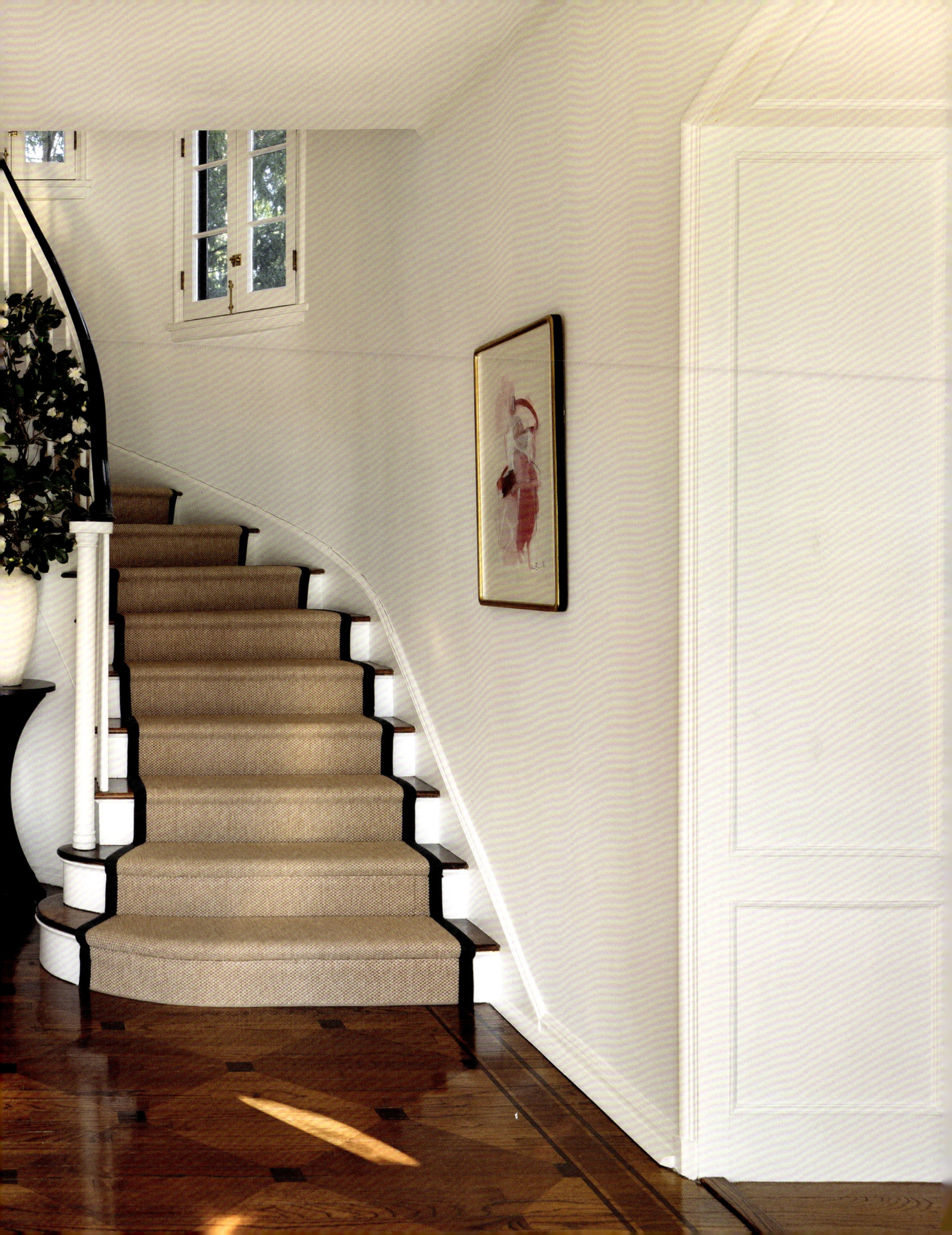

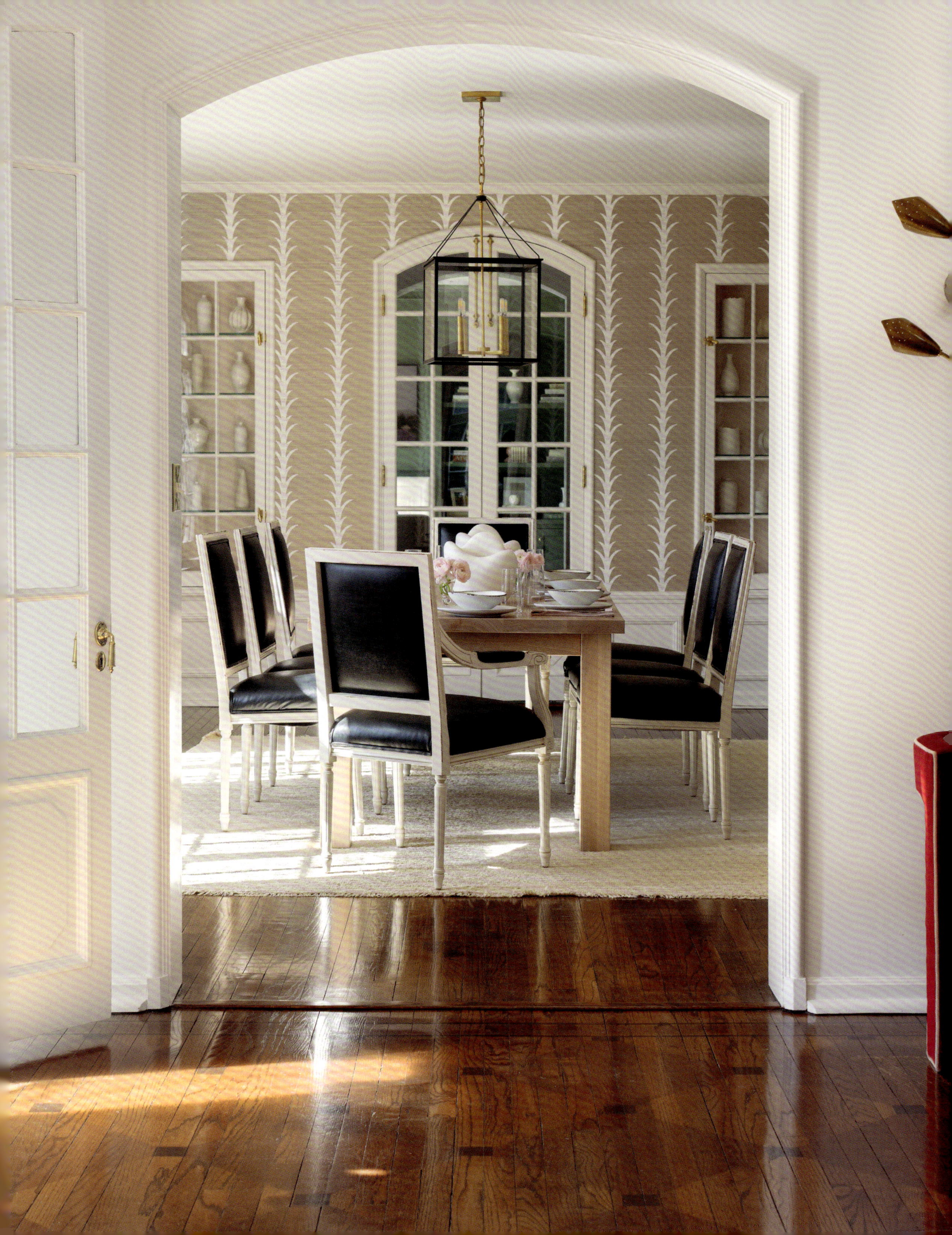

For this home, I was even involved in the house search, which was so special. They wanted a home with a ton of personality but that didn't need a lot of work. They were coming from a prewar building and wanted to replicate its charm, a tall order, as many older buildings have been renovated, their original character removed. At the same time, with three young children, they didn't want to undertake a massive renovation— at least not immediately. When they saw this 1920s French Provincial–style house with incredible original details intact, they fell in love.

We started decorating as soon as they closed on the house, but we didn't tackle the kitchen, bar, and family room—they required a more involved reno—for a few years. The couple was expecting their third child and, given that the home lent itself to a more formal existence than aligned with their day-to-day lives, they wanted to get a sense of how they would actually use it before investing in an overhaul. It's important to realize that a redesign doesn't have to happen right away; often, if you live in a space for a while, you'll have a better sense of what you want out of your renovation.

That was especially true for the kitchen, which we initially discussed expanding by knocking down an interior wall. By the time we got around to renovating it, though, we had landed on something very different —and much more personal.

This room is much more of a multipurpose space than a traditional formal dining room—it's where the kids do their homework and the family plays board games, for example—so we added banquettes for more flexibility in seating options.

Perhaps because we know each other so well, or maybe because of how intimate the process of designing a home is, the couple was not shy to admit that they do not cook. I suspect there are a lot of people who design a big chef's kitchen because they feel like they should, but my thought is that if you're not using all those fancy accoutrements, let's talk about what you are going to use. "I just want a pretty kitchen," the wife said of her prerequisites. We decided to make a traditional galley kitchen that opened into a beautiful courtyard, then take what was previously a breakfast nook and turn it into a butler's pantry that would serve as a little coffee station and offer additional storage. That way, we could preserve the clean aesthetic of the kitchen. We joke that she gets mad anytime her husband so much as makes eggs because, as she says, "This is not a cooking kitchen!"

Because of how the house is laid out, the dining room is a pass-through into the family room and the office, so turning it into a formal dining room would have meant giving up a central area in the home—at least for daily use. Instead, we designed it to maximize usability. The chairs are leather and wipeable and the table is a rustic, wire-brushed wood so that nobody's worried about the kids eating there and making a mess.

Another choice that really made a difference in the dining room was the addition of the banquettes, which transformed the room into a multifunctional space. The kids do their homework there, and the husband and wife use the space when they're working from home; it has become a hub of the house.

Calacatta marble slab backsplashes add a layer of sleekness to this otherwise traditional galley kitchen.

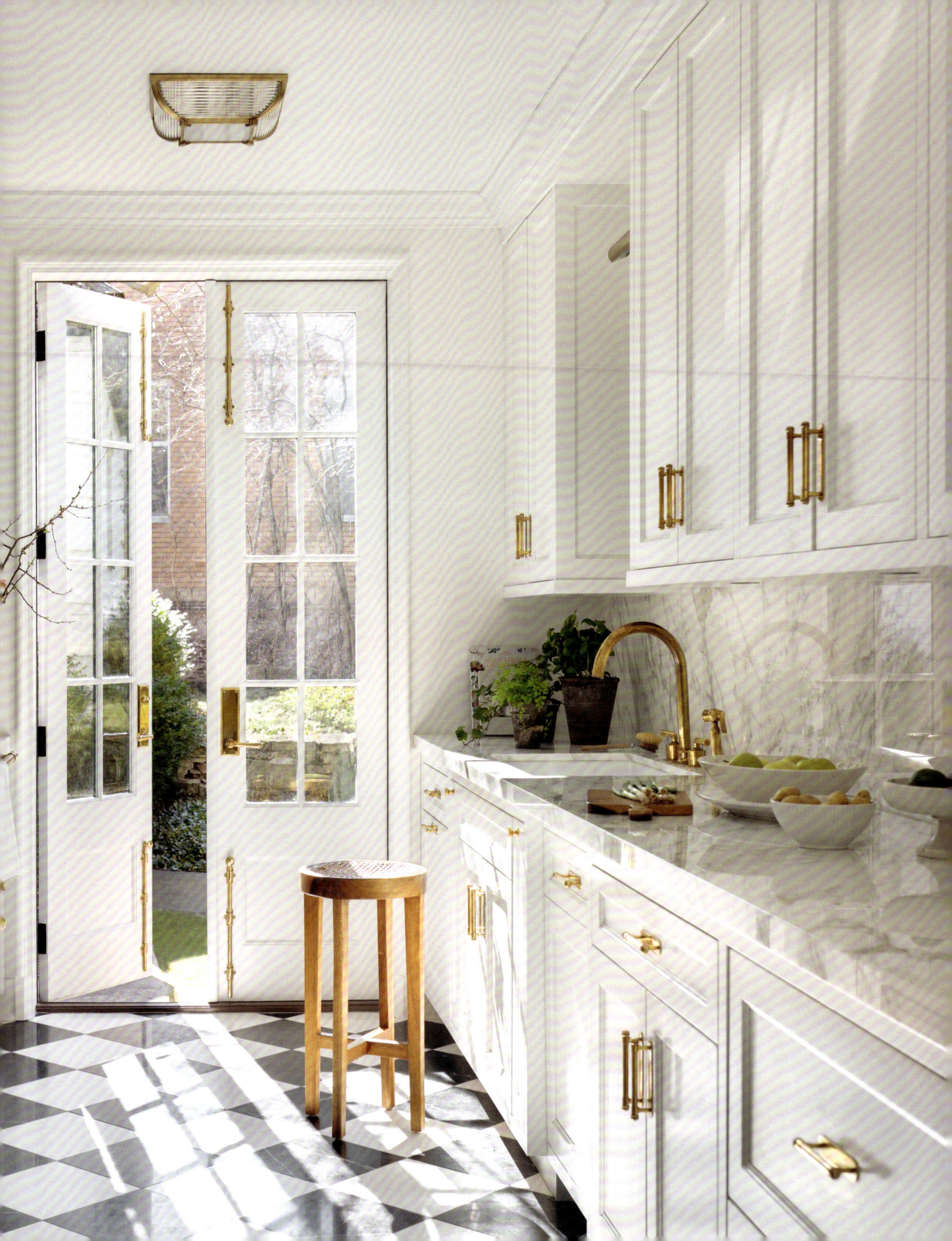

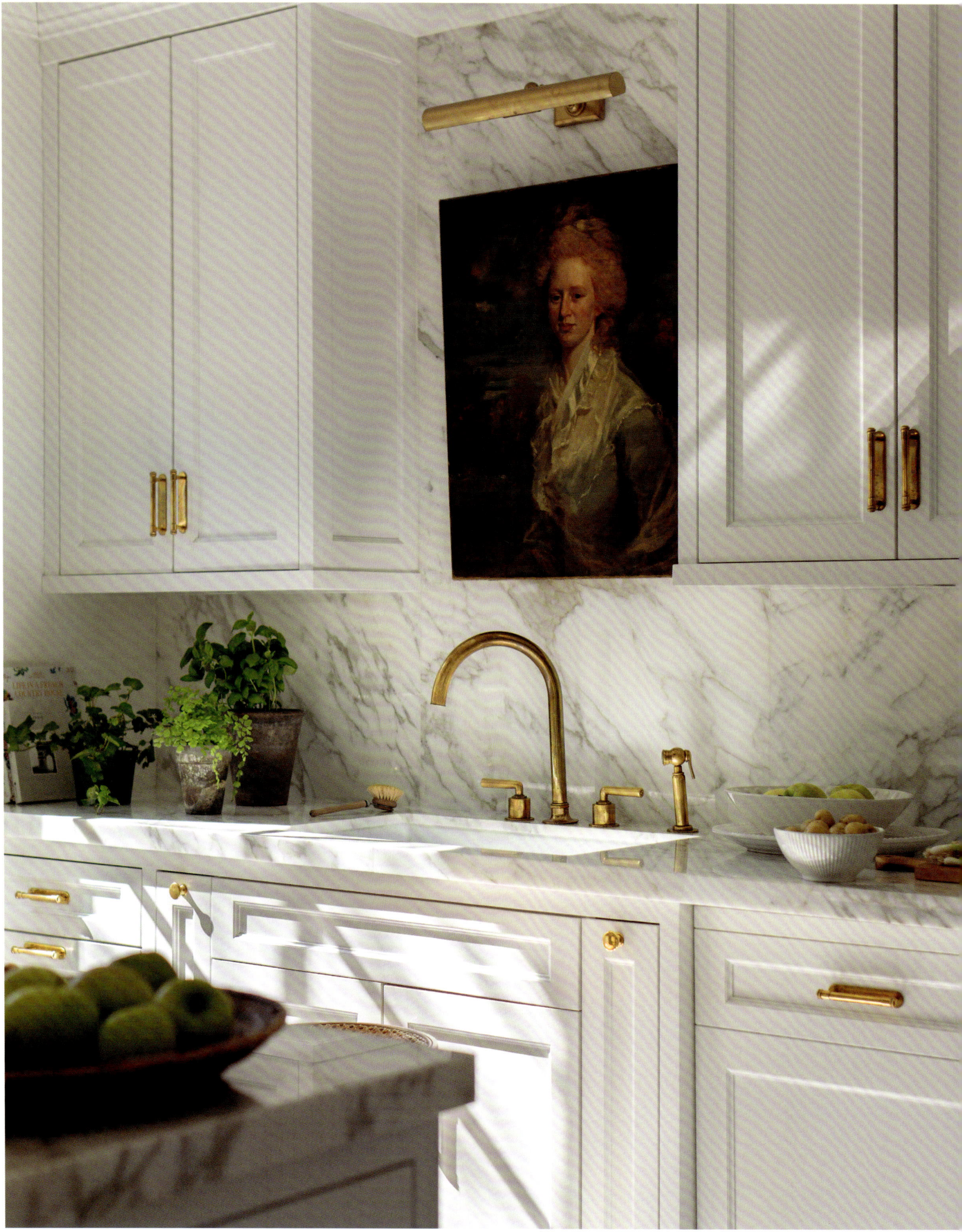

Because the homeowners don't regularly cook, I could add design elements to the kitchen that might typically be off-limits—like original art against the backsplash. The painting's moody palette is nicely juxtaposed against the soft white and gray of the marble.

This room was once a breakfast nook, but we closed it into a traditional butler's pantry for extra storage. The client loved how the movement in the cloud wallpaper, applied to the walls and ceiling, echoed the grain of the marble; it's the perfect subtle contrast to the glossy blue cabinetry.

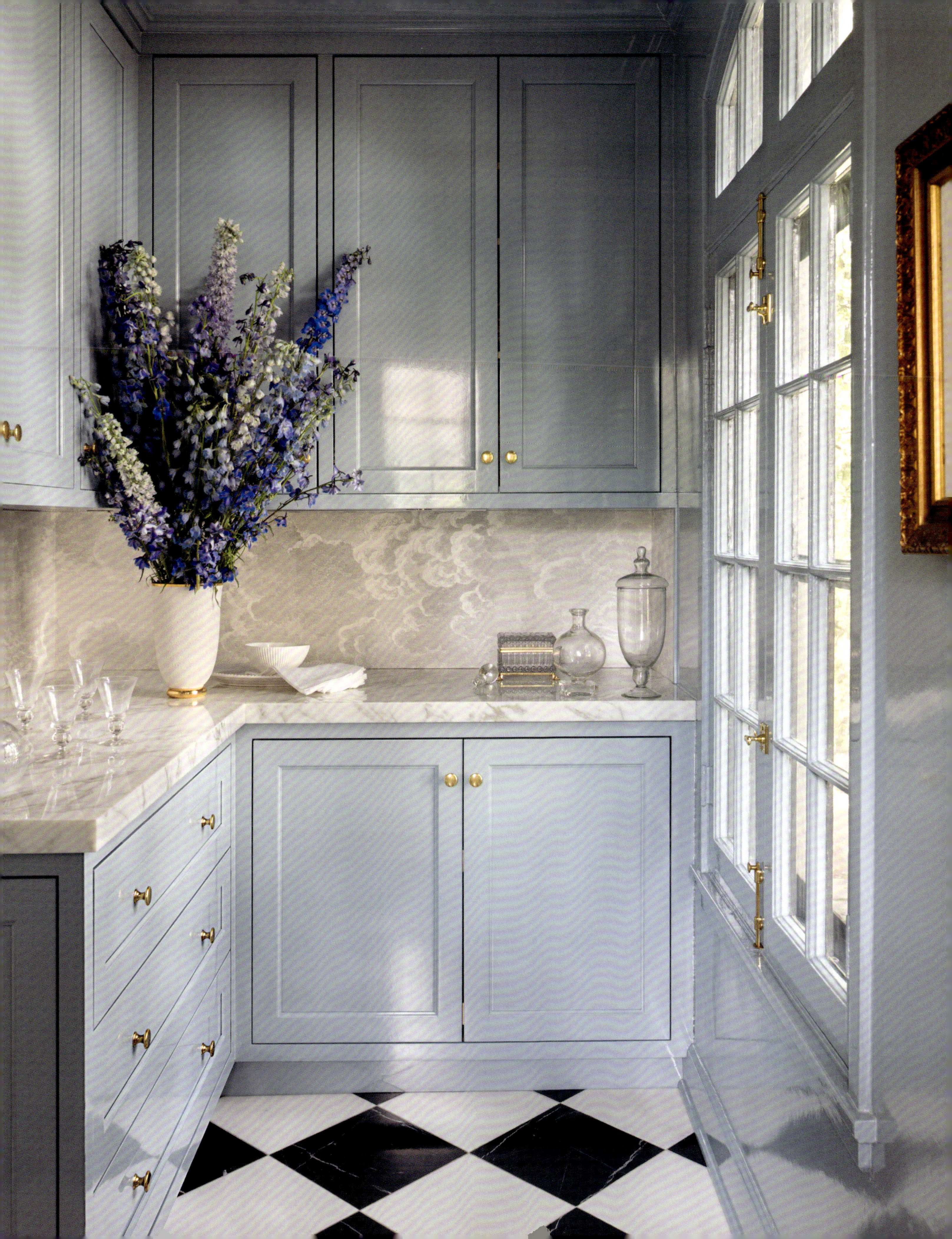

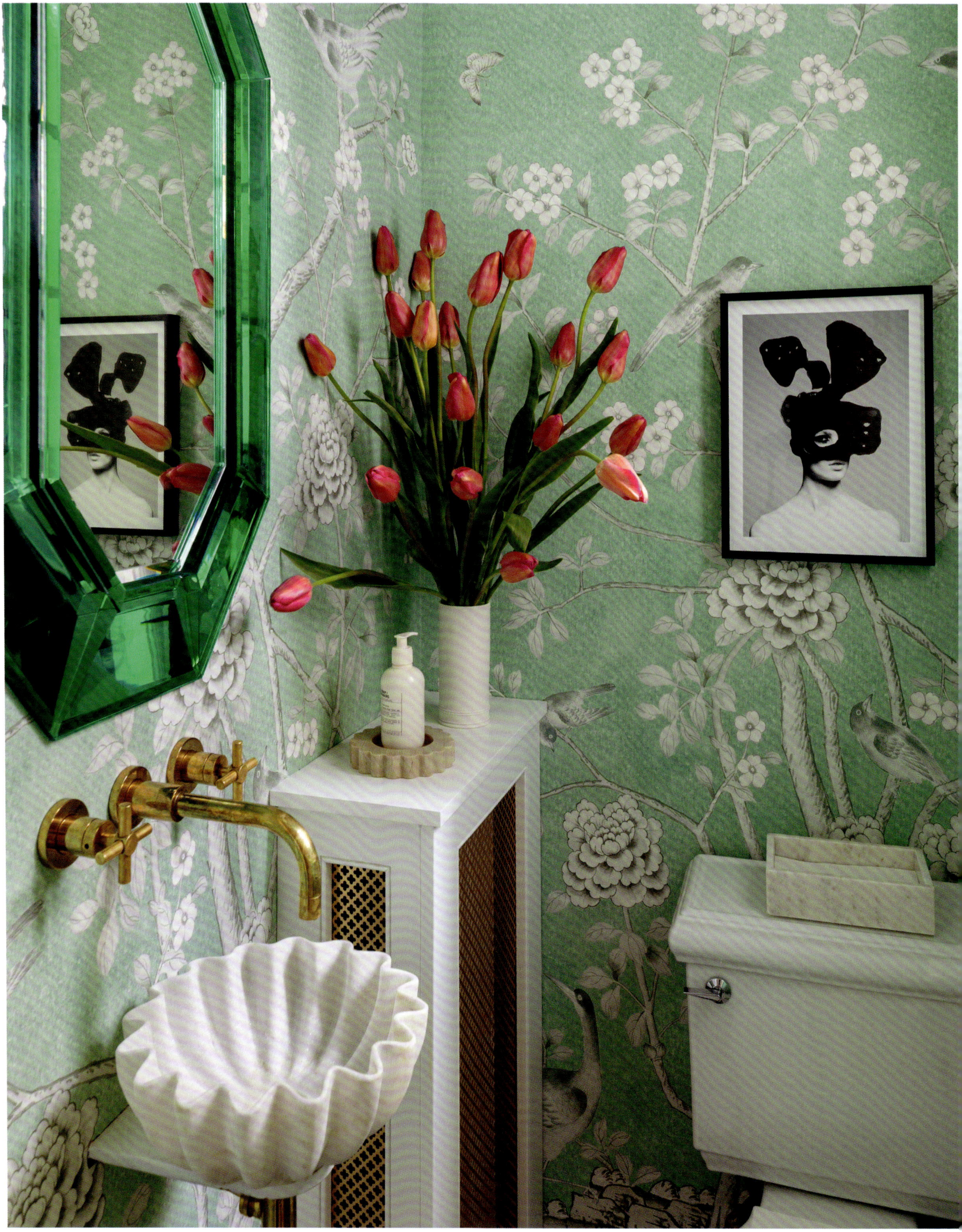

Because they don't entertain much, my clients wanted their family room to function as a cozy space where they could just hang out together. When you're not trying to squeeze every inch out of a space to accommodate guests, you can ask yourself what you need just for your own family to be comfortable. For example, we removed a space that had served as an office from the dining room and turned it into a bar. It is just a pass-through, but with a dedicated purpose.

In my experience, people gravitate toward smaller rooms. So I loved the idea of designing the sunroom as a spot where an adult could go and take a call and the kids could play (their son loves building Legos in here!). Located in the back of the house, off the formal living room, the sunroom has a sense of seclusion.

The sunroom also embodies the overall aesthetic of the house: We felt that we could go a little bit sweeter in here without skewing overly feminine because the rest of the home is so classic. The house has traditional, sophisticated bones, so we wanted the design to bring a freshness to it. If this home were an outfit, it would be beautifully tailored black pants and a classic white blouse with gold costume jewelry and bright pink stilettos—which is exactly what the wife wears.

To that same end, while we went with playful florals and pinks in the girls' rooms, we kept the lines classic and clean. The primary bedroom, meanwhile, is quiet, soft, and relatively neutral in comparison. It's a perfect retreat for two busy lawyers/parents. Ultimately, what I love most about this house is that there are so many different areas where you can settle in and feel comfortable.

Opposite: In the powder room, high-contrast black-and-white photography stands out against the chinoiserie wallpaper.

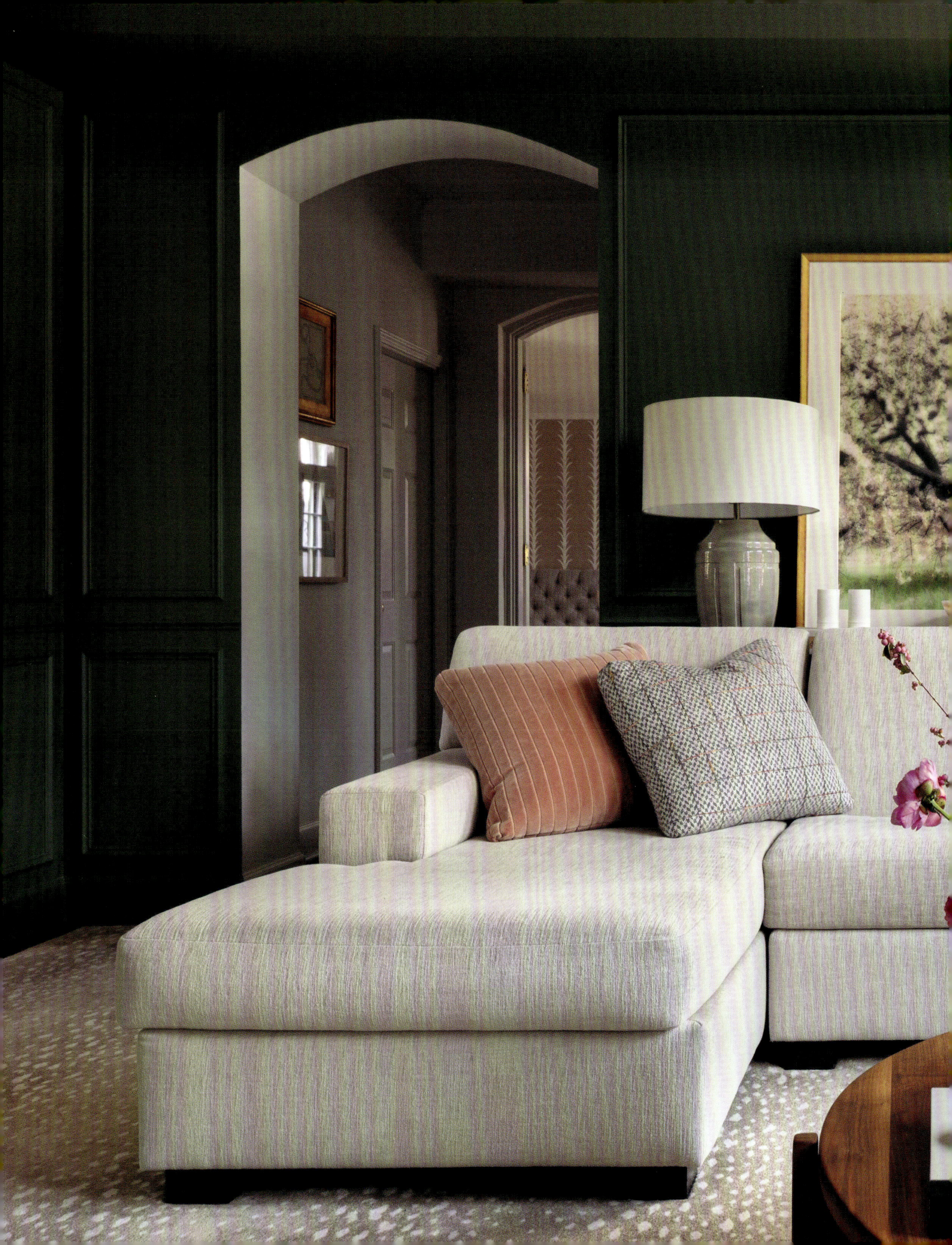

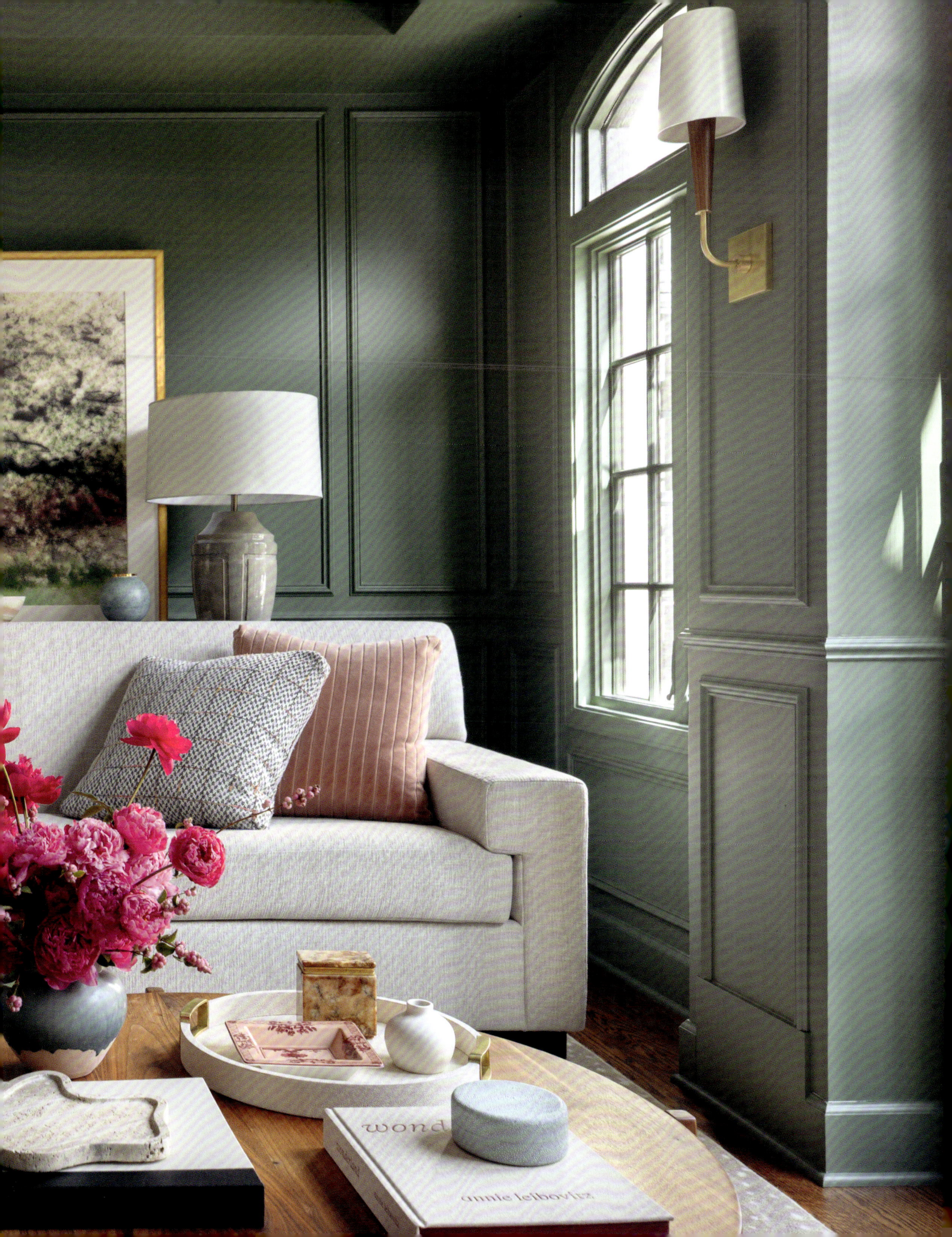
annie leibovitz

"A redesign doesn't have to happen right away; if you live in a space for a while, you'll have a better sense of what you want."

Previous: The art in the family room is by Lynn Geesaman, an artist whose work my mom had in our house growing up. I love that it's photography but it's just as romantic as an Impressionist painting.

MICHELANGELO
FASHION
S IS FOR STYLE
VOGUE
VITAL VOICES
GRAY MALIN
TOM FORD 002

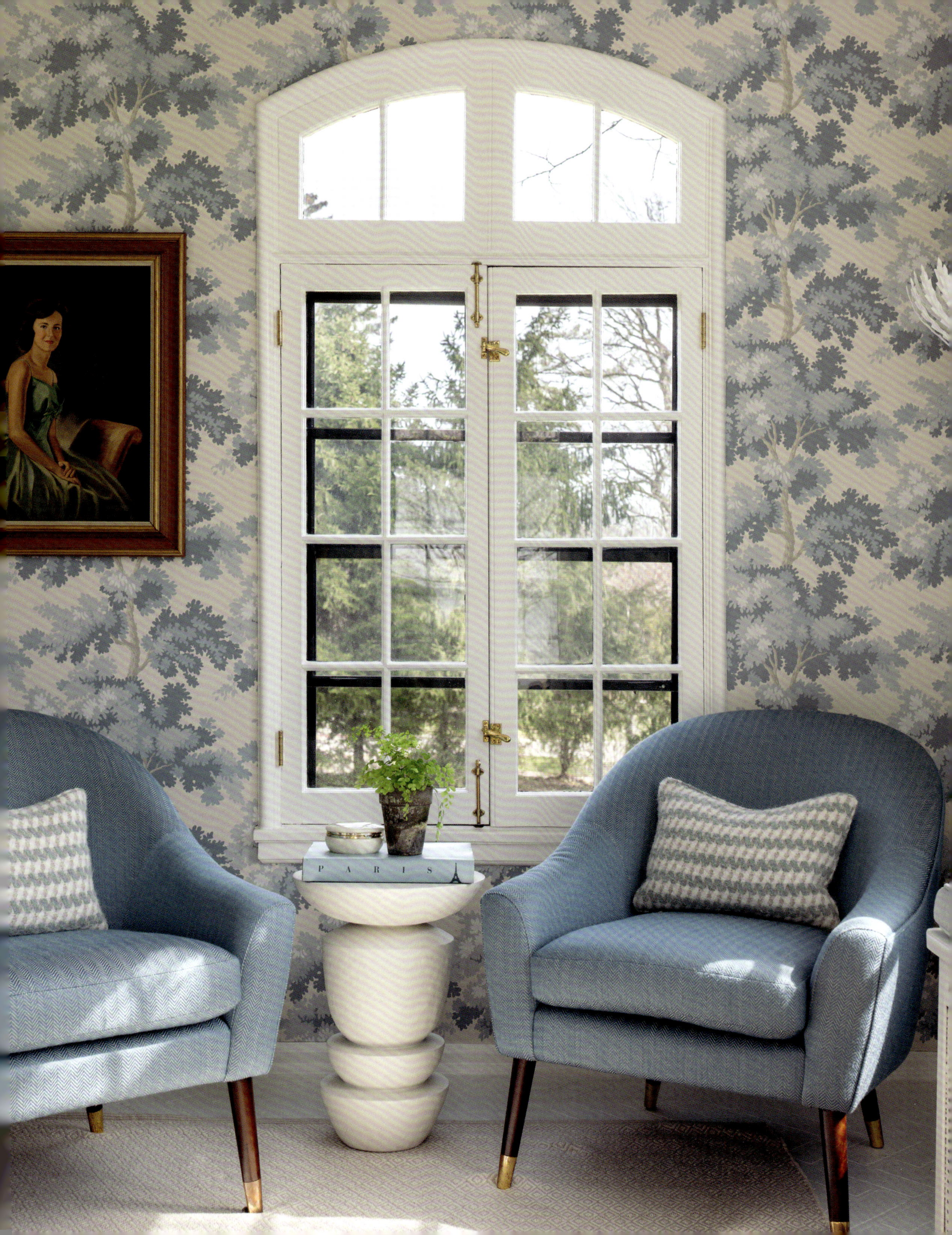
PARIS

In this little sunroom, we wanted to create an airy, ethereal feel that wasn't overly sweet; the blues in this leafy wallpaper pattern strike just the right note of softness behind a portrait of the homeowner's mother.

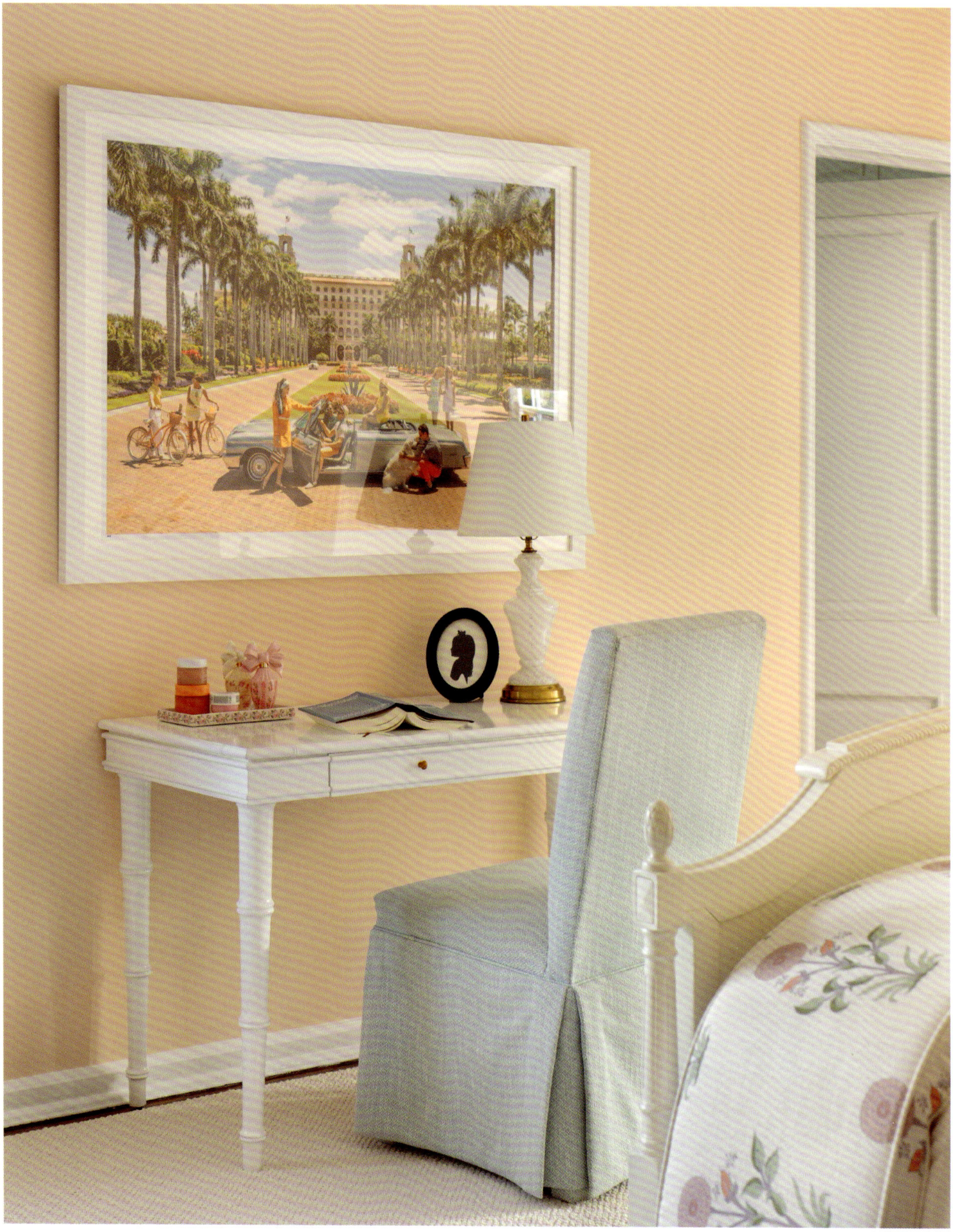

Opposite, above, and overleaf:
The two daughters have Jack-and-Jill
bedrooms, so we designed them with
the same paint color and different but
complementary styles.

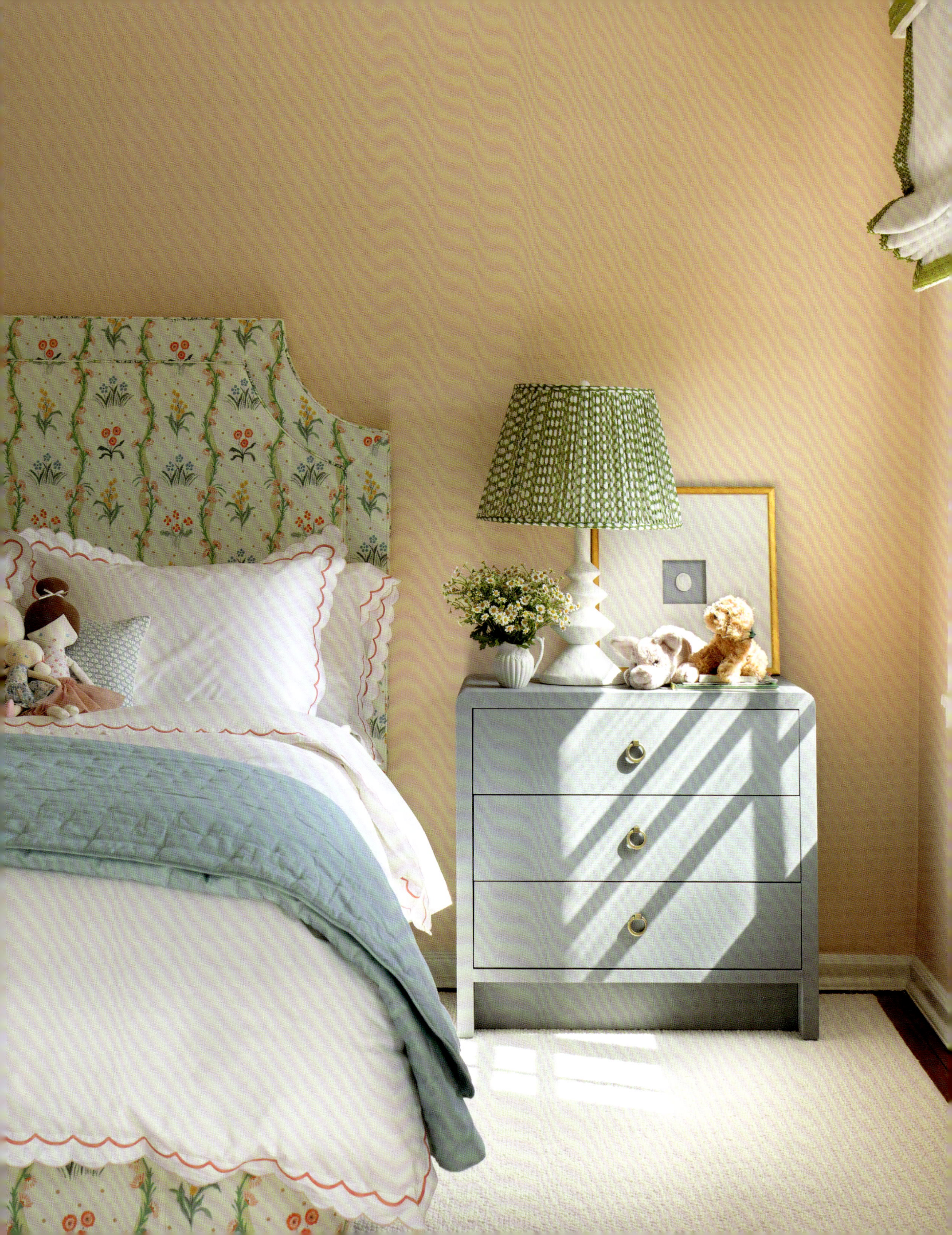

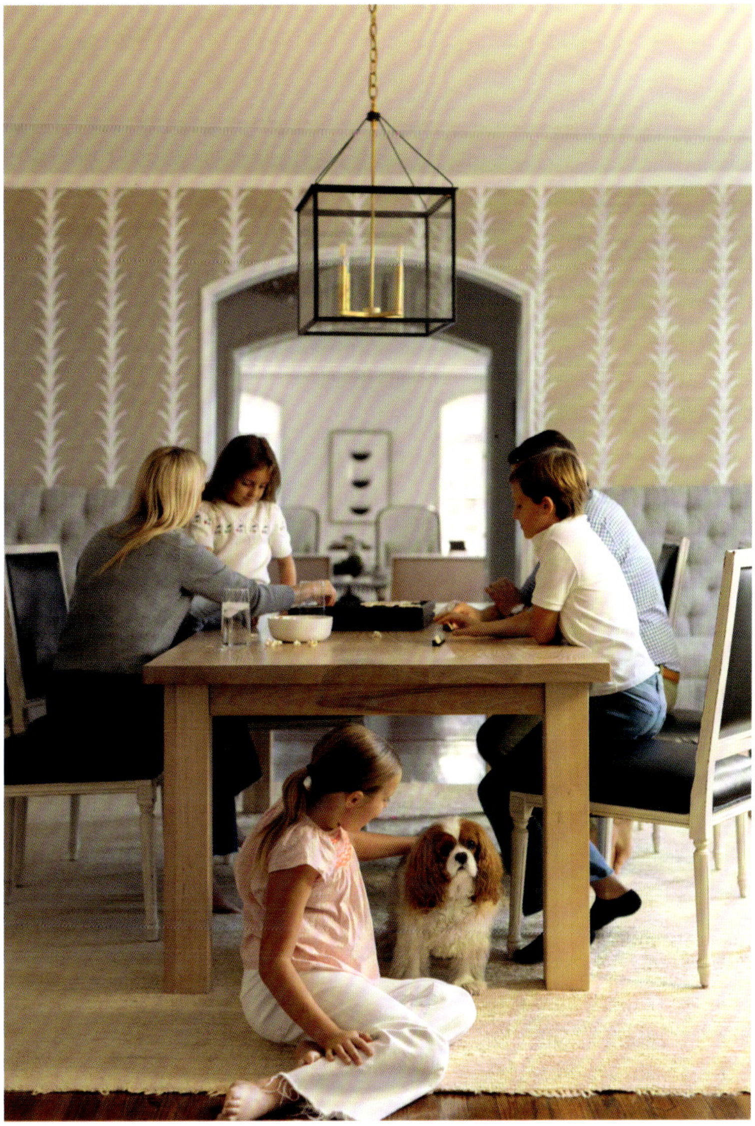

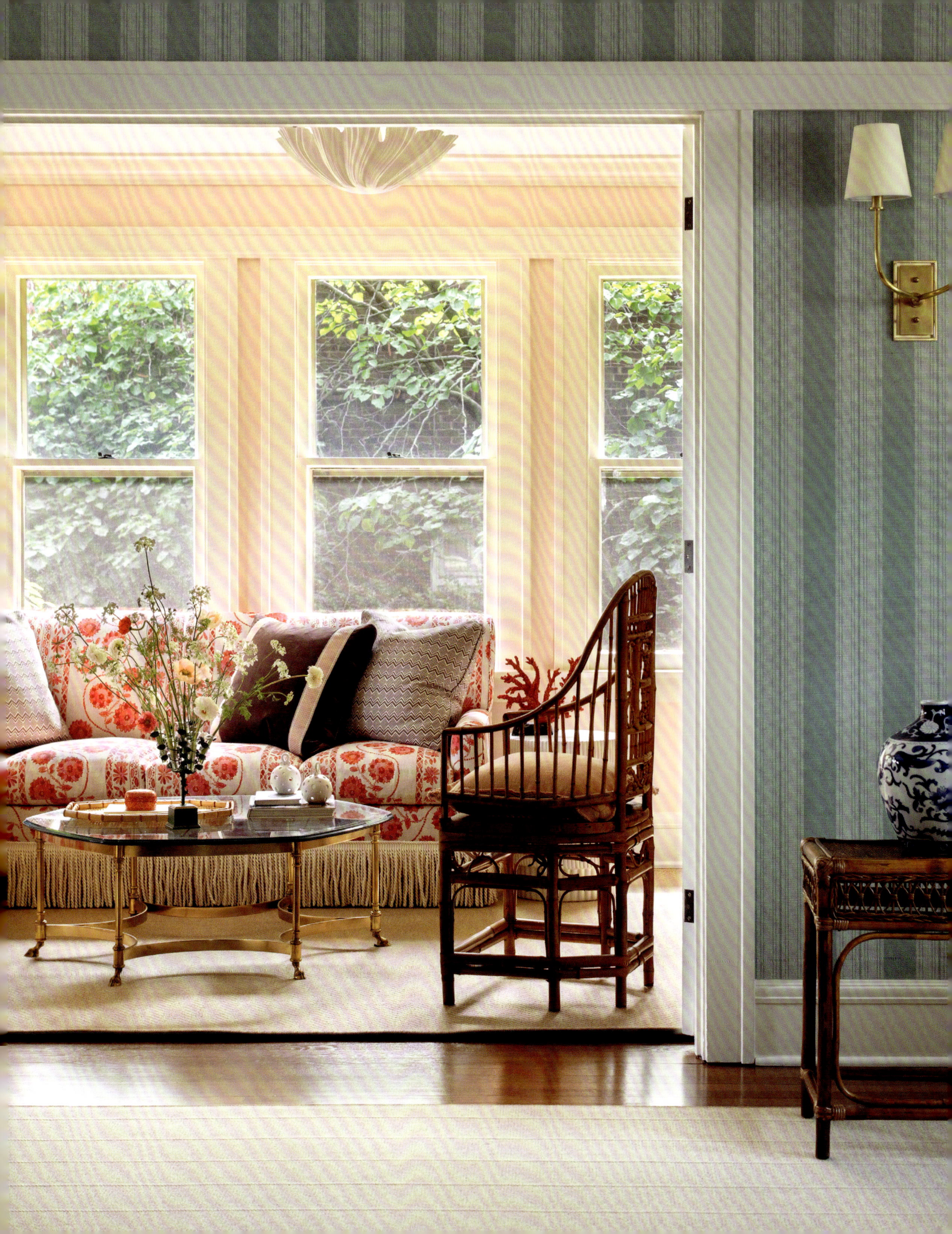

BALANCING ACT

An Arts and Crafts-style home with a traditional and whimsical redesign

Previous: The sunroom off the living room also functions as the wife's office, which she wanted to feel like a light, bright, and superfeminine retreat.

Opposite: The formal dining room is an ode to the homeowner's Southern roots with a traditional mahogany sideboard, scenic wallpaper, and an antique mirror.

When I first met with the owner of this home, she wasn't entirely clear on the stylistic direction she wanted to take: Her inspiration images ran the gamut from 1970s Jacques Grange to heavy neoclassical spaces, to rooms with vibrant colors and floral textiles that nodded to her own Southern roots, and she had a deeply meaningful collection of inherited items that she wanted to incorporate into the design. What she did know was that she wanted color, she wanted pattern, and she wanted an element of unexpected whimsy. Her biggest stipulation, she told me, was that she didn't want her home to feel neutral and impersonal, like a blandly designed hotel. Not only that, but she and her husband have a young daughter, so the house also needed to feel livable for all three of them.

The neighborhood where this home is located is known for bungalow-style houses like this one. The home is prewar, with an Arts and Craft aesthetic, and has some very special architectural details, including substantial moldings and arched windows and trim.

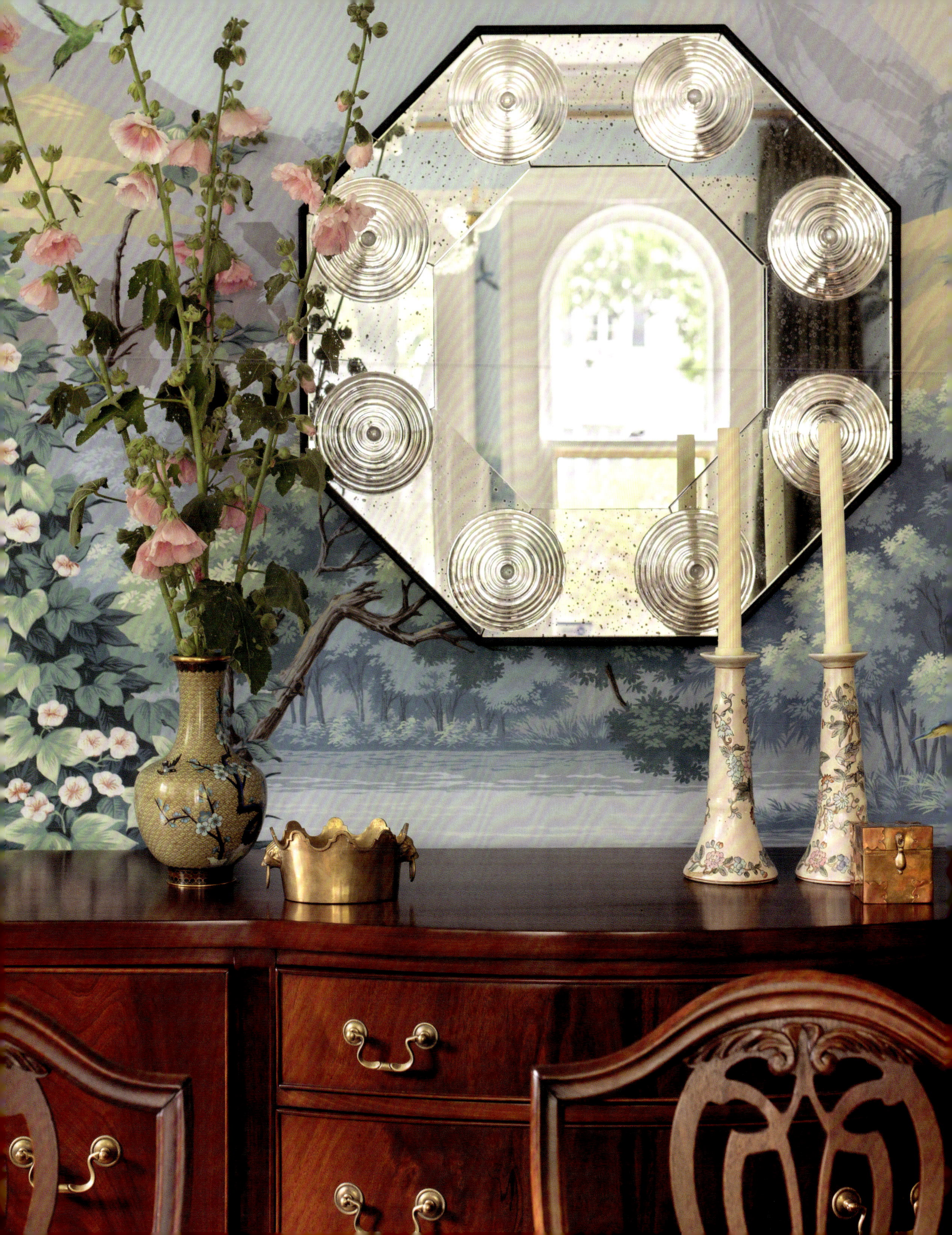

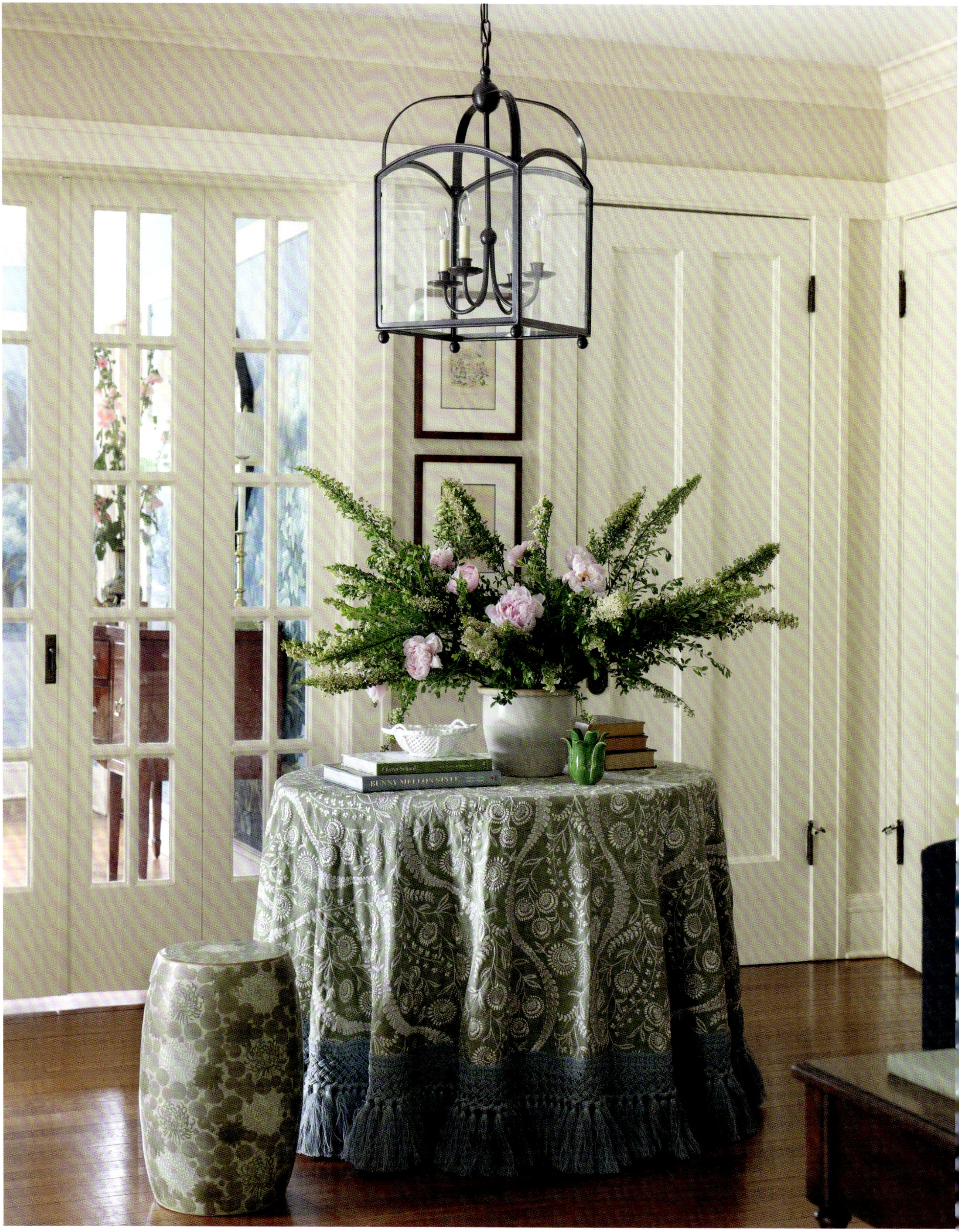
Charm School
BUNNY MELLON STYLE

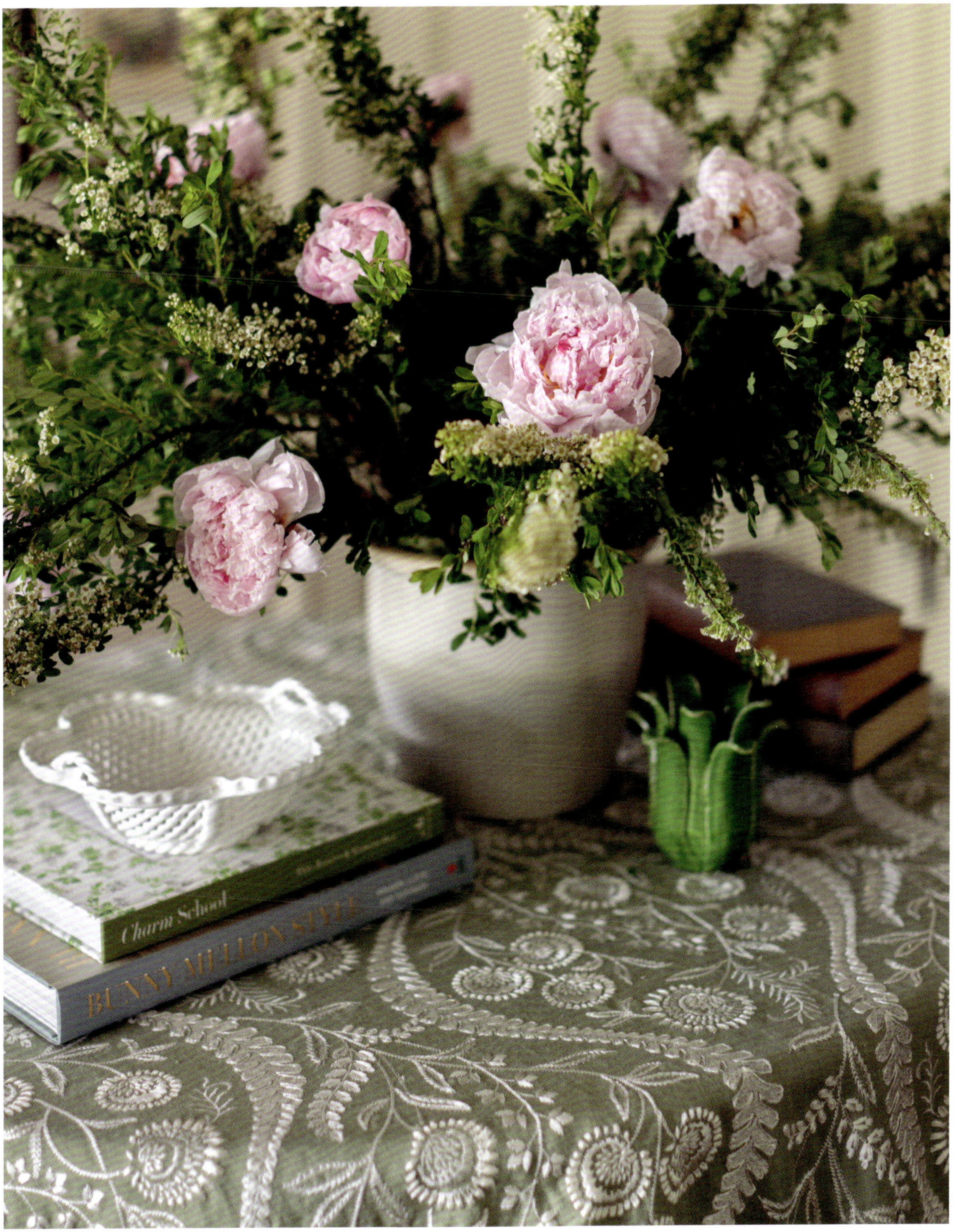
Charm School
BUNNY MELLON STYLE

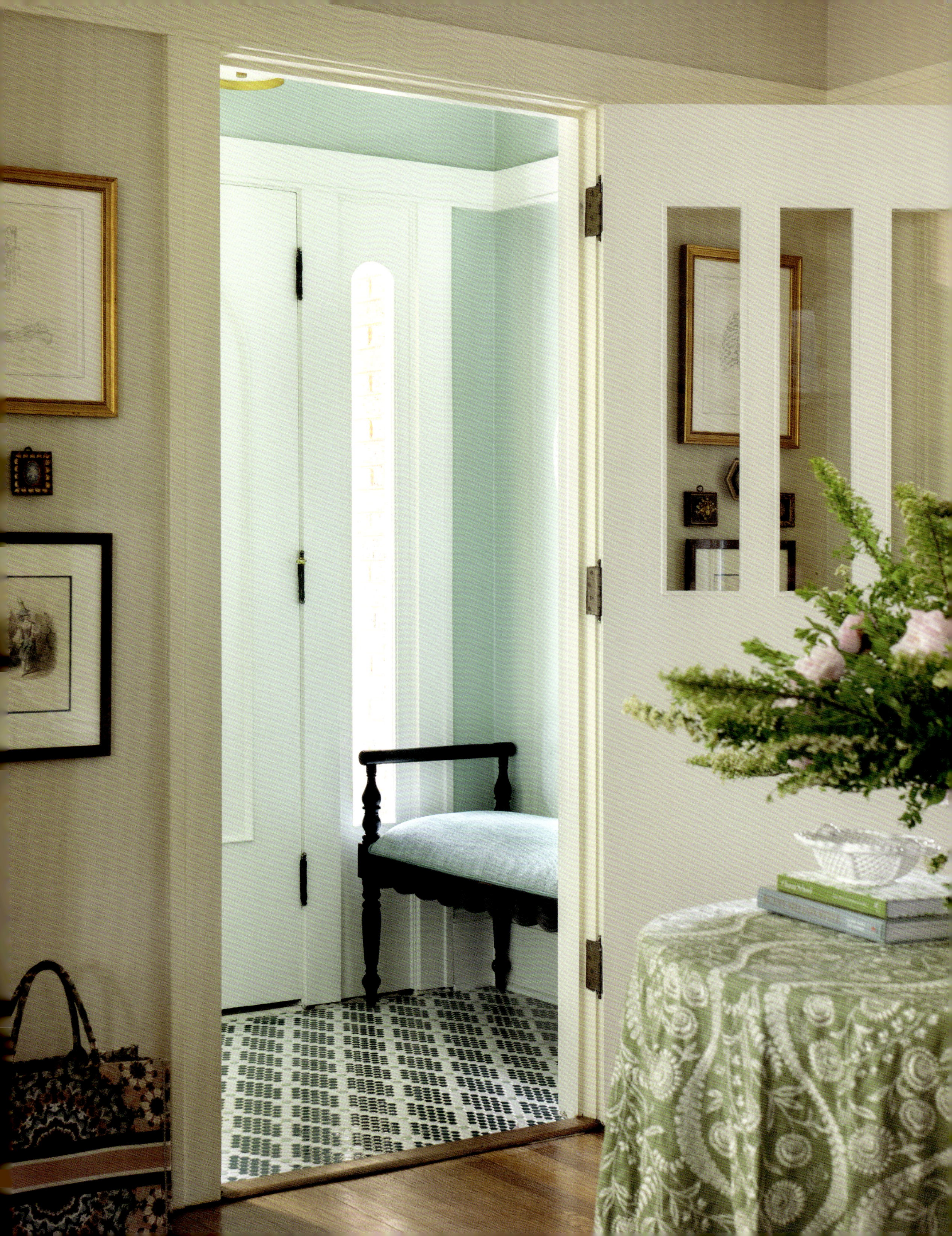

Previous: The entry table's blue-and-green tablecloth, with its oversized fringe trim, hints at the fun twists on tradition that appear throughout the home.

Opposite: This little vestibule provides entry to the larger foyer, giving us the opportunity to do something unexpected. We lacquered the walls in blue-green to reflect light and set the tone for the rest of the house.

Right: A mirror framed in entwined snakes provides an edgy counterpoint to the graciousness of the house.

The architecture of the house was our jumping-off point. From there, we incorporated color and whimsy to match the feel of the inspiration images she had provided. As we worked together throughout the process, she came to trust me more and more, and it was so much fun to watch her fall in love with the design elements that she had been hesitant about as they came to life in the house. A perfect example of this is the kitchen breakfast nook, where the family now spends most of their time. When I first suggested the vine-patterned wallcovering, pleated chintz pendant, and purple banquette, she reeled at the combination. But ultimately she came around to it, and now she—and the whole family—loves it. This joyfully vibrant corner perfectly complements the more quiet, neutral kitchen.

By far the home's boldest room, though, is the dining room. From the beginning, we knew we would use an heirloom dining set that had been passed down through the family. I wanted to ensure that the space didn't seem stuffy or stale with the traditional table, chairs, and corner cabinet. The challenge was to make the room feel fresh. The answer came in the form of the mural wallpaper, the perfect balancing feature: a bit funky, a little whimsical, and a total conversation starter (this couple hosts frequent gatherings of colleagues and friends). The paper's menagerie of tropical birds gives the pattern a bit more edge than typical chinoiserie. To further strike the right balance between the quirkiness of the wallpaper and the sophistication of the furniture, we lightened the weightiness of the dark wood dining set with mossy green drapes and peach-upholstered the chairs. The sparkling Murano glass chandelier was the cherry on top. Our goal was for the home to feel classic but characterful, unexpected, and colorful—and this room speaks to that perfectly.

While this sunroom is also the wife's office, the daughter loves to spend time there, too, so we made sure to incorporate plenty of comfortable seating with the sectional.

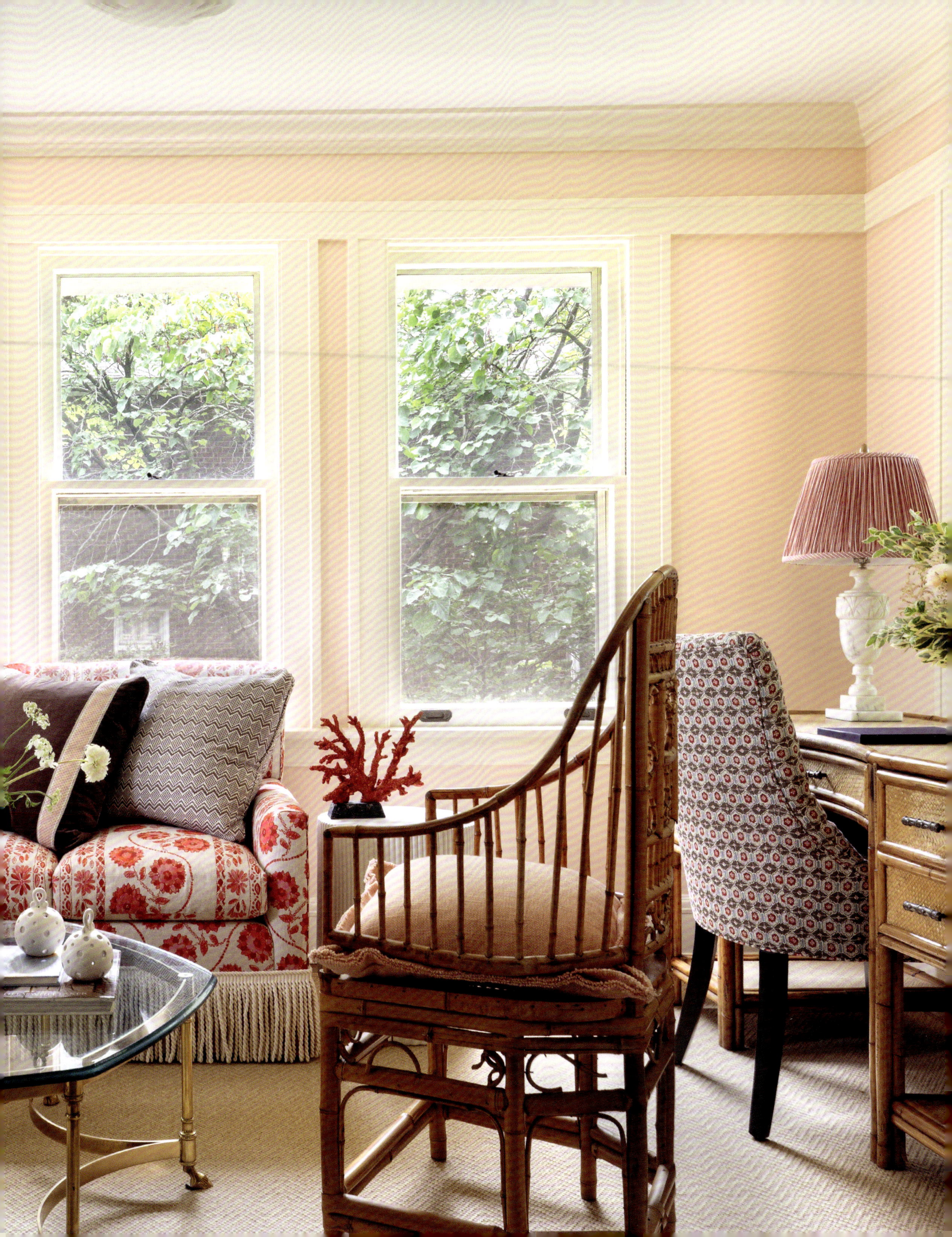

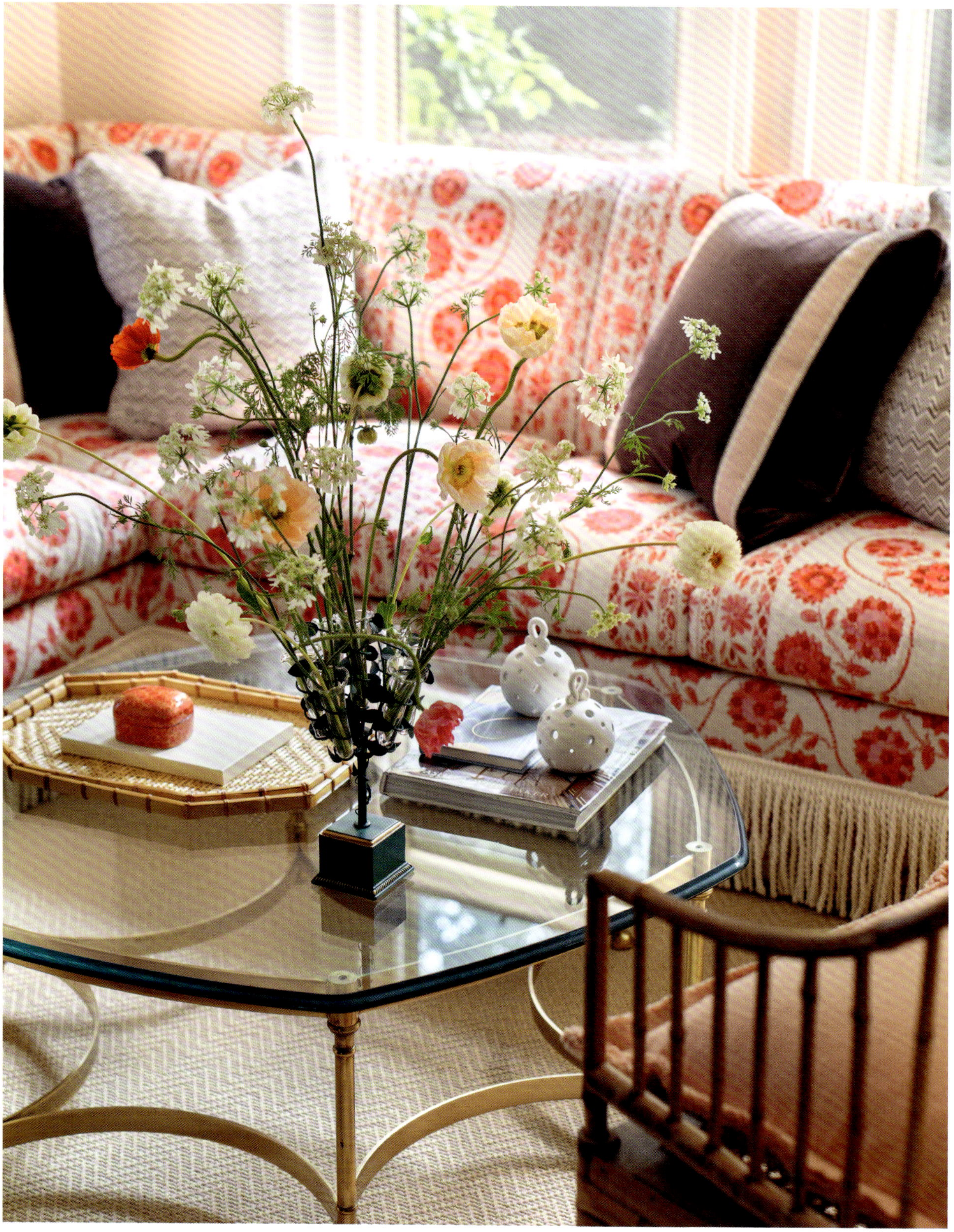

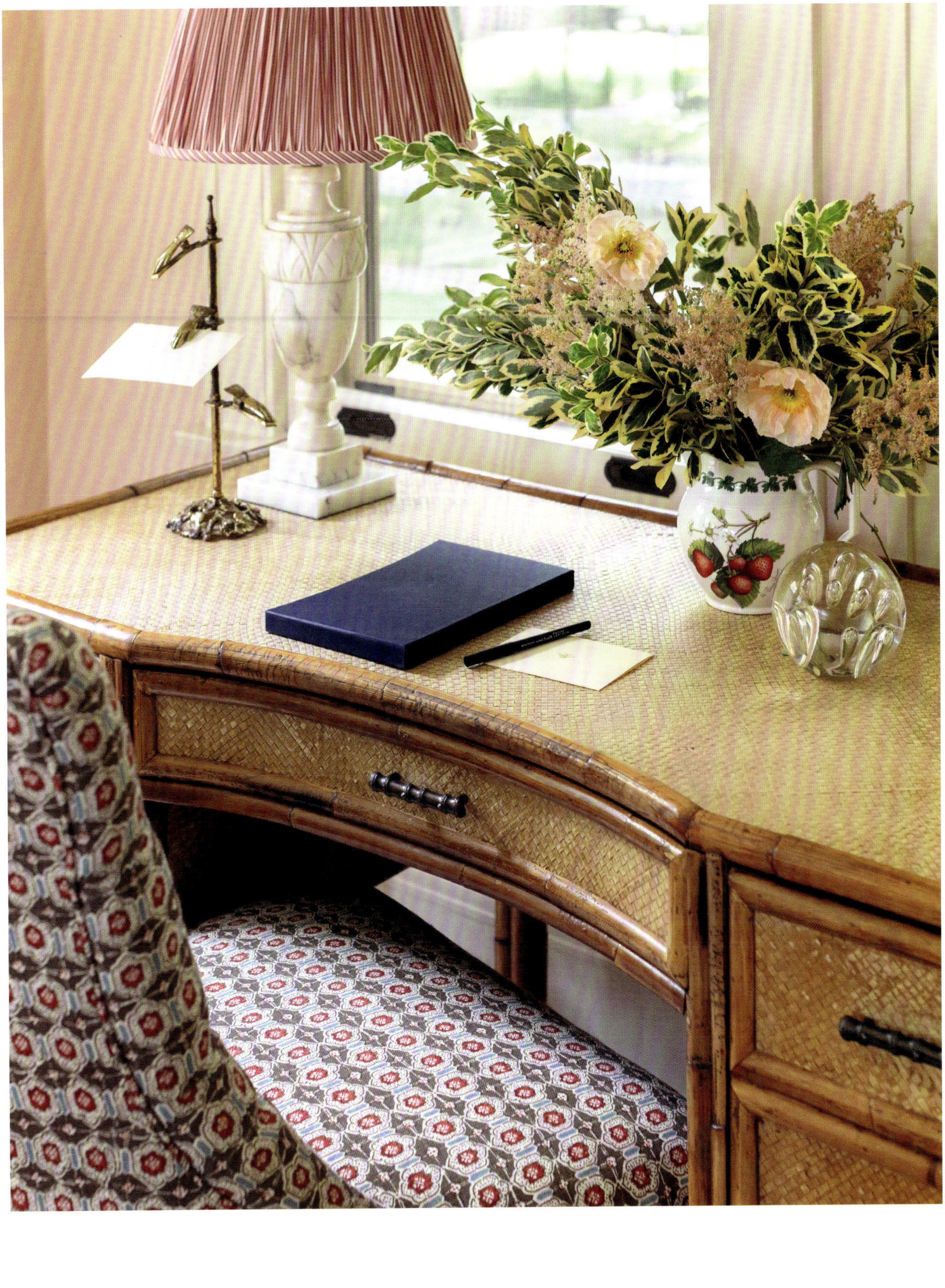

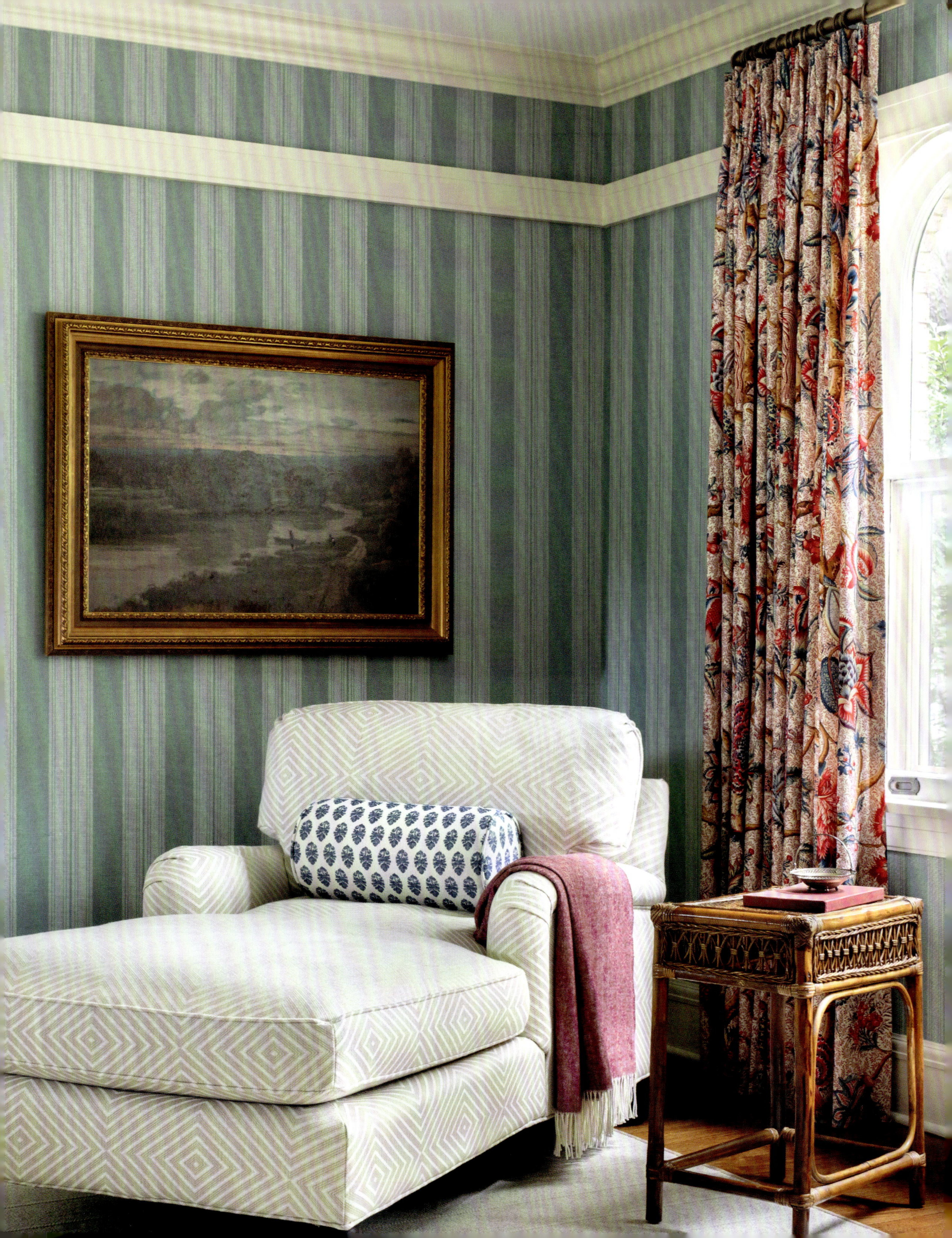

In the living room, we painted the redbrick fireplace surround a fresh, bright white, but preserved the original checkerboard hearth.

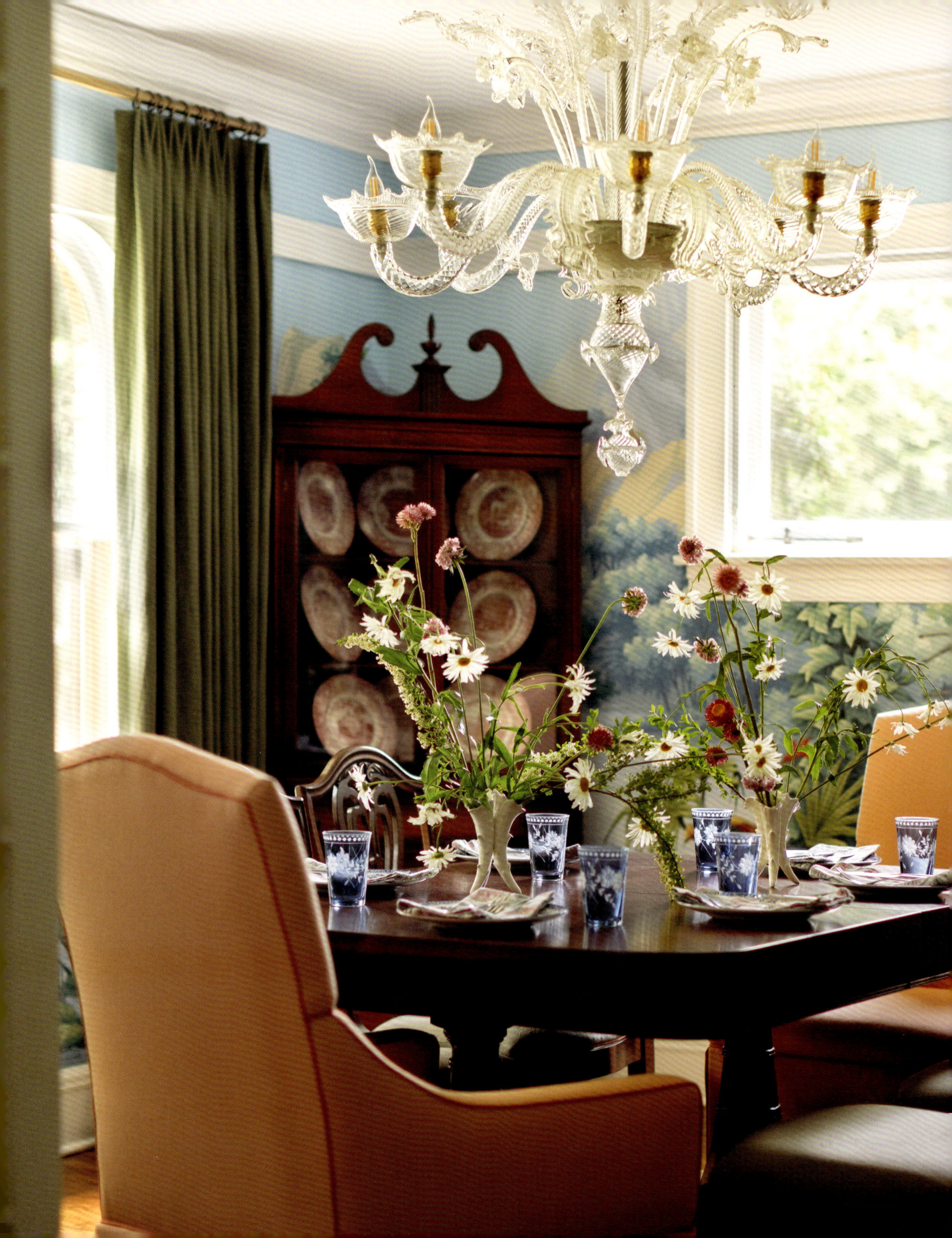

"She wanted color, she wanted pattern, and she wanted an element of unexpected whimsy."

It is especially exciting when a client has a collection of meaningful things that we get to incorporate, and we did so much of that here, finding the right places for the dining room furniture and her grandparents' piano, portraits from her great-grandmother, and even her father's drawings from medical school. As we sourced for the home, we created a mix of the new (sofas and a coffee table) and the inherited, but we also made space for the pieces that she had collected. For the new items, comfort was key—especially in the family room. To the husband, that meant recliners—much to my chagrin! I managed to find a chic set, which I had reupholstered in custom fabric. After all, a room should serve the people who are living in it, and this is a room where they can get cozy. Plus, the addition of abstract art flanked by drapes in Oscar de la Renta's Jessup print gives this room all the elegance it needs.

Left and overleaf:
The homeowners had some very traditional dining furniture from family that we knew we wanted to use, so we balanced that formality with a whimsical tropical-inspired wallpaper. The vintage Murano glass chandelier is the perfect topper.

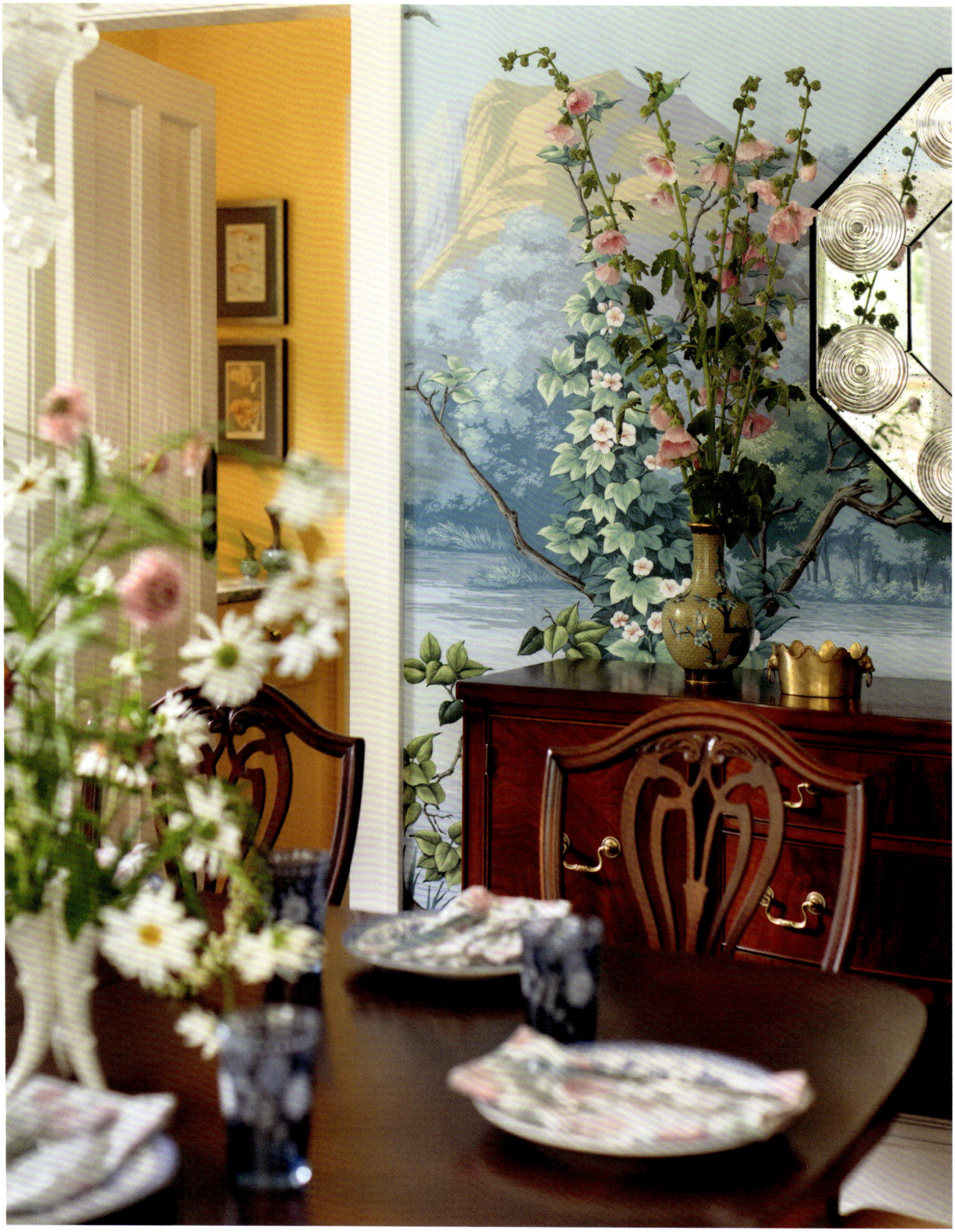

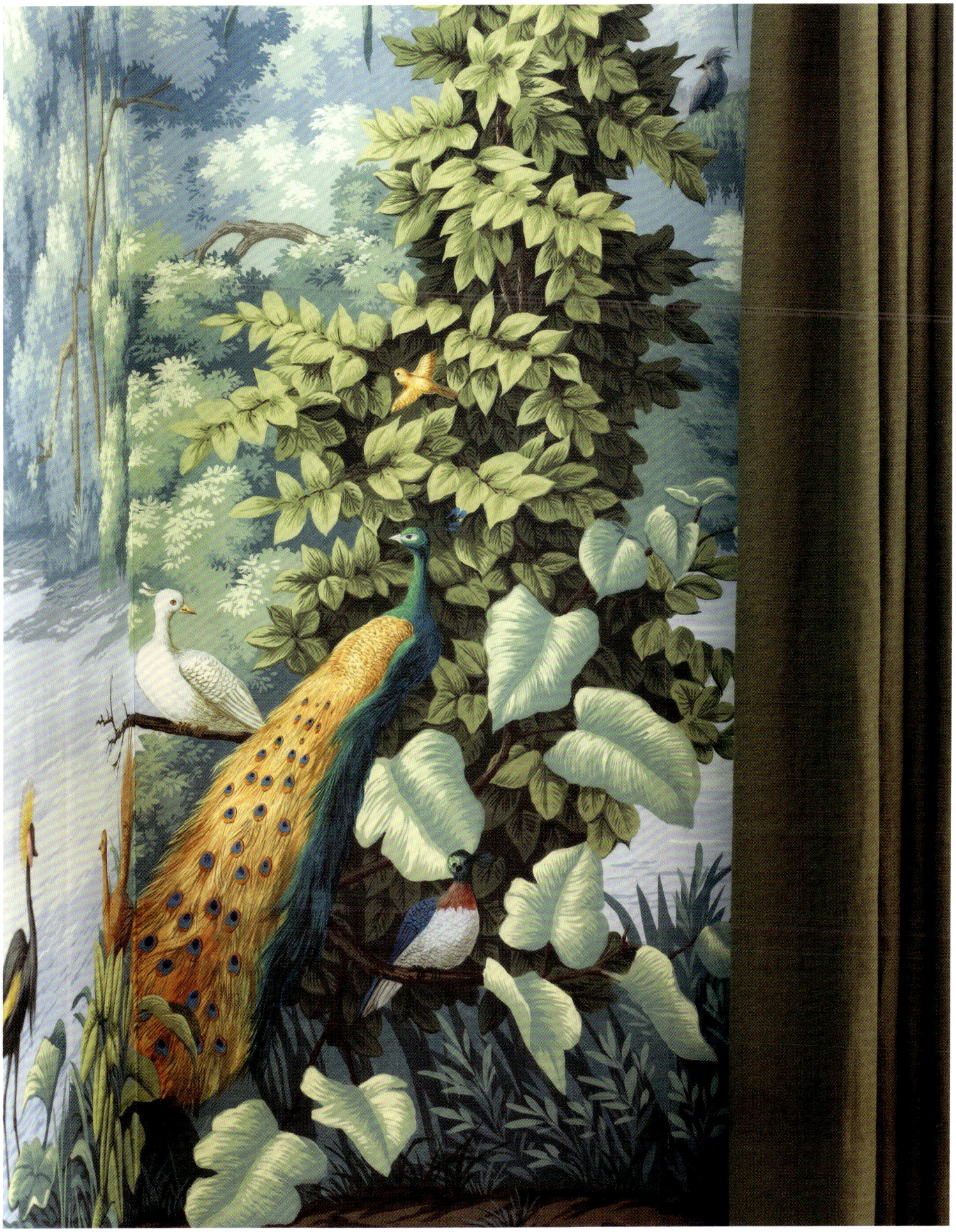

Beyond the family room is a powder room that we covered in a bright yellow Pierre Frey floral wallpaper that somehow brings together the entire ground floor of the home. It ties into the sunflower yellow in the pantry, it echoes colors from the dining room mural, and it's just a cheerful space that radiates Southern charm. The design leaned more feminine in the sunroom off the formal living room, which is the wife's office. She wanted it to be a space where she could work but also where she could sit and read or just relax. I've always loved red and pink together; here the red in the sofa fabric tempers the pale pink of the walls so that the room doesn't feel overly sweet. We sourced an antique desk and lamp and a number of other pieces with history so that the room flows with the rest of the house, but still feels fresh and inviting.

We went bold for the bedroom, much to the initial concern of the husband. The primary bedroom is a big space with very high ceilings, and I wanted it to feel as special as the rest of the house, so we gave it a wall-to-ceiling wallpaper treatment. My goal was to carry the whimsy of the downstairs through into the upper level, but in a way that it was quiet enough that the bedroom still feels restful.

I often say, "Just because it's historic doesn't mean it's pretty." Don't feel beholden to someone's taste from a century ago. In the case of this house, the moldings and interior architecture lent great character and personality, but in some ways that didn't align with this family's style. So, while I strived to maintain some of that original detail, we wanted to make it truly feel like home for its new residents: a lively family home that combined the old and the new, the historic and the eccentric.

I didn't want the butler's pantry, situated between the supersaturated dining room and the white kitchen, to feel forgotten. The butter-yellow walls deliver a traditional Southern look that still feels fresh.

Overleaf: For the family room, the husband insisted on recliners, which are rarely my go-to. But once upholstered in custom fabric, the ones we found from a big-box retailer are actually very chic.

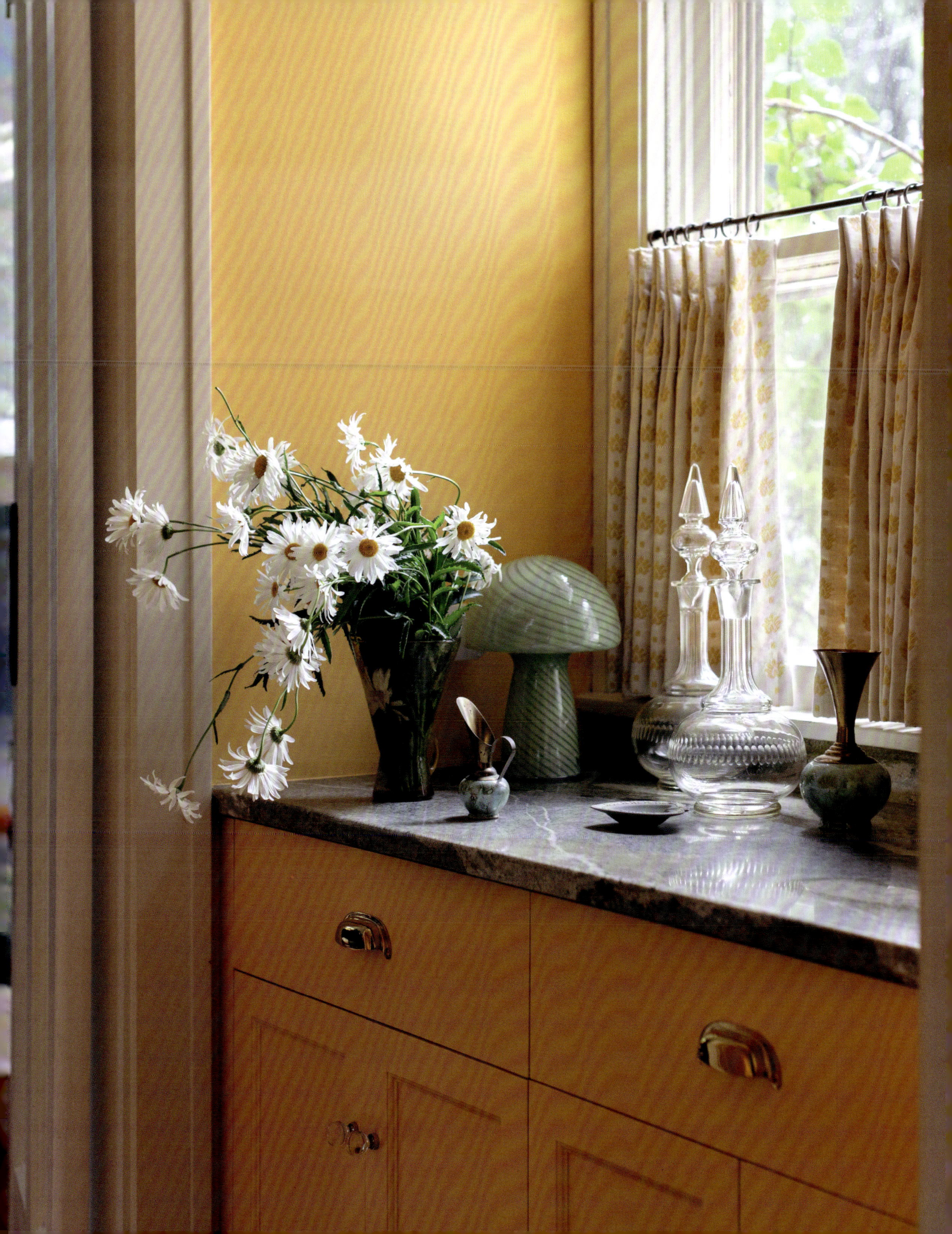

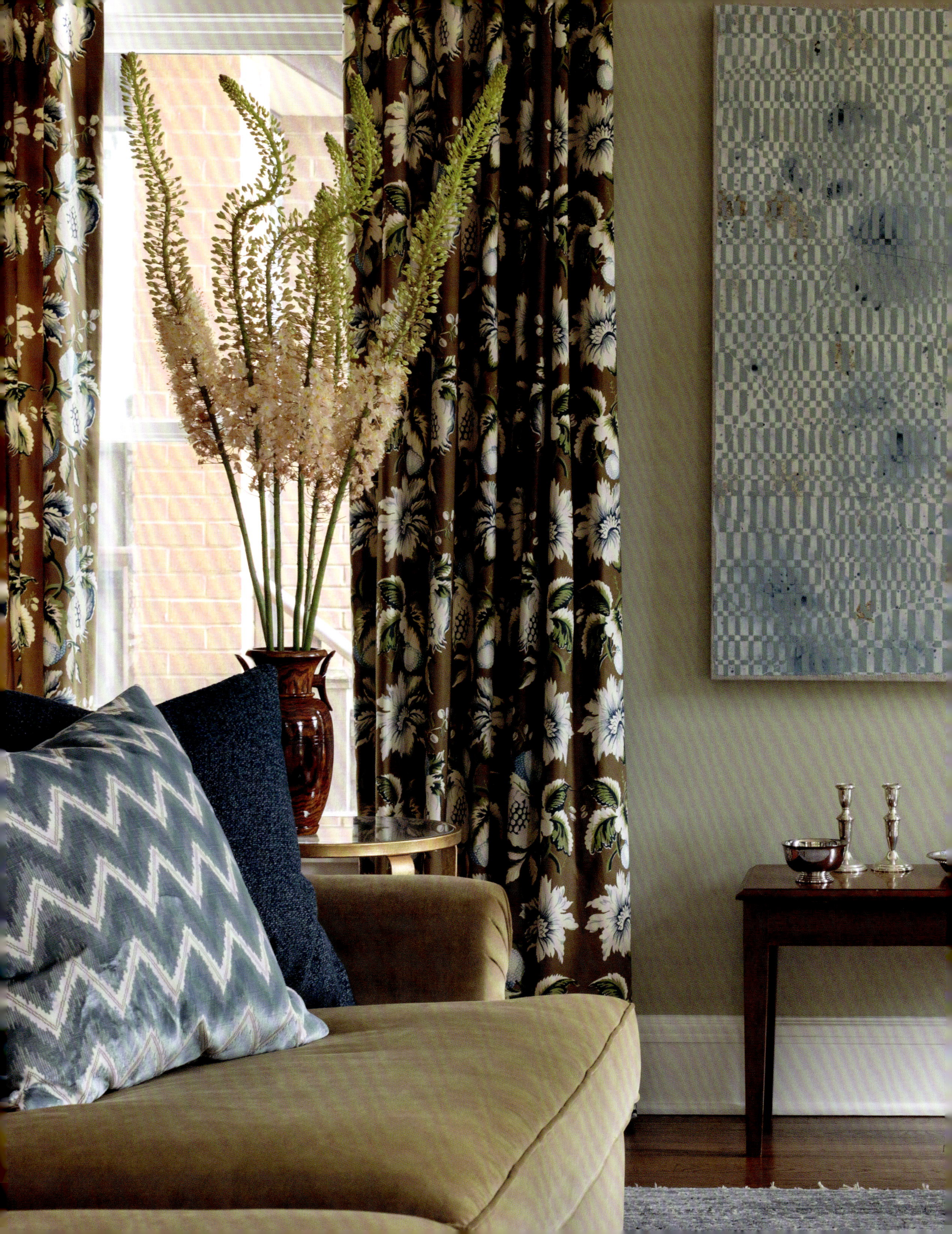

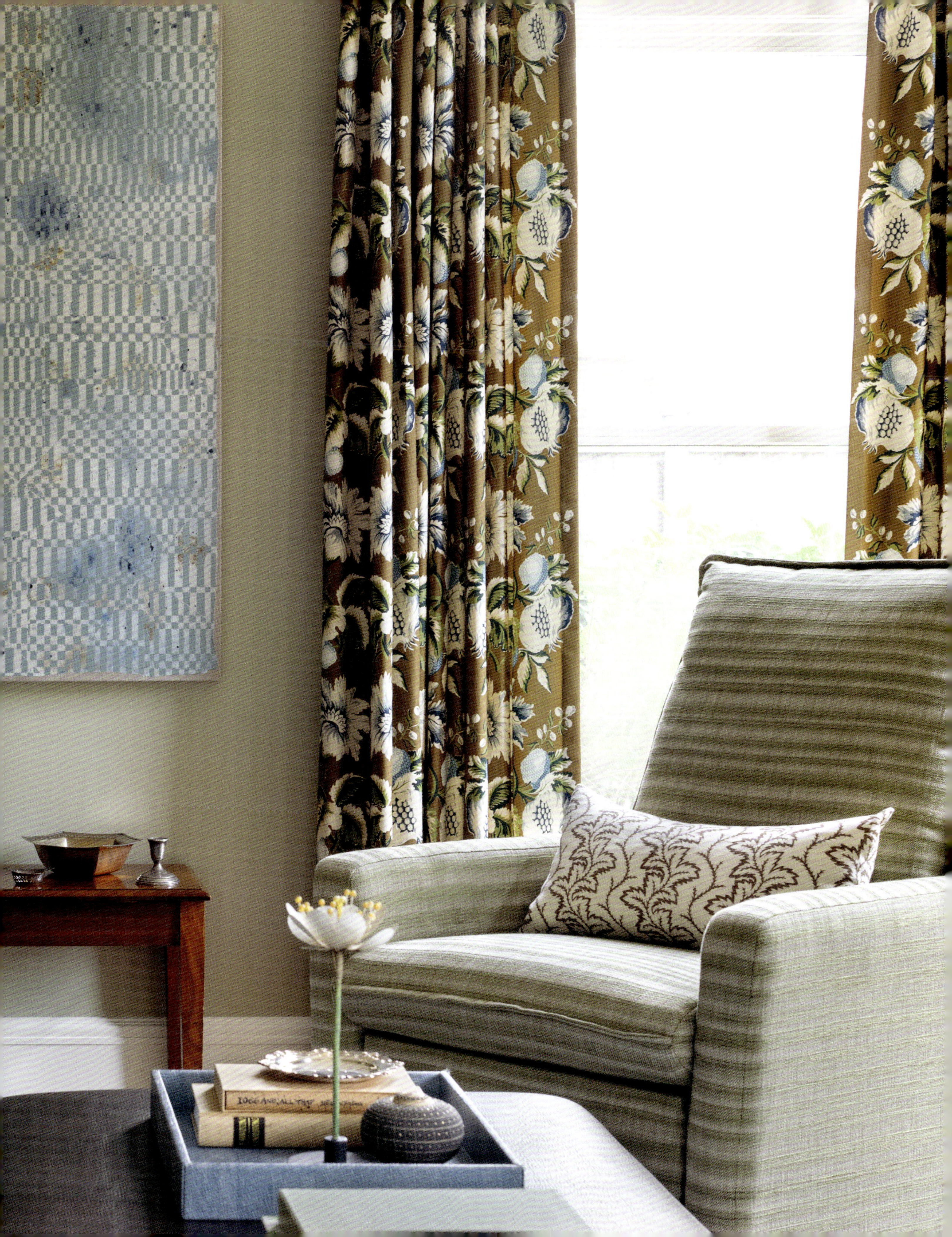
1066 AND ALL THAT

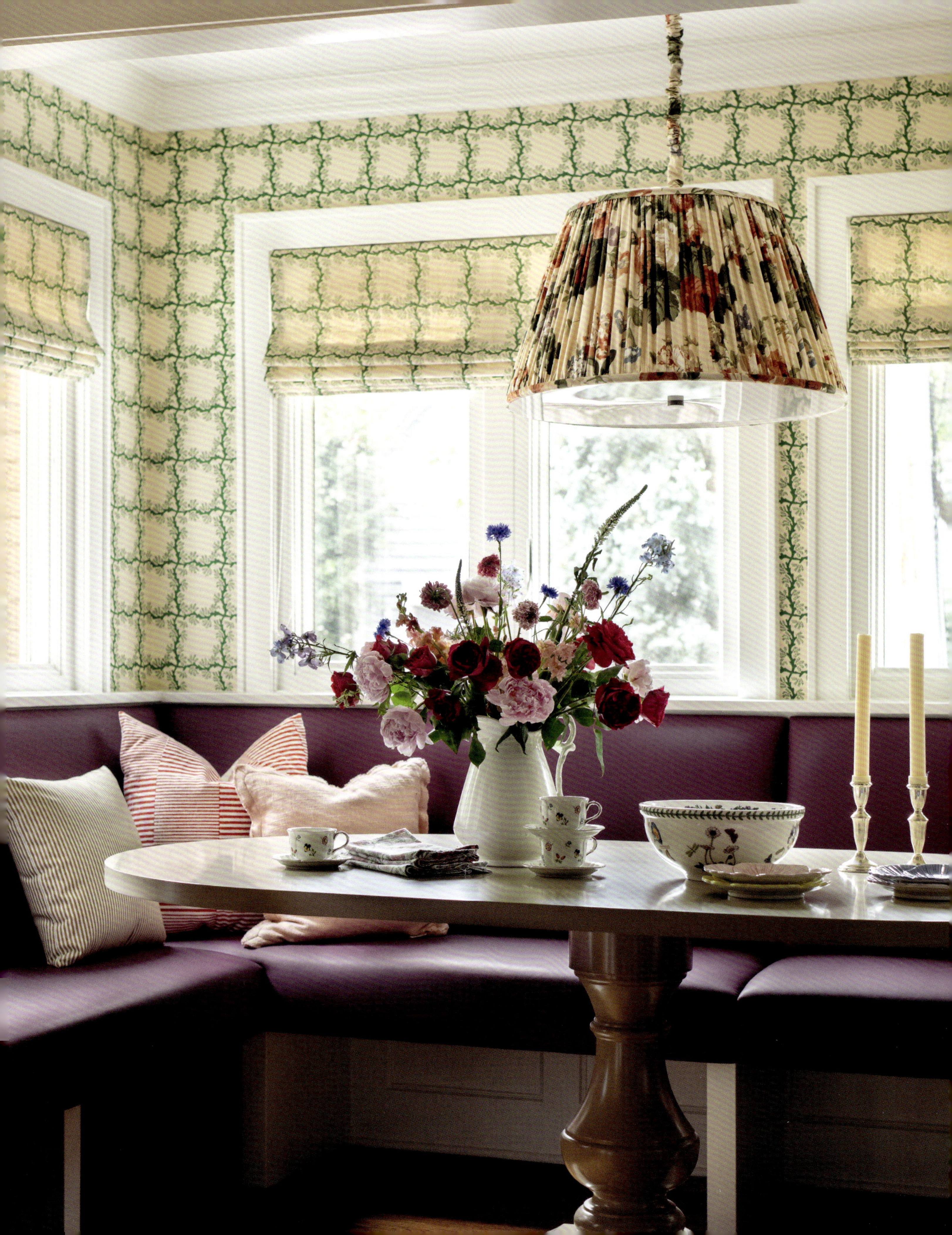

Arranged on vine-patterned wallpaper is a collection of botanical prints that the clients have amassed over several years; now, they can admire them while dining or having their morning coffee.

Overleaf left: This powder room is a case study in making a tiny space impactful. We skirted the existing pedestal sink in a ticking stripe for a graphic counterpart to the bright Pierre Frey wallpaper, then combined it with an antique mirror.

Overleaf right: The mudroom is a high-traffic area, so we kept the functionality of storage and seating area but added warmth with green and wood tones.

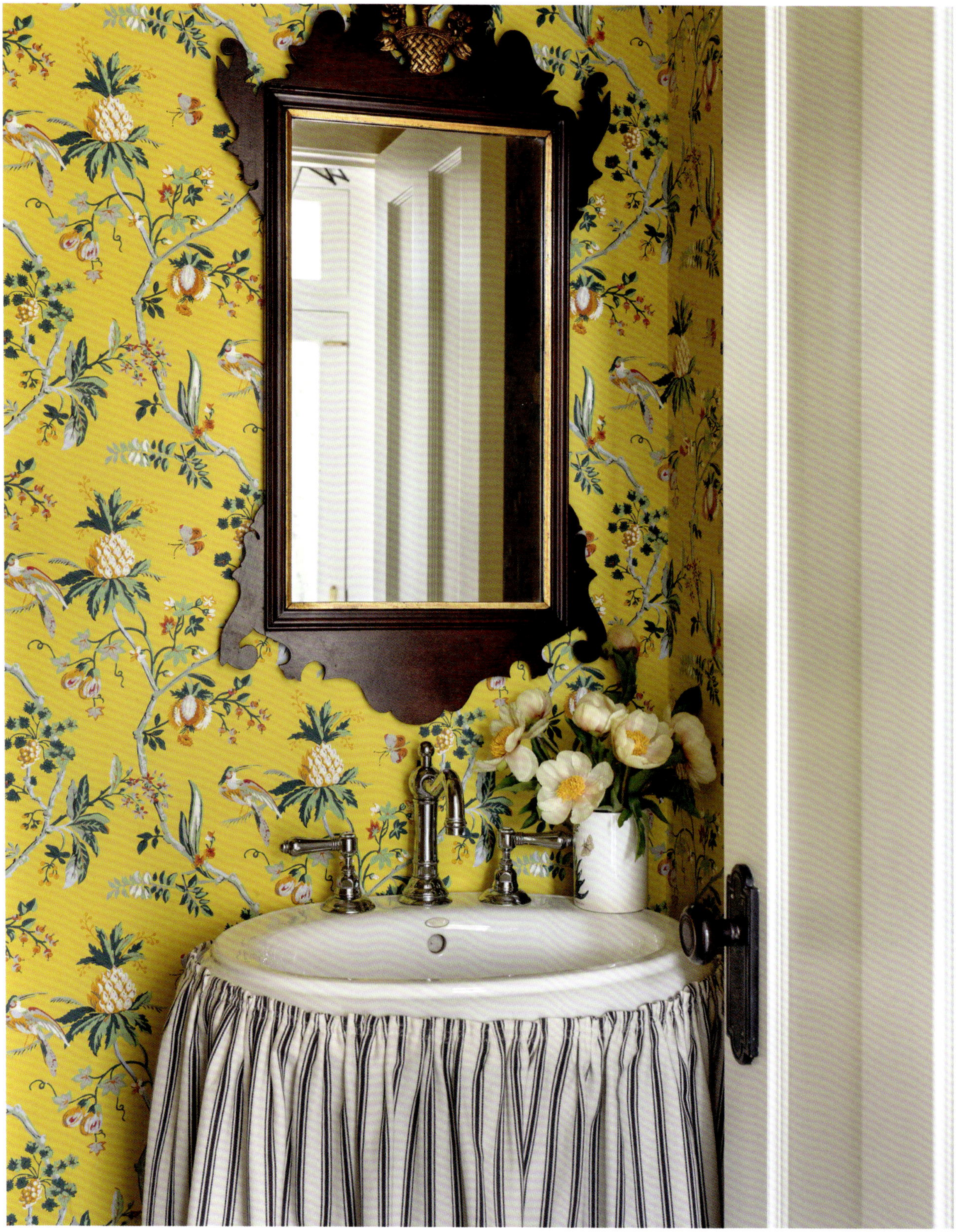

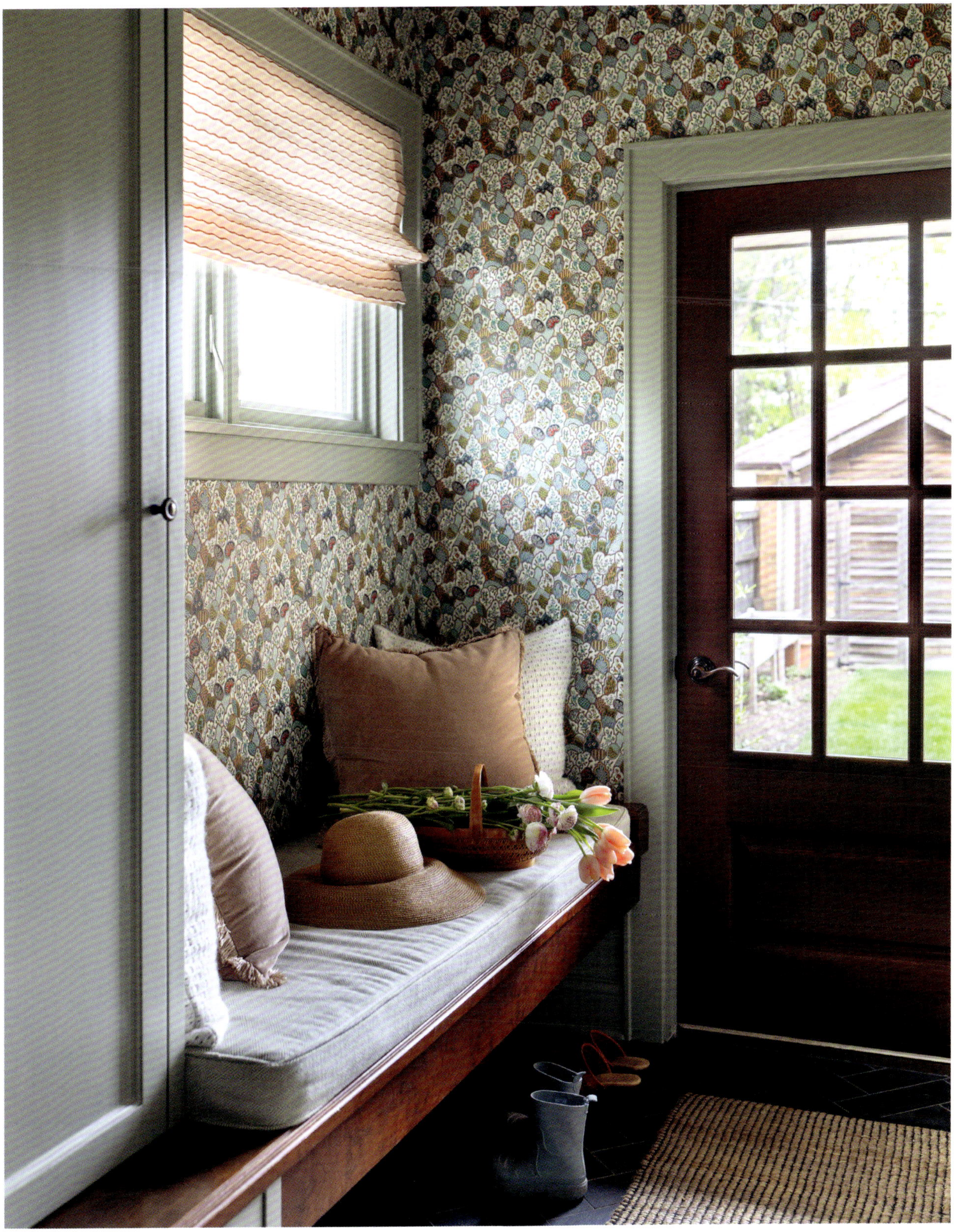

We took a light touch in the kitchen, with the idea that they might do a full remodel down the road; green tiles, brass hardware, and a soft pattern on the counter stool cushions give touches of extra personality without a full demo.

—

Overleaf: The vaulted ceilings in this primary bedroom lent themselves perfectly to this wall-to-ceiling wallpaper treatment, which brings warmth and personality.

—

Page 97: The homeowners' pugs, Bonnie and Clyde.

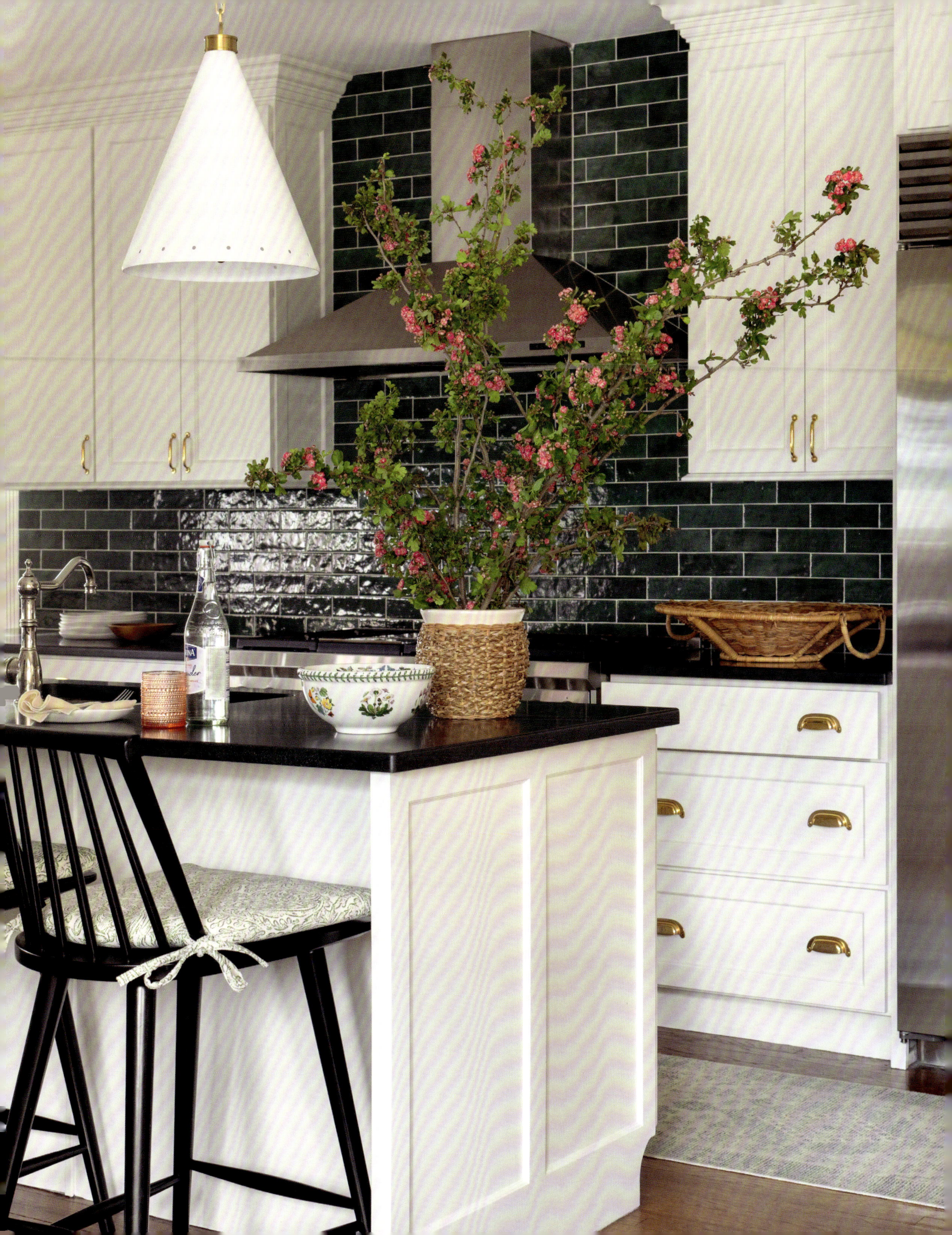

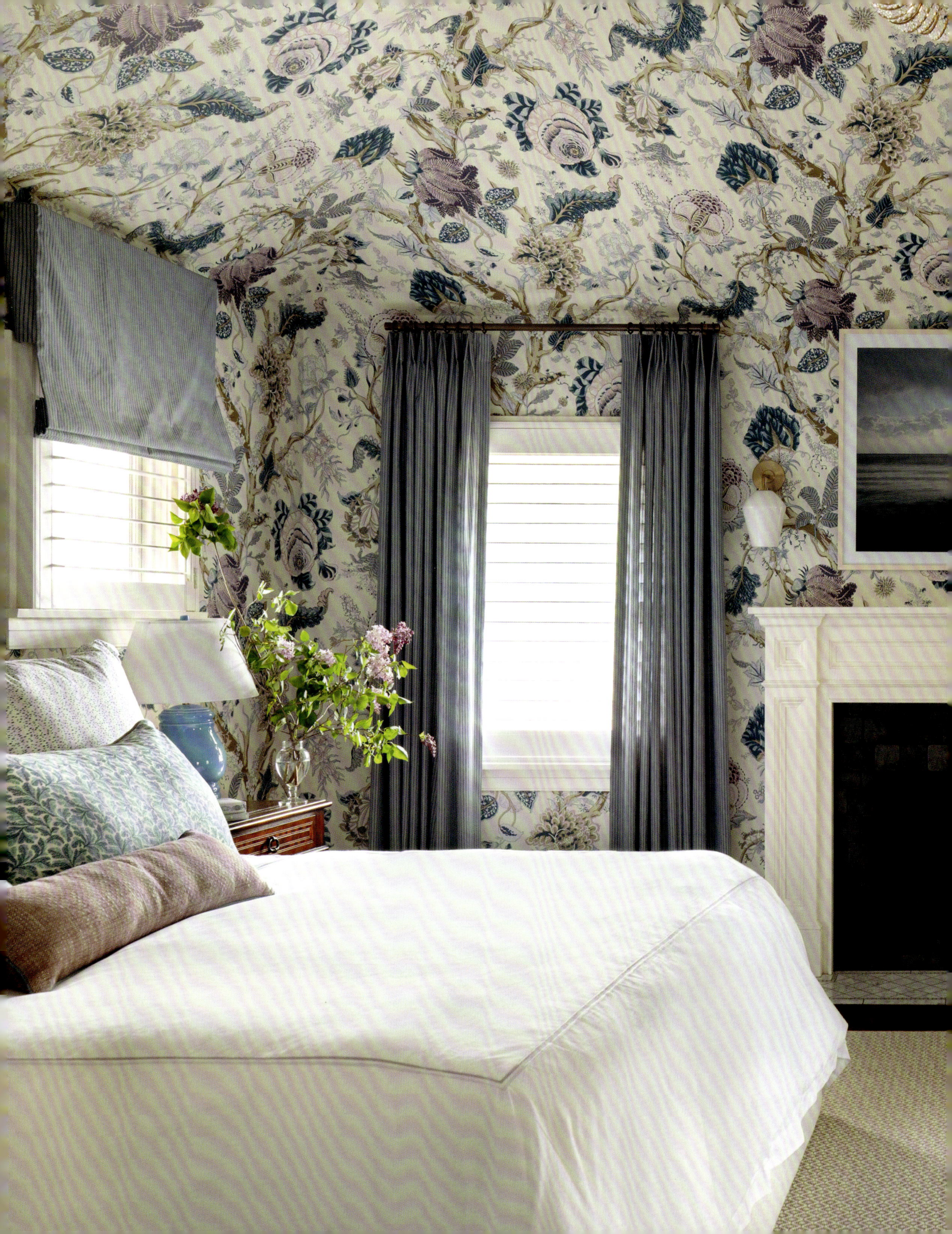

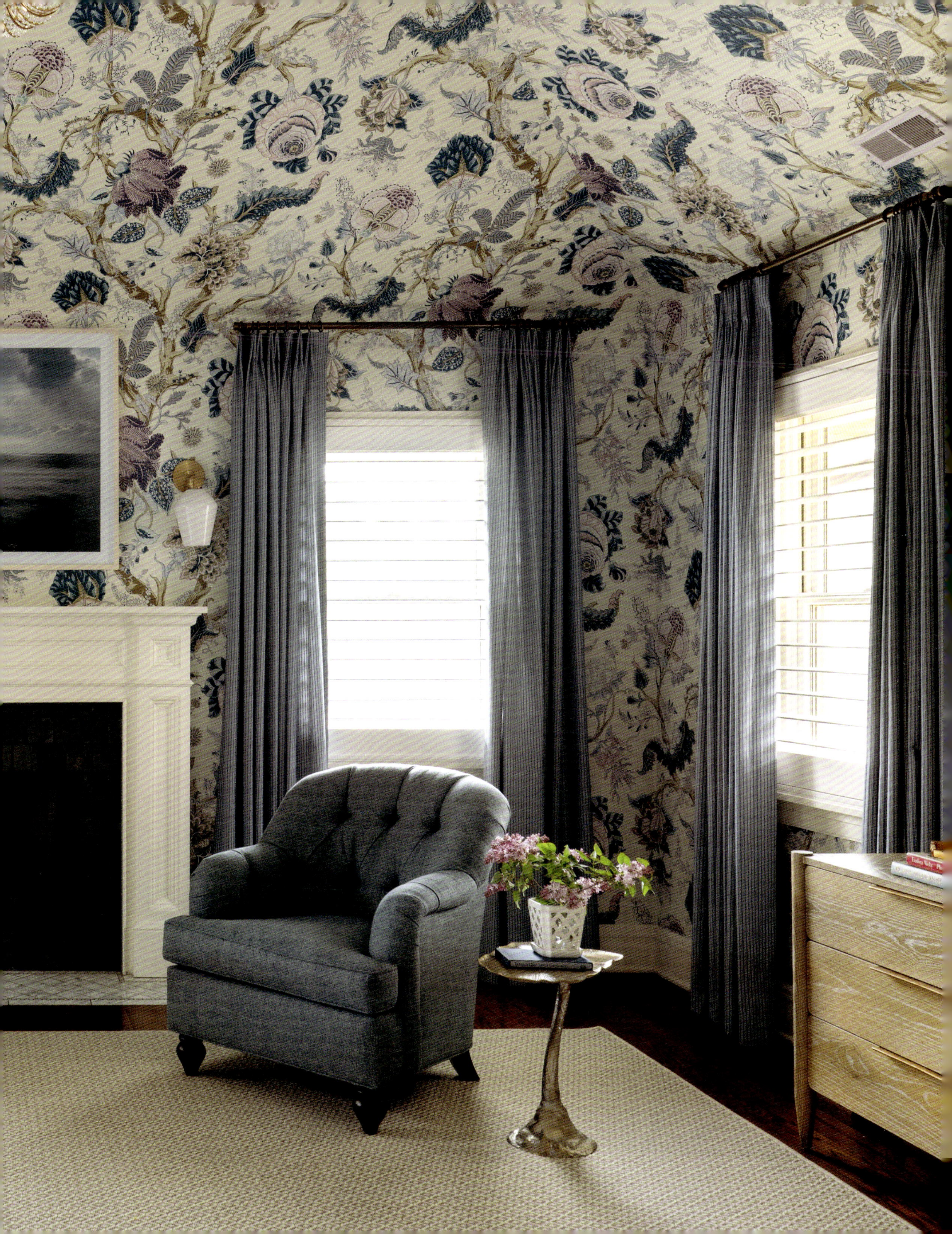

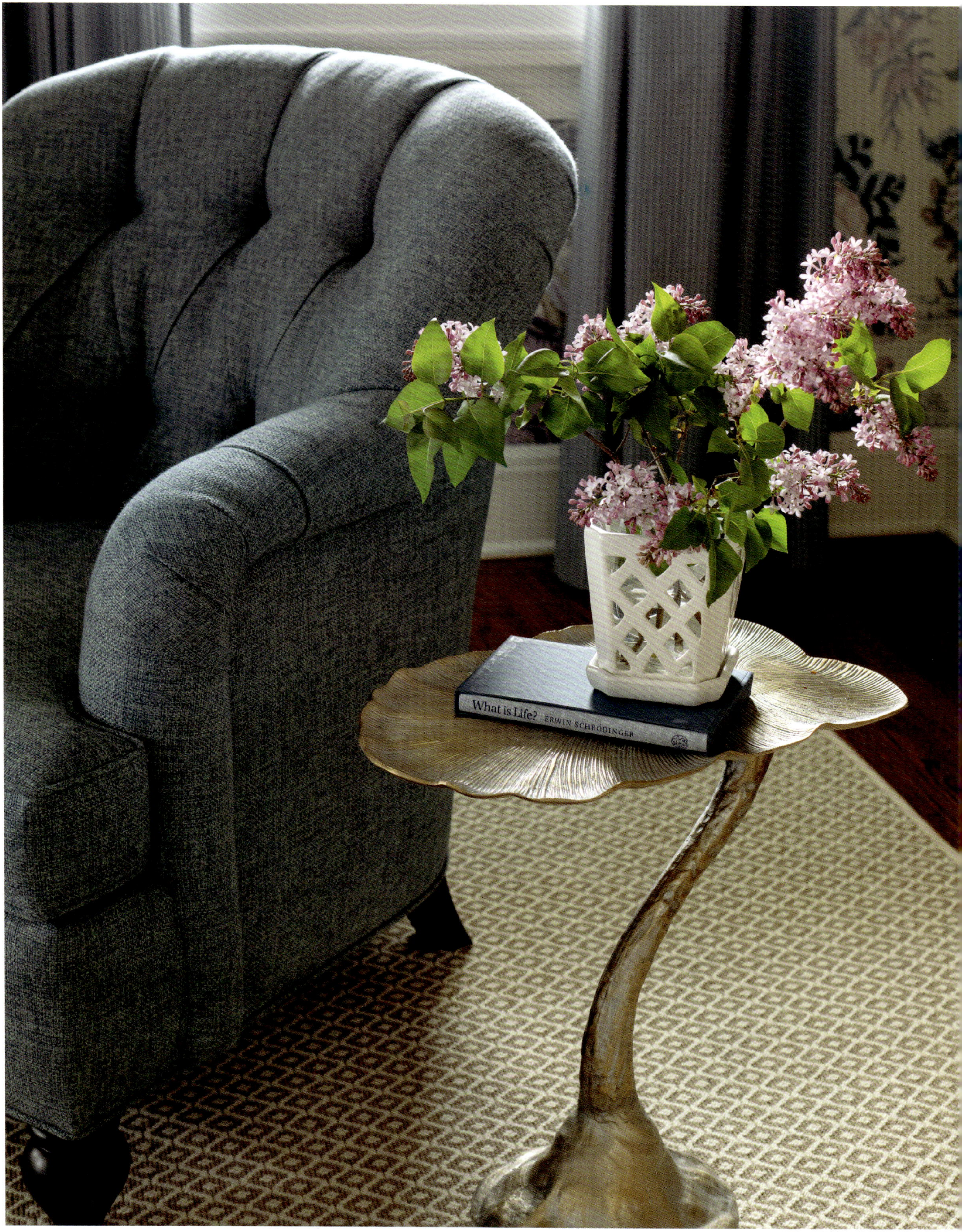
What is Life? ERWIN SCHRÖDINGER

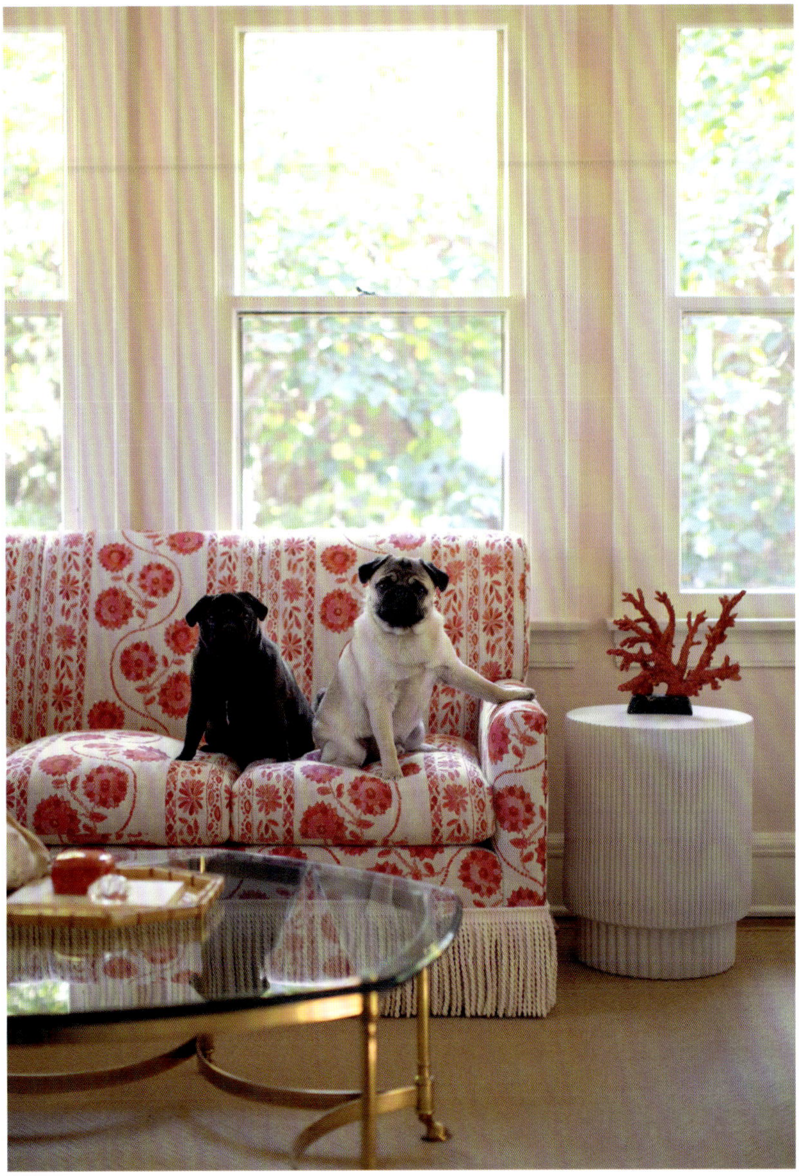

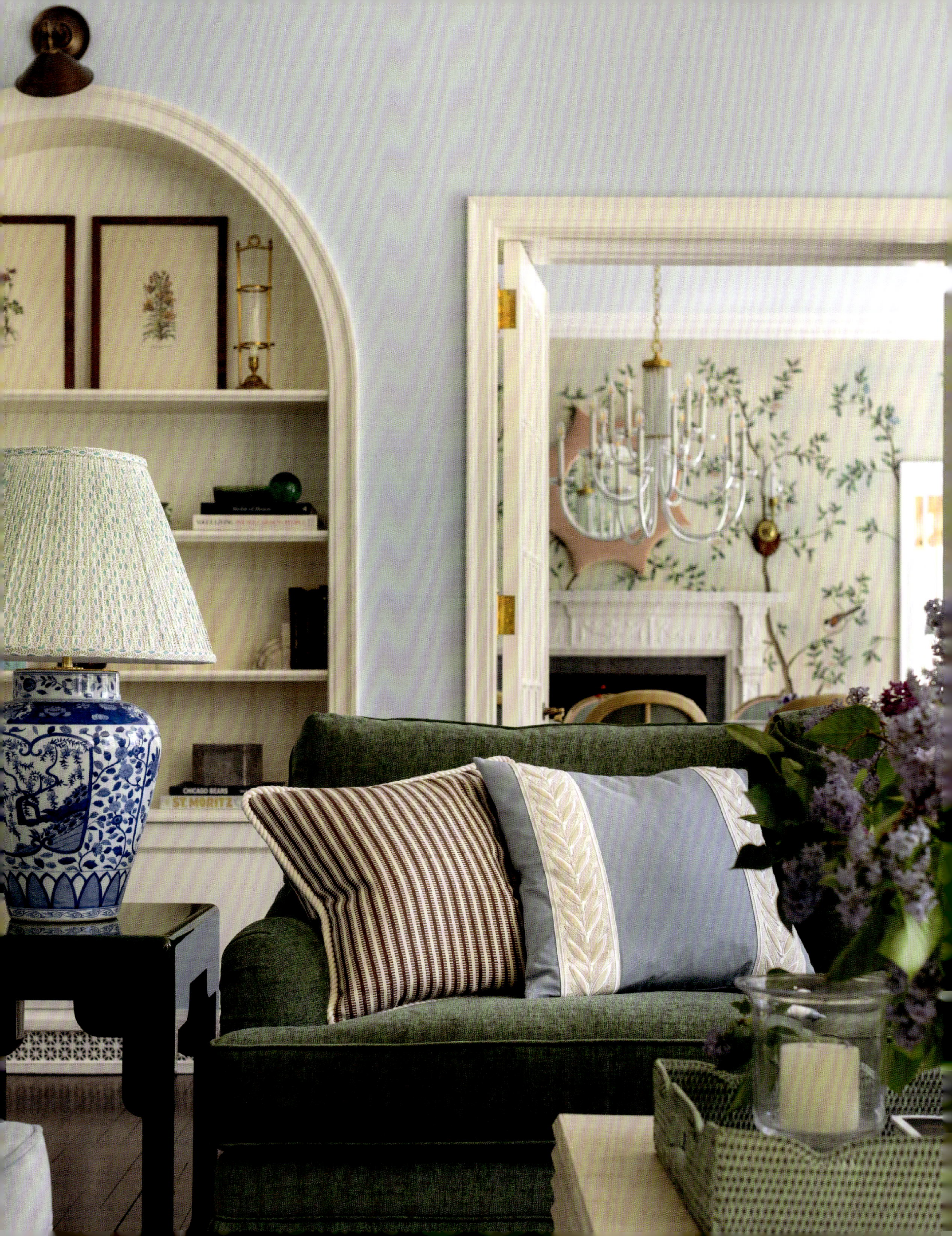
CHICAGO BEARS
ST. MORITZ

FRESH TRADITION

*A storied house turned homestead
for a family that loves to host*

The architecture in this house really speaks for itself, so we wanted to personalize the house without competing with it. That meant using soft textiles in natural tones, like the antique rug in the entry.

In the American Midwest, a hundred-year-old house is pretty much as historic as you'll find. When these clients tapped me to design their 1924 home in the suburbs of Chicago, I was elated. The couple, who have three children under five, both grew up in the area, and when this house came on the market, they jumped on it. It's easy to see why: The home has incredible bones and, thankfully, had been beautifully restored through previous renovations, retaining its original charm.

The structure of this house was formal and traditional, but with a young family moving in, we were tasked with respecting the history of the house while making it feel fresh. As the wife put it, "We love the bones, but we want it to feel lighter, brighter, and more youthful"—just like their adorable family. As with many of my projects, we began with the question, How do you want to live in your house? Even though this family has young children, they entertain a lot. Since they are both from the area, they—like me—frequently host large family gatherings, everything from football game viewings to traditional Thanksgiving dinners.

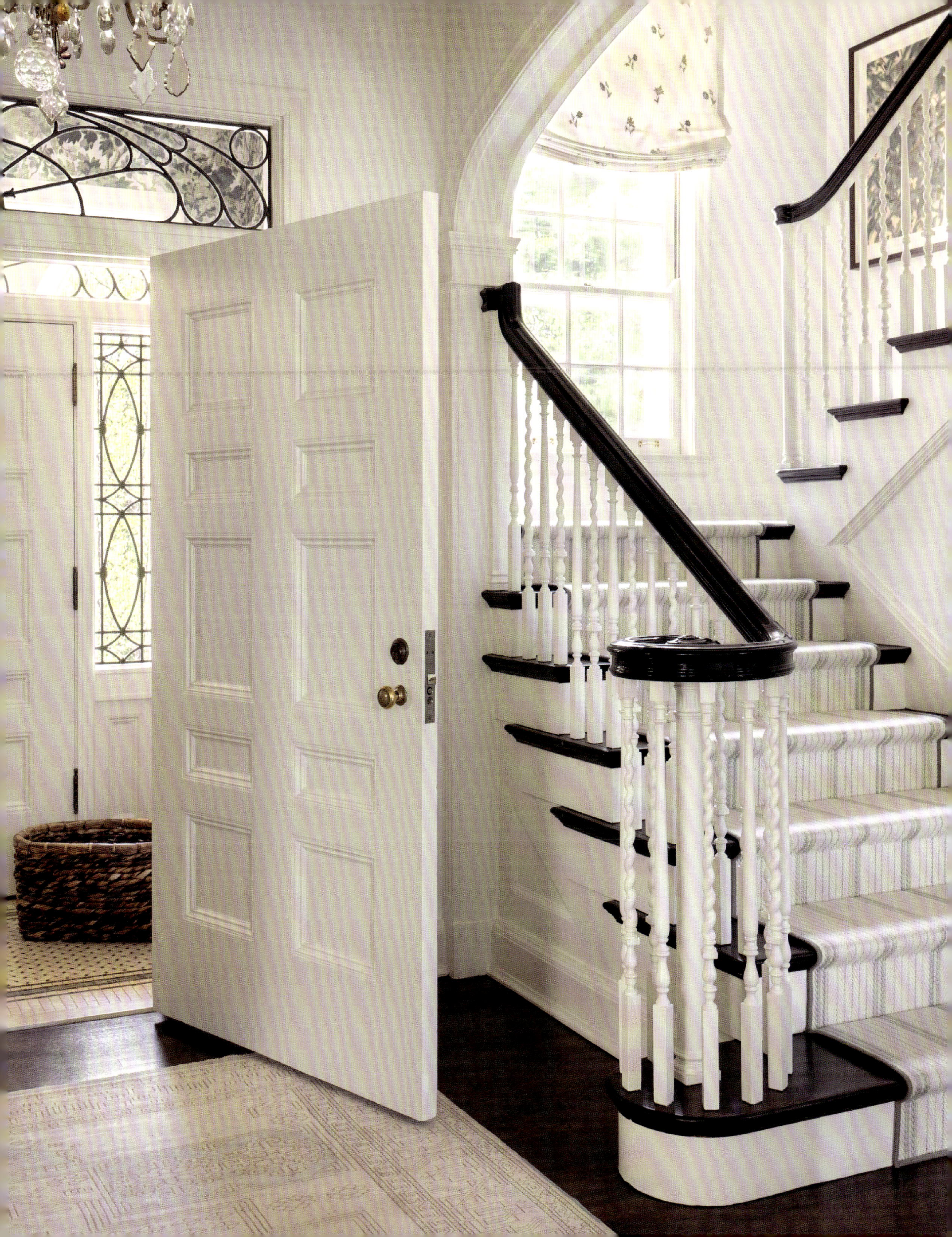

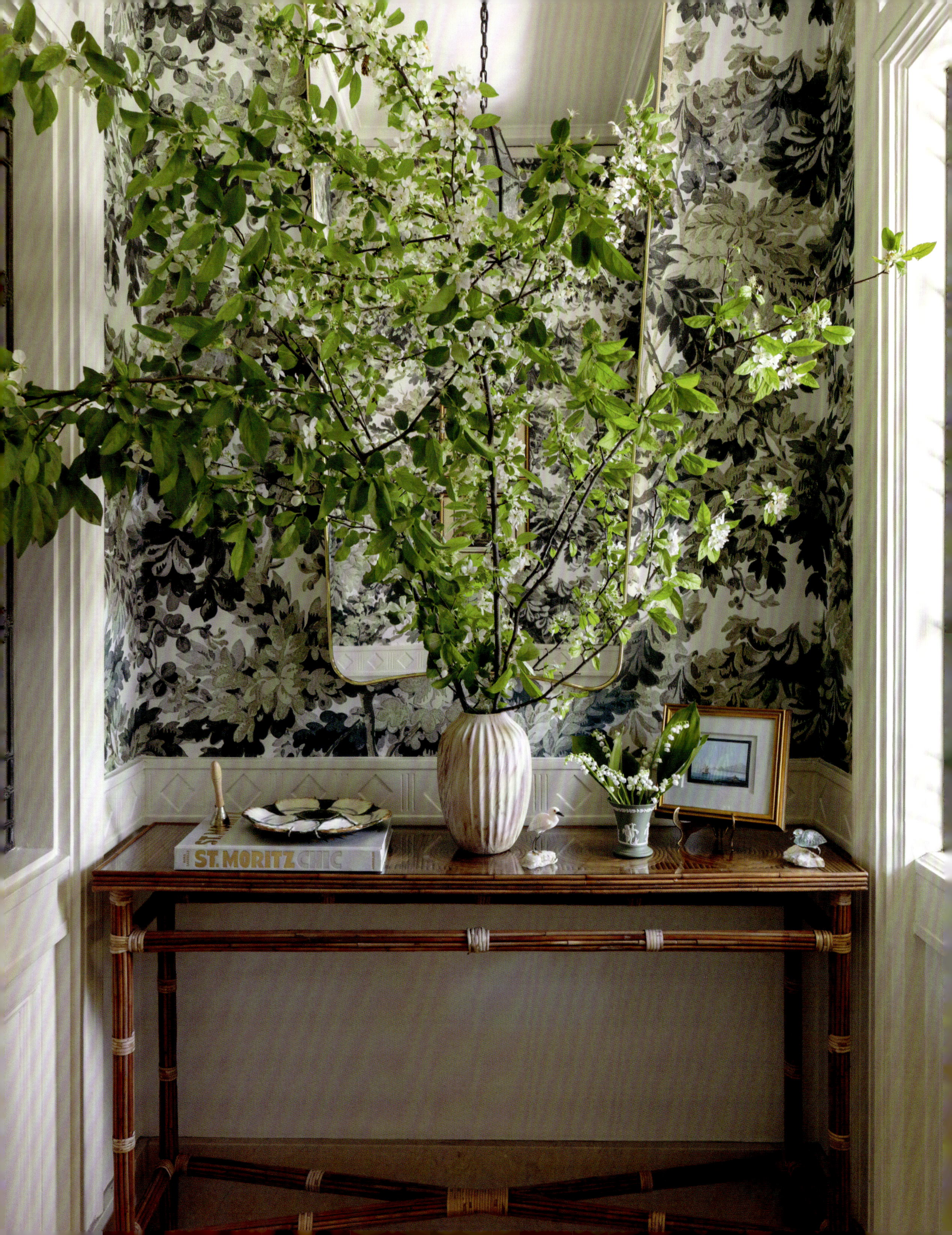
ST. MORITZ CHIC

Opposite: Since the entry vestibule is completely closed off from the foyer, we wanted to give it its own personality. The leafy wallpaper provides the perfect transition from outdoor foliage to the color palette inside.

Above left: Pairing an antique Italian gilt and tiger-print upholstered chair with a trio of oyster plates adds character without detracting from the architecture.

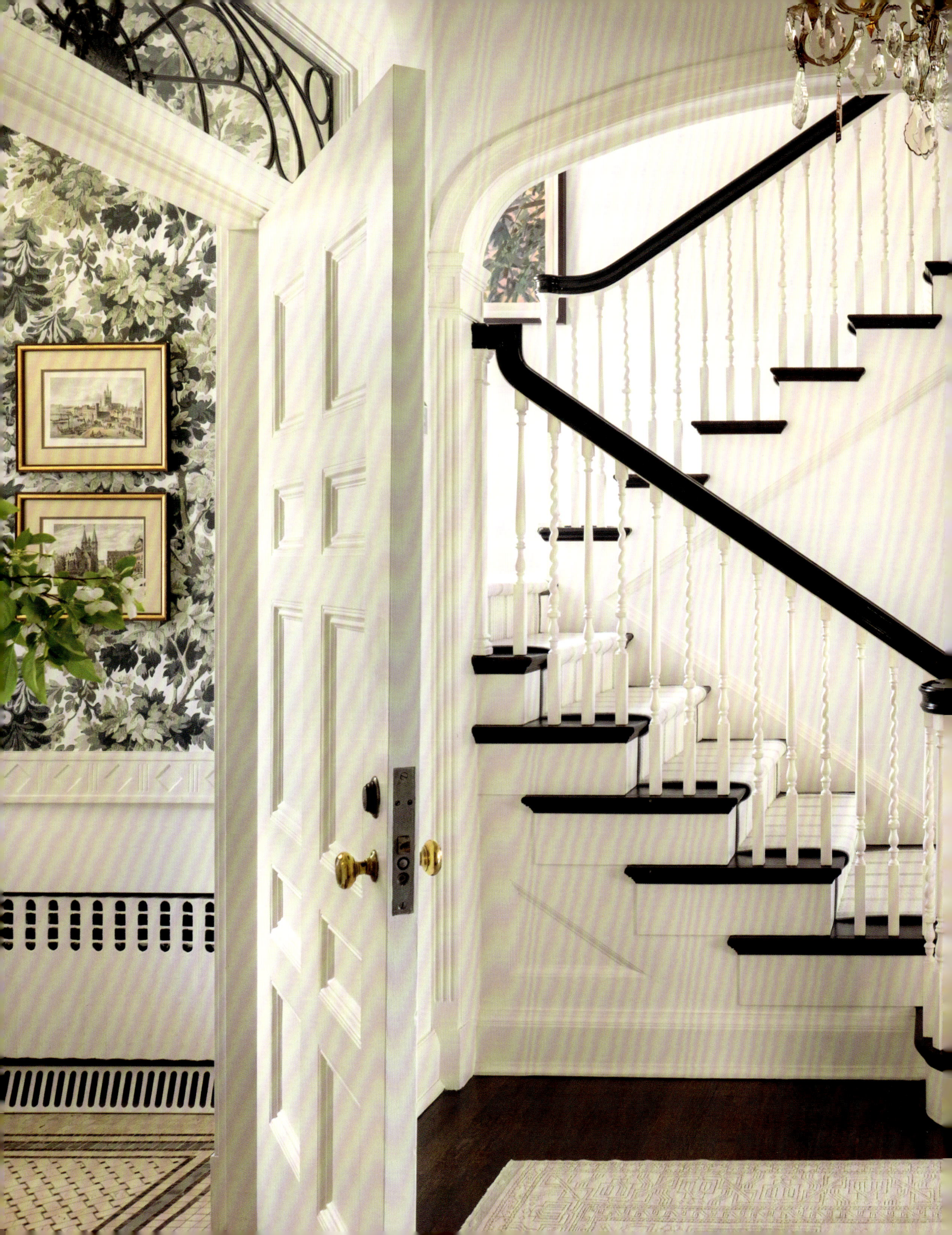

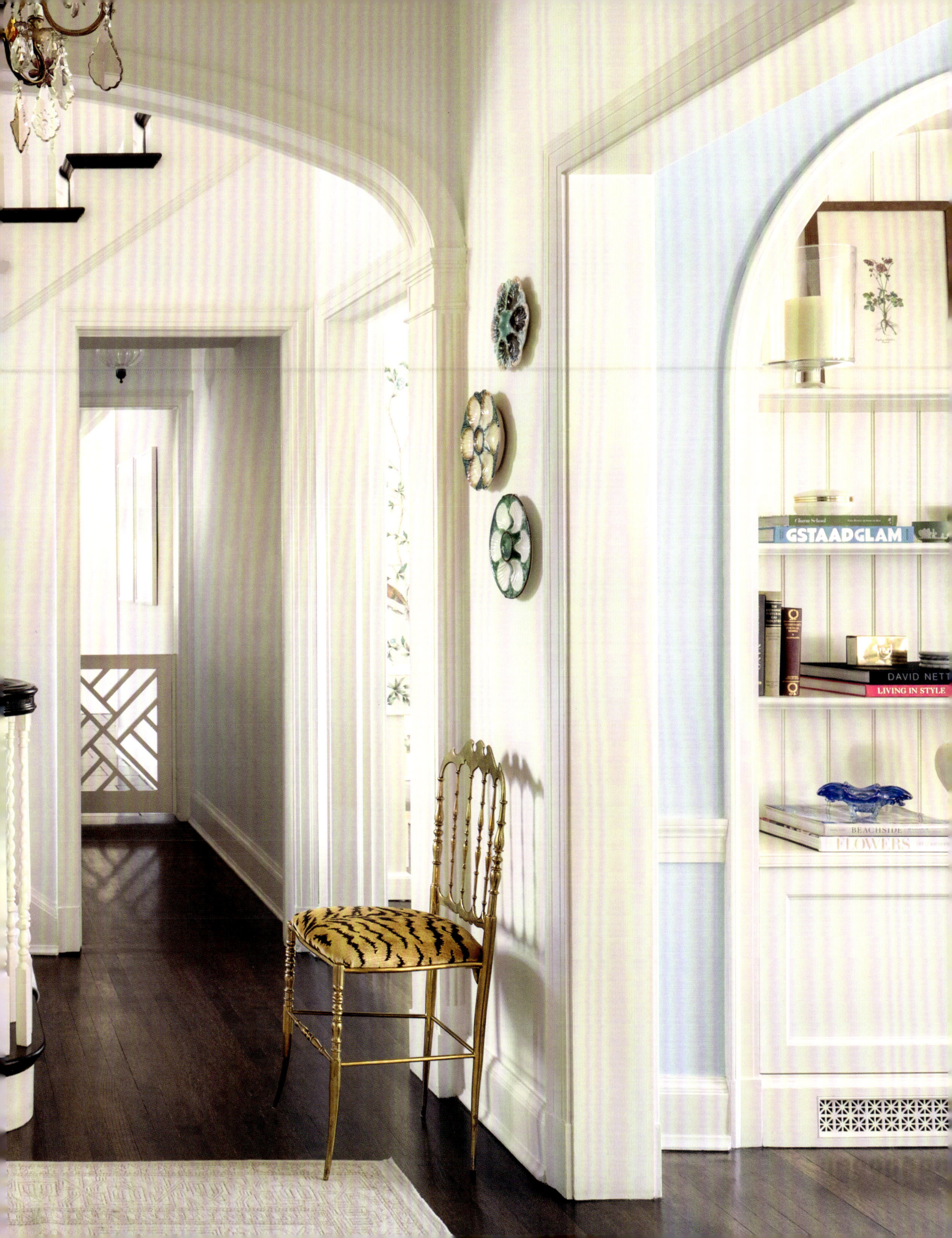
GSTAADGLAM
DAVID NETT
LIVING IN STYLE
BEACHSIDE
FLOWERS

A big part of our strategy, then, was to embrace the history of the space while rethinking how it could be used. For example, the home has a large, formal living room, and while we didn't want to diminish the fact that it's a big formal living room, we wanted to reimagine it in a way that invites people to really use it.

The wife had grown up in a house with a living room that she never went into, and she was adamant that she didn't want that in her own home. That said, long, formal living rooms are tough. People sometimes struggle to arrange them in a way that is conducive to informal entertaining; it's easier to create beautiful, creative layouts for more formal entertaining, but for just hanging out and watching a game, it's tricky.

We probably tried fifteen different arrangements. We presented several options to the homeowners, and they were fine—nice enough, but none quite clicked. Then, at one point during the design process, my husband, kids, and I went to my grandmother's house in Michigan for the weekend. Her great room was a similar size and shape to the clients'. We were a big group that weekend—six adults and nine kids—and it was total chaos, but it worked so perfectly. We could all get comfortable. All of a sudden, it hit me: We needed to replicate my grandmother's layout. I came home, drew up a floor plan that matched my grandmother's—two sofas and a pair of chairs surrounding a large ottoman—showed it to the clients, and they immediately, excitedly, approved it.

In the living room, two sofas laid out in an L shape function almost like an elongated sectional, with plenty of seating for a large group to watch football together while maintaining a note of formality.

—

Overleaf: We pulled the overall color palette for the room from the Schumacher & Co. chintz on the armchairs, which incorporates the perfect forest greens, soft blues, and neutrals.

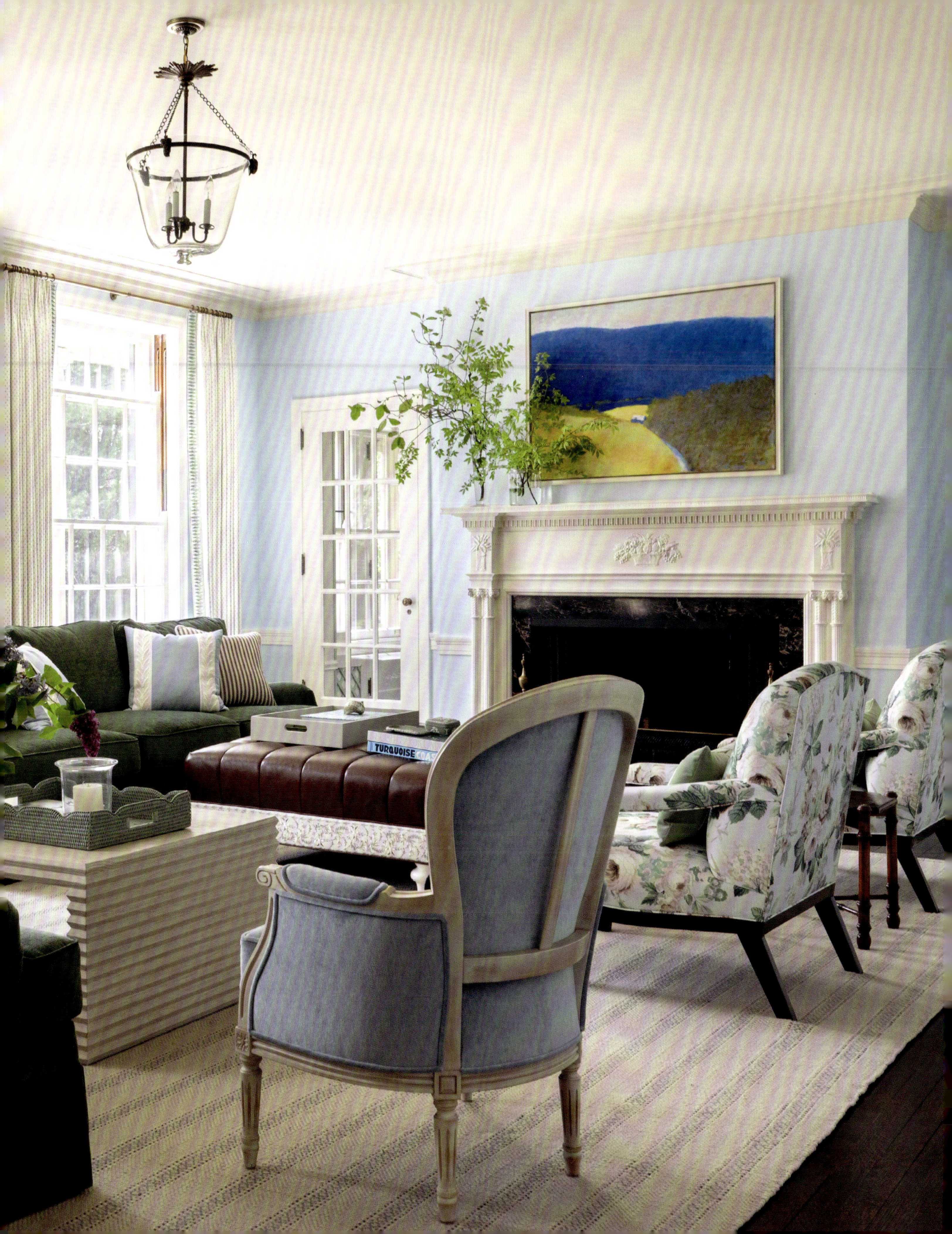
TURQUOISE

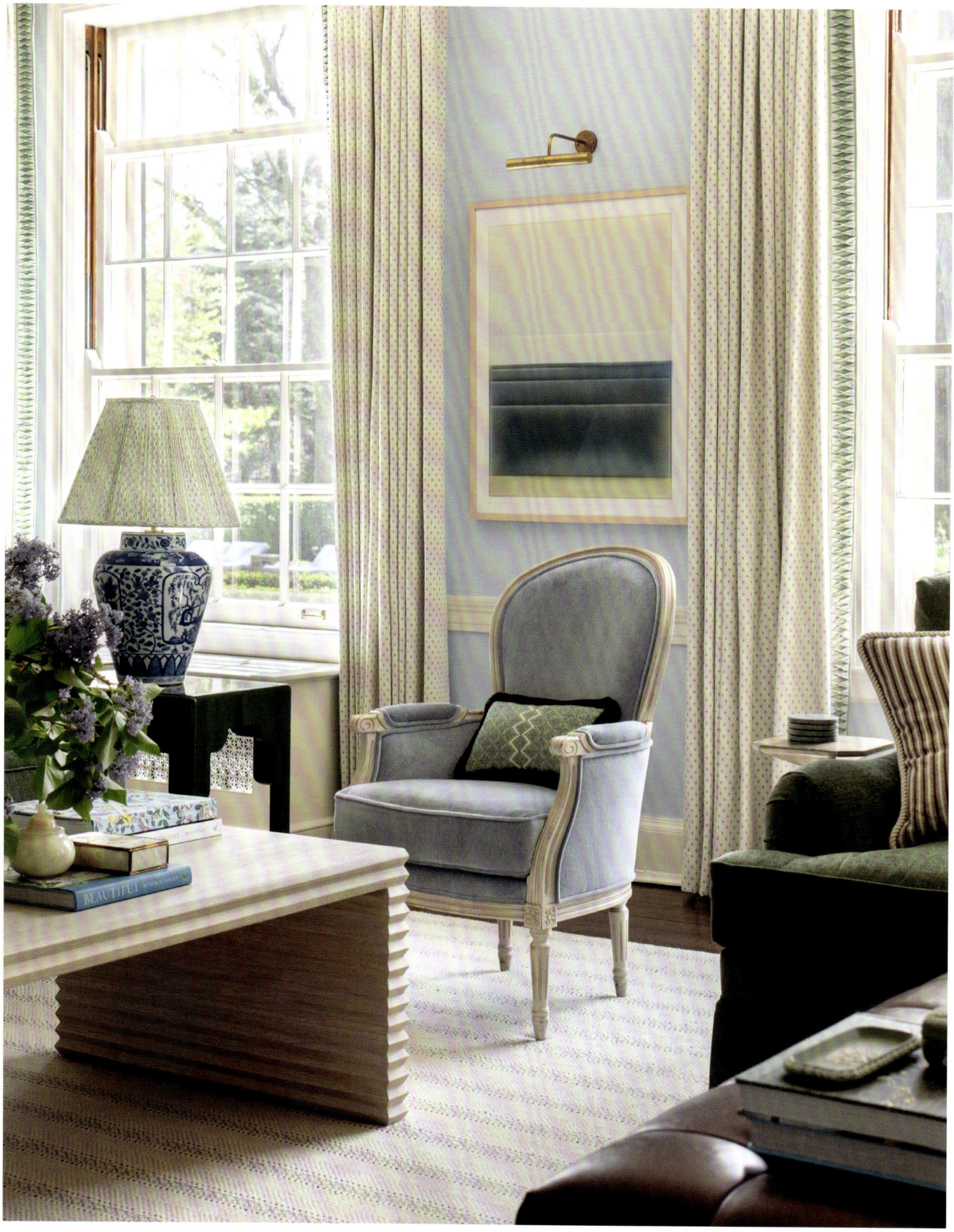
BEAUTIFUL

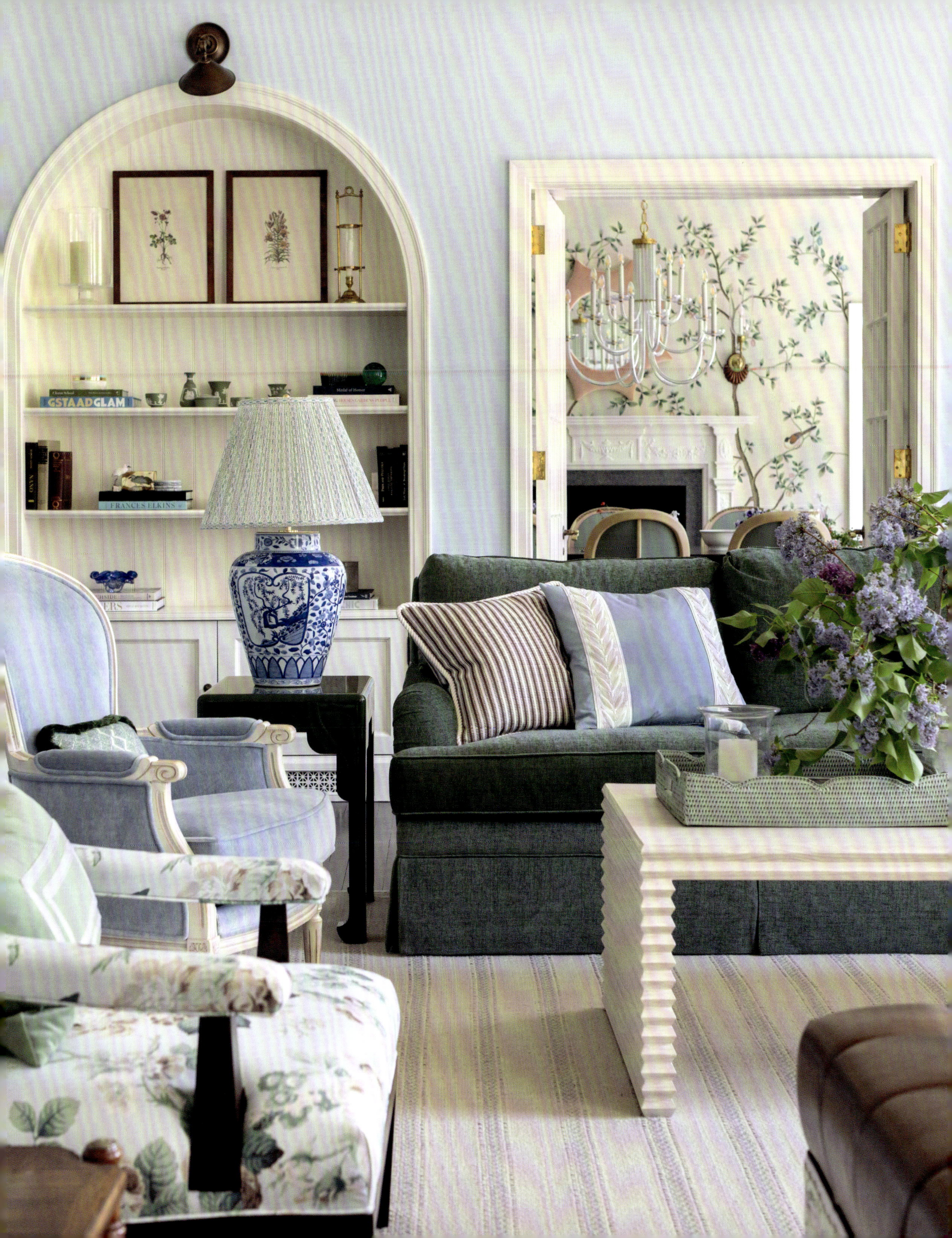
GSTAAD GLAM
FRANCES ELKINS

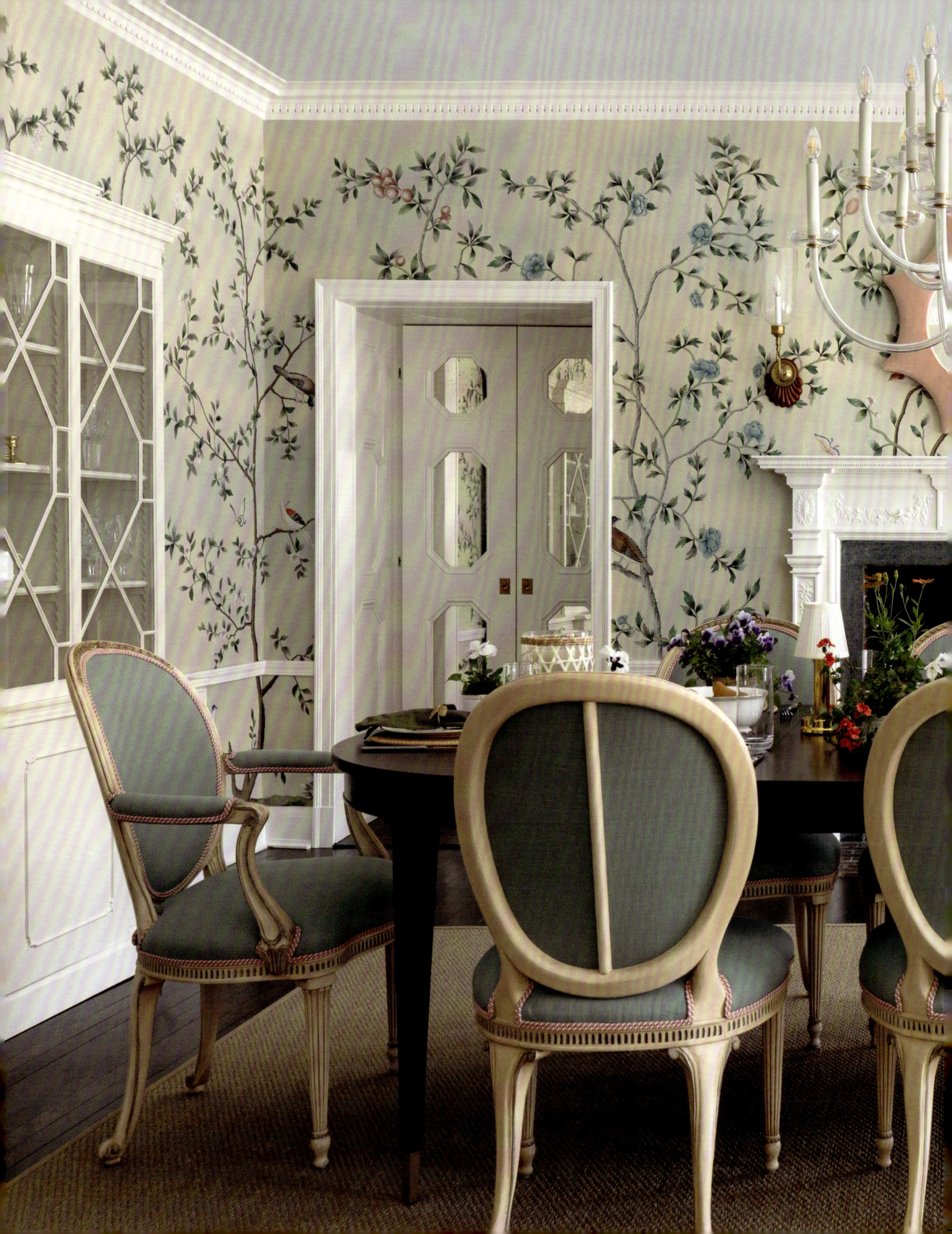

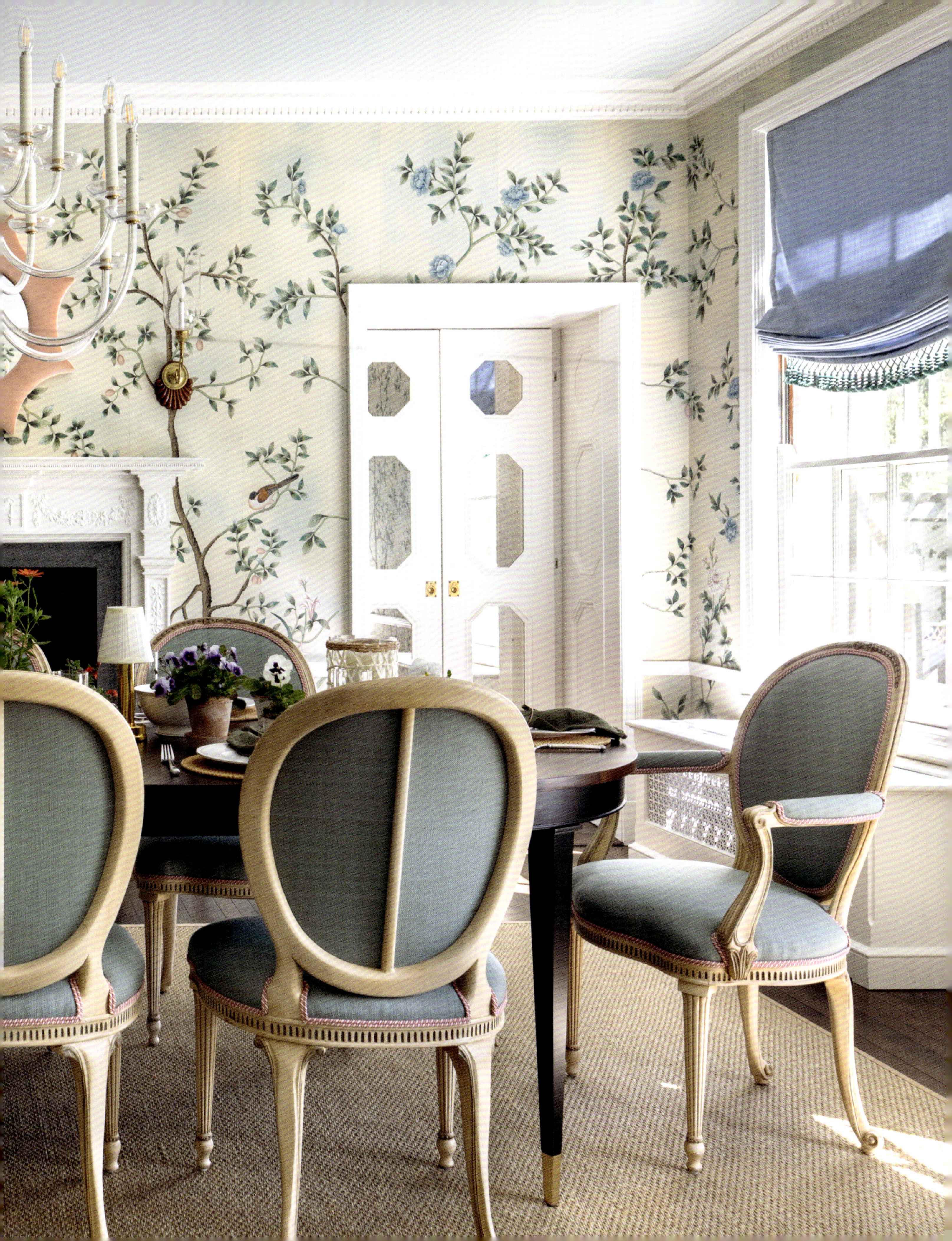

With the living room layout settled, we wanted a fresh color palette to perfect the space. The walls were previously plastered in a deep, dusty blue, which made the room feel dark and serious. The clients love blues, however, and told me that, left to their own devices, everything would be a nautical blue-and-white scheme. While that didn't feel entirely appropriate for this house and its decidedly noncoastal location, it served as a great jumping-off point for me. Pairing their beloved blues with rich browns and mossy greens gave us the ability to reflect the beautiful landscape outside, which is visible from most rooms of the house. This natural influence was the impetus for the de Gournay wallpaper in the dining room—a forest of delicate flowering trees. It is a perfect example of a new, timeless take on a classic pattern. The sconces in this room were from the previous owner, and I love that we got to reuse them, now pairing them with a playful starburst mirror upholstered in pink velvet—underscoring the successful juxtaposition of the classic, the elegant, but also the fun.

The dining room leads into the sitting room and, just outside, the pool. In the sitting room, we wanted to create a beautiful space that would also stand up to wet kids passing through. Enter durable rug and performance fabric. In this room, which is full of furniture in traditional shapes, we had a ton of fun layering colors and patterns.

I always think that given the choice, people gravitate to small, cozy rooms. The sunroom, off the living room, was previously a forgotten space, but it opens onto a quiet courtyard on the side of the house where their kids play. It needed to be something really special to encourage its use. I wanted it to feel like part of the garden, so the treillage was a perfect choice for the space. The lattice also complemented the room's beautiful barreled ceilings. We added a mix of antiques and new pieces (the custom backgammon table paired with two-hundred-year-old prints)—which is really the theme of the house. I didn't want anything to feel so old or so new; it was a constant balance.

Previous: In the dining room, deep, paneled doorways—original to the house—are an architectural counterbalance to the elegant wallpaper. I love how the de Gournay paper reinterprets the blue, green, and neutral palette in a way that nods to tradition but feels fresh—especially when paired with a bold, velvet-upholstered mirror.
—
Right: The red-and-white ticking trim on the dining chairs is a quietly surprising pop of color.

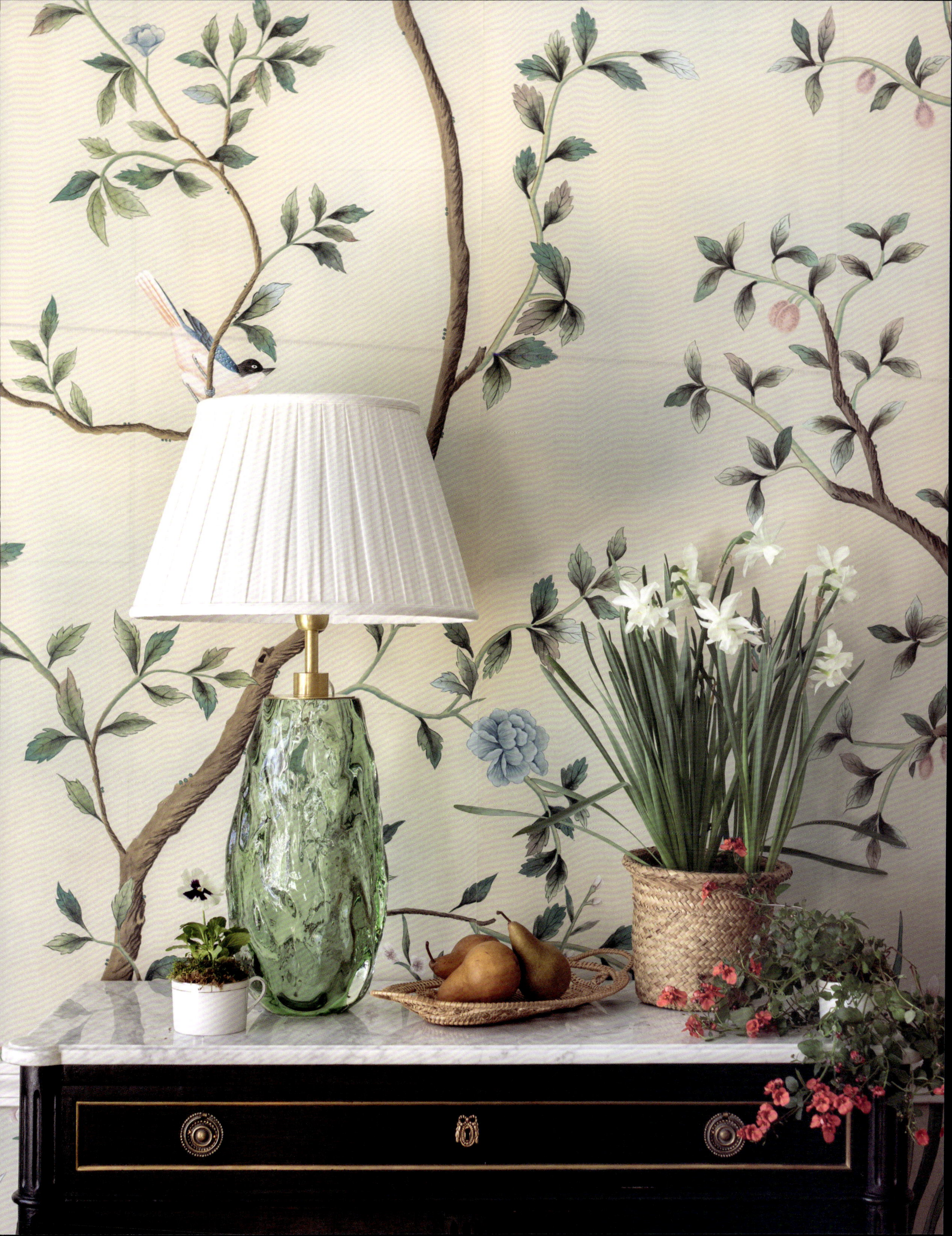

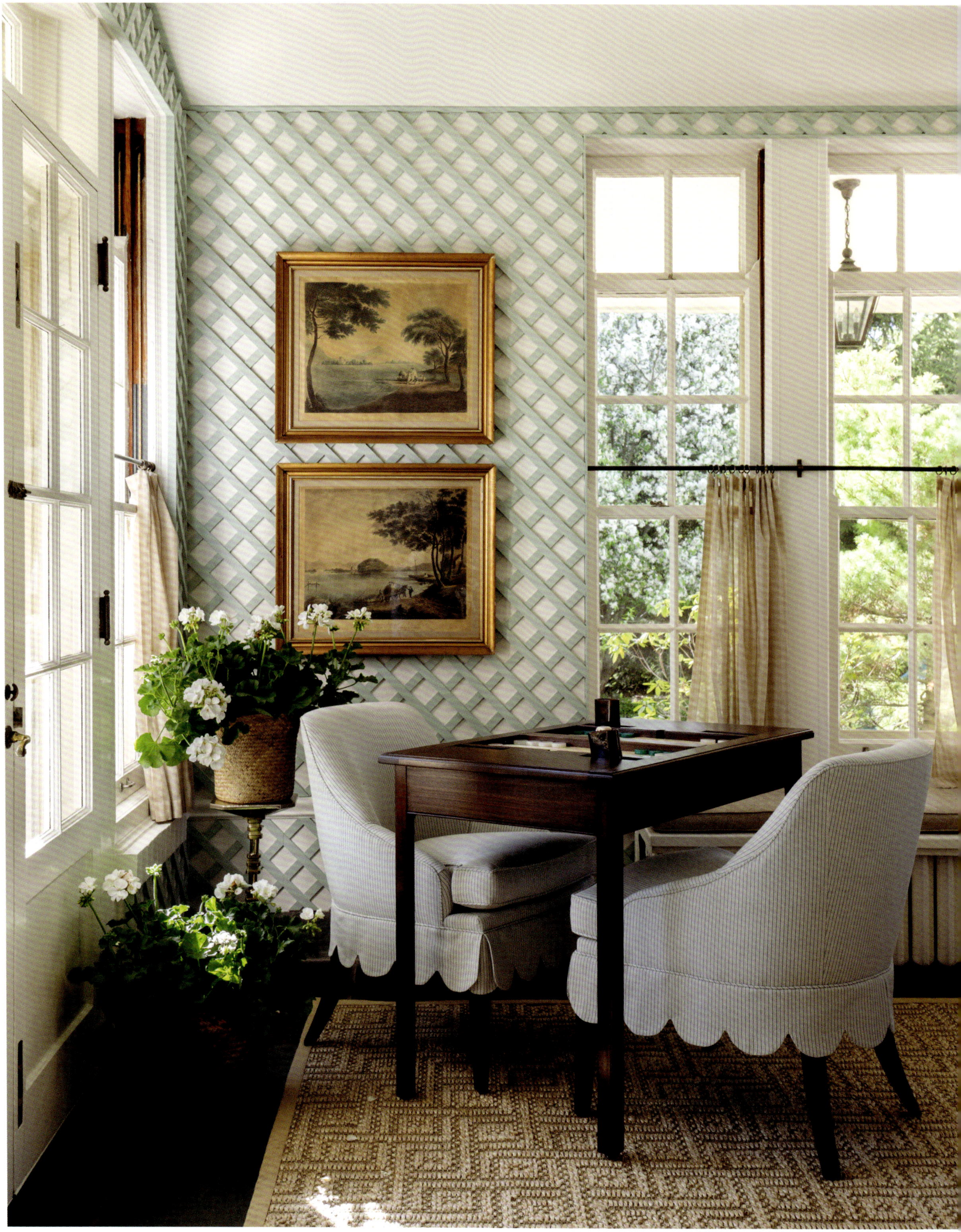

This sunroom looks out to the swing set in the backyard, so it's the ideal spot for adults to watch the kids play. Putting a cozy sofa, game table, and piano in the trellis-covered room makes it feel like an indulgent place to rest.

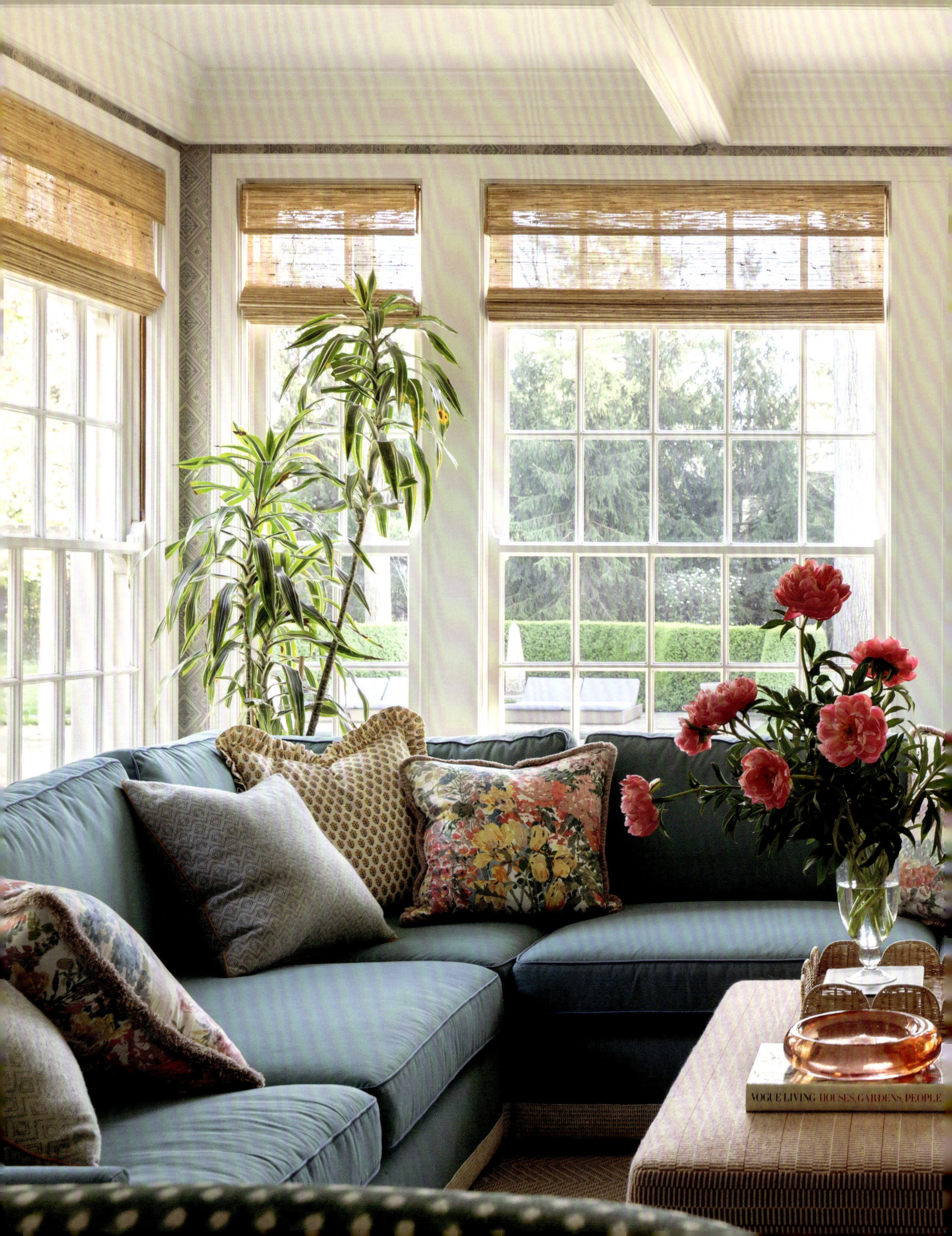
VOGUE LIVING HOUSES, GARDENS, PEOPLE

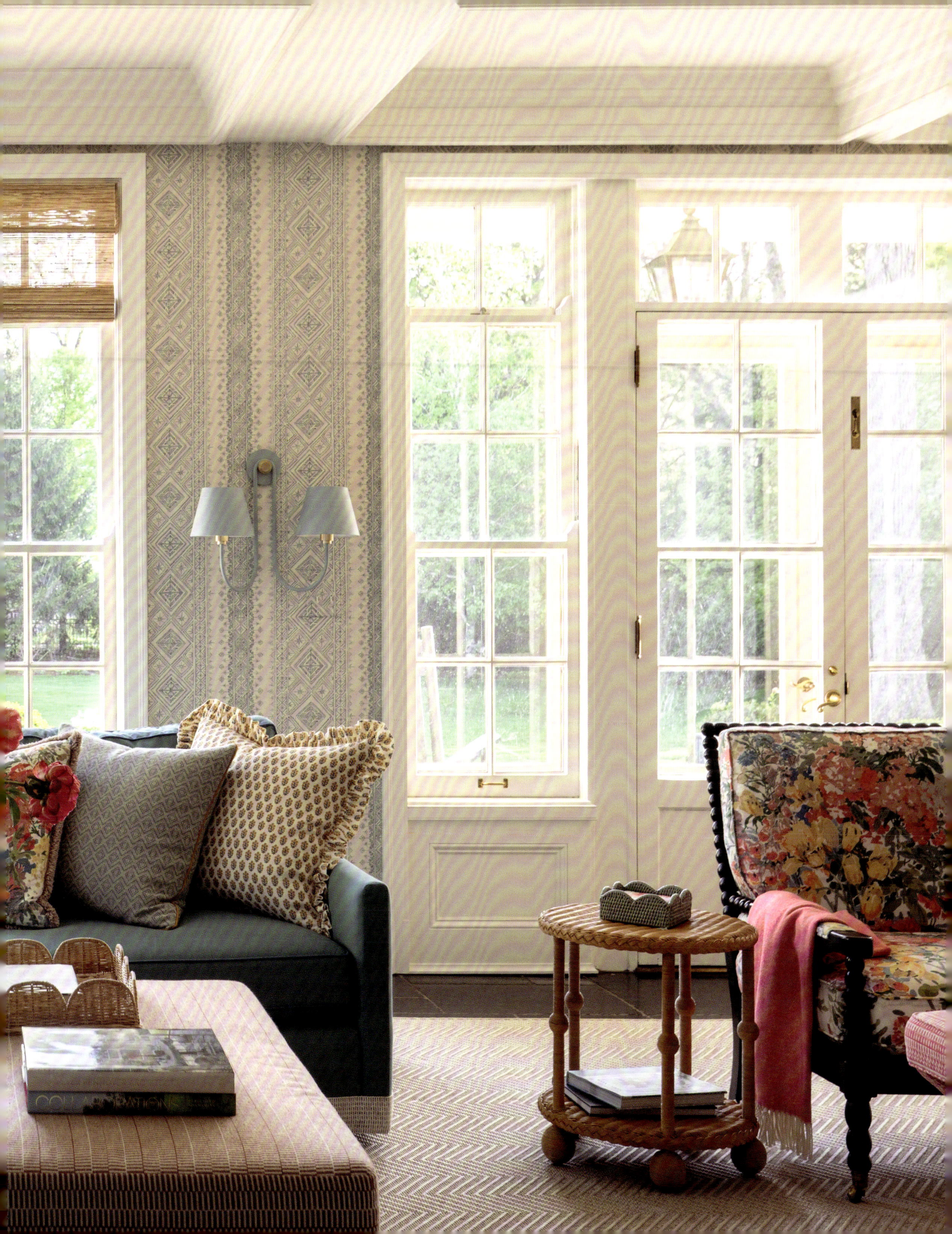

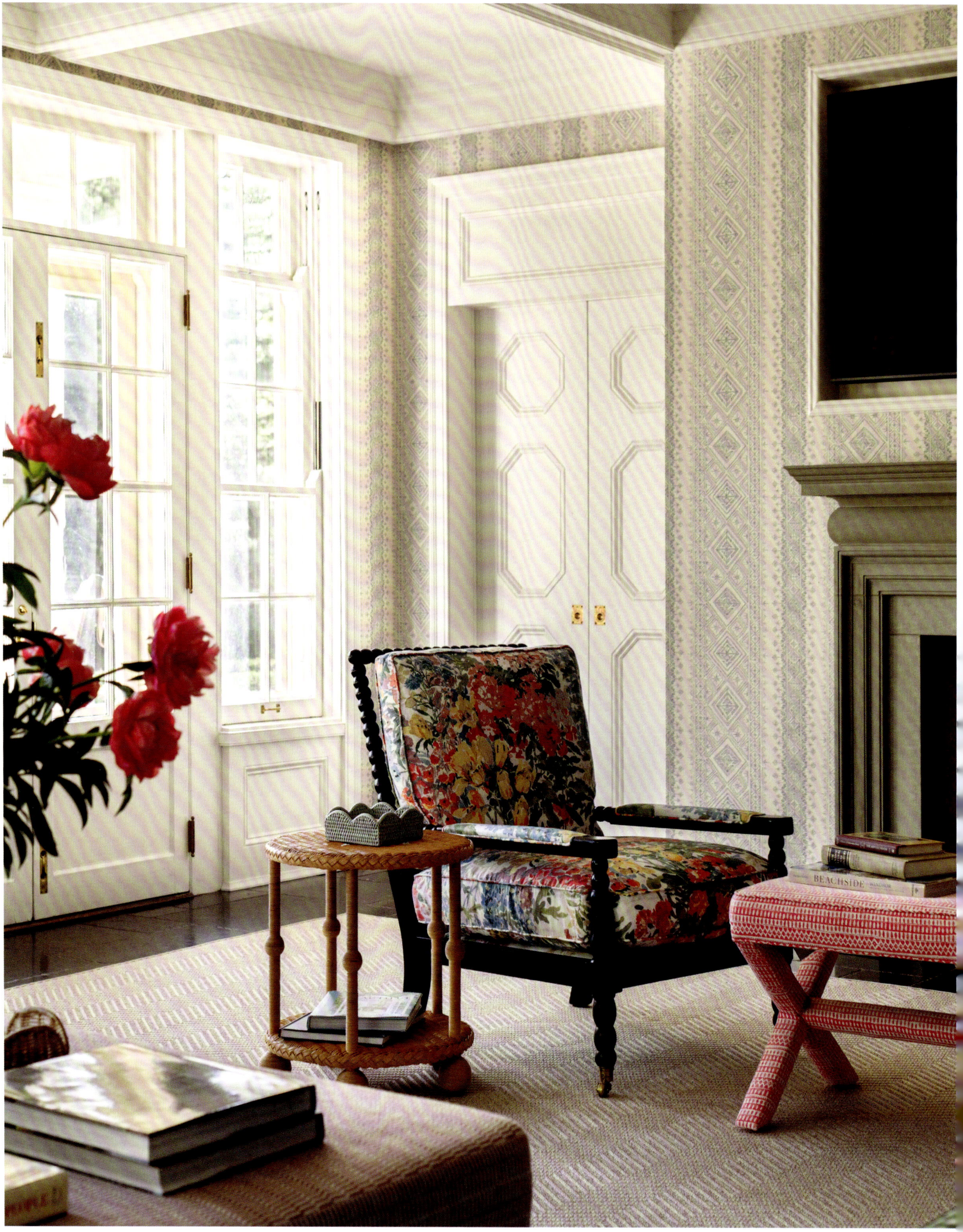
BEACHSIDE

The mix of color and pattern in the sitting room was both an aesthetic and a functional decision; every element of this room is super forgiving of tiny feet running and climbing through it.

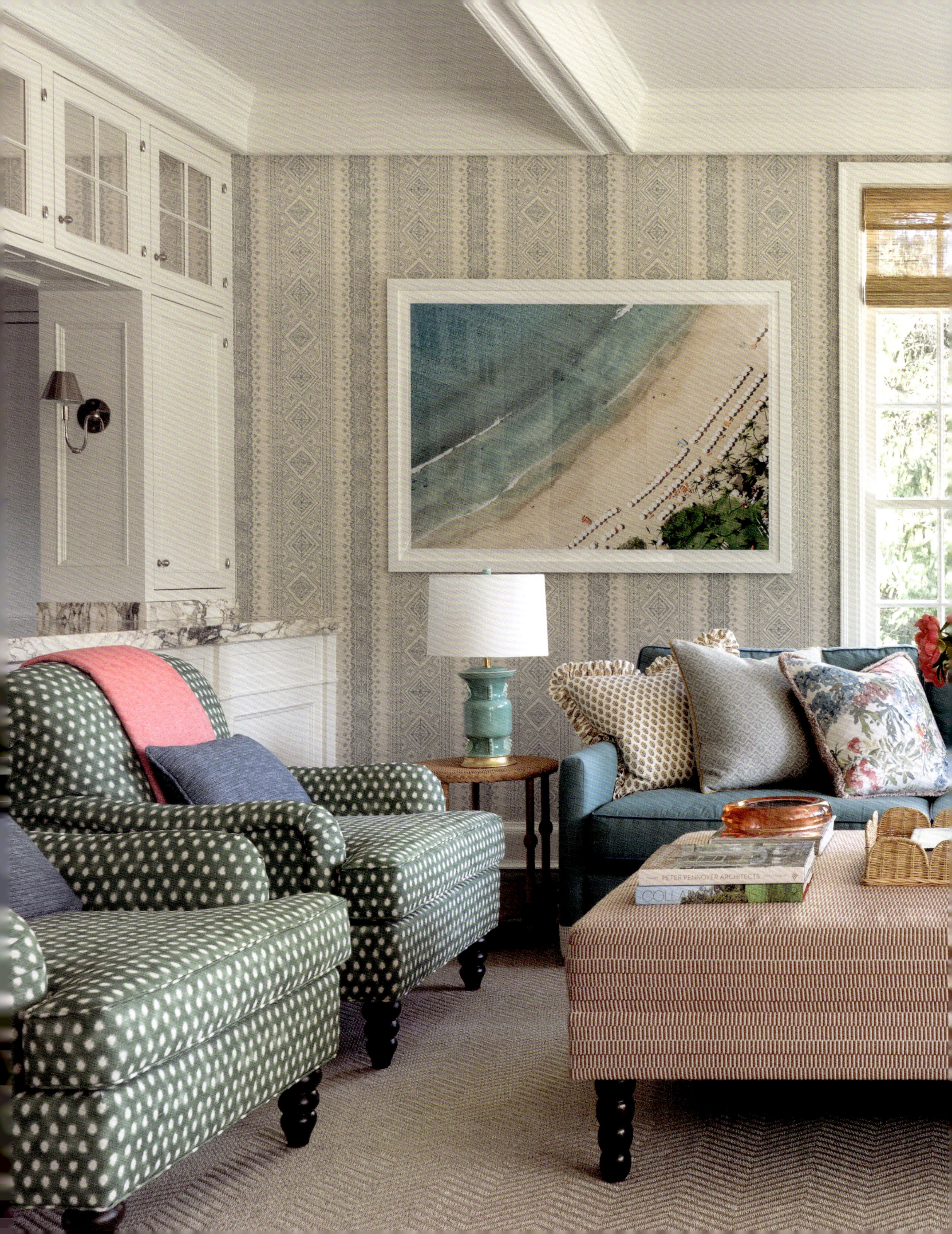
PETER PENNOYER ARCHITECTS

> "With a young family moving in, we were tasked with respecting the history of the house while making it feel fresh."

The final element for freshening up the home was adding contemporary art. The couple's sister-in-law is an art consultant, and they loved the experience of working with her to bring their dream home to life. The wonderful pieces we sourced with her assistance became key visual and personal additions to the project, and the design encourages the family to carry on their collecting. You'll notice that not every shelf or wall is filled in; I wanted to ensure that the family has ample space to layer over time, giving them the backdrop to build their own history into their home.

The family vacations frequently in Hawai'i and bought this Gray Malin photograph because it reminded them of their time there. I love that the palette in here ties into the art without feeling the least bit beachy.

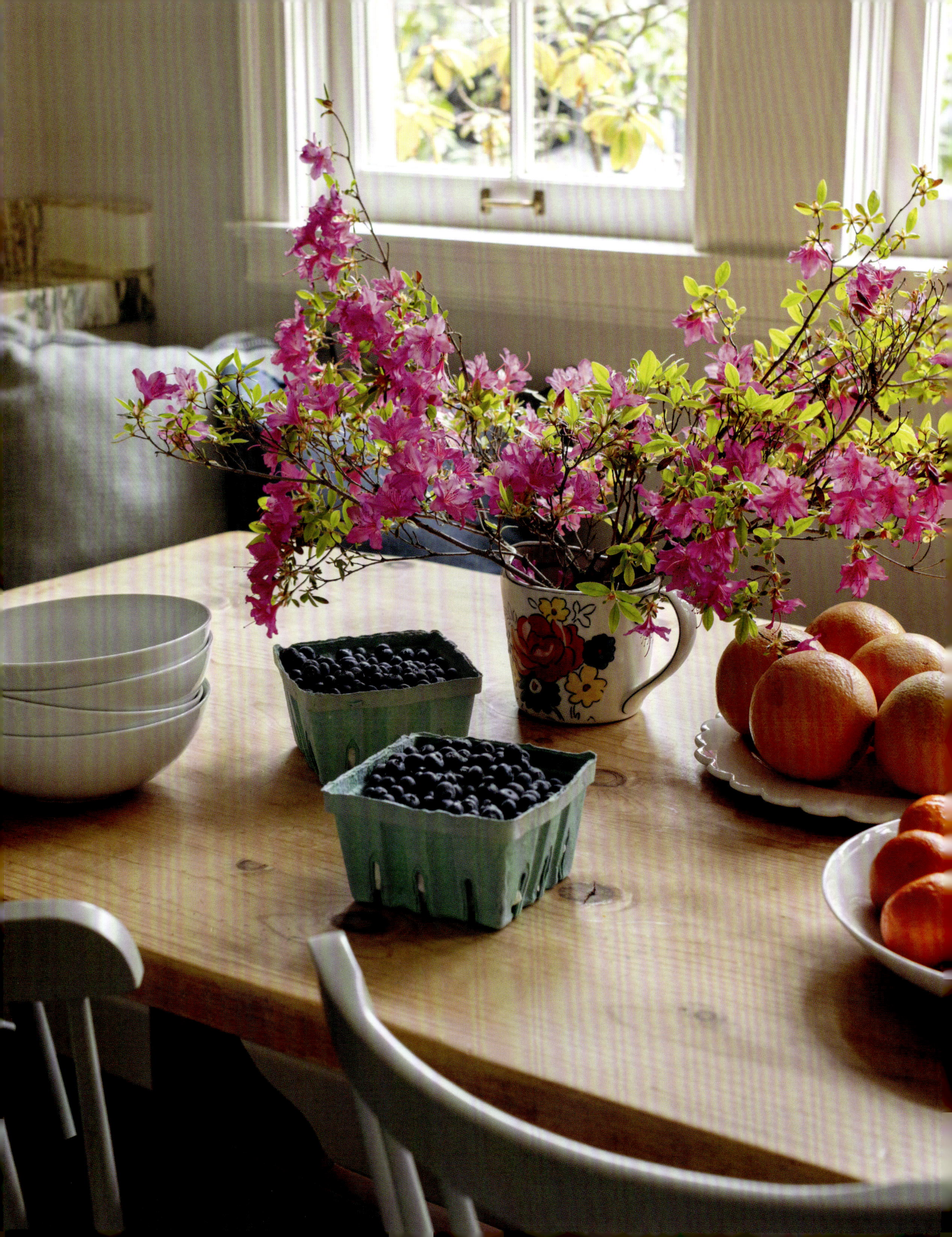

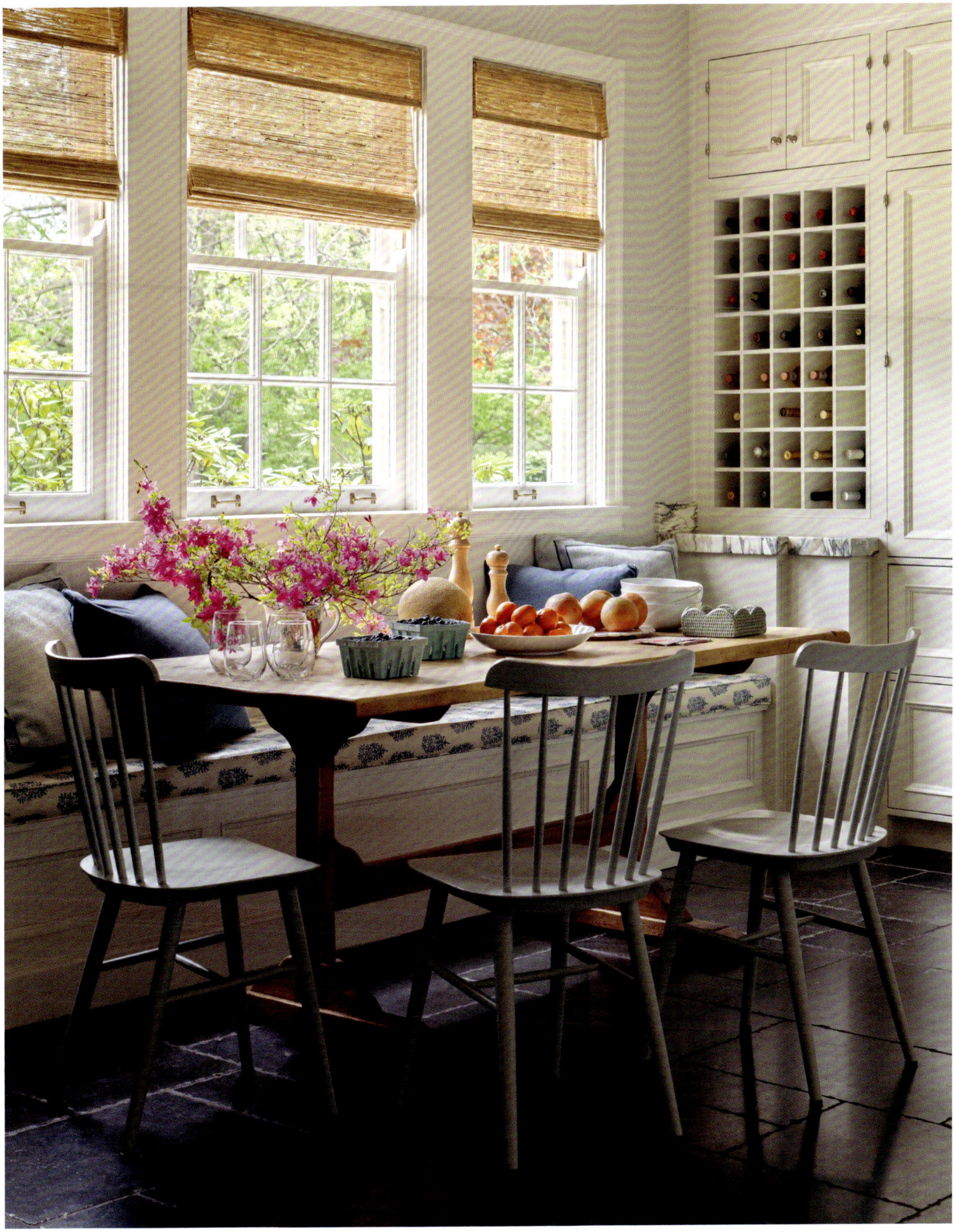

Previous: A banquette with performance fabric plus a table that will patina elegantly is the right recipe for a family breakfast nook. We built tons of storage into the adjacent cabinetry for everything from dishes to wine bottles.

Above left: I love going bold in a powder room, and these cameos from Bridie Hall in London were the perfect pop against peacock-blue lacquered walls.

Above right: Pleated grosgrain ribbon trim along the moldings makes the lacquer pop even more and adds textural contrast.

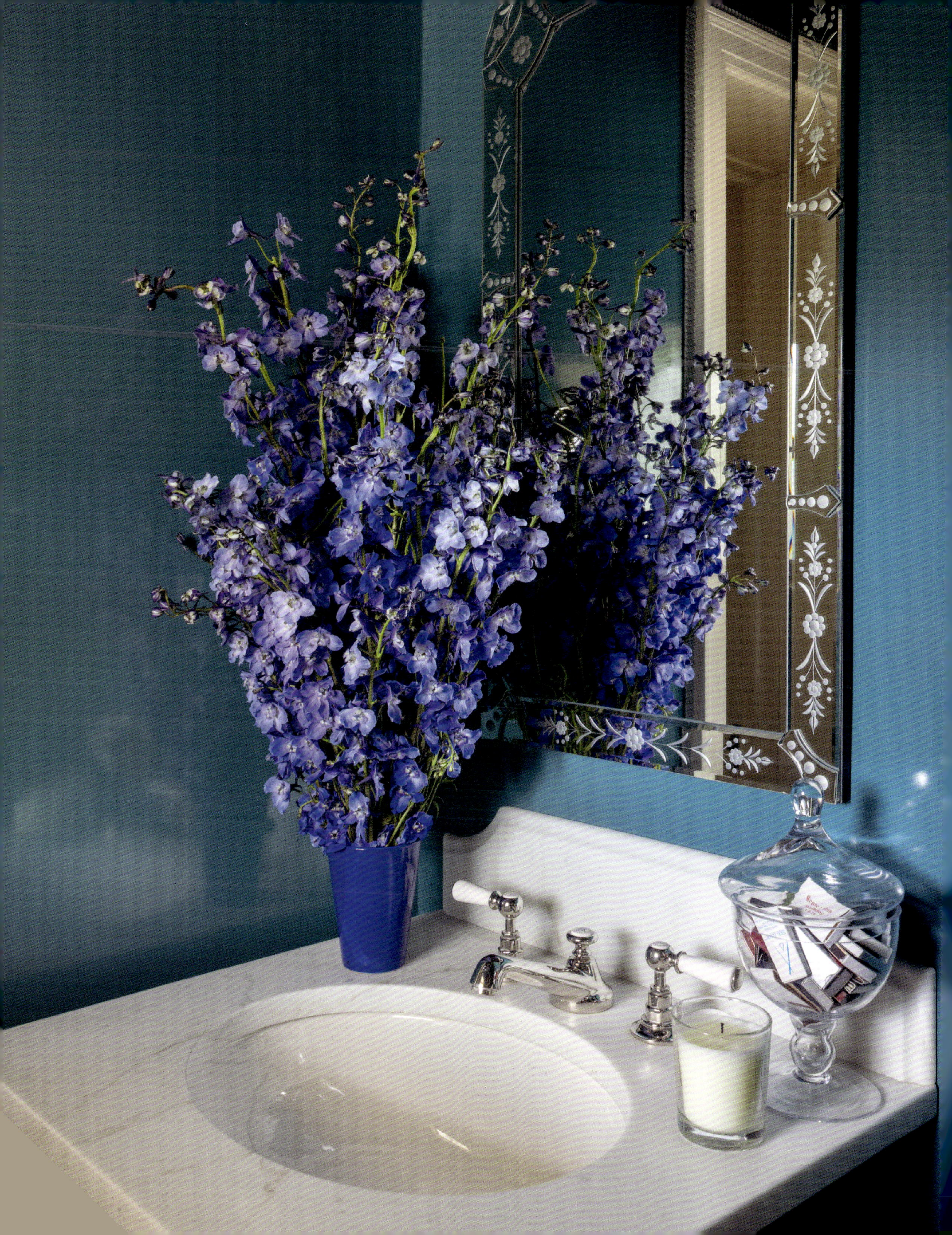

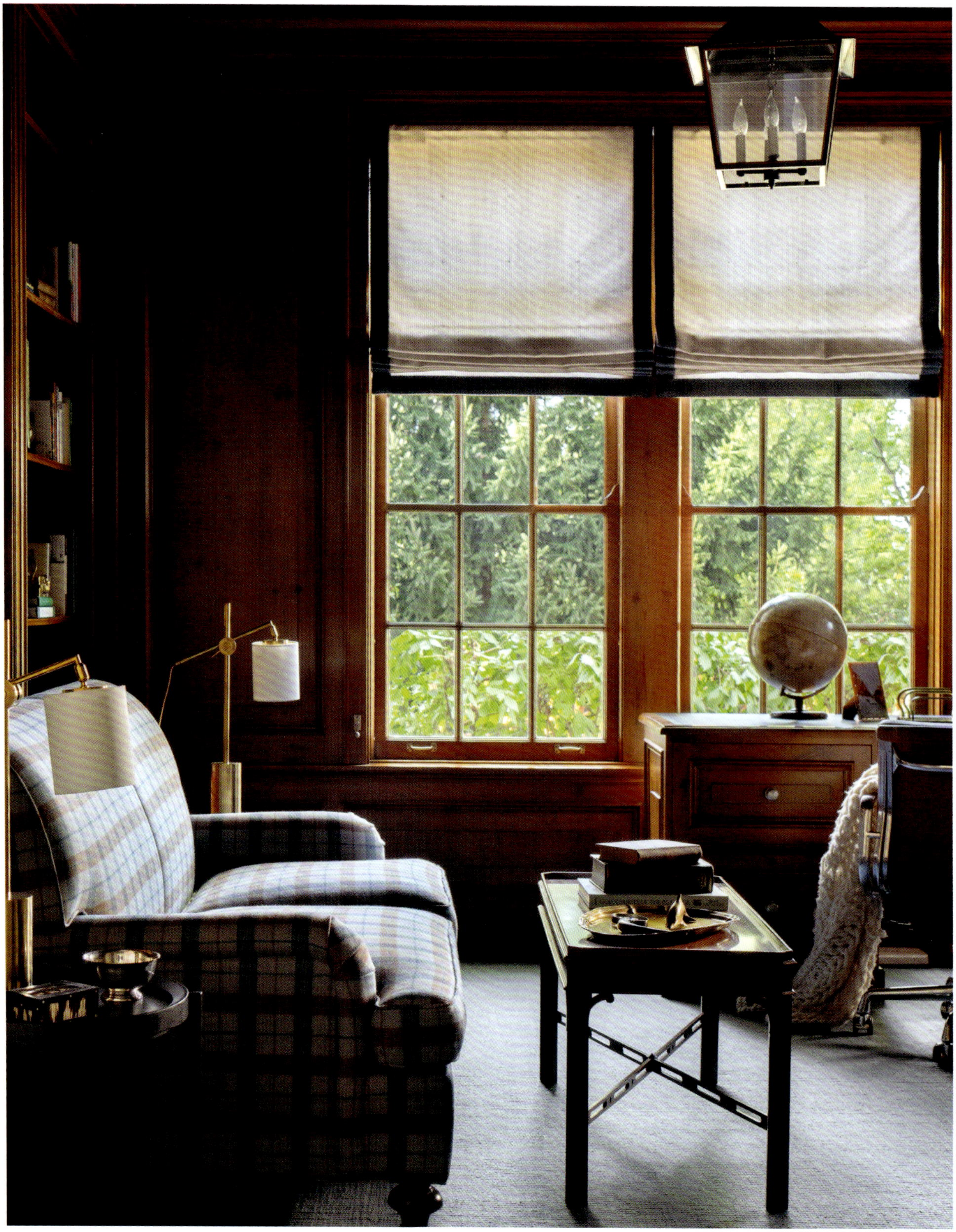

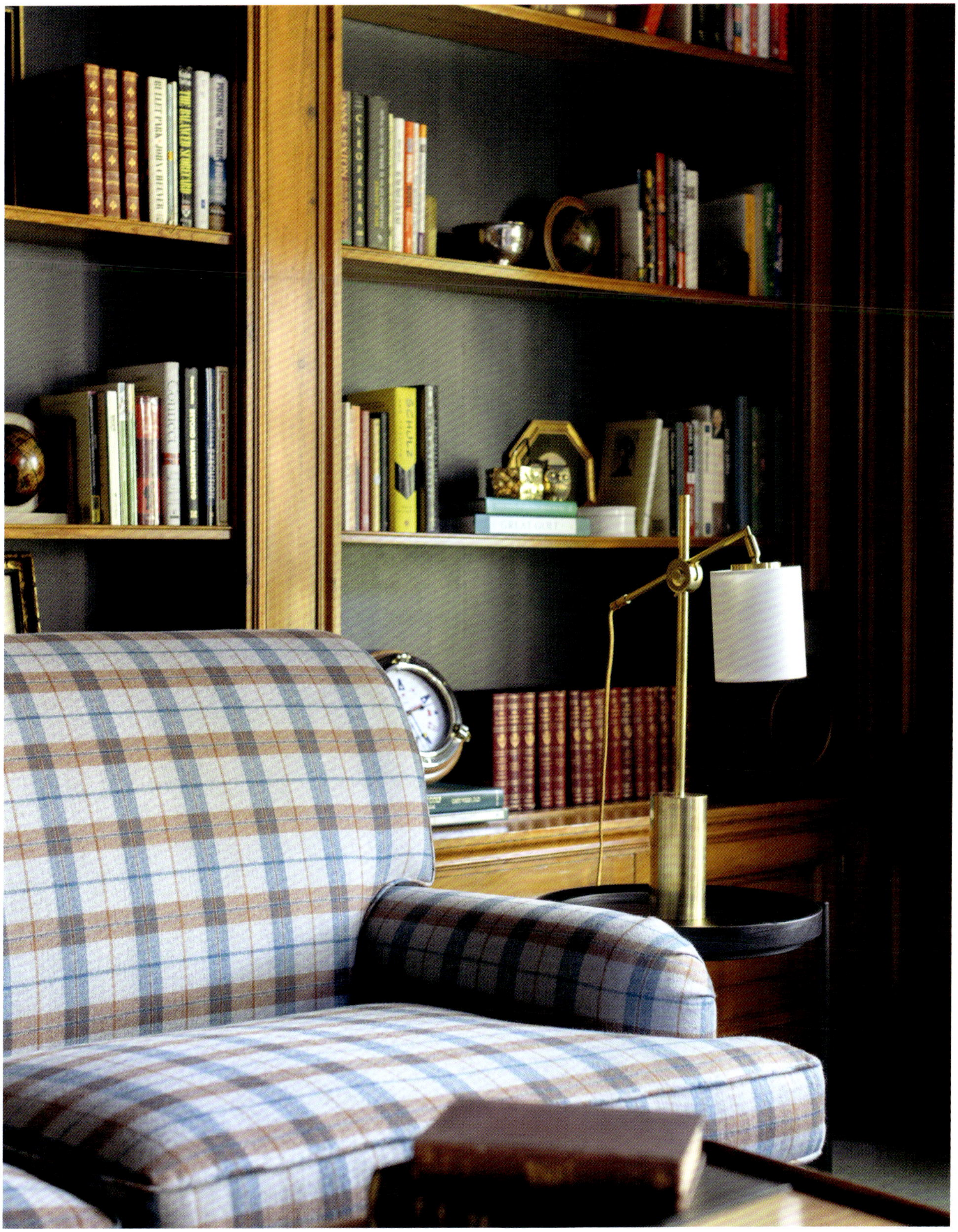

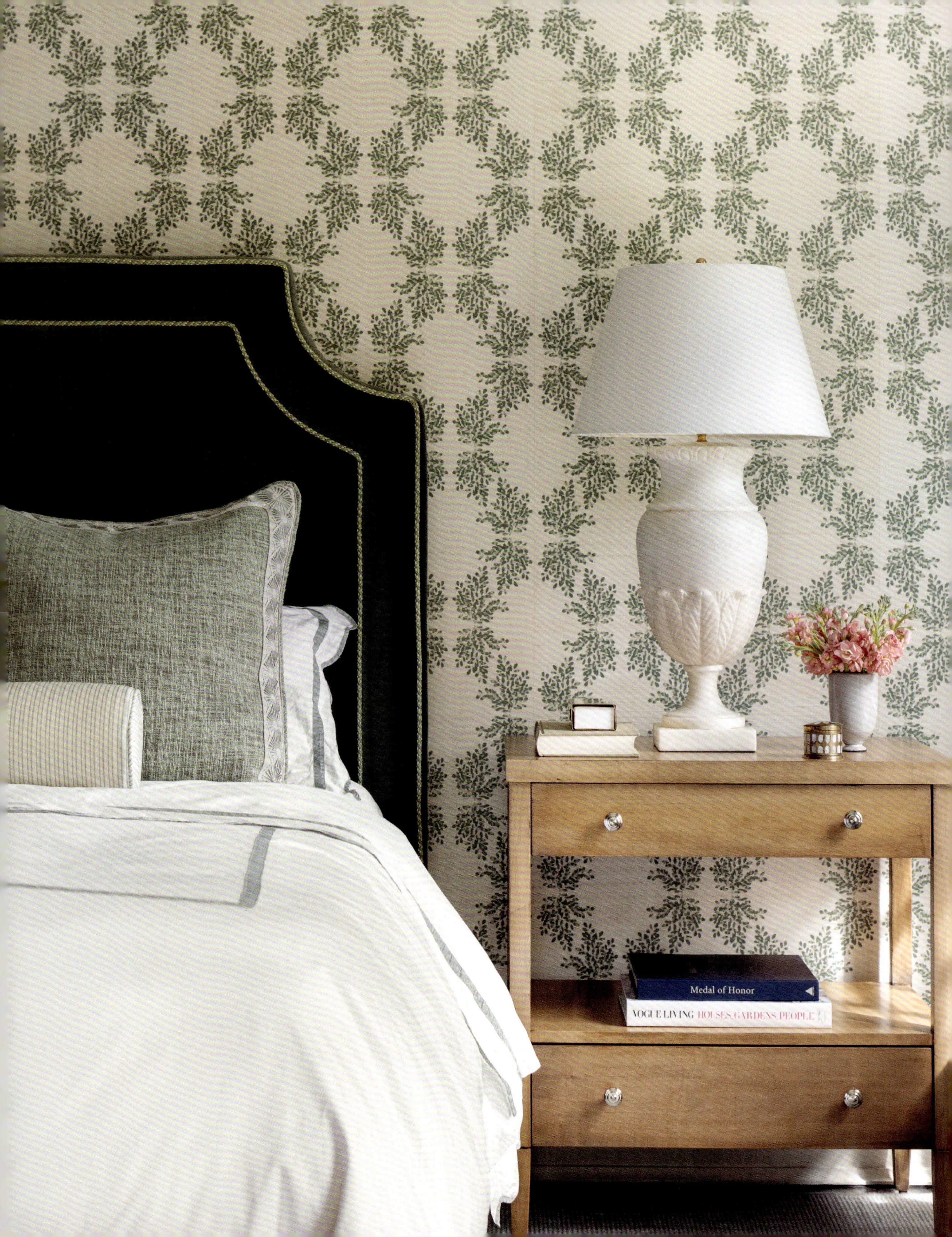
Medal of Honor
VOGUE LIVING HOUSES GARDENS PEOPLE

Previous: A blue-and-brown plaid gives the study a grounded, masculine feel that still relates to the overall palette of the home.

—

Opposite and right: This wallpaper pattern, which I designed, presents a more graphic, modern take on a vine motif, striking a balance between classic and contemporary.

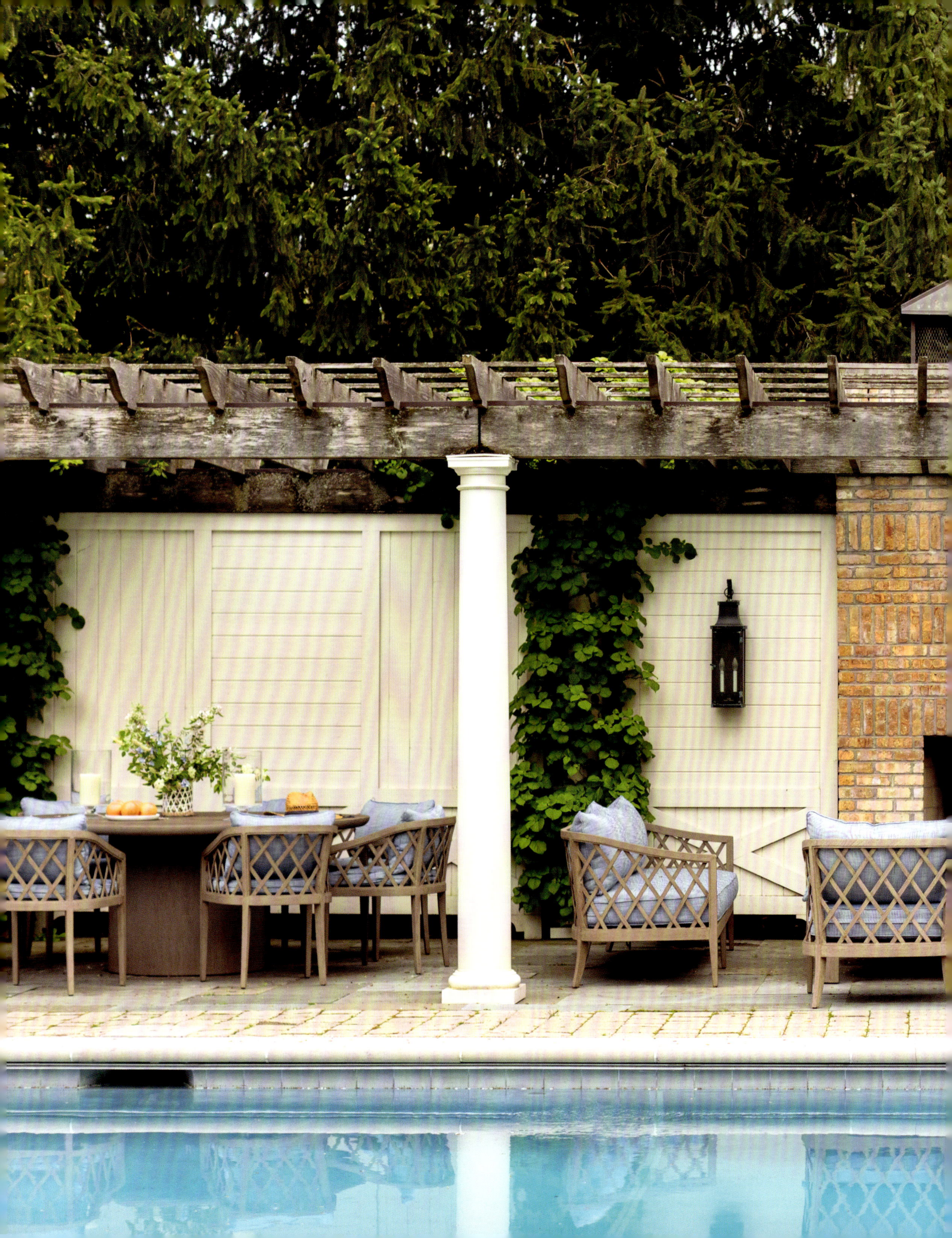

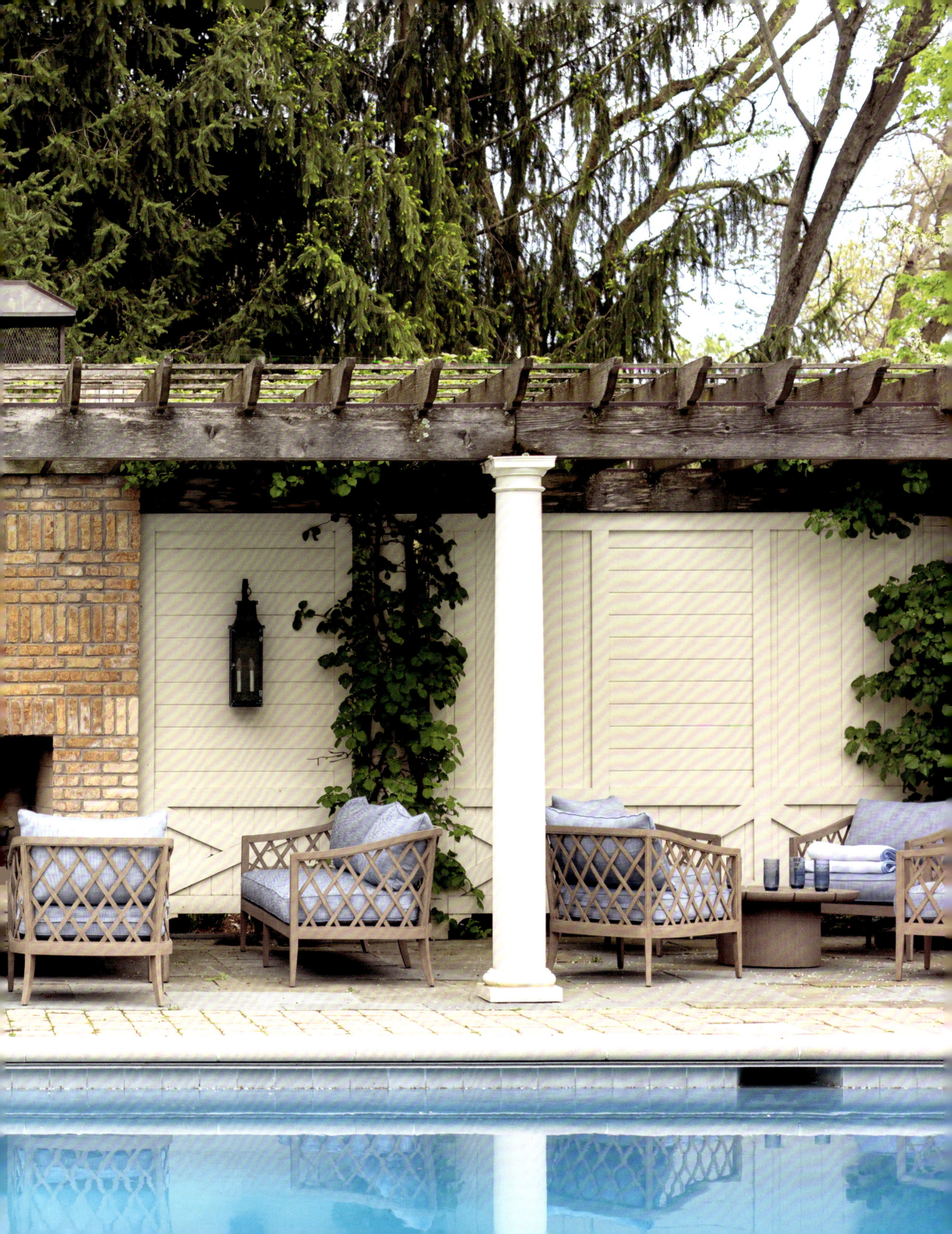

Previous and above: The family spends a lot of time outdoors in the warmer months, so we extended the livability of this house by arranging areas for lounging and dining beneath the long pergola.

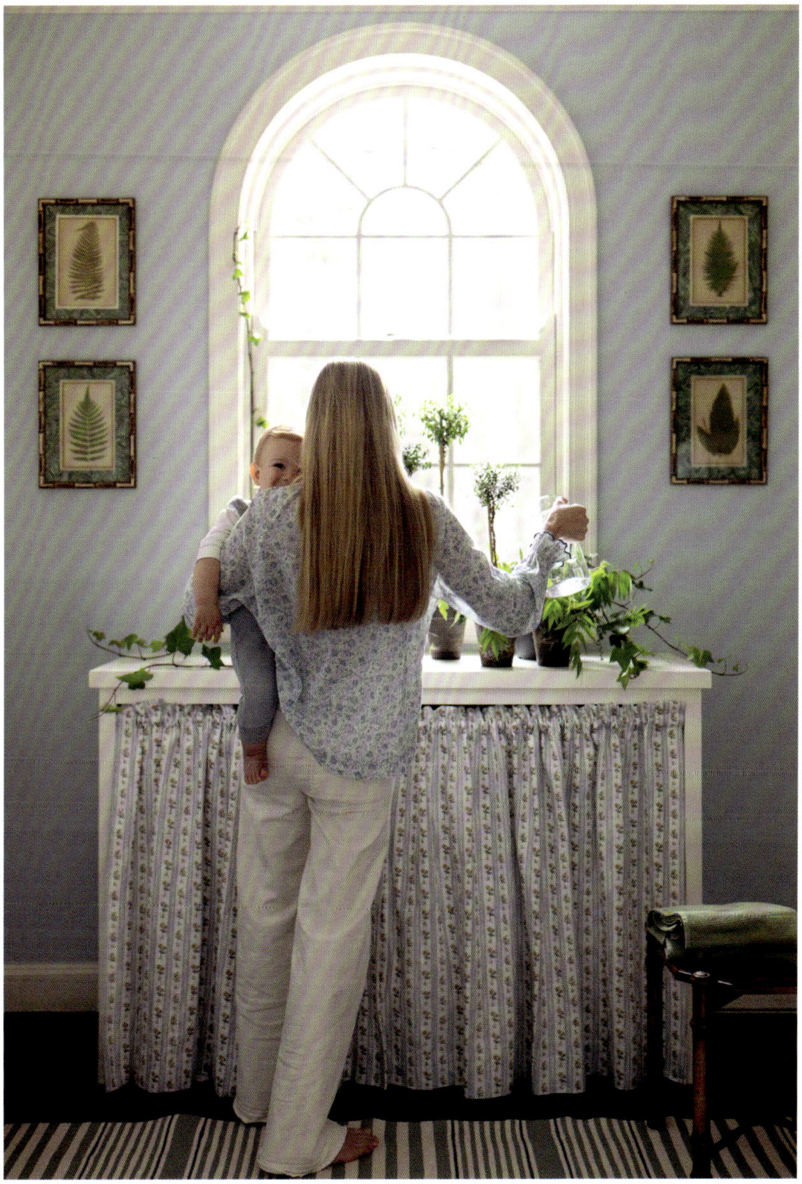

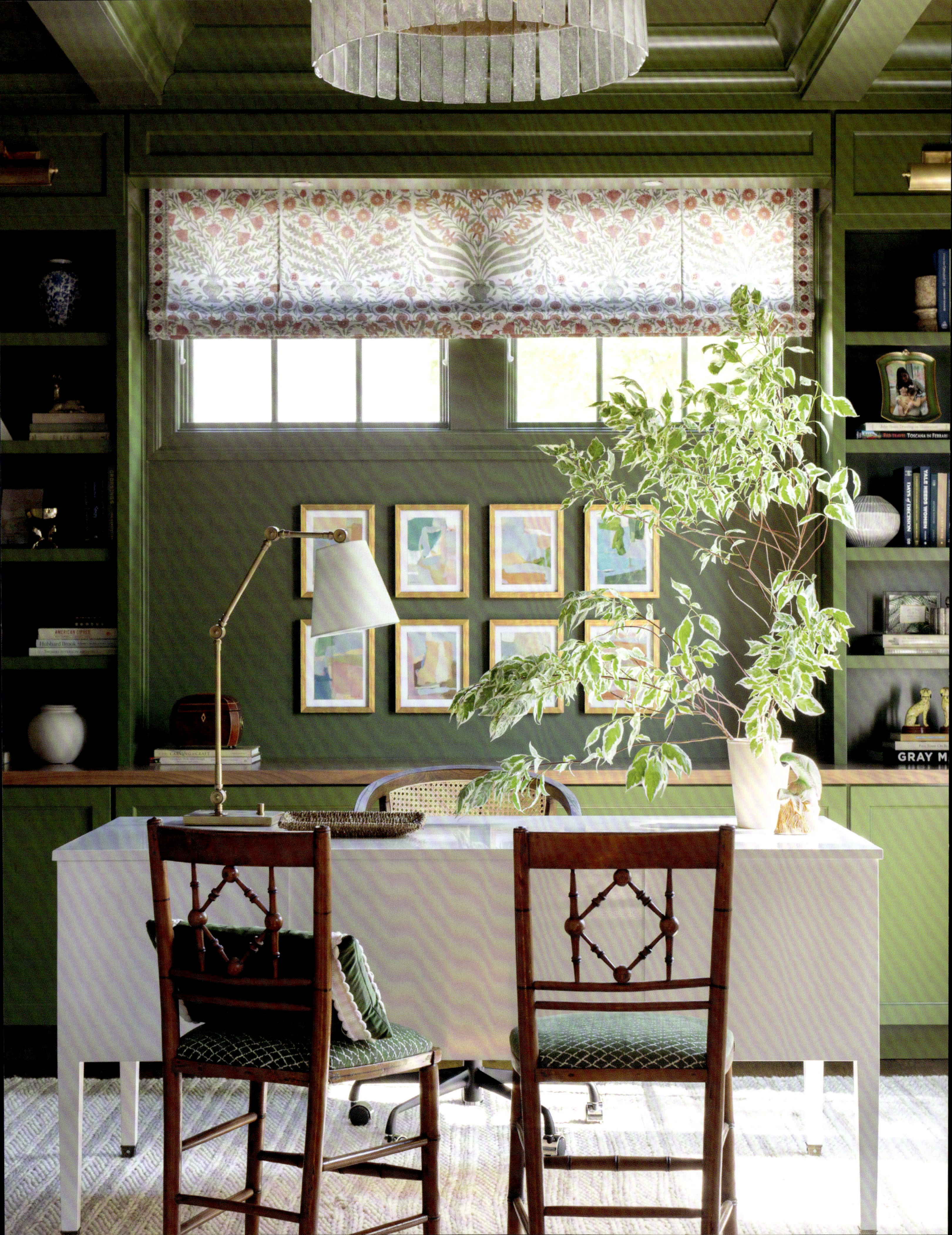
GRAY M

NEW OLD HOUSE

An inviting new-build

with a sense of history

Previous: In the home office, the small size and positioning of the windows close to the ceiling made any wall treatment tough, so we embraced the challenge and turned the wall into the ultimate Zoom backdrop with a grid of abstract art.

Even those of us who love old homes will be quick to admit that their restoration, upkeep, and formal floorplans aren't for everyone. These clients, a couple with two young daughters, loved the idea of an old house, but just didn't feel like they could stomach all the work that an old house requires. The home they found—a shingle-style new construction with an East Coast feel—was about halfway built when they brought me on board. Given that the construction wasn't yet complete, we had the opportunity to make some key decisions on interior finishes and layout that usually come only with a ground-up build. Throughout the project, our guiding question was, How do we add depth and character to the house without making it feel contrived? Or, as our client put it, How do we make it feel like it's been here? Ultimately, the answer was to bring in antiques with history and patina and pay close attention to textile choices.

While the clients wanted the kind of elegance and character you'd find in an old home, it was important that it didn't feel "dainty or breakable." It was also

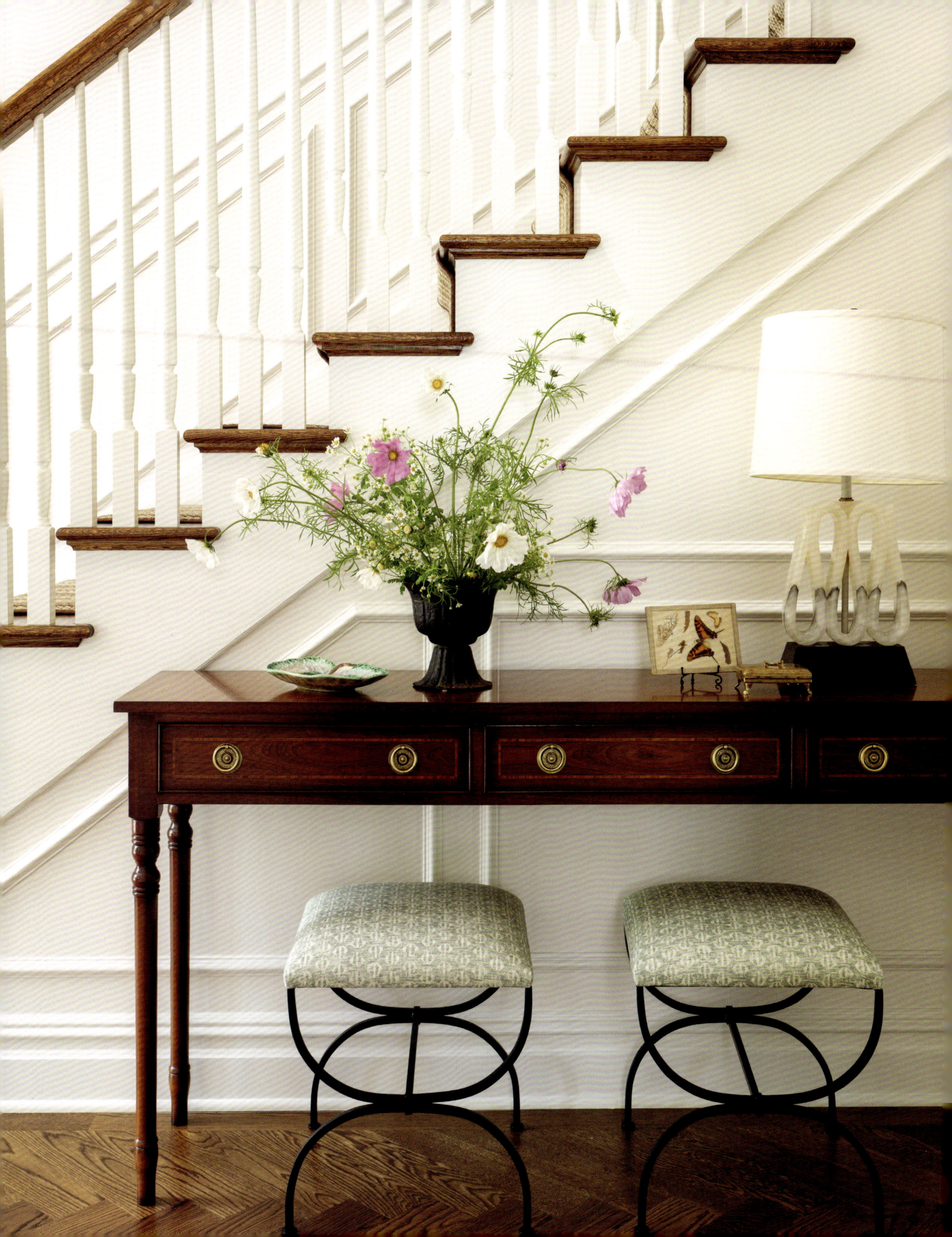

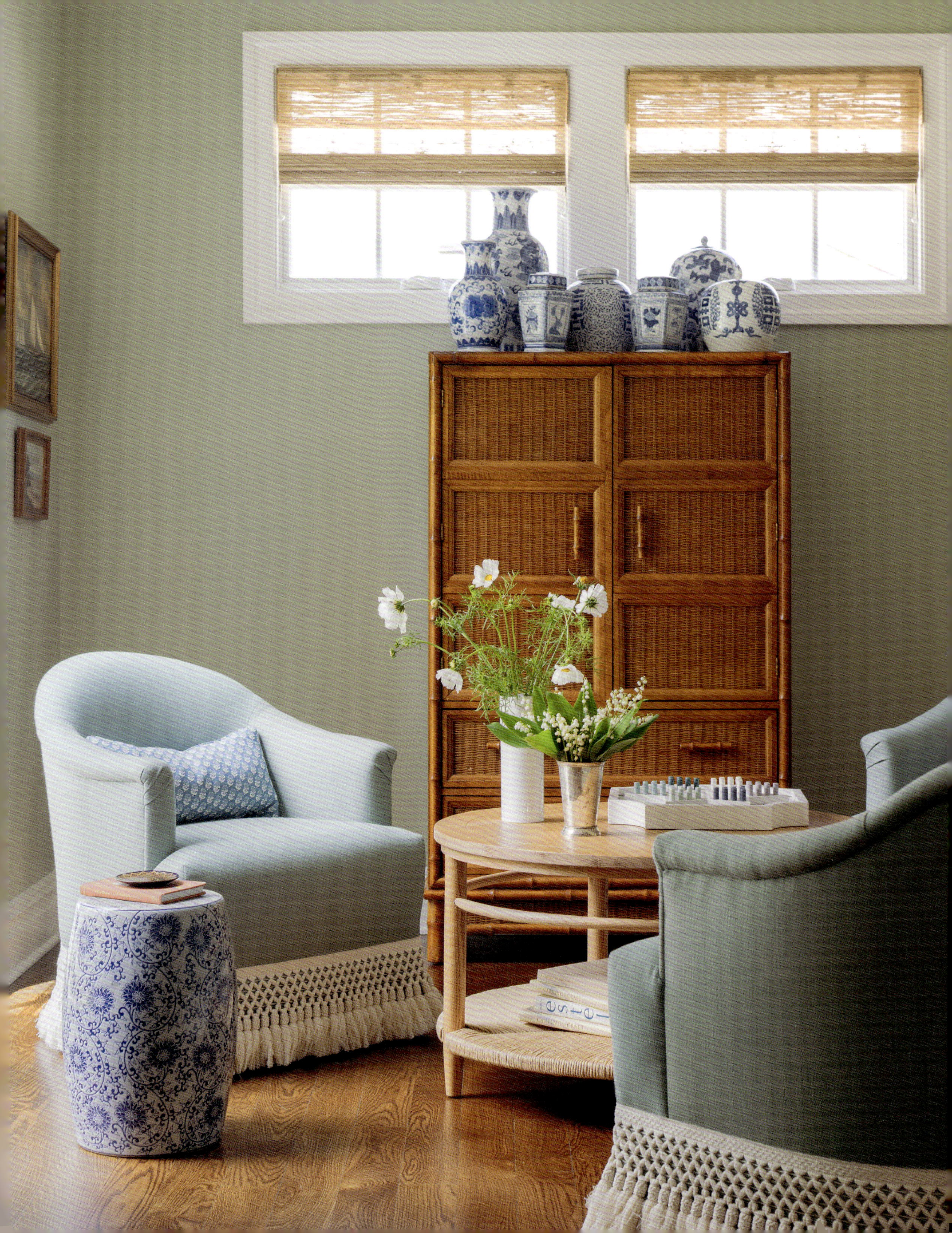

In the lounge off the wine room, an antique bamboo cabinet holds glasses and barware for easy serving when the family entertains.

The laundry-slash-mudroom is right off the kitchen, so we wanted to ensure that the space is pretty in addition to being functional. Powder blue cabinets and walls and a checkered marble floor do the trick!

—

Overleaf: The goal with the kitchen was to make everything not feel so new. A patterned tile, woven stools, and linen window treatment add much-needed warmth and texture.

critical to them that every space be functional, not just pretty. These two directives coalesce pointedly in one of the home's most unusual features, and a surprisingly central element for the family: the wine room. The couple are big wine collectors. In the home's initial plans, this small space was designed to be used as a study, closed off from the adjacent family room. Luckily, since I came on board during the building process, we were able to pivot to a more unusual layout that better aligned with the family and their personal interests. Instead of closing off the wine room behind a door, we incorporated it into the living space, creating one large L-shaped area that connects the wine room and a "lounge" outside it on one side and the family room on the other. We wanted this space to be super functional when they and their children are at home, but they also wanted to be able to entertain larger groups. Now, the wine storage area essentially serves as a design element of the family room—easy for them to access when they're hosting or just enjoying wine themselves, or, as I observed on a recent visit, a place where the girls can set up games and play. I love how it creates a completely unique backdrop for this family.

When it came to the home's aesthetic, we let the Cape Cod–style architecture and the house's location just blocks away from the lake inform an elevated coastal feel. This look aligned well with our efforts to "create" a little history and patina, as in the dining room, where the wallpaper's creamy white background feels like a more historical alternative to a bright white and blue. We emphasized that creaminess with the dining chairs, which are upholstered in a butter-yellow herringbone fabric (performance, of course!).

While these homeowners were what I'd call "color cautious," they came around to some unexpected pairings, especially when the combinations made sense in context. The best example of this is without a doubt in the large home office, where grass green paired with burnt orange and creamy neutrals is unexpected and fresh. This space was originally meant to be a formal living room, but my philosophy is that there's no reason to have a room that you won't use, and with most of the family's gathering happening in the kitchen and wine room, this space would have been totally overlooked. We decided to turn it into an eye-catching office, complete with a wall of abstract art by Christina Baker that's the perfect backdrop for Zoom calls. It also happens to be the very first room you see when you enter the home, so it really makes a statement.

I encouraged the couple to add color in the kitchen, but they preferred a clean white. We settled on a

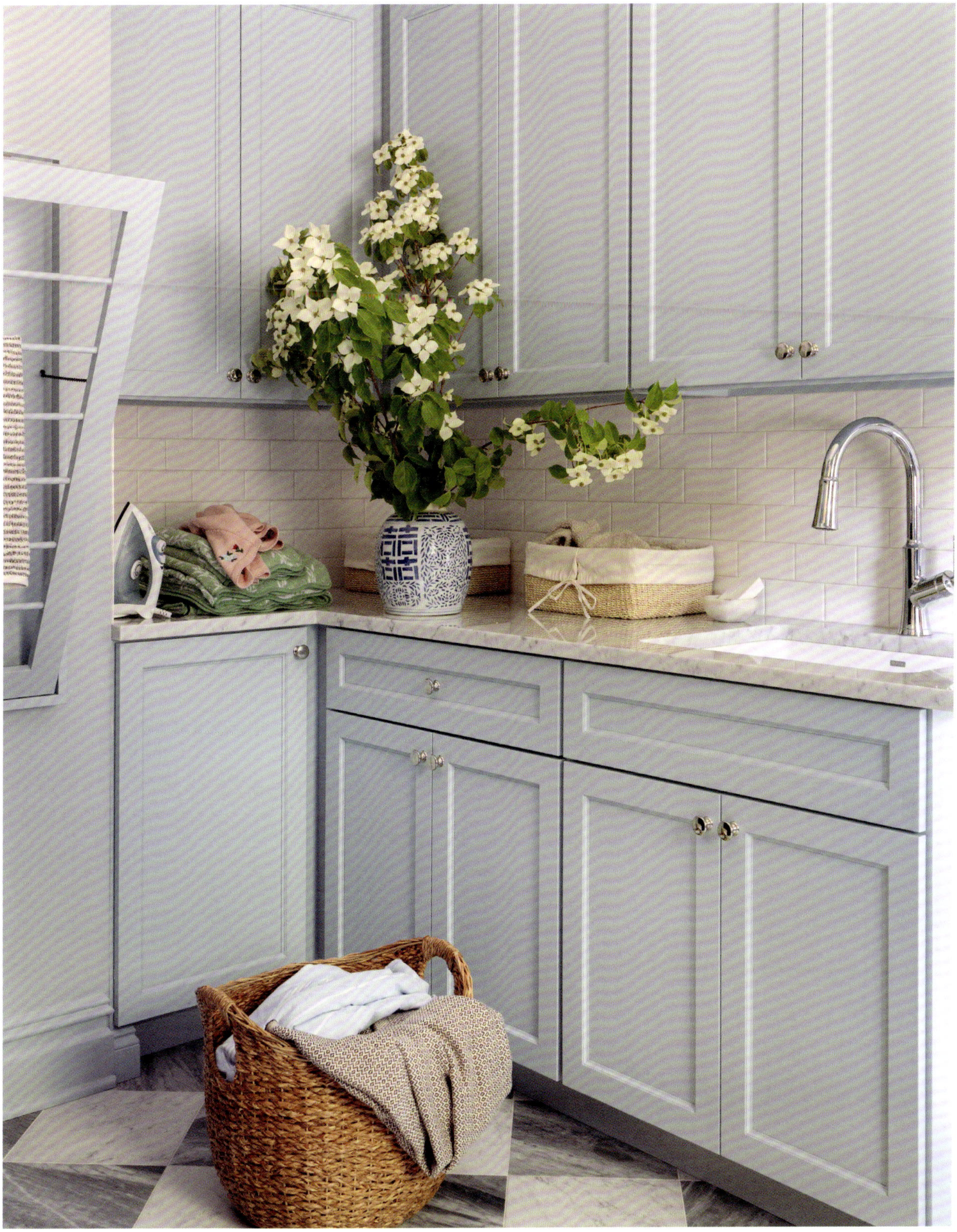

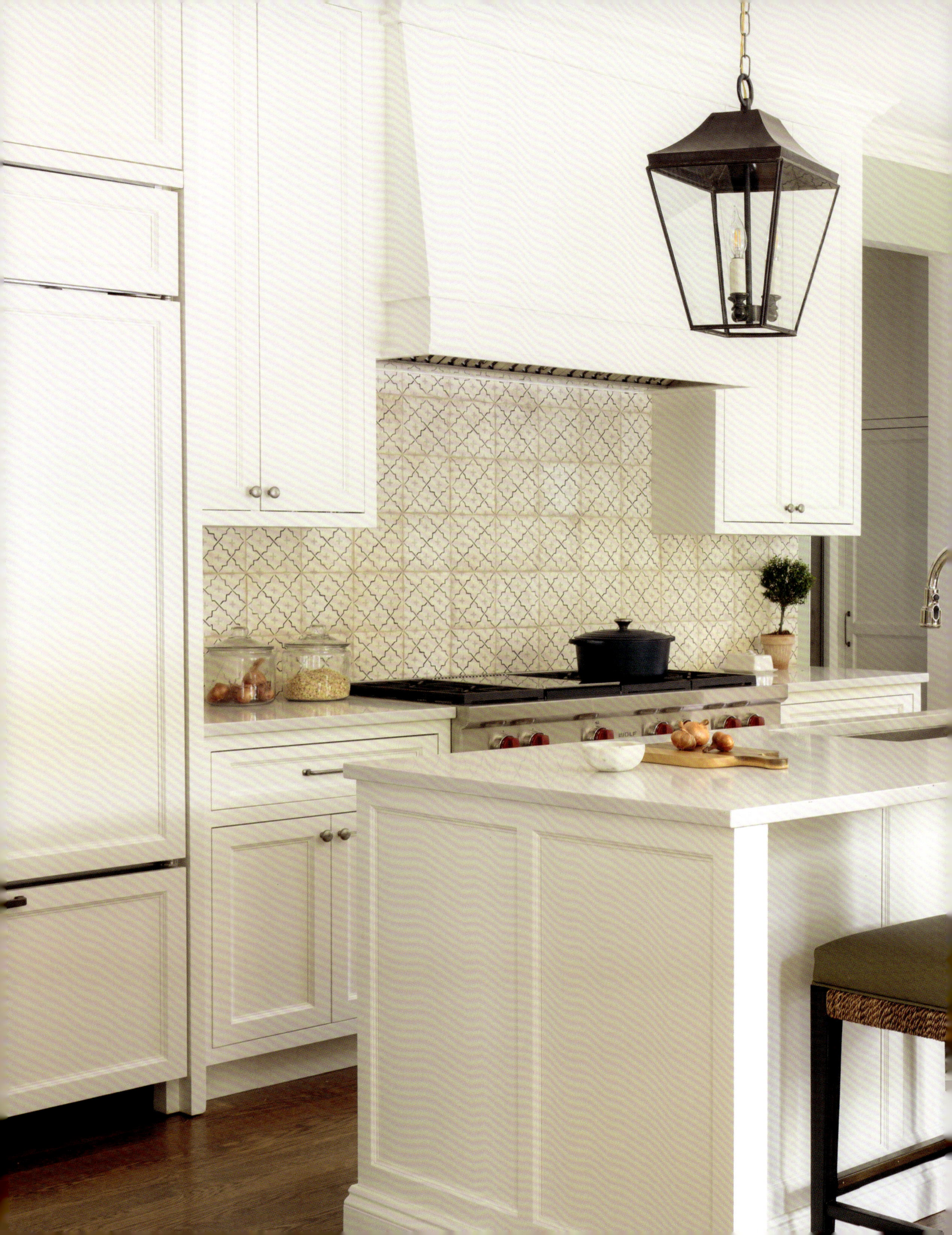

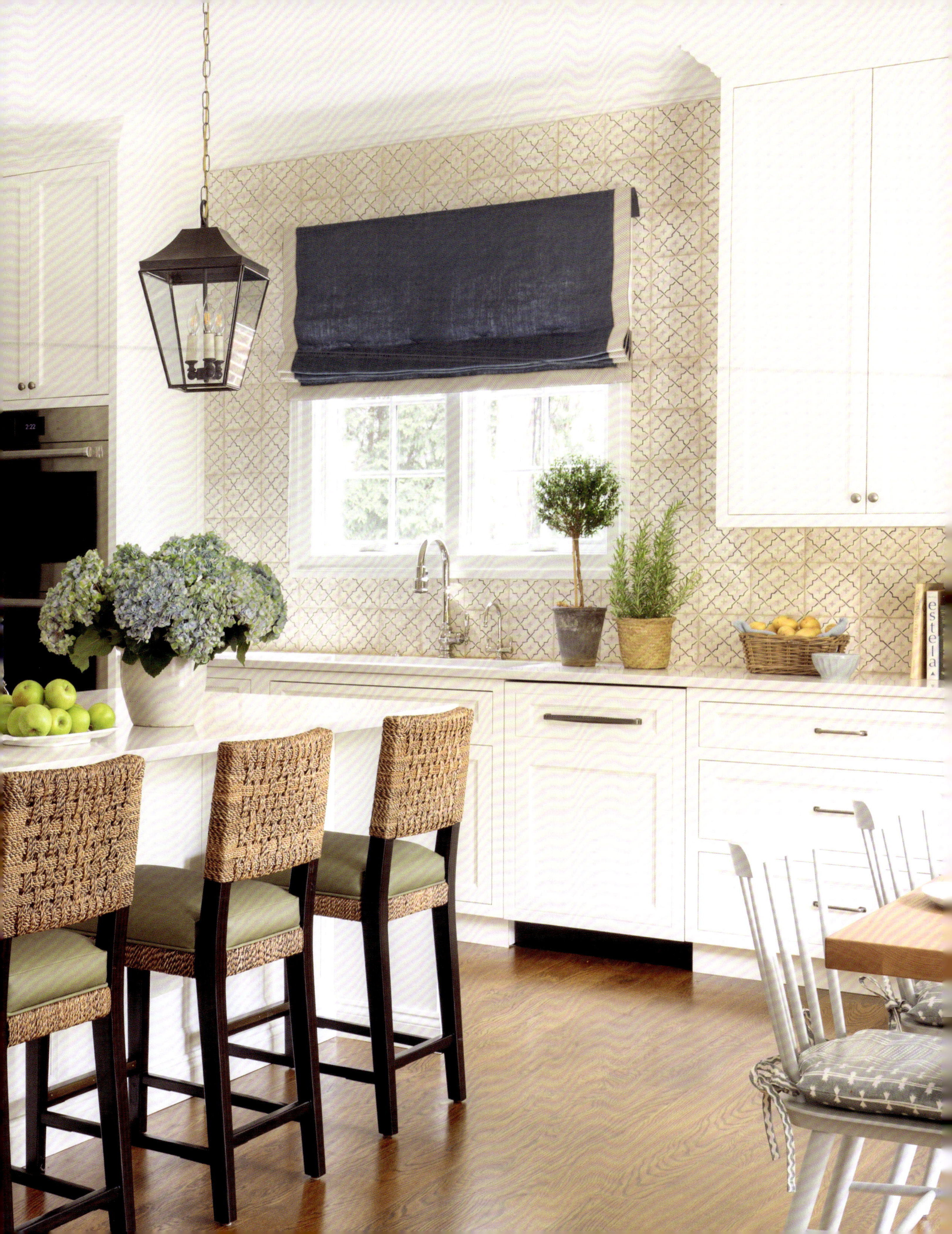
estela

warm white, a shade with some depth that pairs nicely with the greens and blues in the family room. To incorporate more visual interest, we installed a hand-painted terra-cotta backsplash, then filled the space with textured organic materials like raffia, linen, and wood.

I managed to get my color fix in the first-floor mudroom/laundry room, where we selected a sky blue for the cabinetry and leaned into the Cape Cod feel with checkered marble floors. With its fold-down drying rack, built-in bench, and tons of hidden storage, this unassuming space may be the best fulfillment of the clients' request that every square inch be functional—but it has some competition: Even a nook under the stairs got carpet and wallpaper for an upgrade as a tiny play area!

Ironically, although we filled the home with antiques in pursuit of a historic feel, we used almost no furniture that the family had previously owned. This made it even more imperative that we source furniture that looked like it had been collected and layered over time. We wanted furniture that looked good together but not like it came as a set: upholstery fabric in a mix of materials, textures, and pattern scales helped create that collected look. The few existing pieces of furniture were the wood and rattan bed and gold leaf and antique mirror nightstands in the primary bedroom, which were a wedding gift from the husband's grandmother. That we use that bed and nightstands was the couple's only furniture request for the entire home. I love being able to incorporate furniture that's meaningful, and working with this bed that I might not have otherwise chosen, was a fun challenge. It has such a presence, and it provided the jumping off point for the entire room and adjoining bathroom, where we went with light walls and subtle patterns to balance the weight of the furniture. The ensuing design is elegant, welcoming, and playful with a strong grounding element—a perfect metaphor for a good family home.

An antique quilt draped over the sofa adds visual interest underneath an overscale abstract painting by Caleb Mahoney.

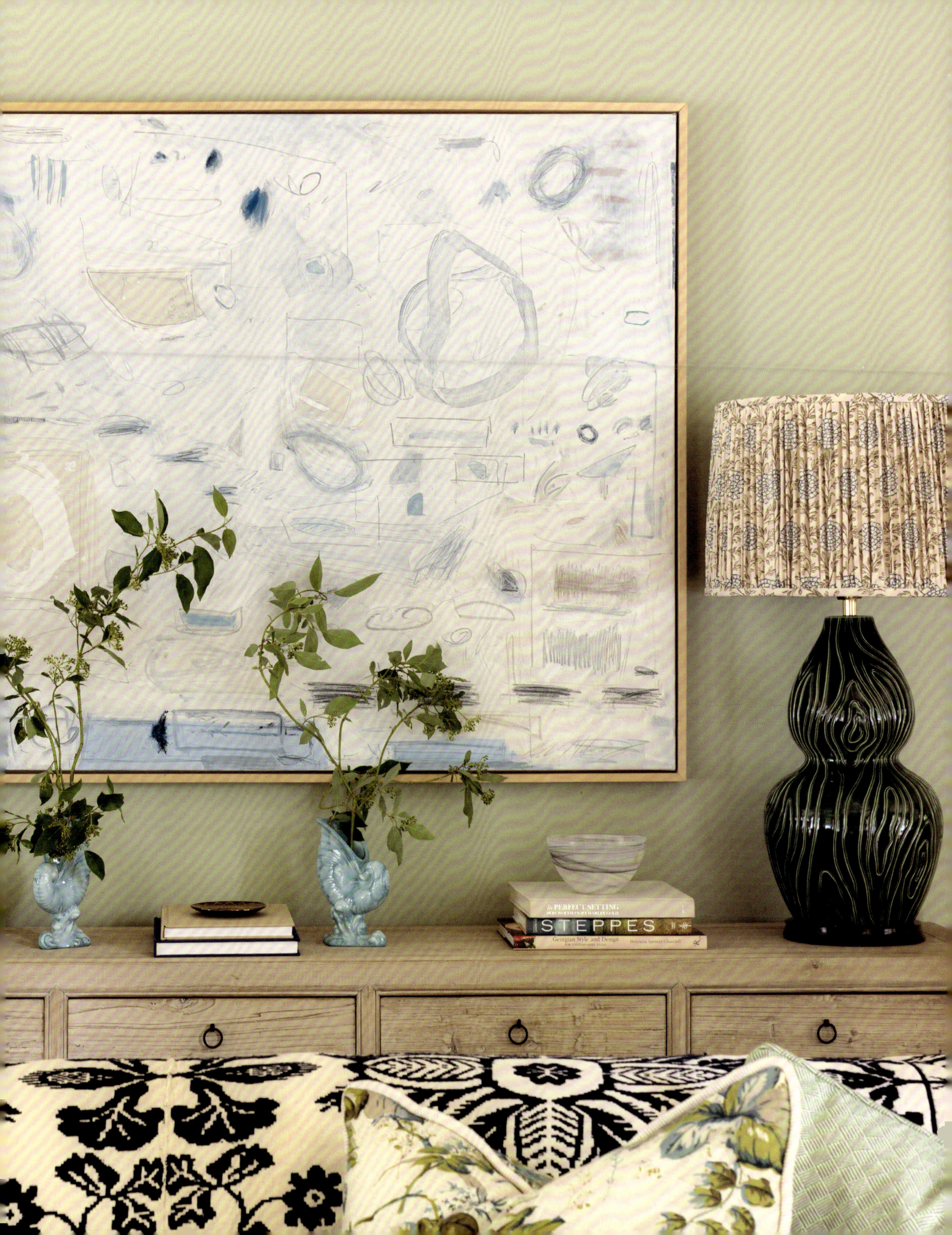
PERFECT SETTING
STEPPES
Georgian Style and Design

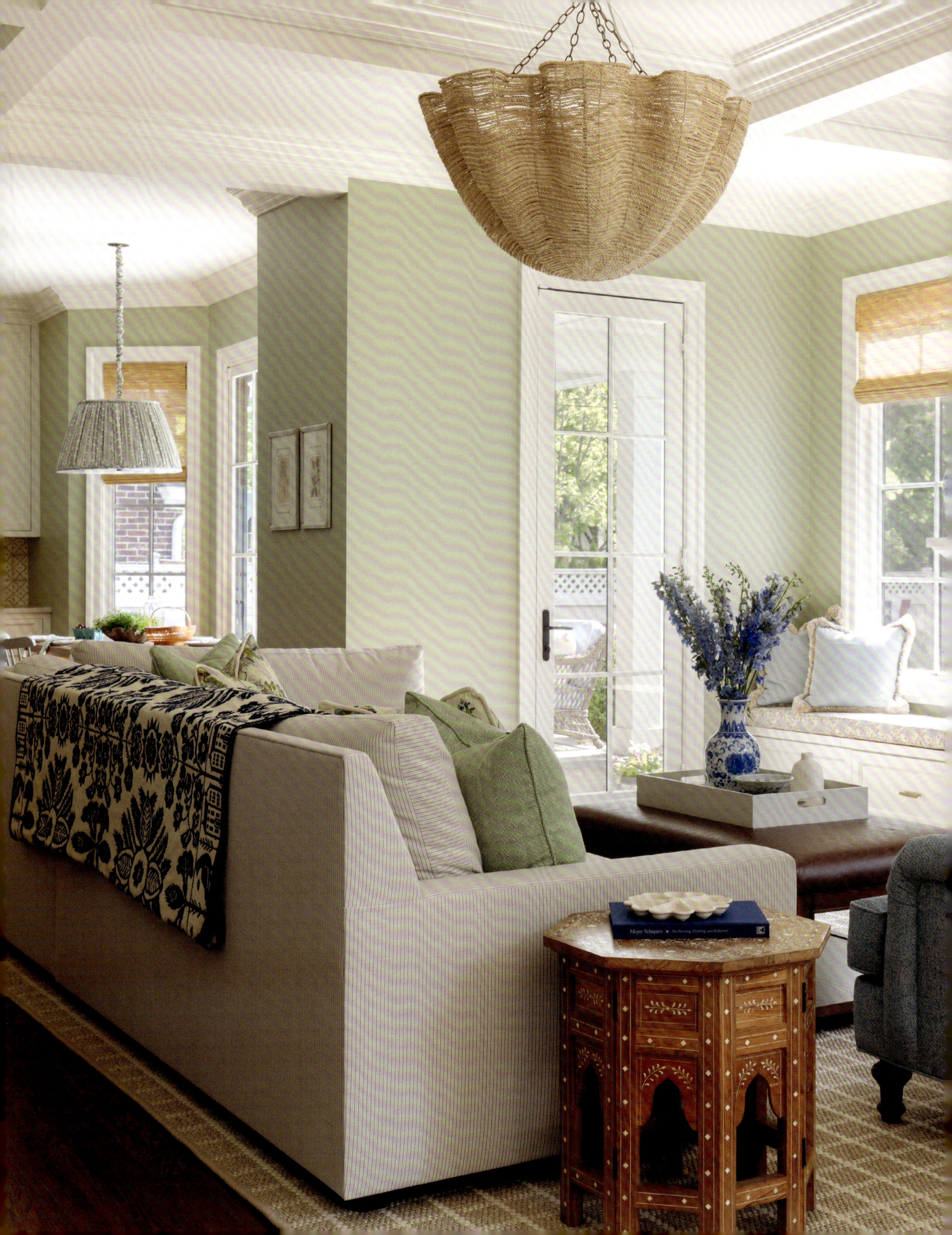
Meyer Schapiro

"How do we make a new house feel like it's been here? By bringing in antiques with history and patina and paying attention to textile choices."

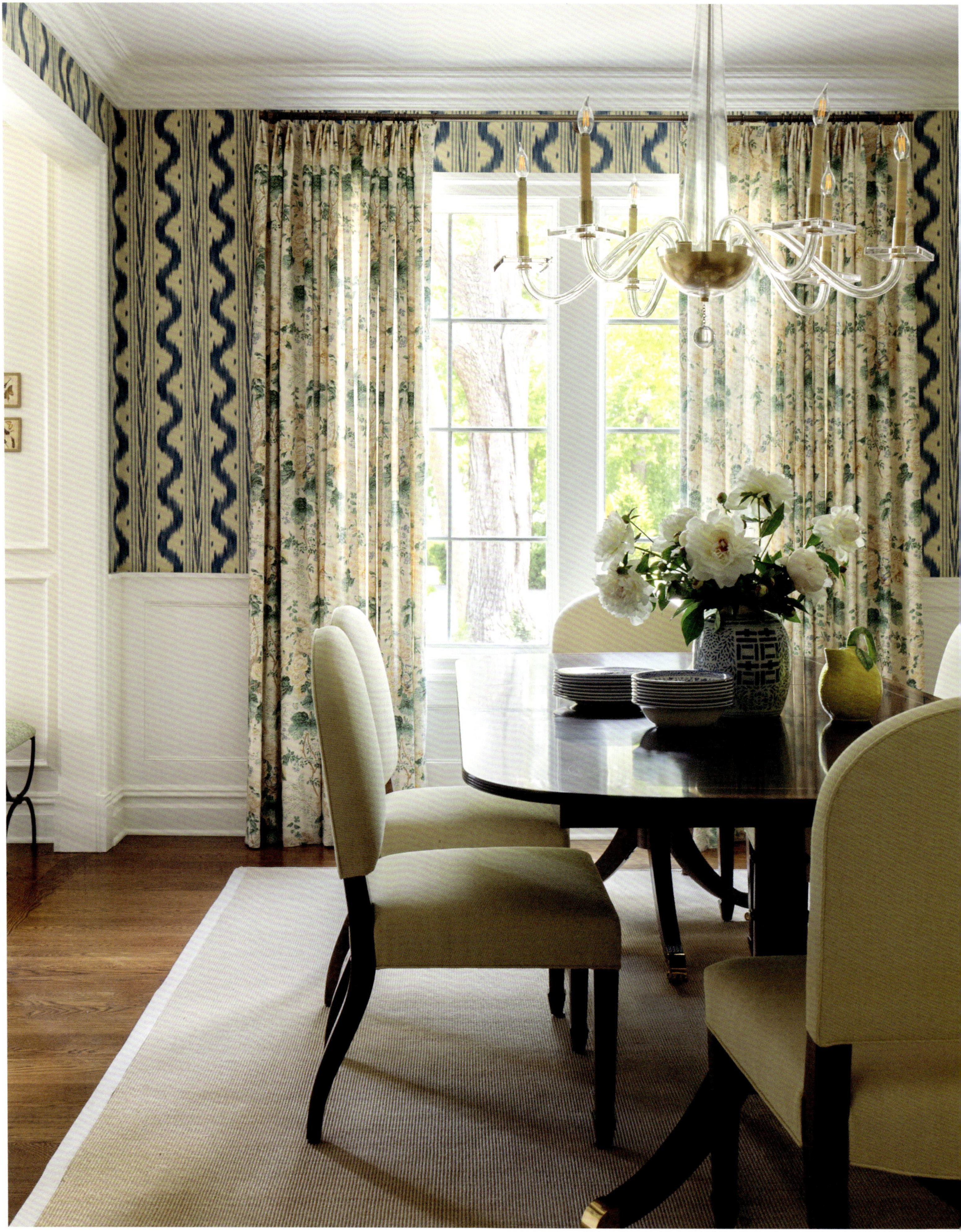

In the dining room, we presented a fresh interpretation of the classic combination of blue and butter yellow by mixing prints and textures. I love how the chairs read almost as neutral, even though they're yellow herringbone.

—

Overleaf right: Pairing ikat stripe wallpaper with very traditional chintz floral drapery is an unexpected combination.

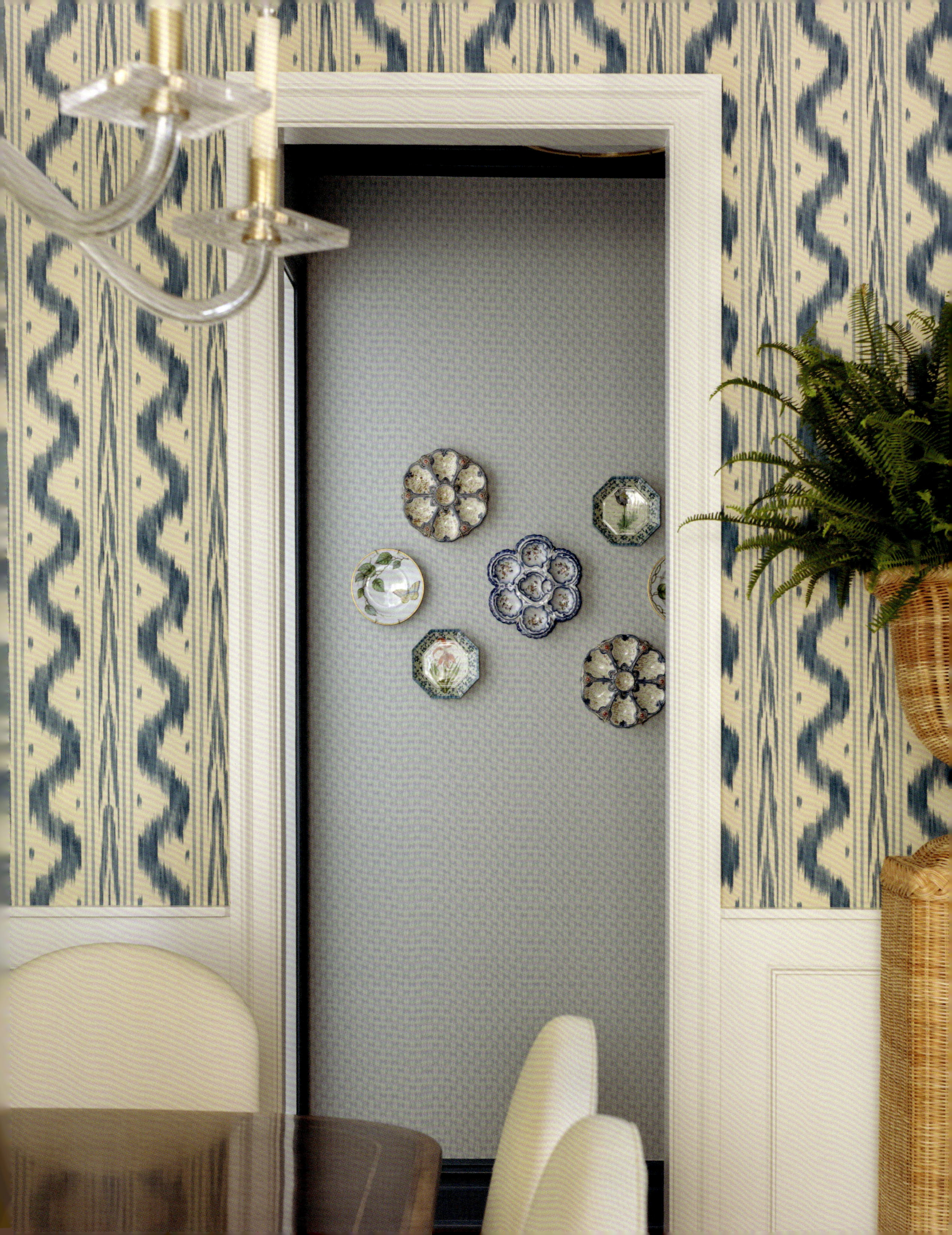

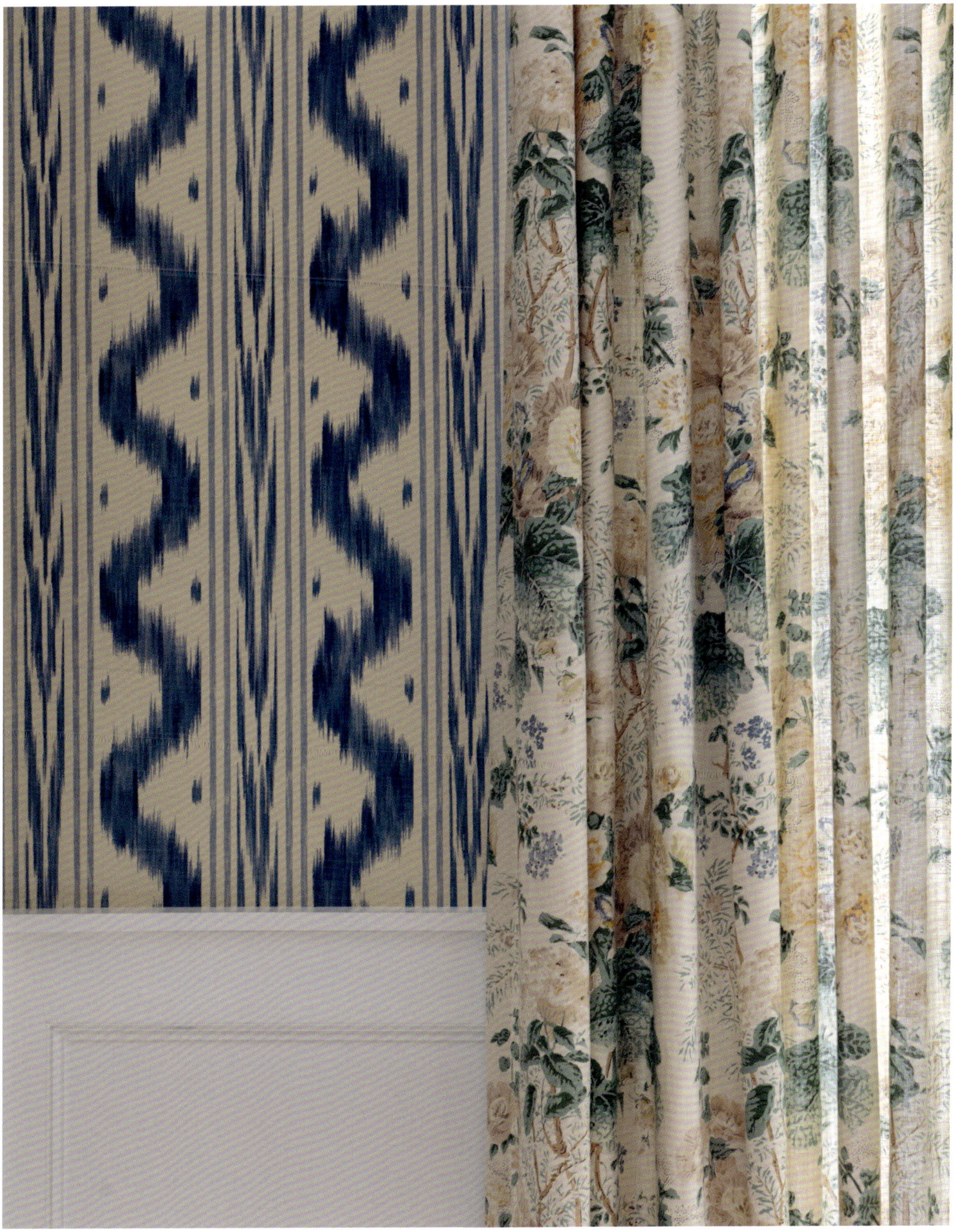

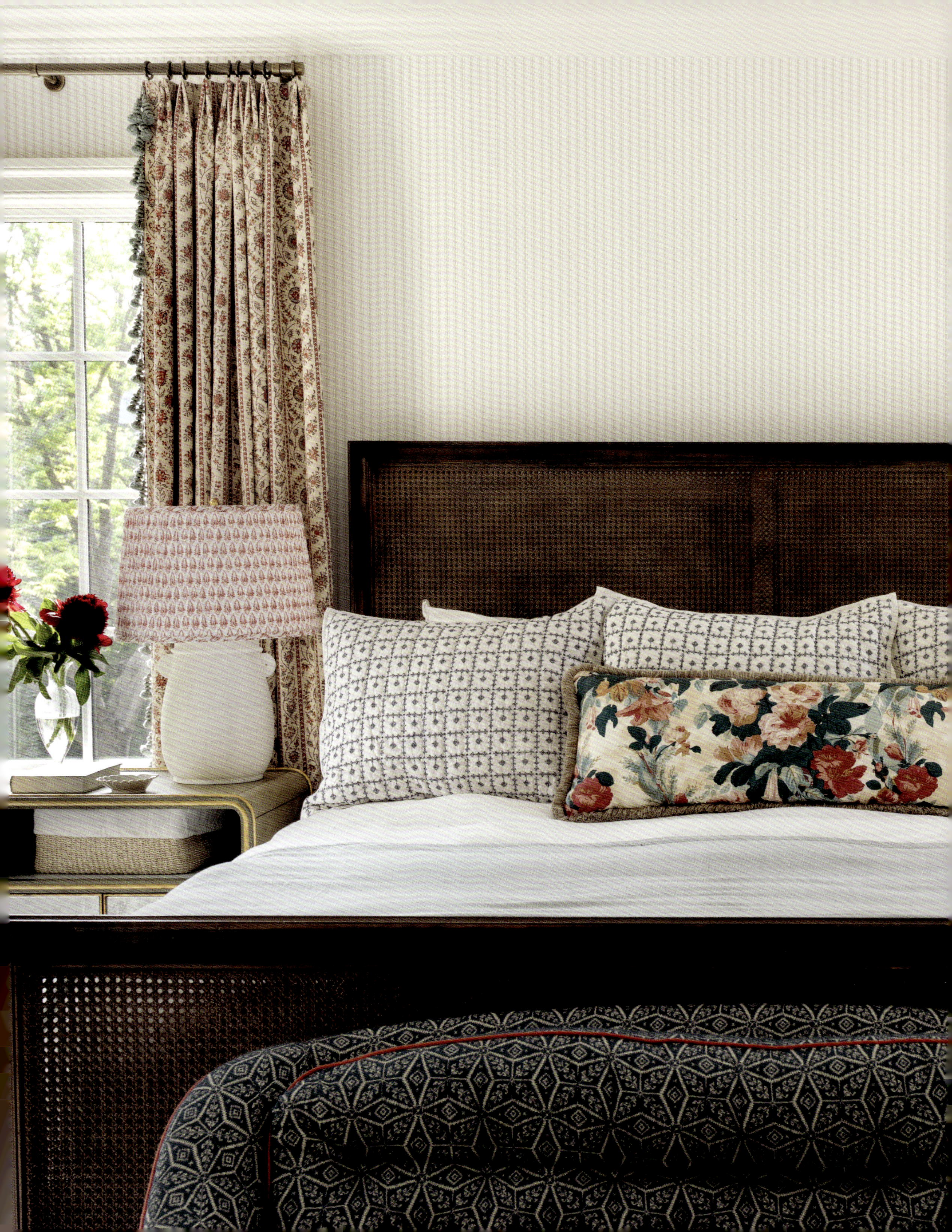

The bed and nightstands in the primary bedroom were wedding gifts to the homeowners, so it was important to keep them. We brought in a light-colored wallpaper and soft florals to contrast with the heavy furniture.

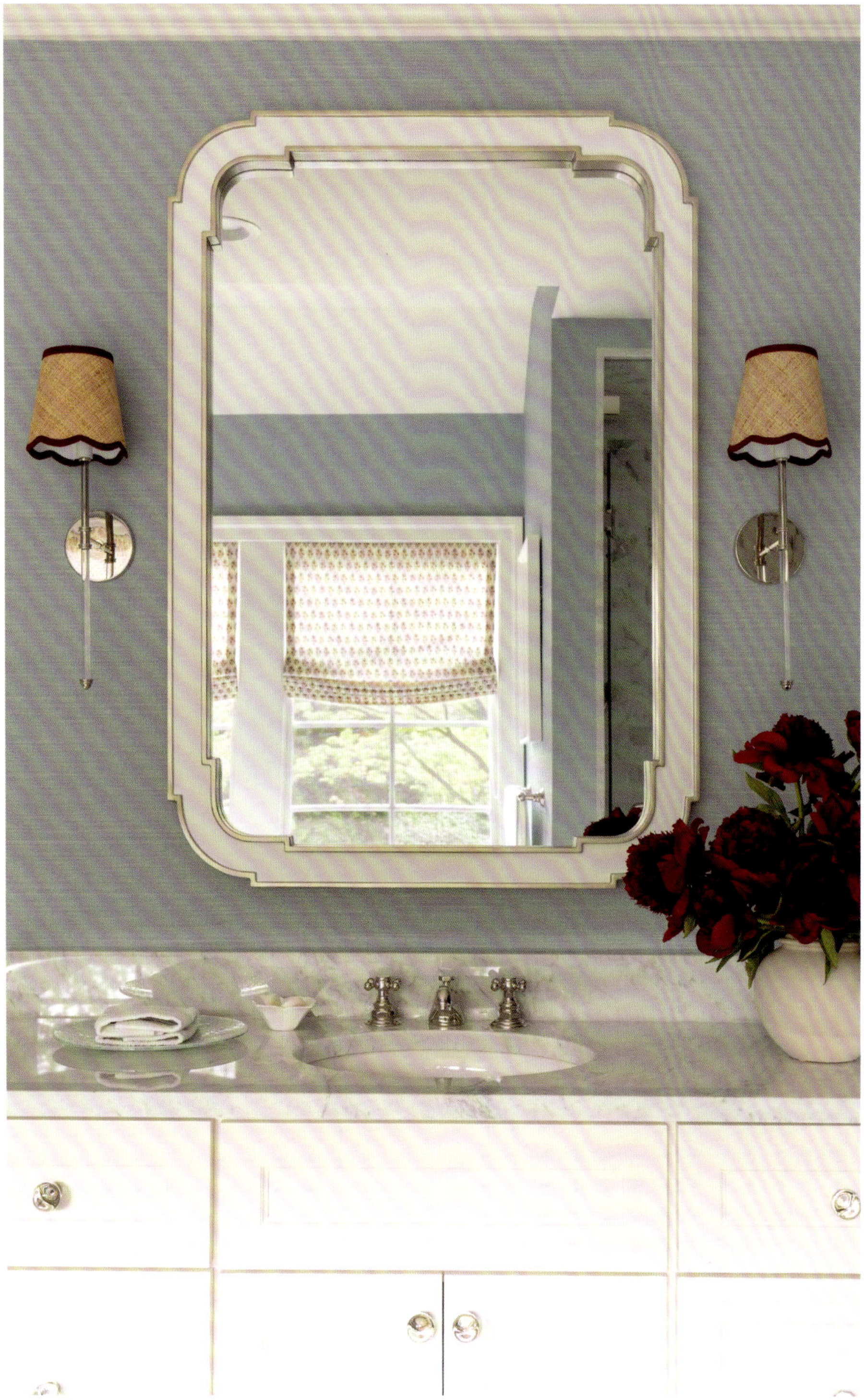

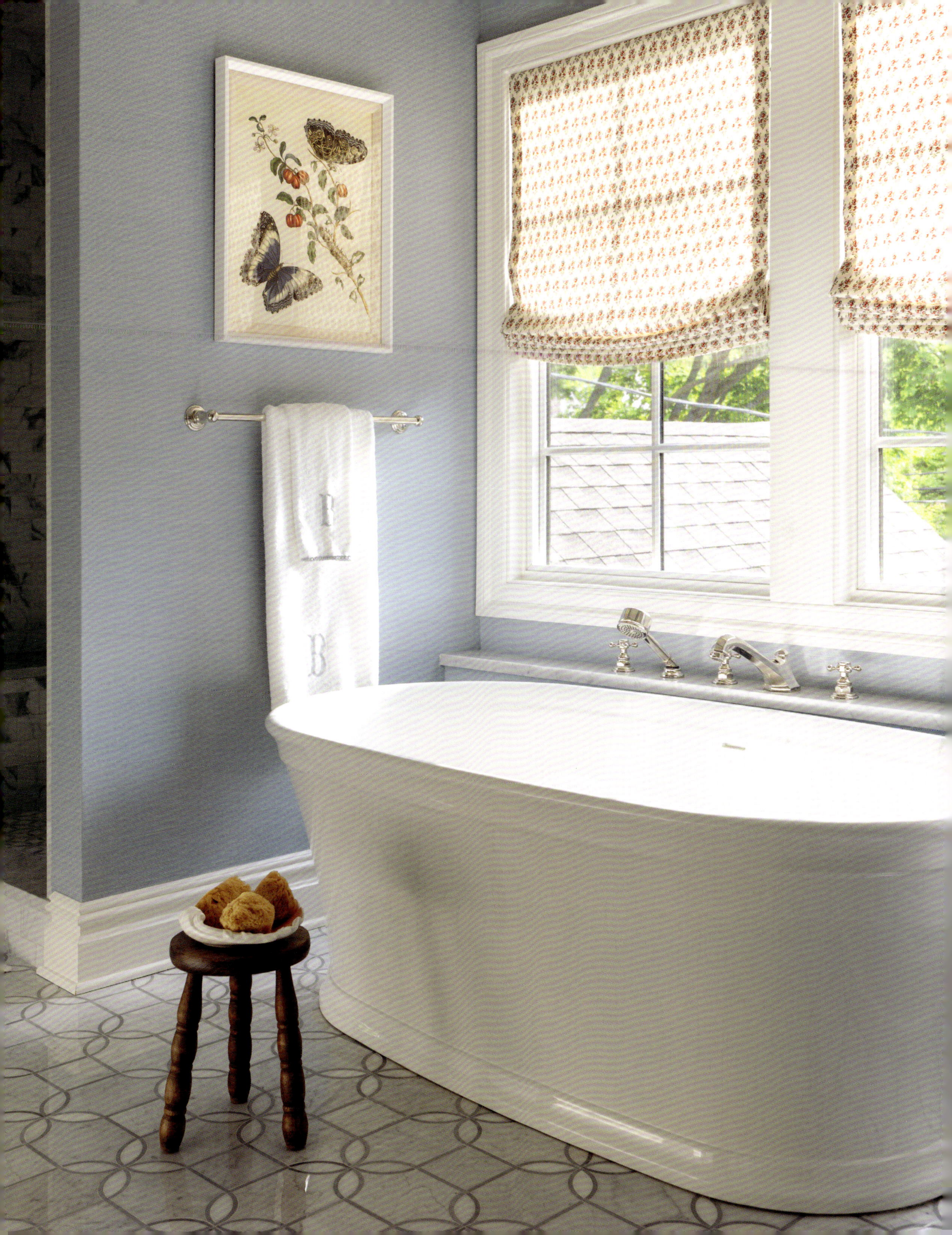

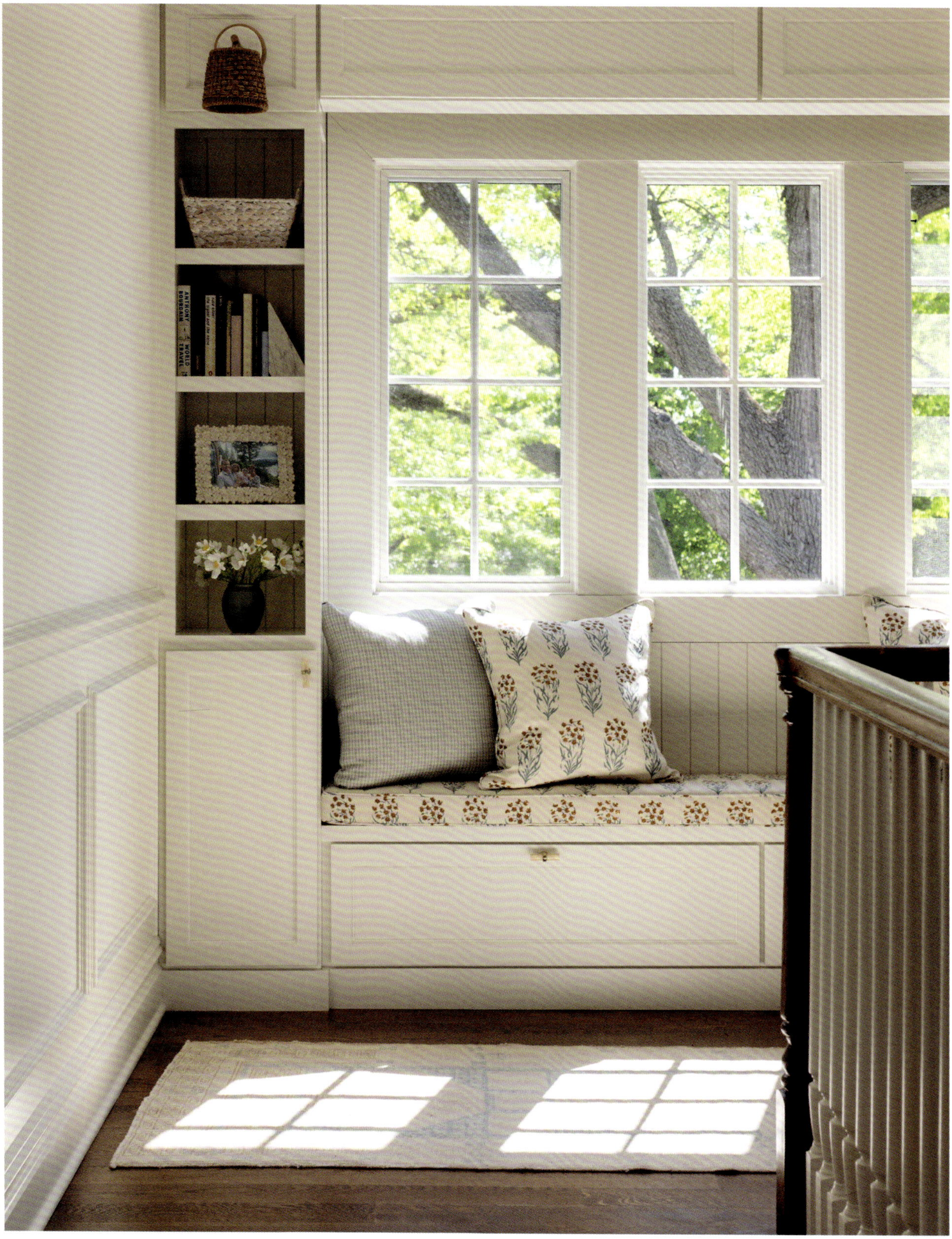

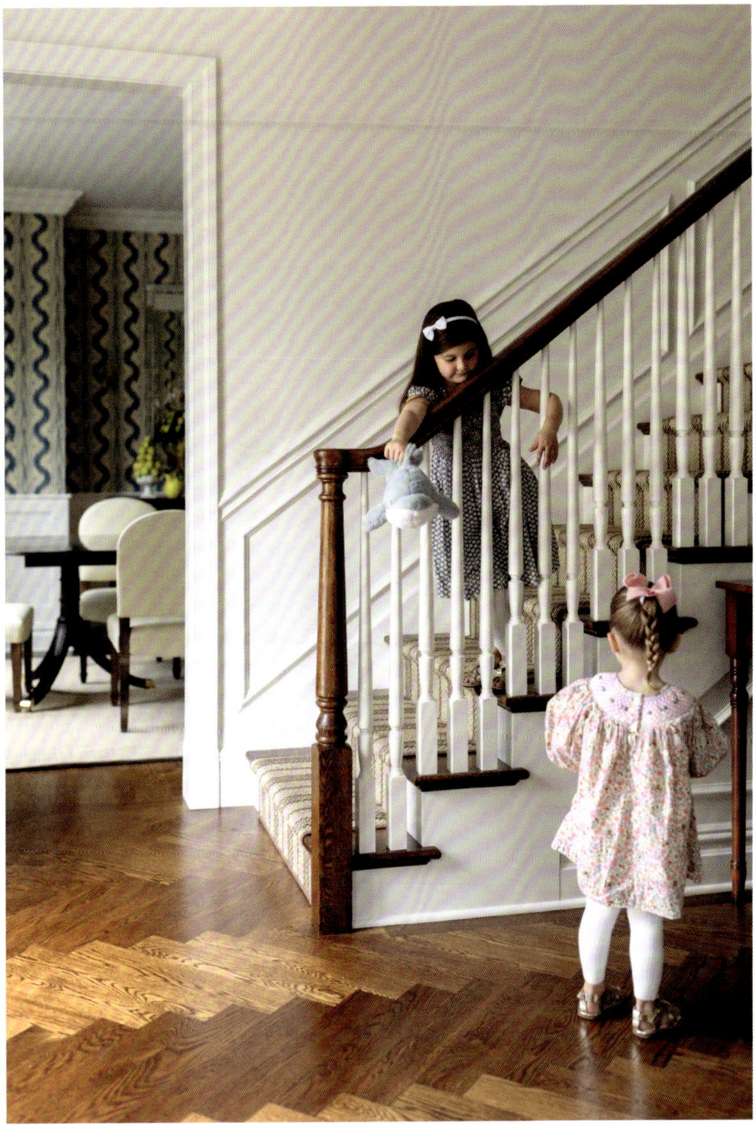

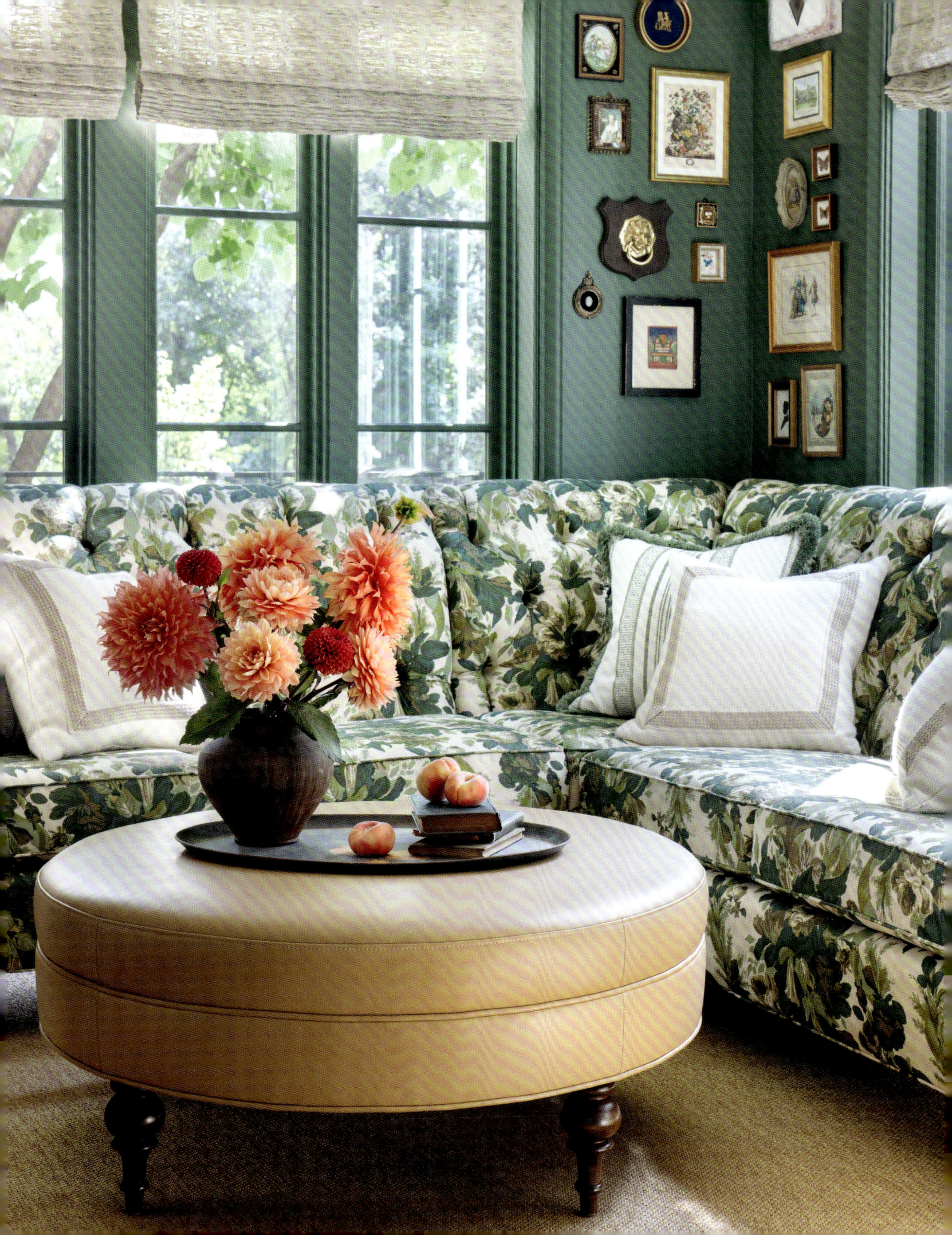

HOUSE PEOPLE

A forever home for my sister's growing family

Previous: Grouped against a green wall, my sister's collection of miniature artworks makes a strong statement and serves as a memento of her travels.

In the speech that I gave at my younger sister's wedding, I said, "When I think about my sister, I think about her wrapped in a tartan blanket in a chair by the fire." My family has always called ourselves "house people," and, like me, my sister is a homebody who's happiest when cozy in her space with her family. Unlike me, though, she's a staunch traditionalist and an unabashed maximalist with a strong aversion to modern furniture and blank spaces, which made designing a home for her an exciting challenge. The first directive she gave me was, "I don't want a single white wall." What she did want was a warm and layered home that incorporated her collections and sense of sentimentality while making (literal and figurative) space for her future family life.

When my sister and her husband, after spending many years halfway across the country, began house hunting in the neighborhood we had grown up in and in which I now also live, they invited me to join them. They fell in love with a French Tudor–style house that had been updated beautifully by its previous owners, who understood that it was a piece of history and required special care (they even went so far as to source wood for an addition from a tree on the property that needed to be cut down).

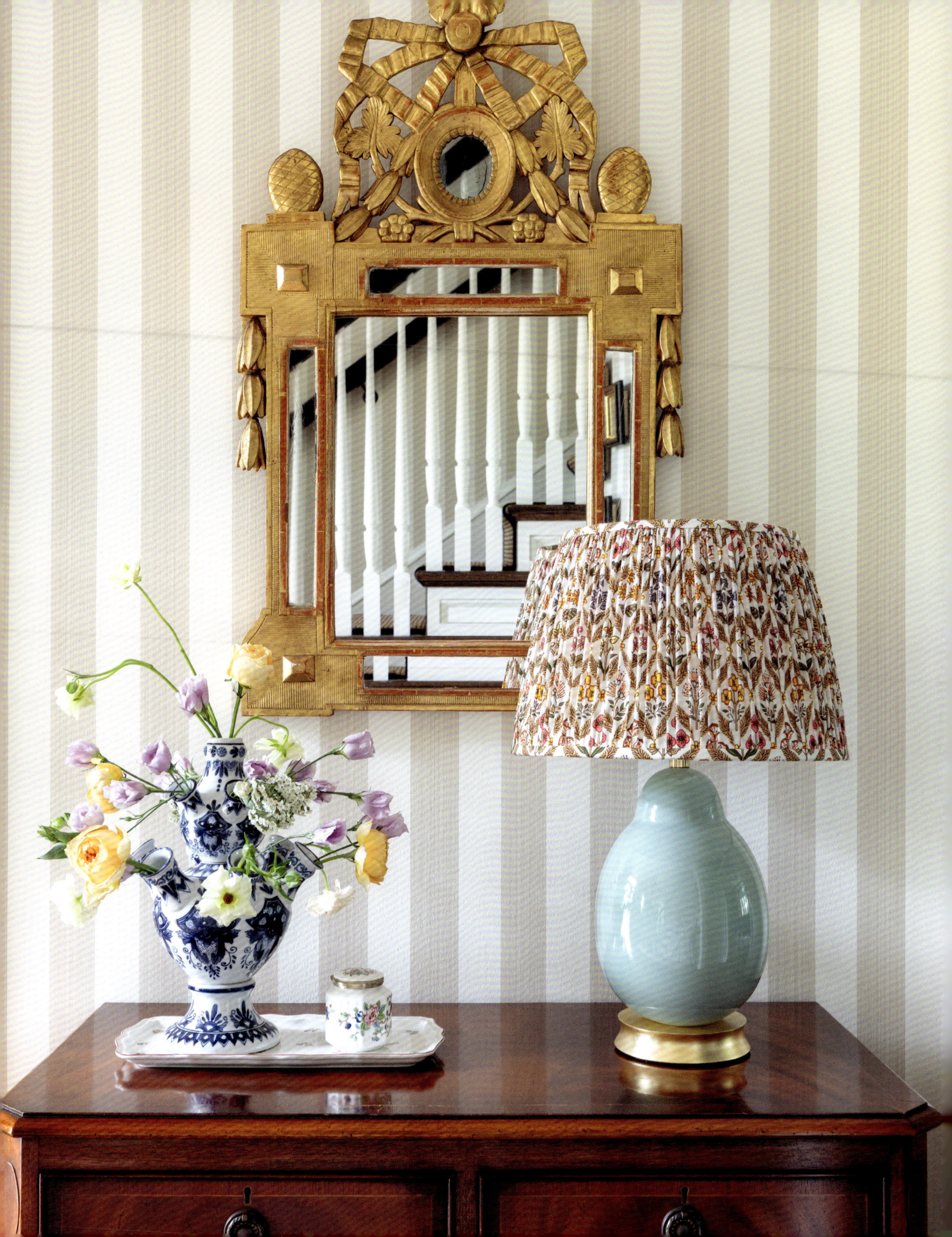

The most neutral my sister went in her colorful home was in her request for a tonal striped wallpaper in the entry—a graphic, grounding treatment that would prove the perfect foundation for the maximalism inside.

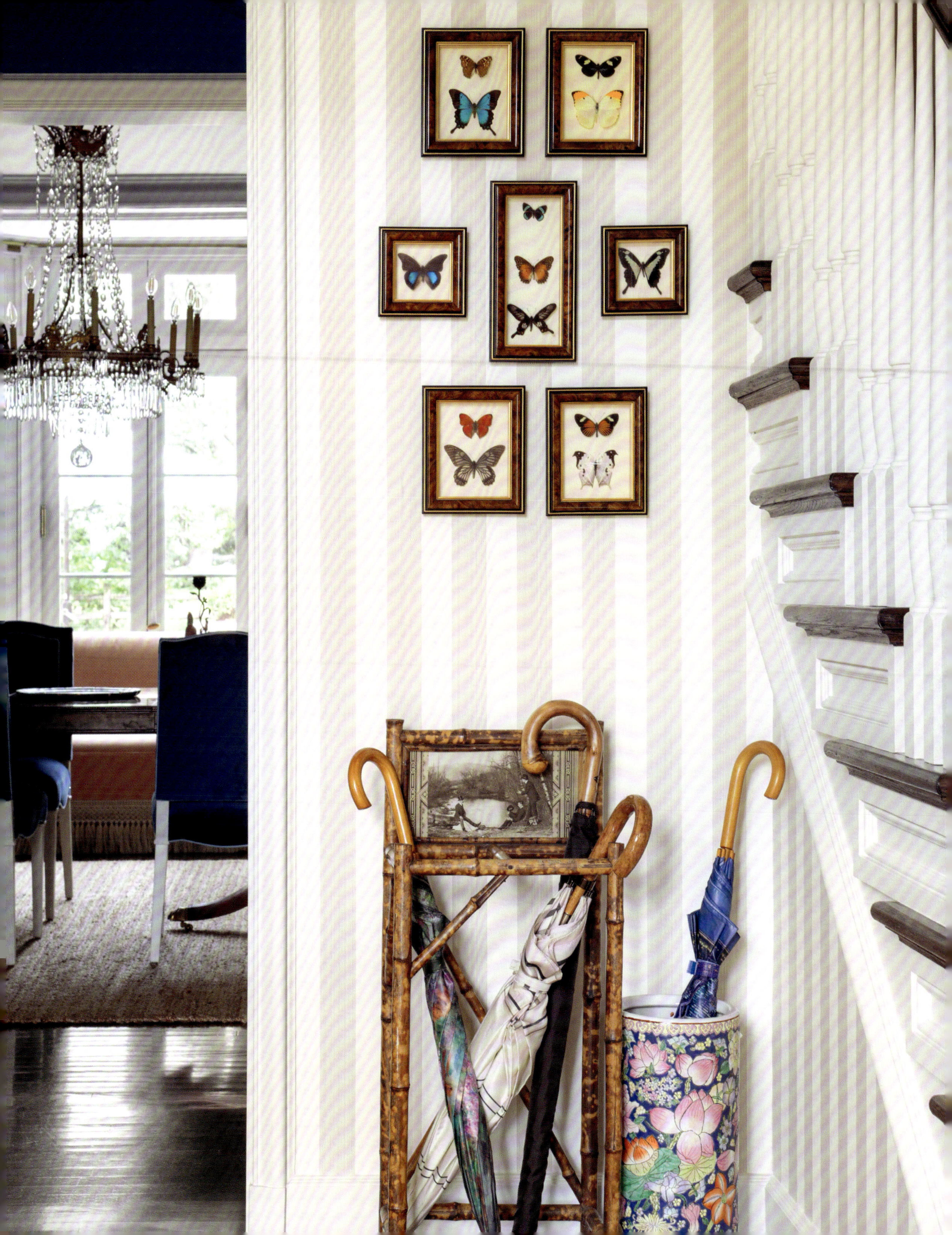

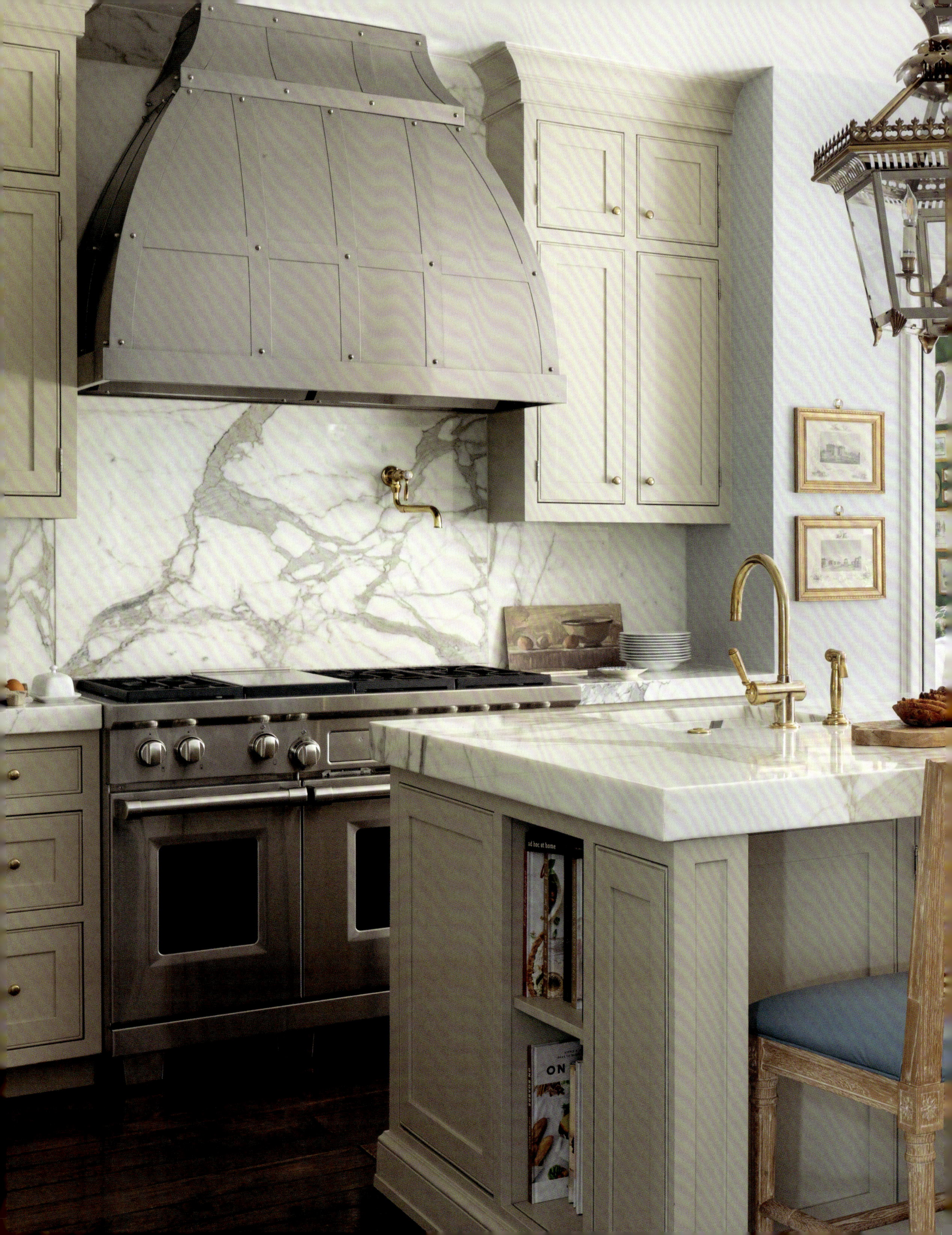
ad hoc at home
ON

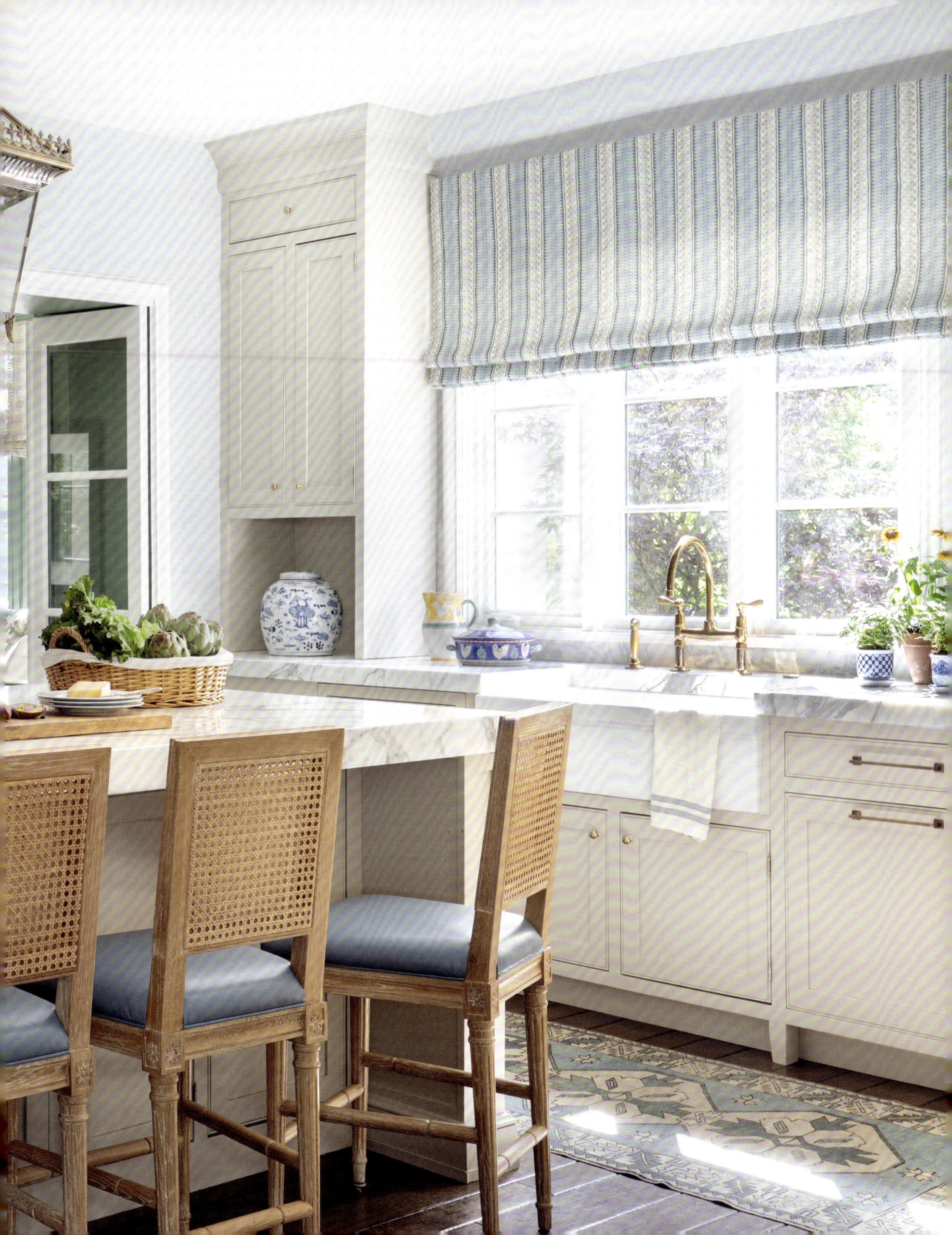

HARVEST
TARTINE ALL DAY
ina garten make it ahead
NEWLYWED KITCHEN
DEFINED DISH
NATHAN TURNER'S I LOVE CALIFORNIA
IT'S ALL EASY
JACK'S WIFE FREDA
Cravings
CHRISSY TEIGEN
ON BOARDS
Cookie Perfection
momofuku milk bar
ALISON ROMAN
COOK90
THE FOOD LAB
Carmen's Recipes

"I believe in the power of a good white wall as a palate cleanser—especially in a home with as much pattern and color as this one."

Opposite and overleaf: Of course, an all-white kitchen was out of the question. I think the pale blue grass cloth on the wall and the soft taupe cabinetry make for a beautiful new take on a classic.

The really great thing about committing to a forever home is that you're not looking at resale, or marketability, or curb appeal; you're looking at what you truly love. For my sister, that meant designing a home wholly to make her and her family happy, both with how it looked and how it functioned. After all, at the end of the day, you want your home to be attractive, but you also want to live in it, to be comfortable enough to manifest the dreams of what your life will be.

One significant advantage of this project is that it's been decades in the making: My sister and I spent years fantasizing about what this home would look like. While she was living in tiny apartments in San Francisco, she'd send me images torn from magazines or saved to Pinterest: British rooms bedecked in florals, sofas in the Lee Jofa Althea print that had covered our grandparents' living room, samples of bright wallpapers and vivid textile patterns. Throughout those years, she was also preparing for her eventual home in another way: by collecting. My sister is a total magpie; she's always amassed pretty things, whether they're miniature paintings, butterfly specimens, or blue-and-white ceramics found during her semester abroad in Copenhagen. On her trips home, she and I would visit antique stores, and she'd give her purchases to me for safekeeping "until I have a house for them." So there was never a question that her future home would be a layered, maximalist, collected one. As a designer, I was determined to create a space where my sister and her husband and children could feel comfortable without sacrificing the collections and antiques she loved for babyproofed furniture and tables covered in kids' toys.

When my sister and her husband first closed on the property, they were hoping to start a family; by the time we broke ground, she was pregnant—just in time for us to add a nursery to the plans. With three children of my own, I could share insights from life with young kids. Though I knew that she preferred open bookshelves, I suggested we compromise with some closed storage with plenty of out-of-reach shelving. Thousands of baby toys later, she is now very appreciative. And while she was initially hesitant about a sectional, preferring a more traditional, formal design,

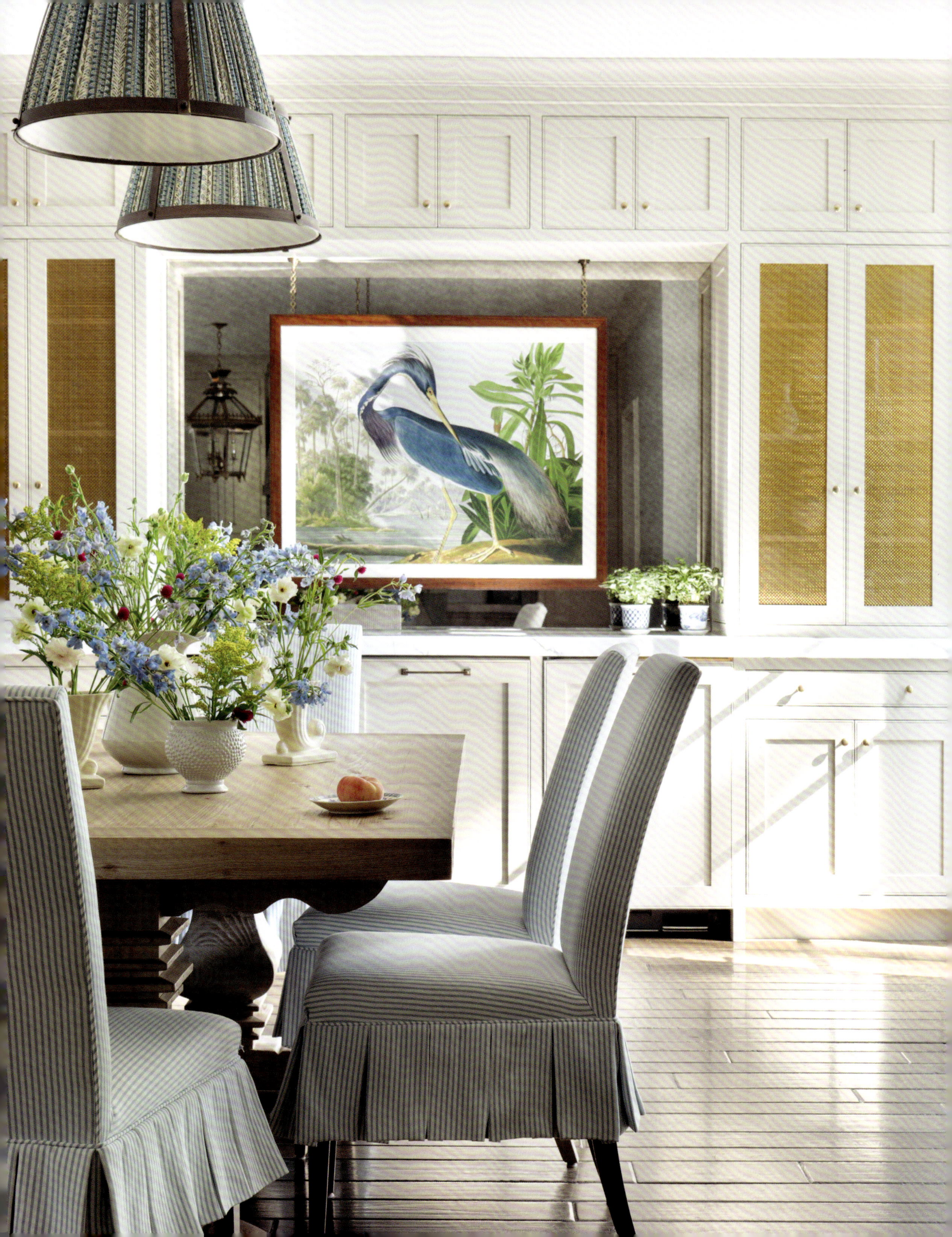

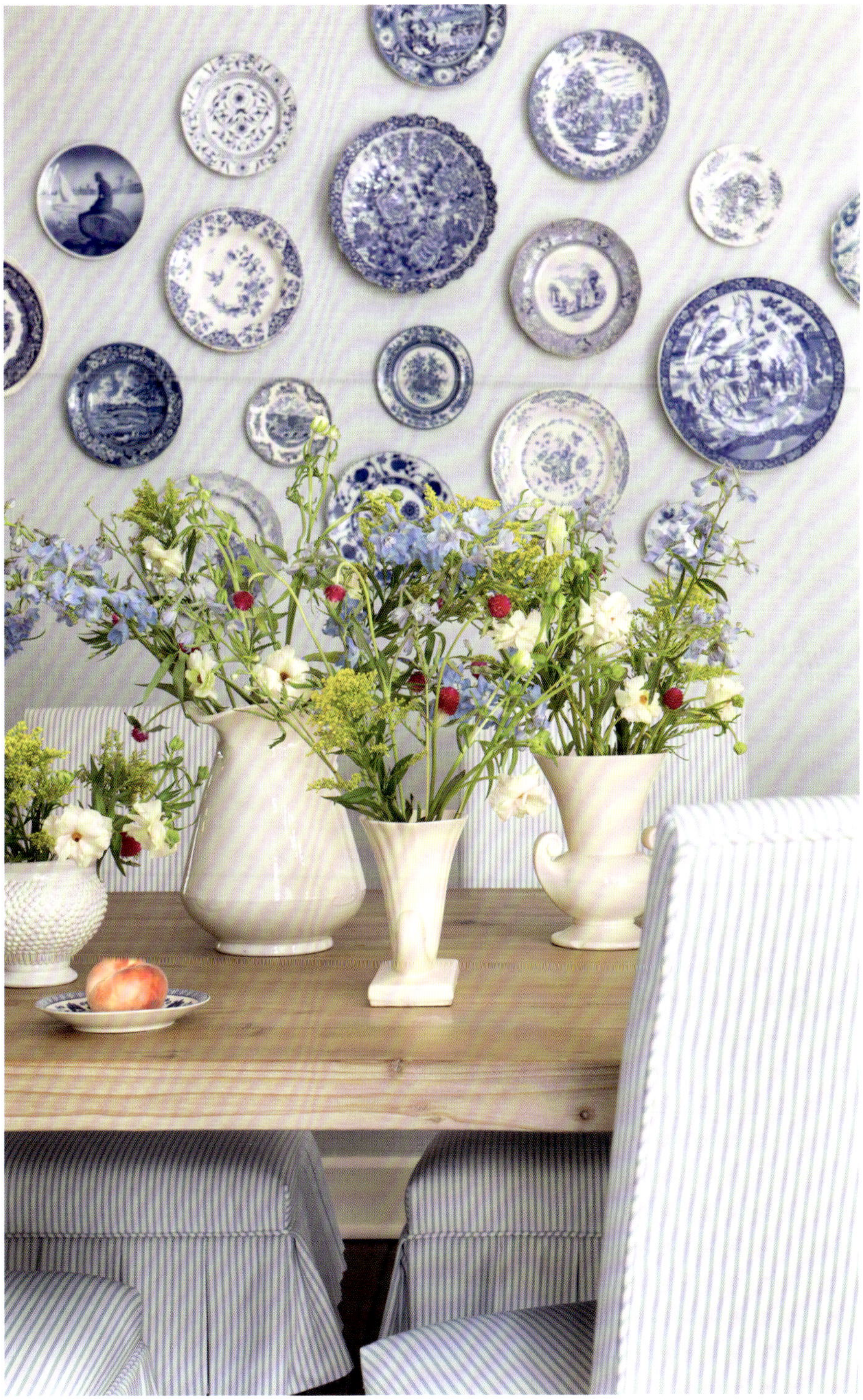

she changed her mind after envisioning nights when her husband would watch sports and she'd needlepoint beside him (illuminated by ample task lighting), or, later down the line, family movie nights with kids and adults snuggled together. Similarly, we adapted a space off the kitchen to serve as a sitting room and play space so that the children could have somewhere to play while their parents cooked dinner. Now, this and the sectional are the most trafficked spaces in the whole home.

  The home's color palette, of course, was dictated by my sister's adamant aversion to white paint. No one would call me a minimalist, but as a designer, I believe in the power of a good white wall as a palate cleanser —especially in a home that has as much pattern and color as I knew hers would. Without that to rely on, we needed a strong palette to unify the ground floor. We found our inspiration in the dining room wallpaper, a delicate chinoiserie-style mural with saturated colors. The paper's cobalt accent proved a perfect shade for the walls in an anteroom, and we pulled out a warm, peachy hue as the primary color in the living room. For the sunroom, a leafy green upholstery feels like a (literally) natural companion to the botanical mural and is complemented by a verdant wall and organic sisal rug. Even the more pattern-filled family room off the kitchen pulls from that dining room wallpaper, its sofas an indigo blue and armchairs an orange-and-green-dominated floral.

One of the things my sister liked most about the house was that it didn't feature an open floor plan. She has always favored more traditional, formal living, and that's what she wanted in a home.

Overleaf: The terra-cotta of the living room walls is a warmer neutral alternative to white or gray that allows for more pattern mixing than a supersaturated tone.

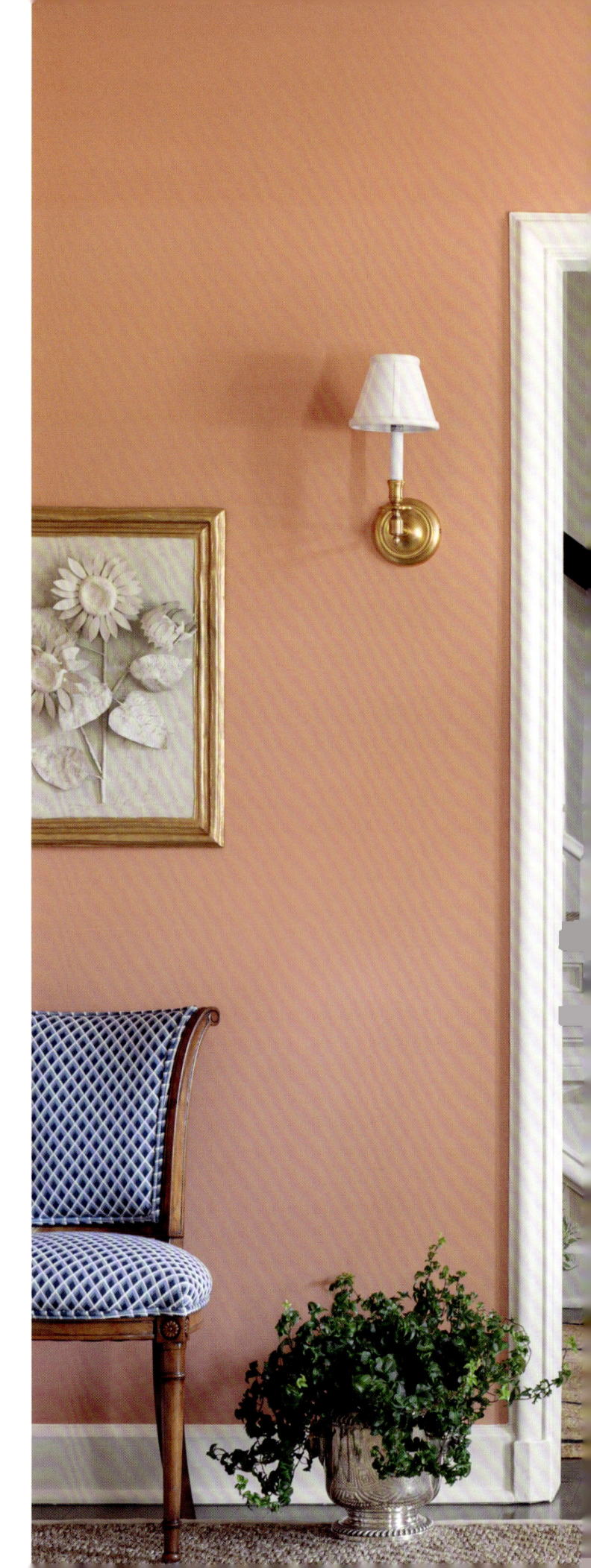

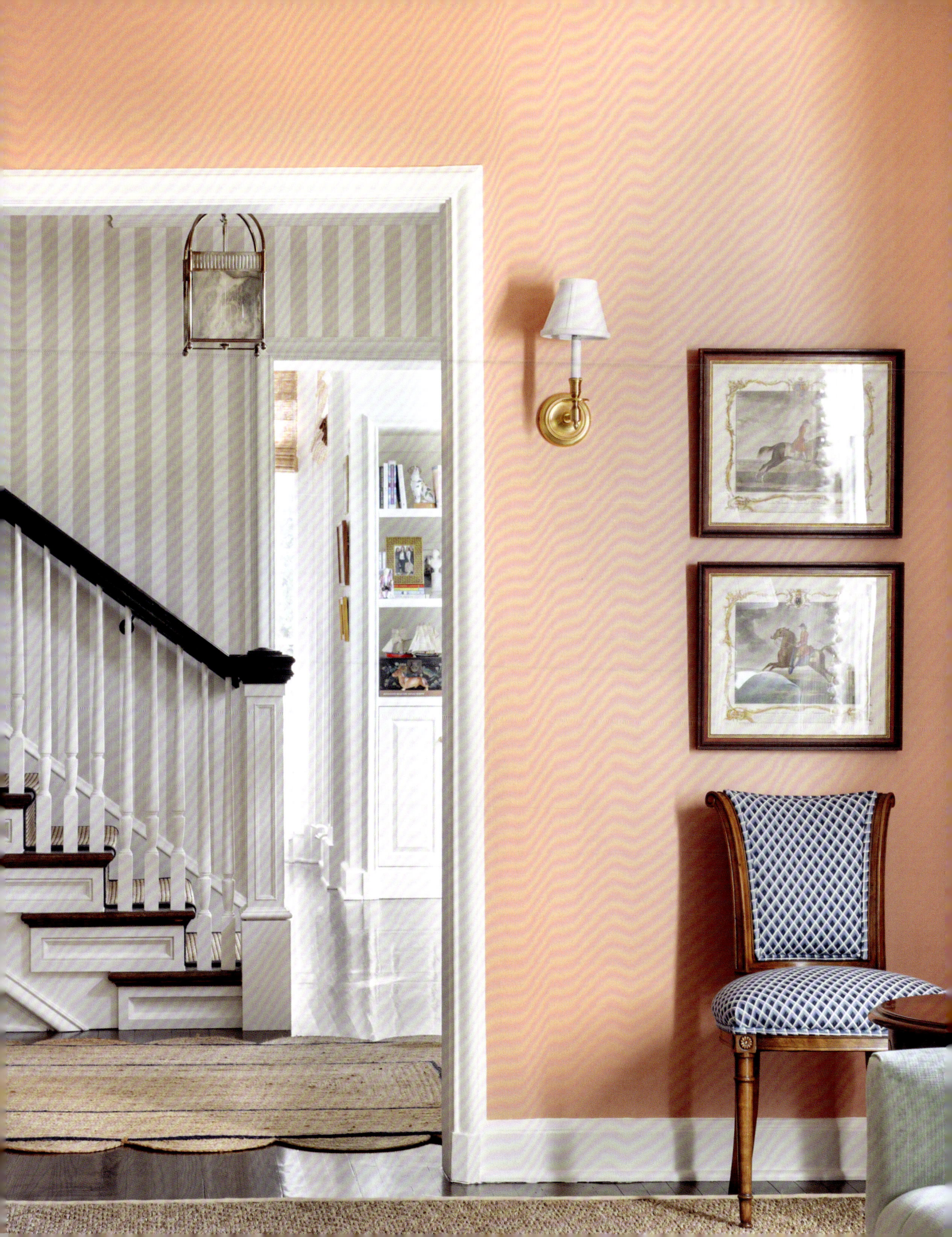

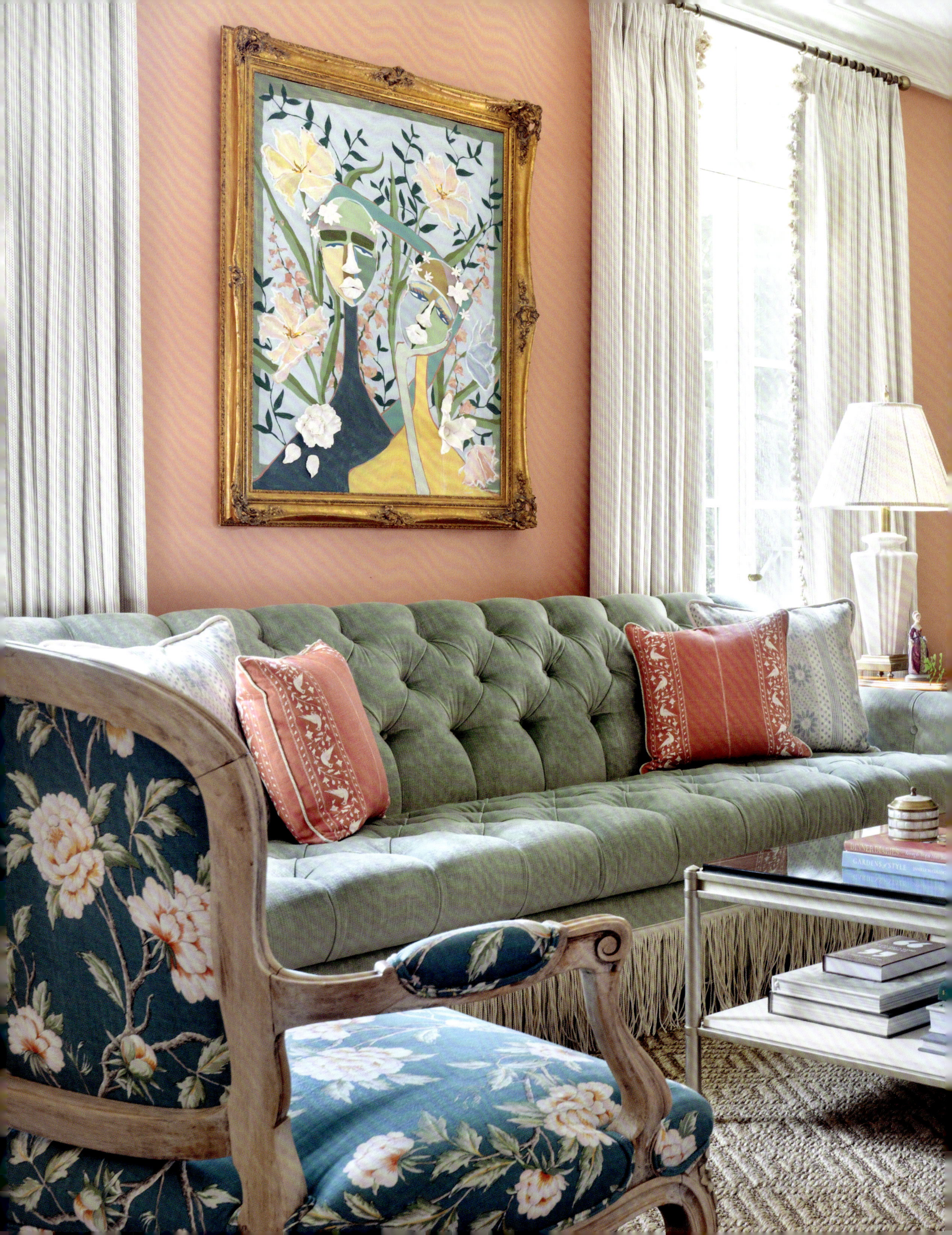

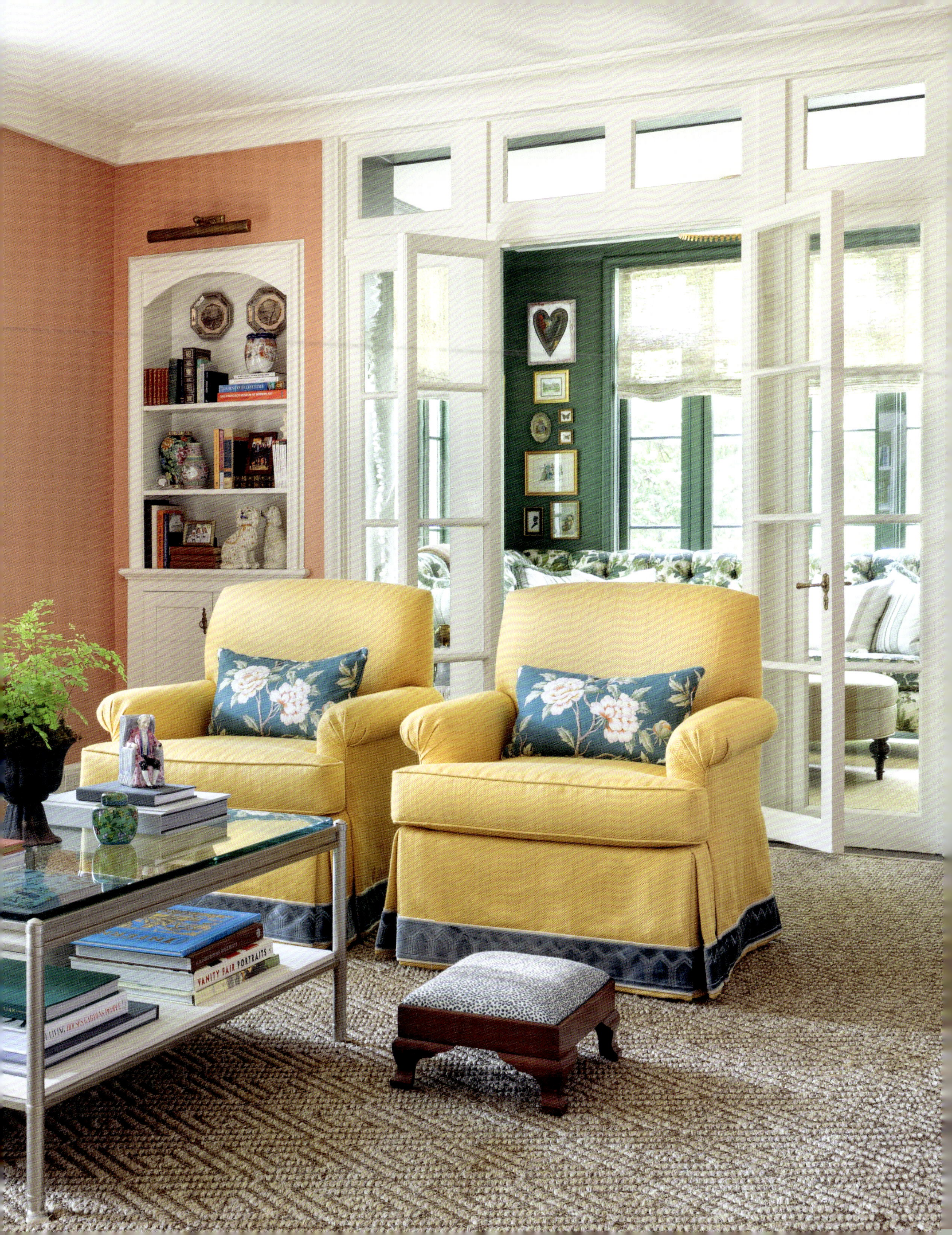
VANITY FAIR PORTRAITS

My younger sister has a vibrant, bubbly personality, and it was a thrill to translate that into interiors. In the living room, one of the biggest ways we did that was through art. When I asked her what she envisioned in the space above the fireplace, she said, "Something like a portrait of a dog in formal attire." My sibling translation of that was: something that feels rooted in tradition but is also playful and whimsical. The Caroline Boykin mixed-media work we selected is exactly that: a fun, contemporary way of looking at portraiture in a stunning antique gilt frame; it adds the unexpected.

If her design personality is colorful, exuberant, and floral, our middle sister, an artist, is the opposite: cool, modern, geometric. The three of us joke that we couldn't be more different aesthetically—and yet we're very close. Of course, we had to incorporate some of her art into the home, and I love how her abstract pieces play against the antiques and bold colors.

The biggest "controversy" of the project was my insistence that the family room be painted white. Its nearly floor-to-ceiling windows left almost no wall space, making wallpaper look odd and any color feel flimsy against the views beyond. I dug my heels in and insisted she try it in white, even offering to pay for it to be repainted if she really hated it. We brought in warmth and visual interest by covering doors with gathered fabric in a small-scale print and grounded the space with wicker furniture. Six months after moving in, though, my sister had it repainted a light green—but she hated it so much she painted it back to white the next day.

All jokes aside, she pushed me, in the best way. I would say, "Okay, we're done with this room," and she'd respond with, "Nope, we need another layer." To this day, every time I come over, she's added another needlepoint pillow to the sofa, or hung more of her beloved blue-and-white china in the kitchen. I'm delighted that I was able to help her create the foundation for a space that she could continue to really live in—in the particular way that she does—going forward.

After she moved in, my sister wrote me the most beautiful letter: "You created this nest where I can raise my chicks. This is where my life is going to happen." And when you boil it all down, that's the single most important thing we as designers do.

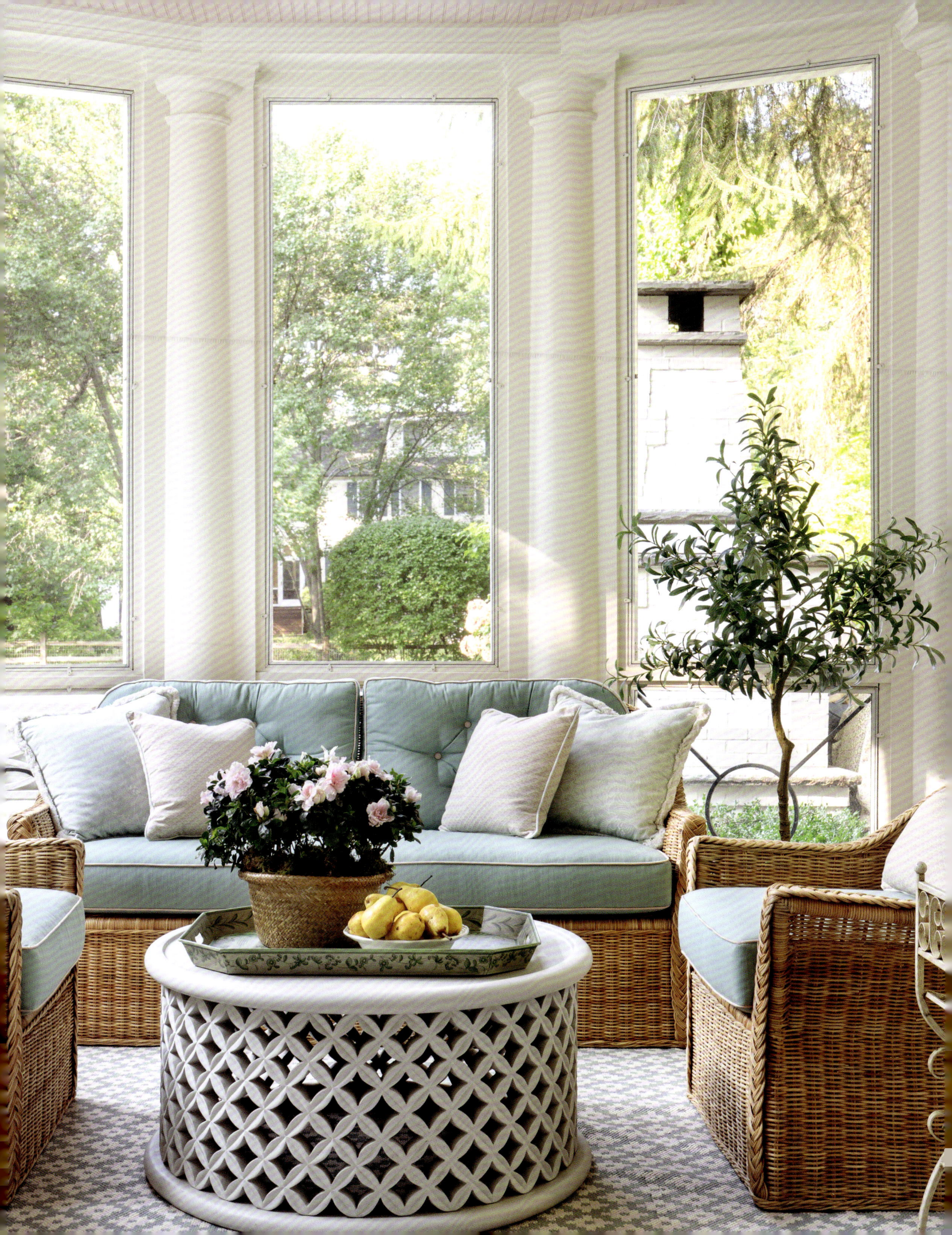

Against my sister's original wishes, this room stayed white. We actually painted it a pistachio green after she put up a fight, but she quickly returned it to a clean background.

—

Overleaf: Though the dining room isn't used every day, it's the first room you see when you enter the home and a main thoroughfare. It feels like something of a showpiece for the home. We pulled the accents of blue from the gorgeous de Gournay wallpaper, whose palette unifies all the home's bold colors.

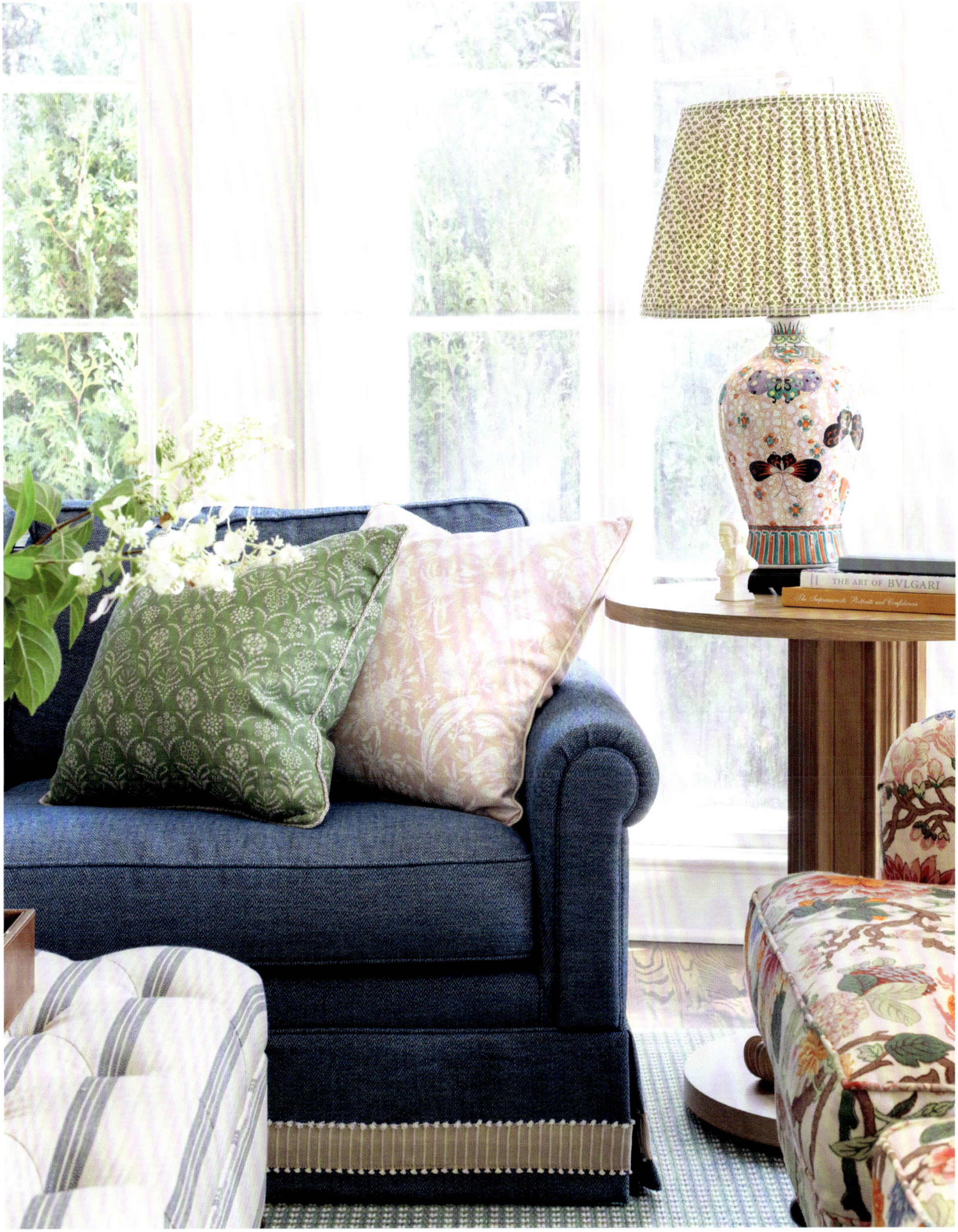
THE ART OF BVLGARI

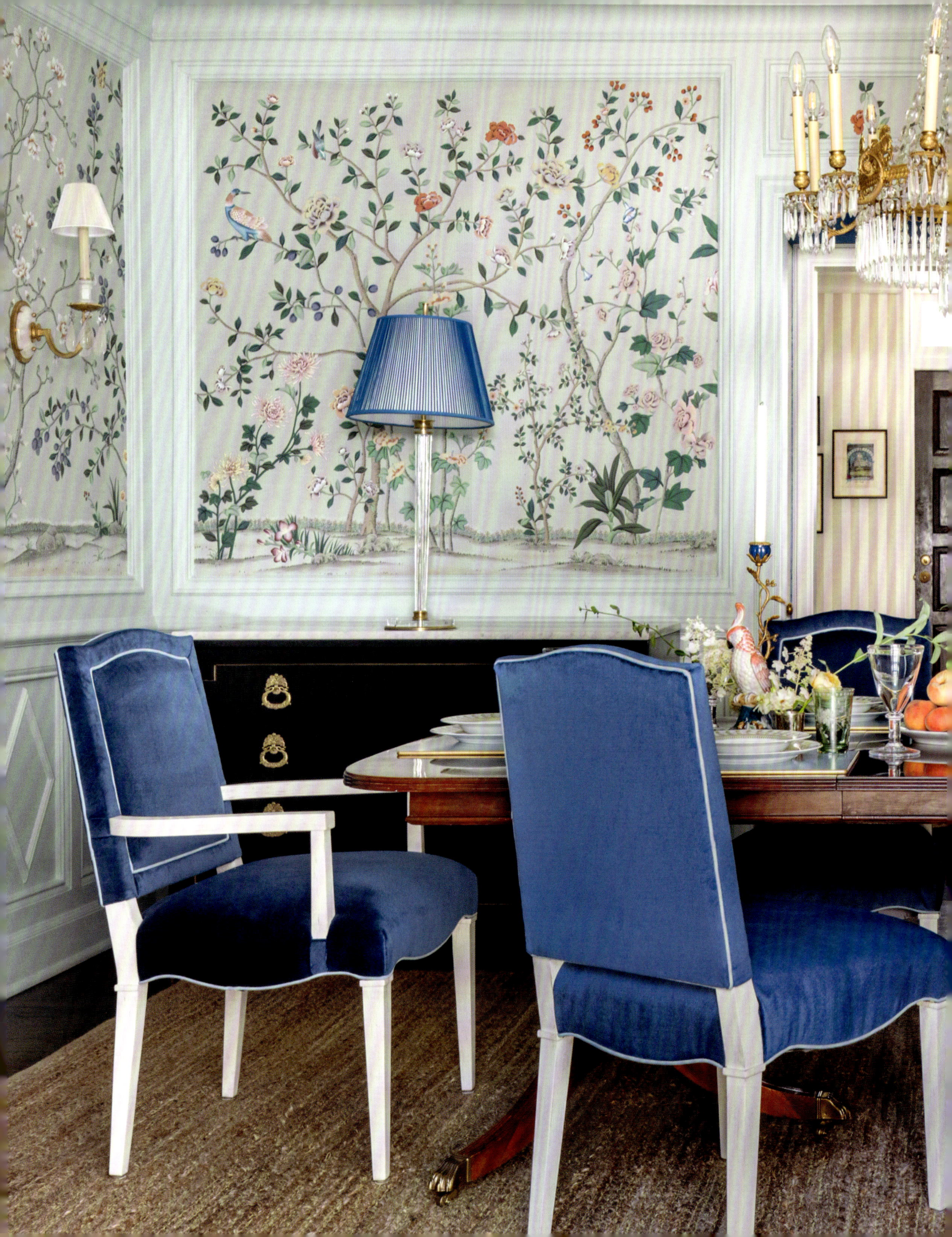

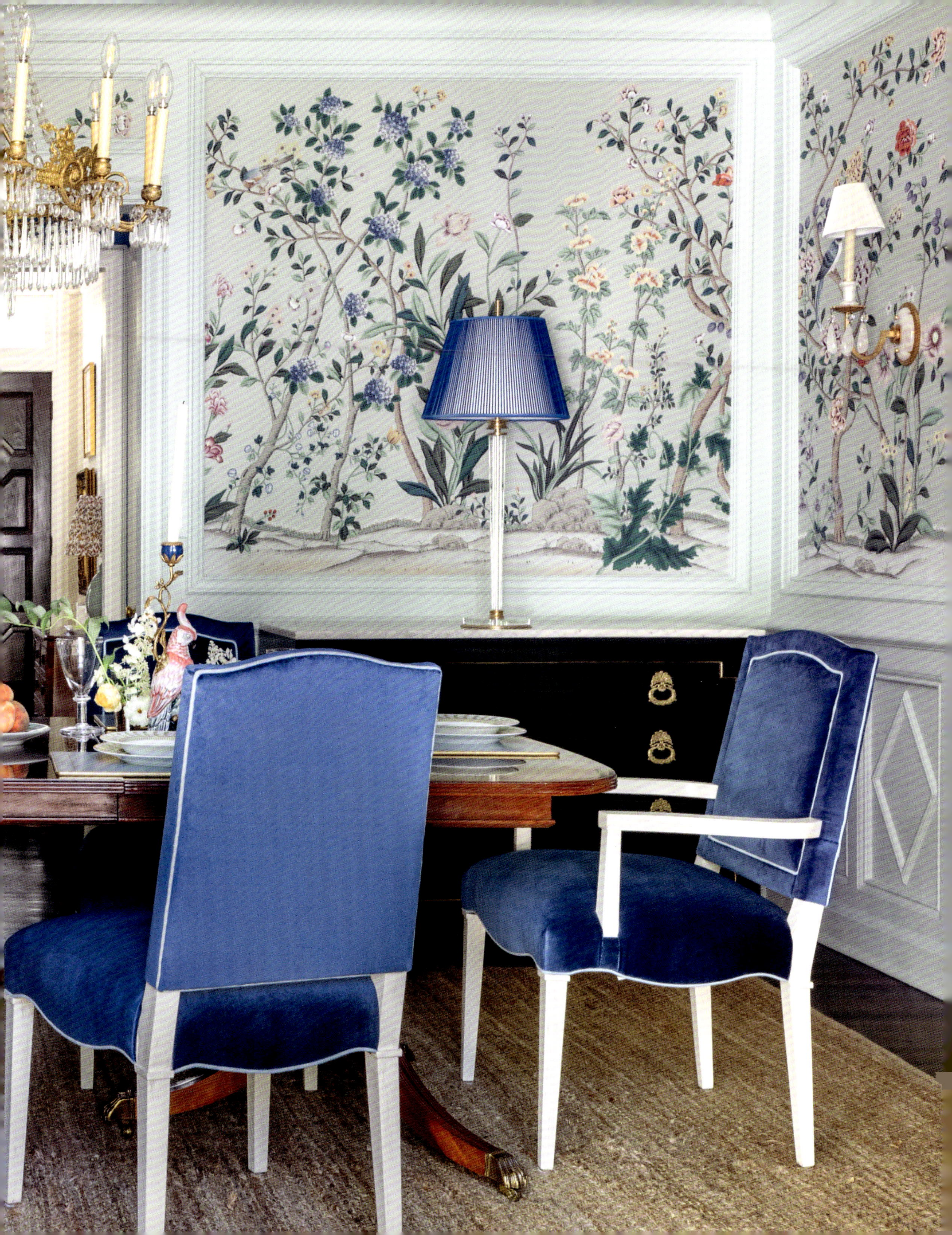

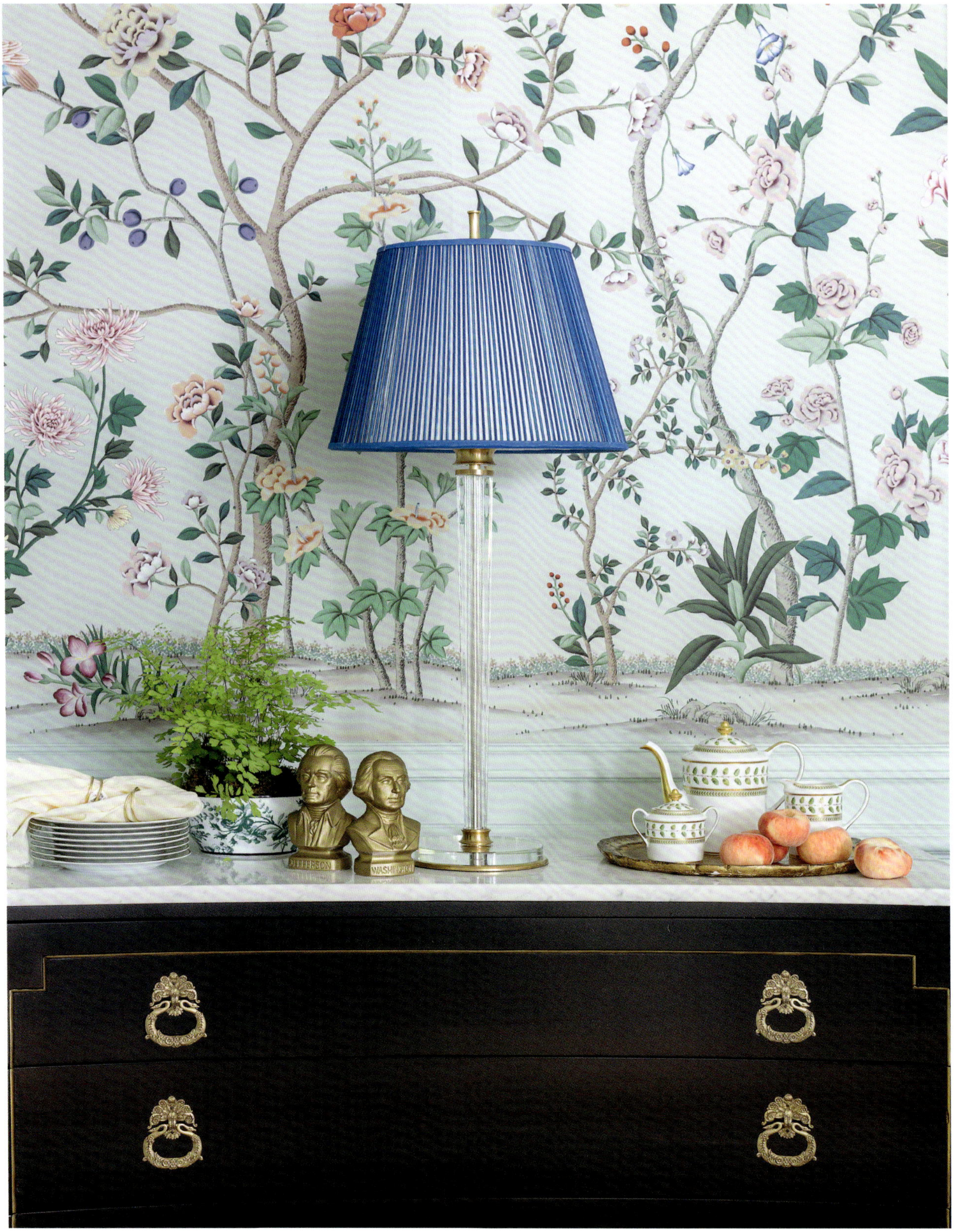

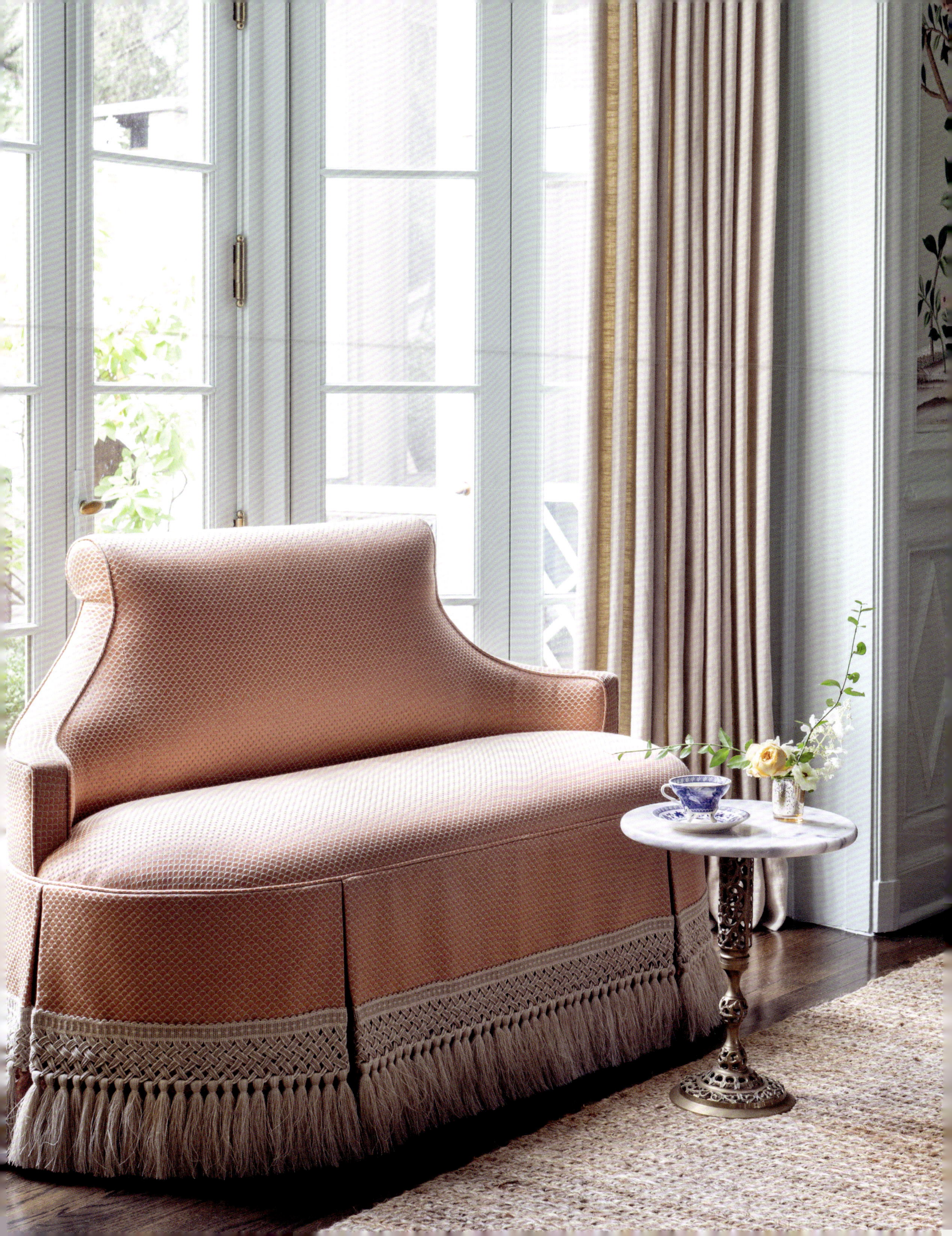

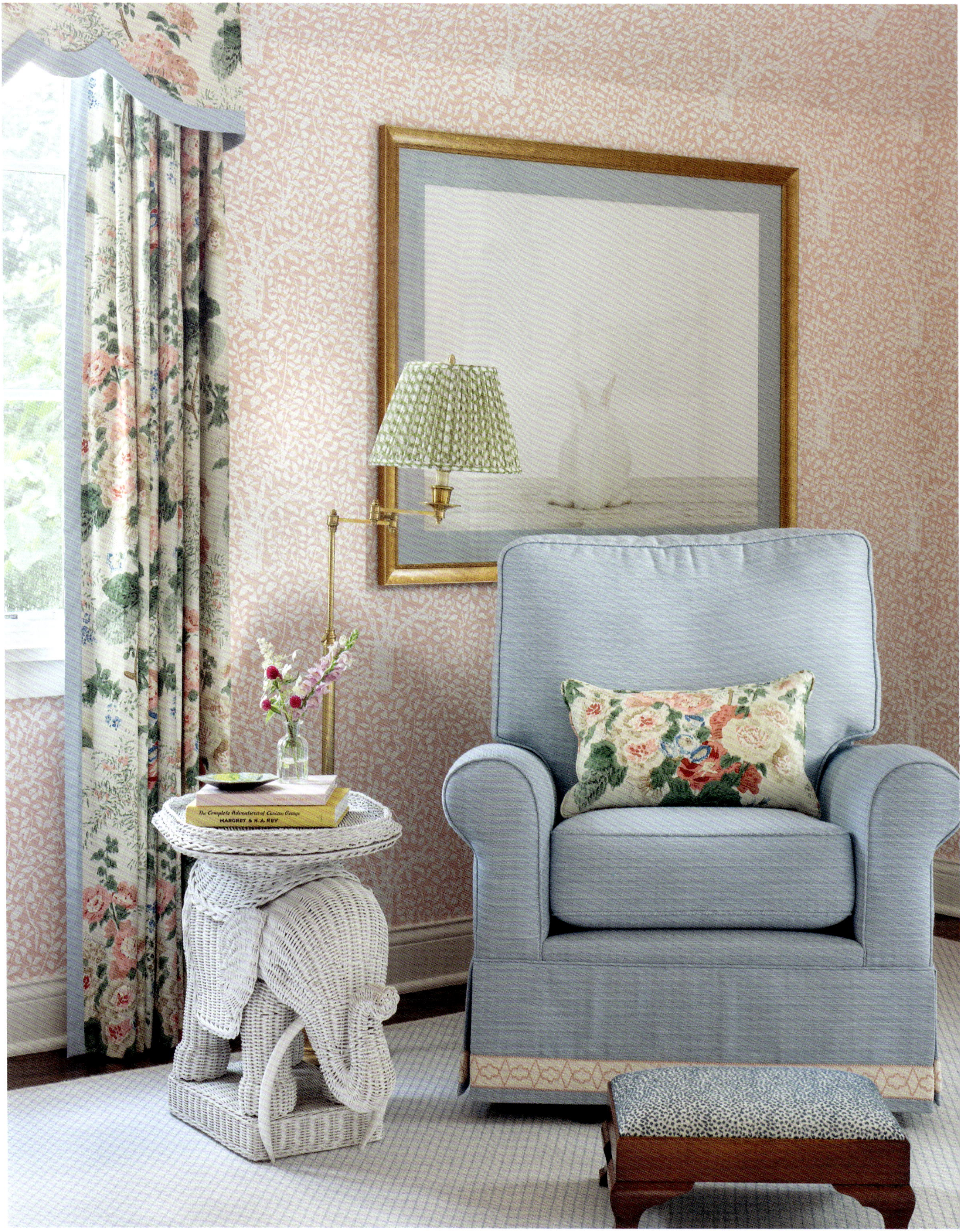
The Complete Adventures of Curious George
MARGRET & H. A. REY

Opposite and above left: When long lead times quashed the idea of a sofa upholstered in Lee Jofa's iconic Althea print, which had graced our grandparents' living room, we decided to use the pattern in curtains in my sister's daughter's room. They're a visual connection across four generations – and a pretty but sophisticated touch that she'll grow with long beyond the baby stage.

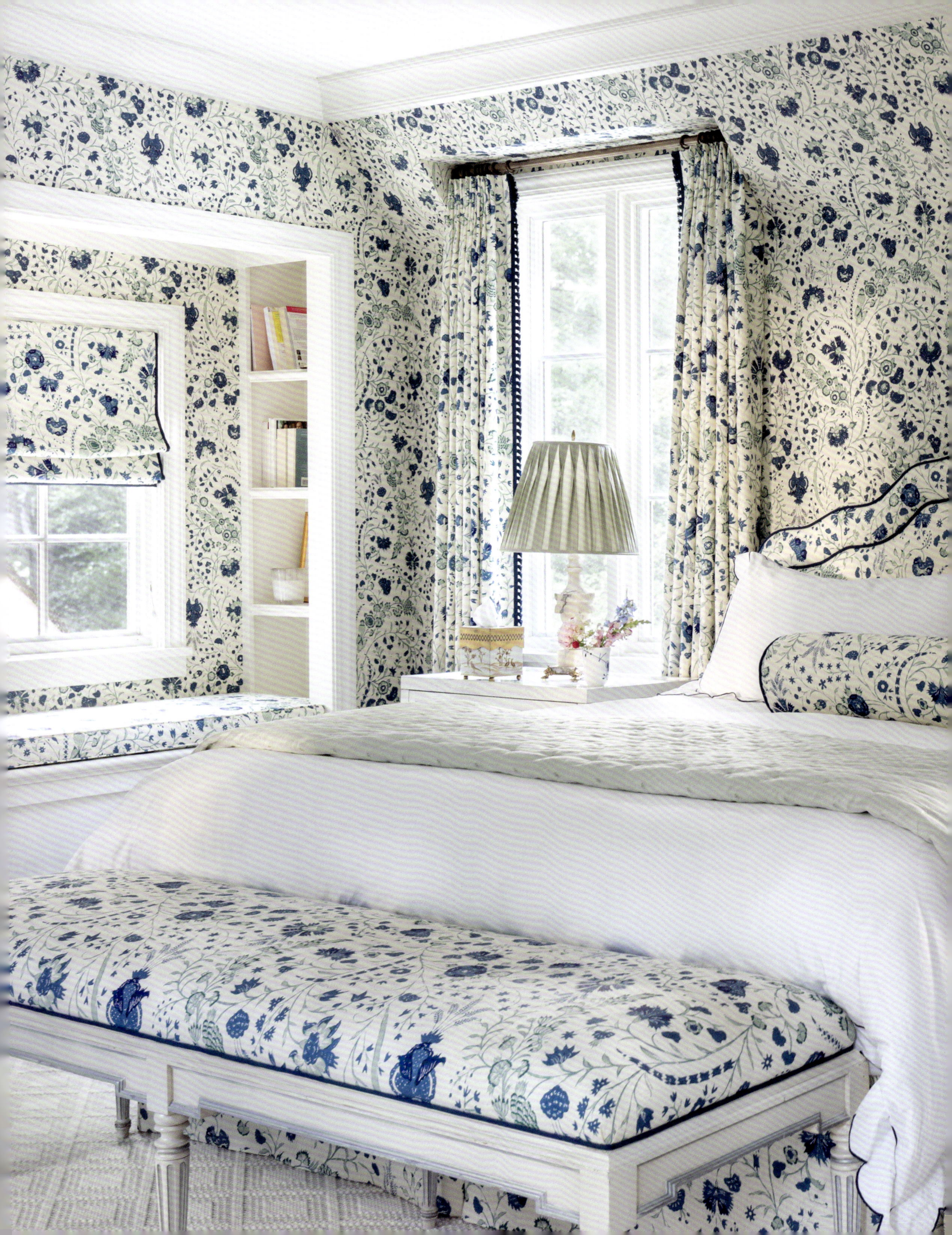

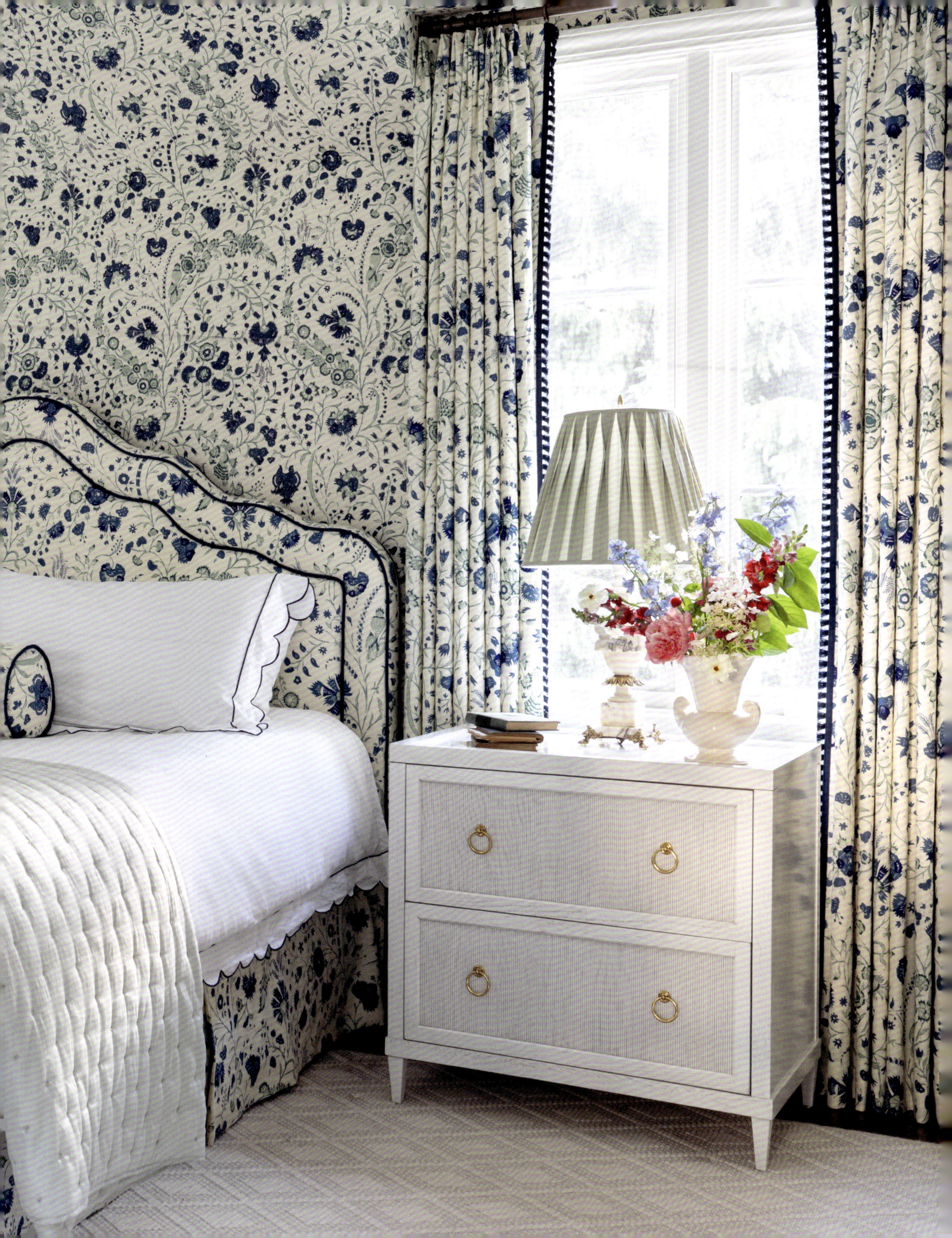

Previous, left, and opposite: The beautiful Soane Britain pattern that swathes the primary bedroom, Dianthus, reminded my sister of our grandparents, who used a similar, English-inspired allover print application in their bedroom.

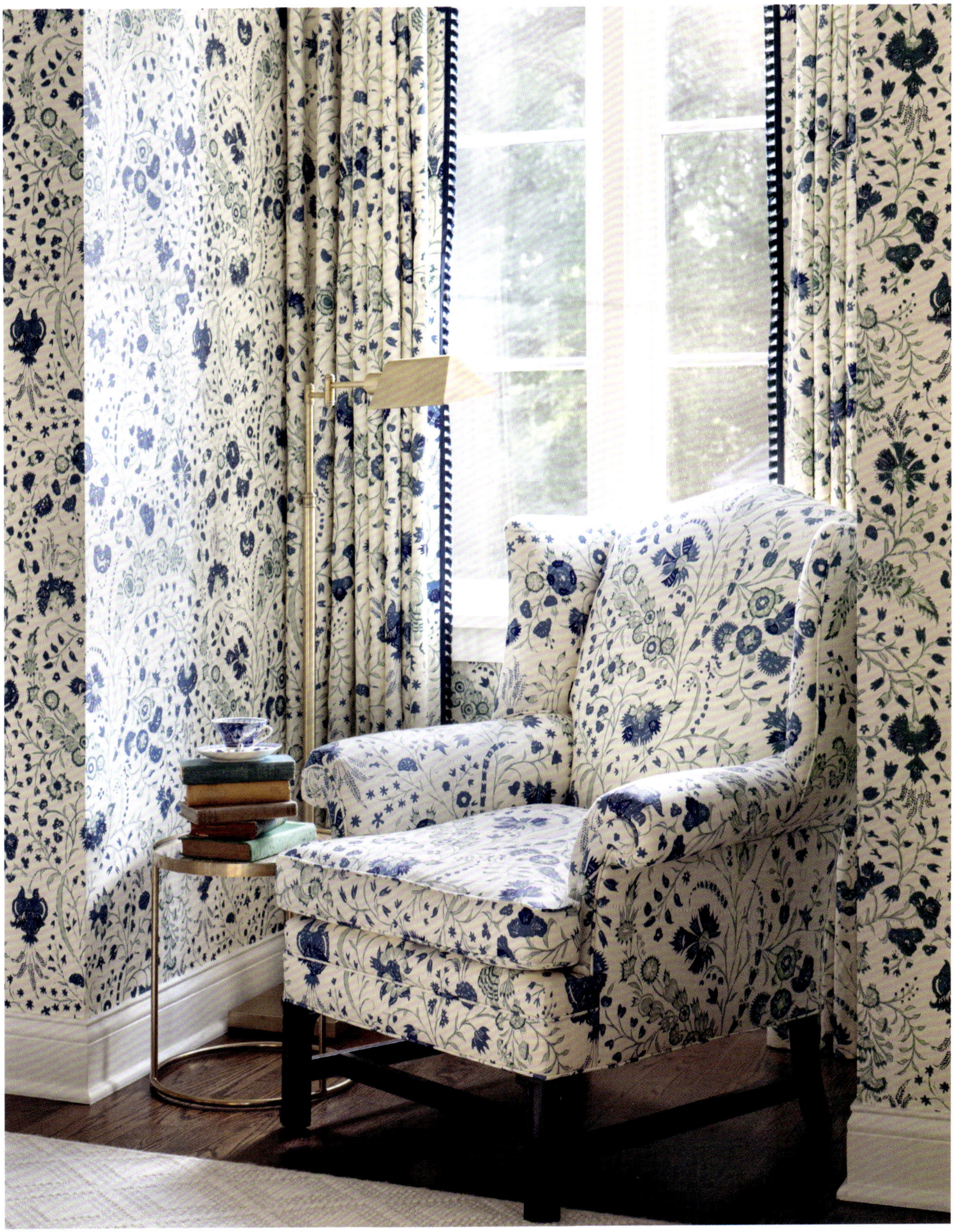

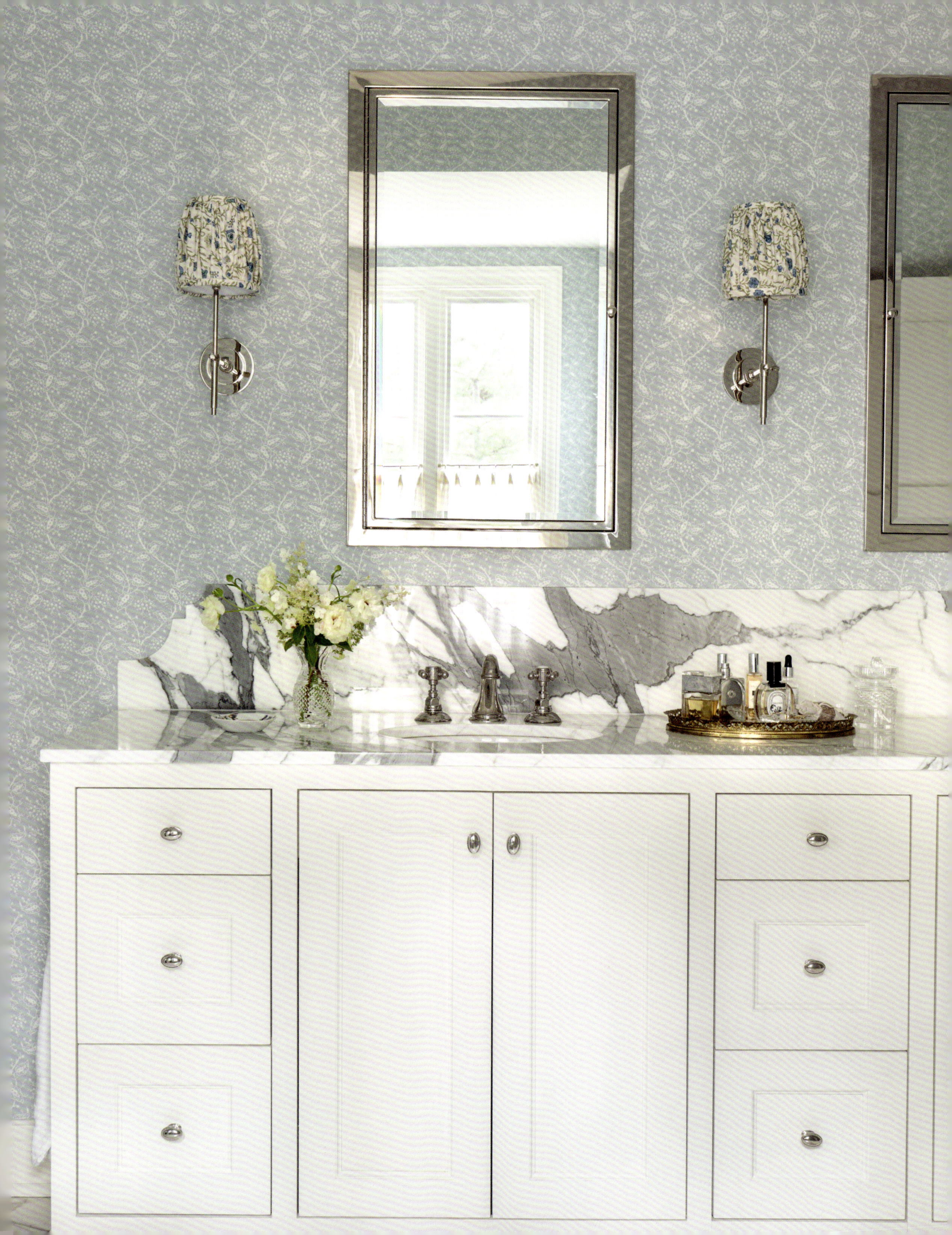

The bathroom was an exercise in layering patterns and materials to ensure that the space felt just as inviting as the bedroom it was connected to.

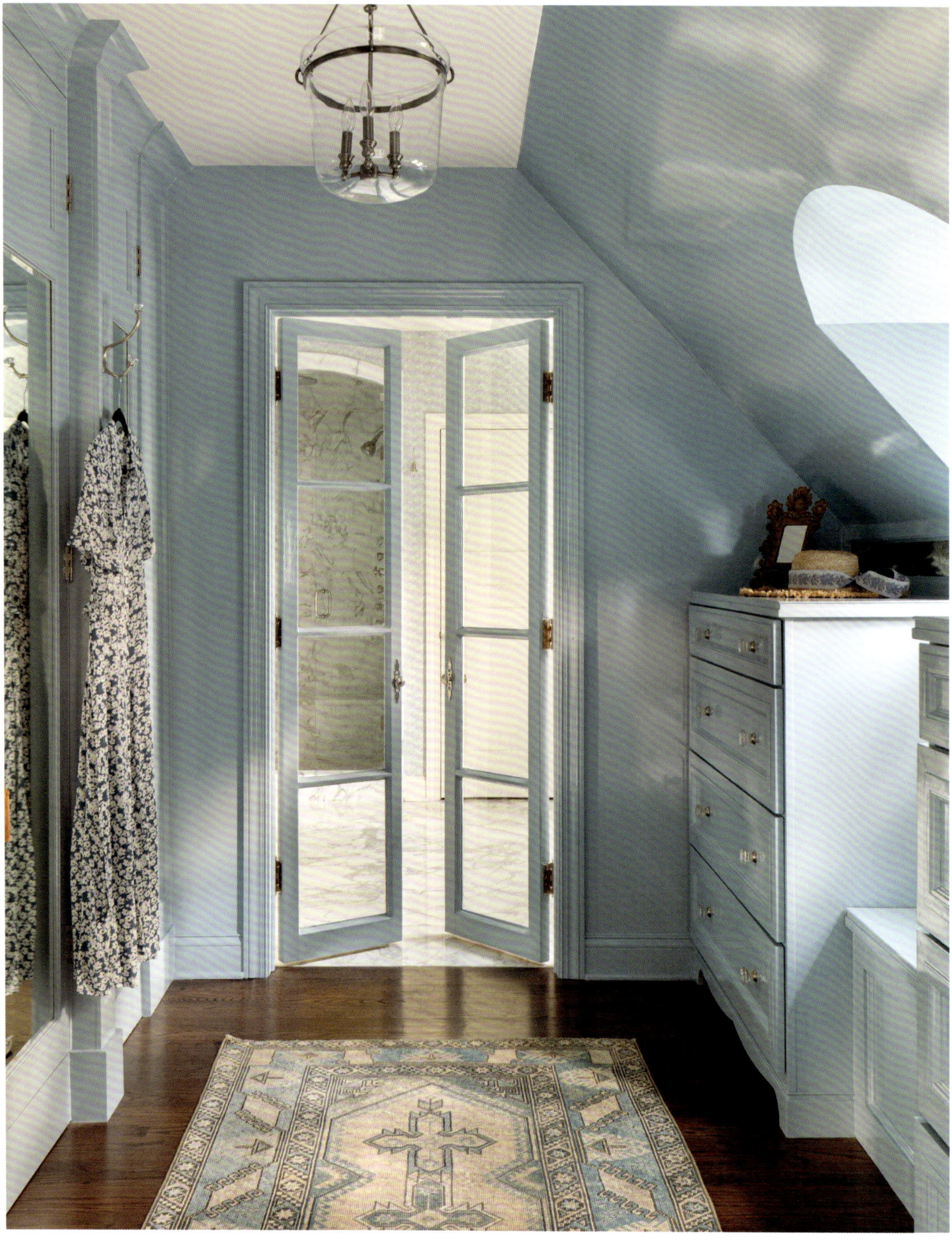

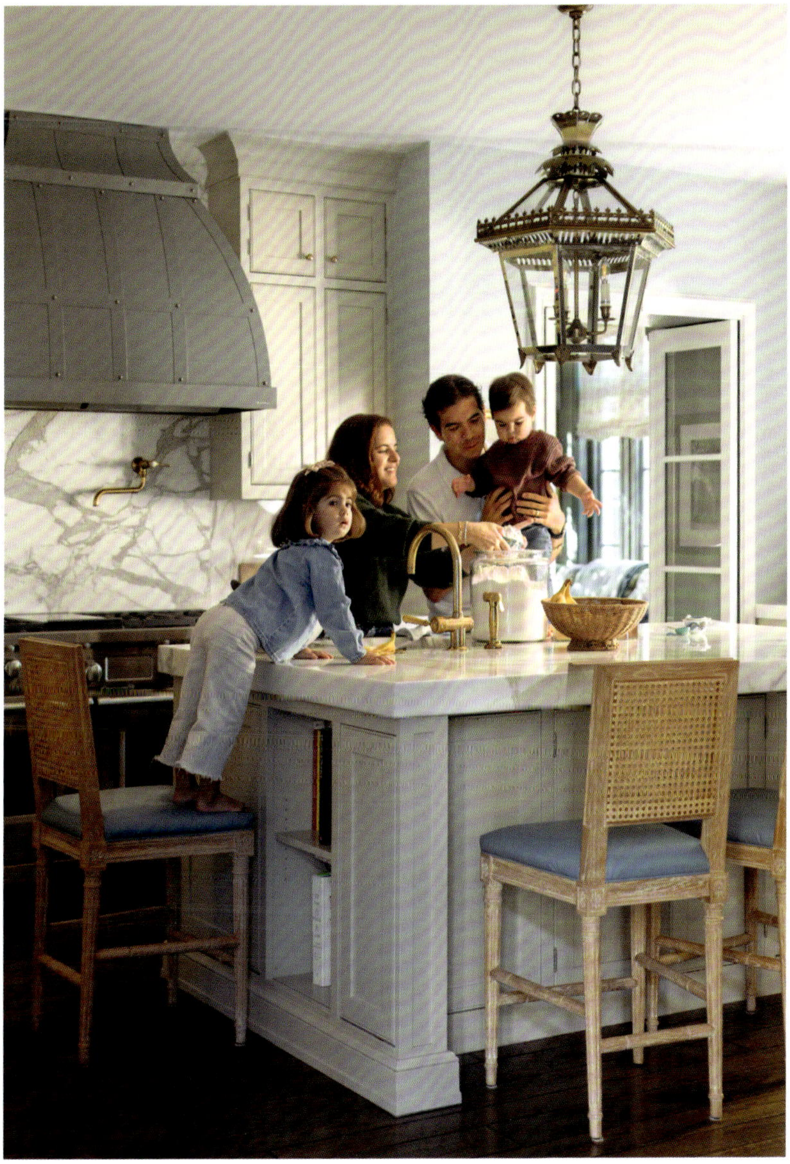

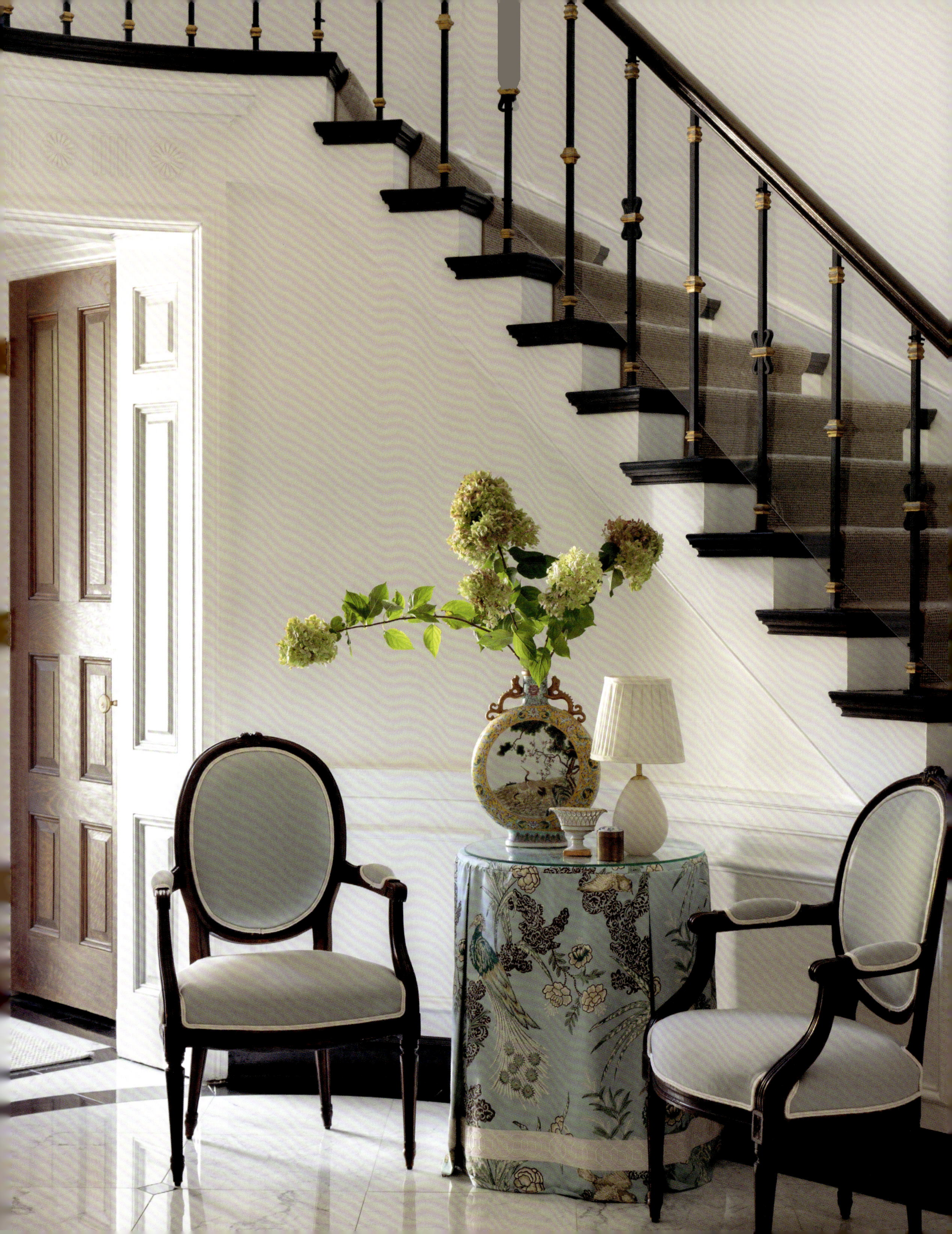

GREAT ESCAPE

A historic family home with a backyard getaway

Previous: This home has a stunning grand entrance with a curving staircase that allows space for a seating area and elegant, skirted table.

Despite how it seems from design TV shows, decorating a home is rarely a quick process. This project is a prime example. Eight years ago, I got a call from a young couple who were just starting their family. They had found a hypertraditional, historically protected 1920s home, and, while they were ready to decorate, they weren't entirely sure of what they wanted. They hadn't yet pinned down their personal style, and they didn't quite realize what it would take to furnish a house of this size. But they were ready to learn. Over the course of the next several years, we worked on their home in stages: We started with the basics and then added layers over time. Gradually, the couple became more open to taking risks with color and pattern, and the design started to reflect that. This evolution culminated most recently in the addition of a pool house, which they built to match the existing historic structure but with a completely different feel and a new purpose.

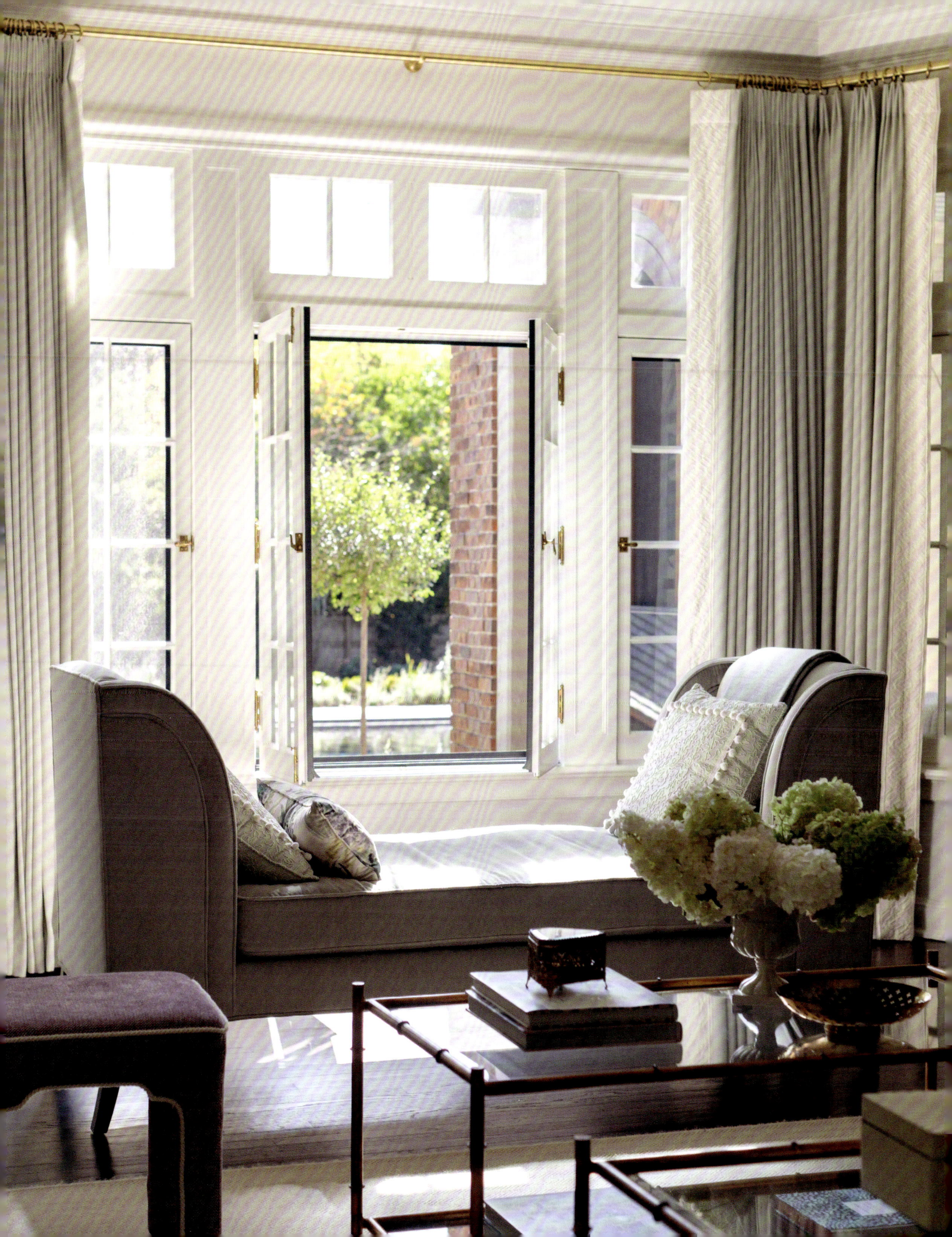

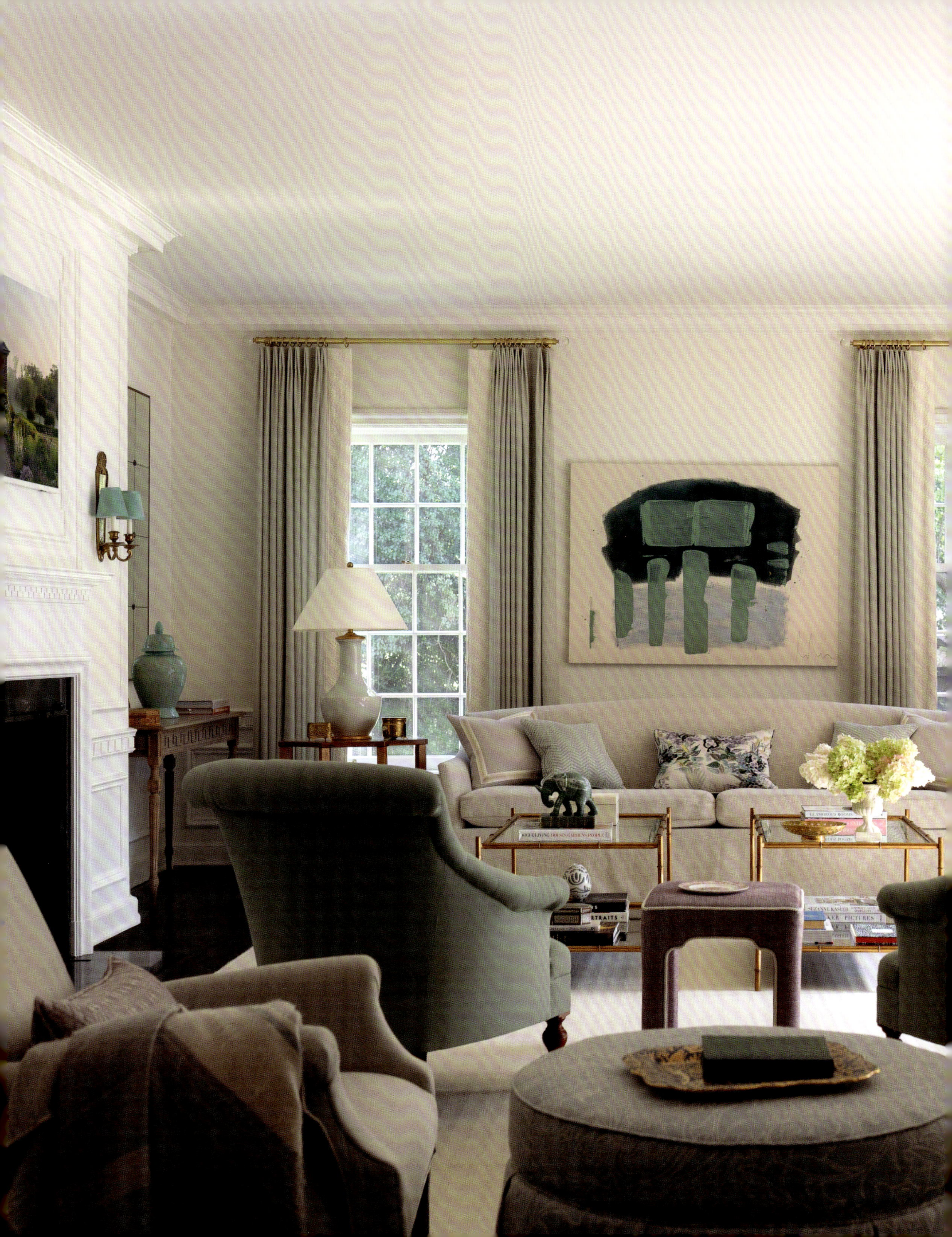

"The space didn't have to feel formal, but it had to feel special."

When working on historic homes with such spectacular architecture, it's important to me that we don't distract from the bones. In this case, that made our job of decorating over many years much simpler; it's easier to tolerate living without tons of layers if your backdrop is beautiful. The first part of the design process was all about taking that light touch and changing small elements to add some personality. The kitchen, for example, had been redone by the developer who bought the house before my clients, and, although it wasn't the couple's dream kitchen, it was very nice and very complete. So we kept the structure as it was and added things like new window treatments, counter stools, and light fixtures to make it feel truer to them. Not every room needs a complete overhaul to feel updated!

In the dining room, we also went simple, with white walls, an antique table, and pale blue chairs that work with the colors in the rest of the house but don't compete with the incredible millwork and original hardwood doors, which are really the focus here. That space has stayed pretty much the same since we first installed it nearly a decade ago, which is really a testament to the timelessness of its design.

To keep this large space from feeling overwhelming, we designed it to be super multifunctional, with discrete areas for entertaining, gathering as a family, and relaxing alone.

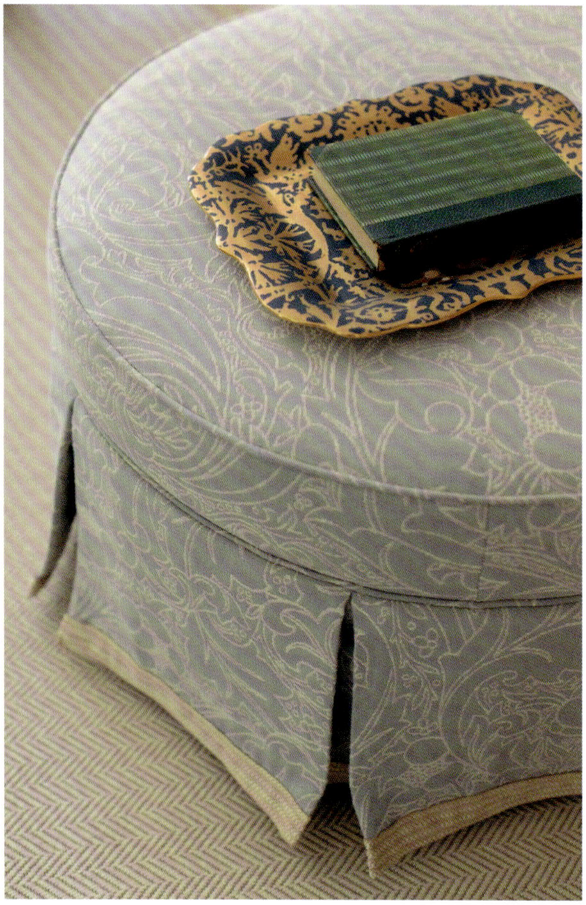

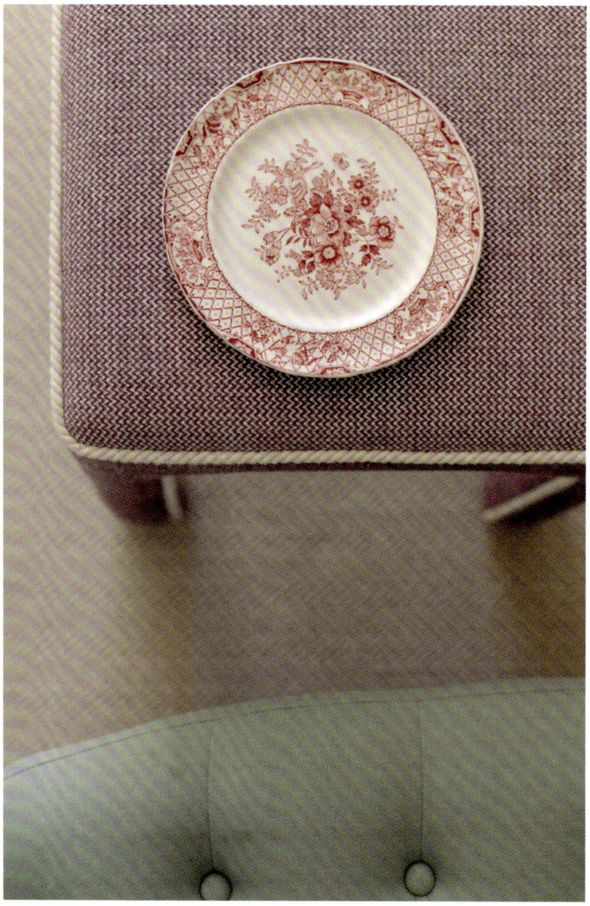

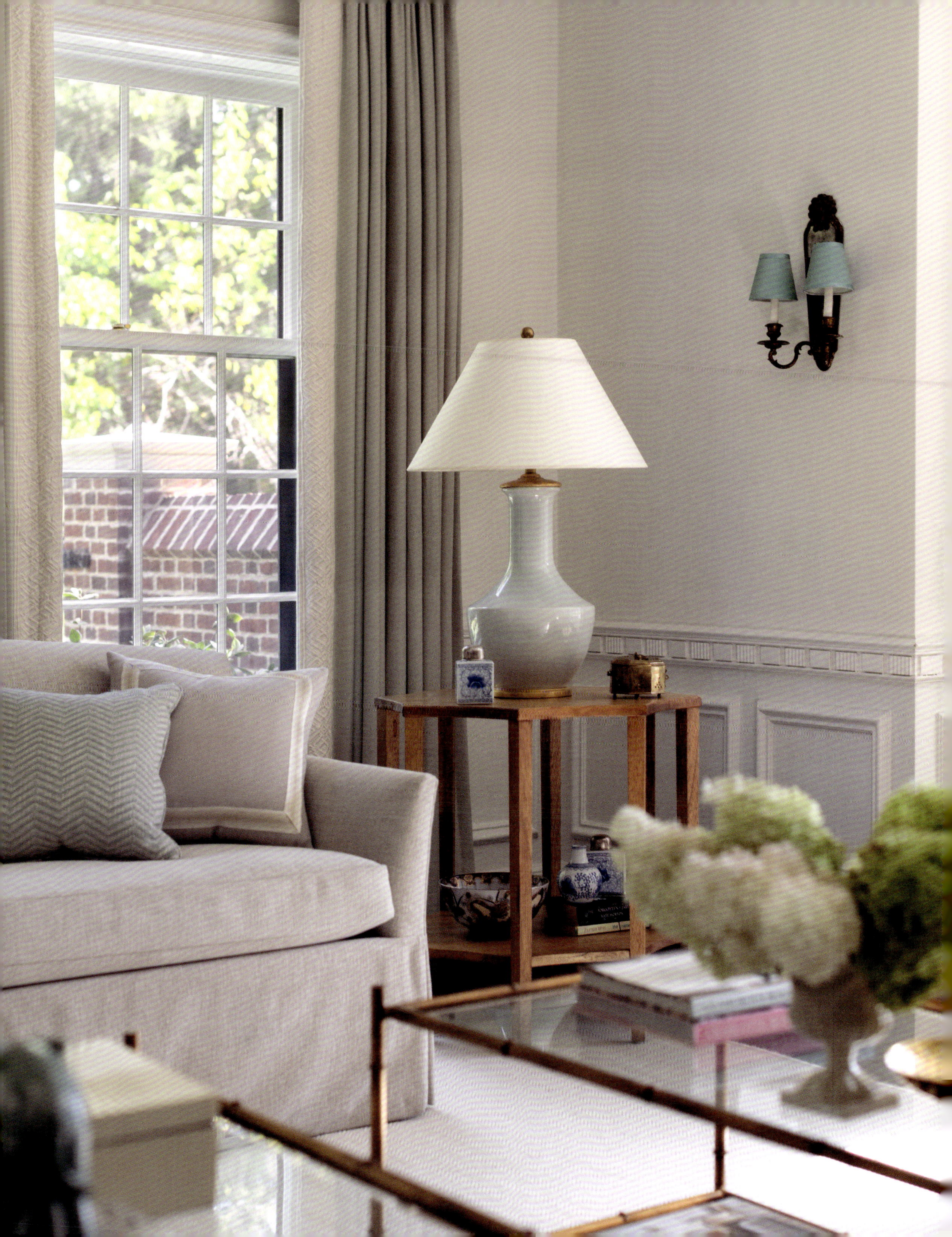

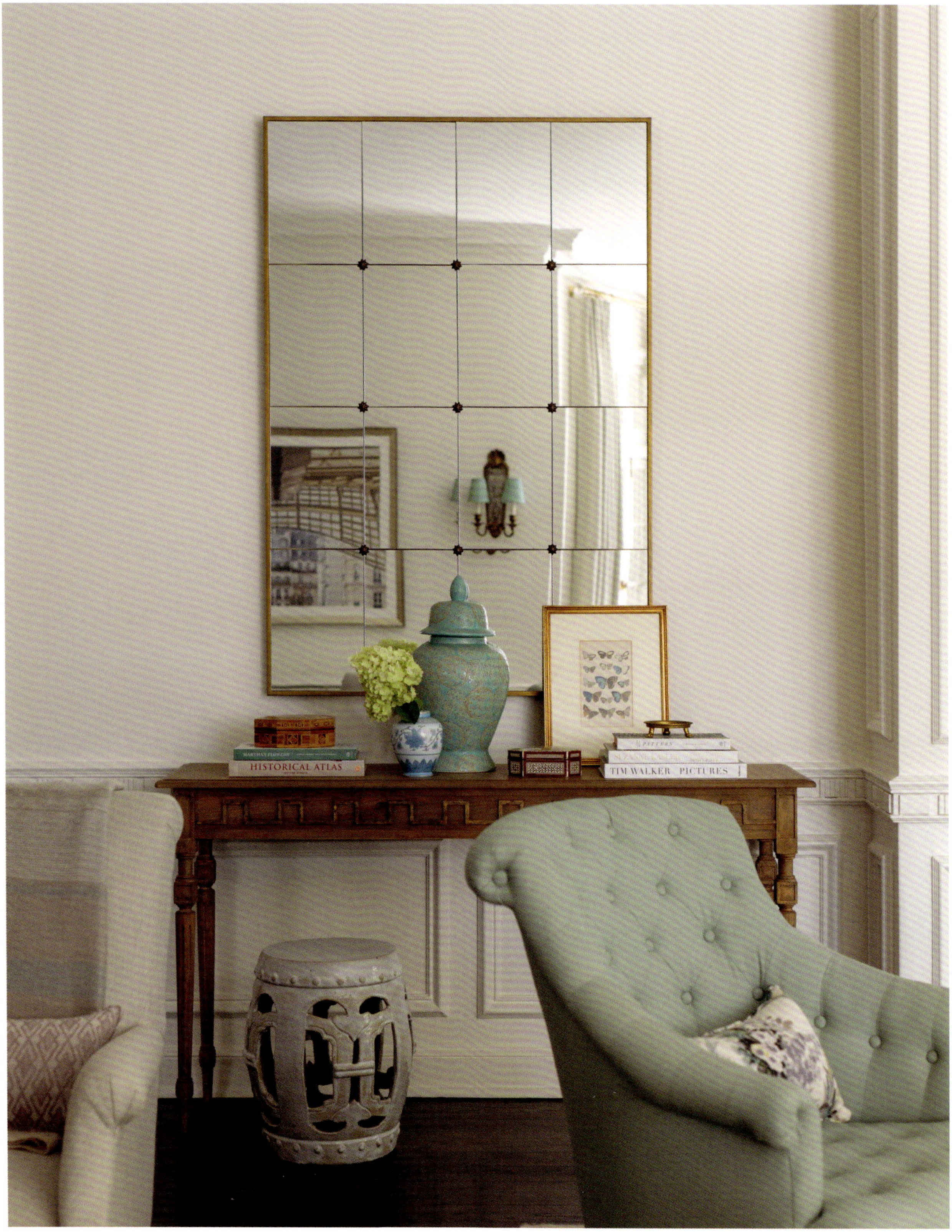
HISTORICAL ATLAS
TIM WALKER PICTURES

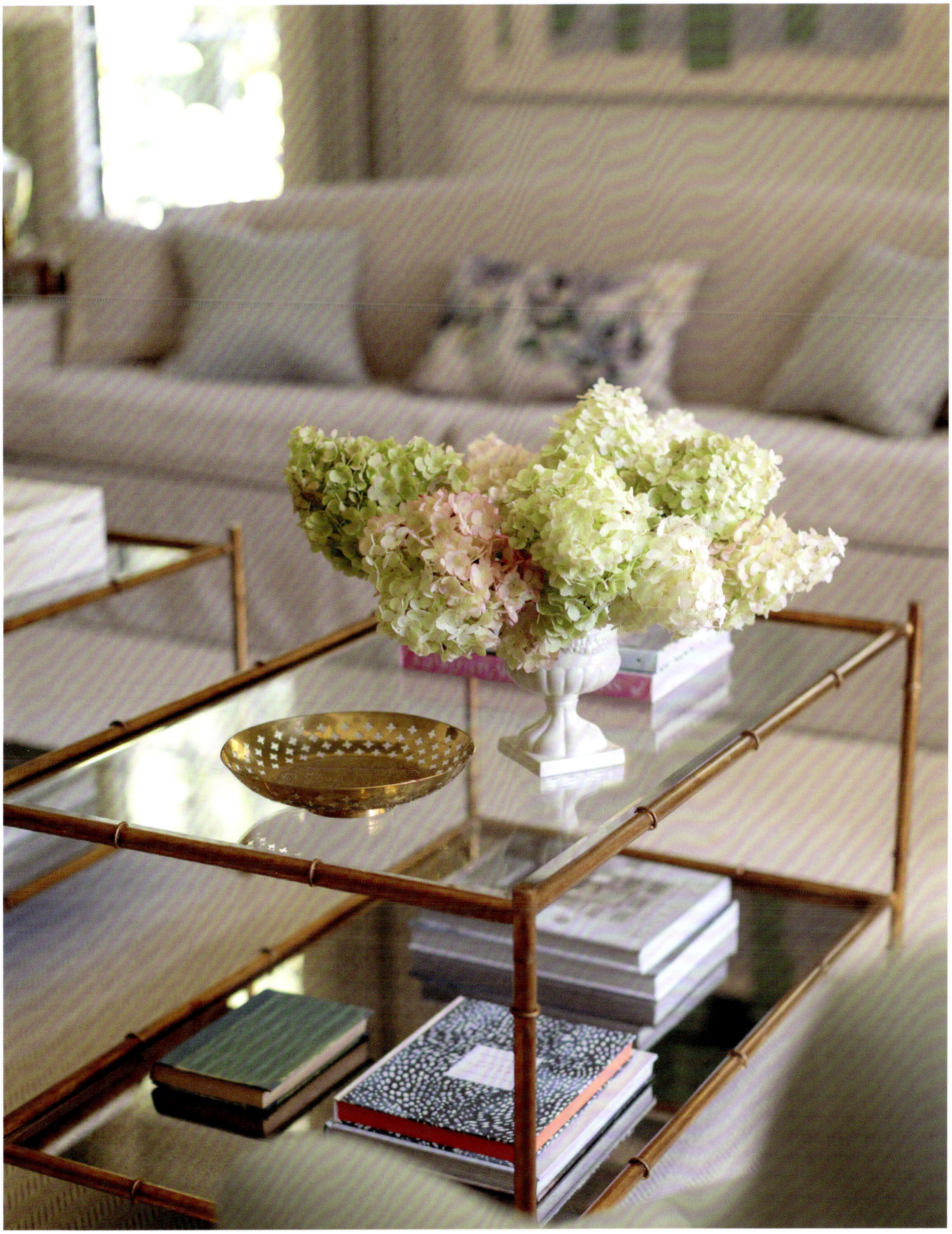

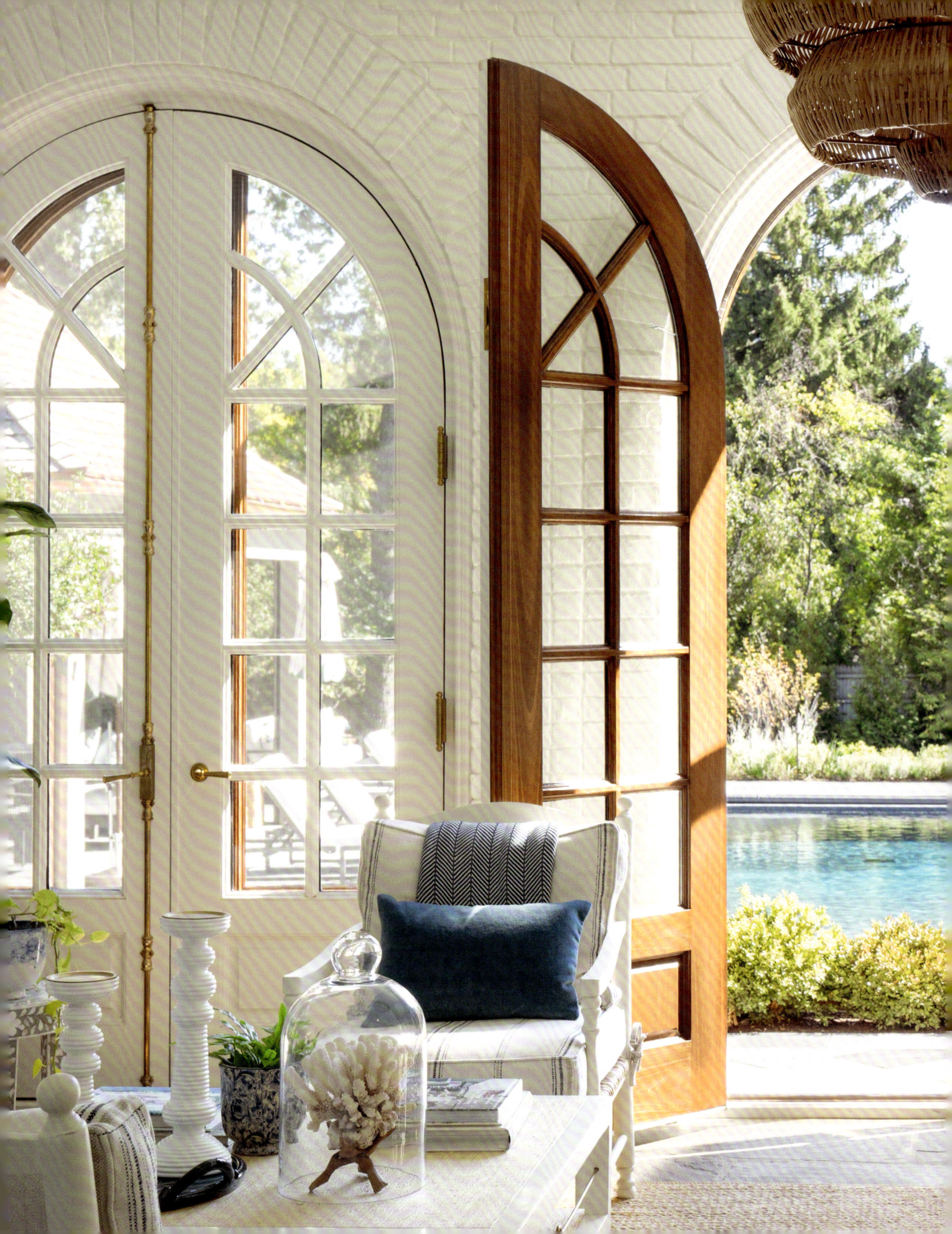

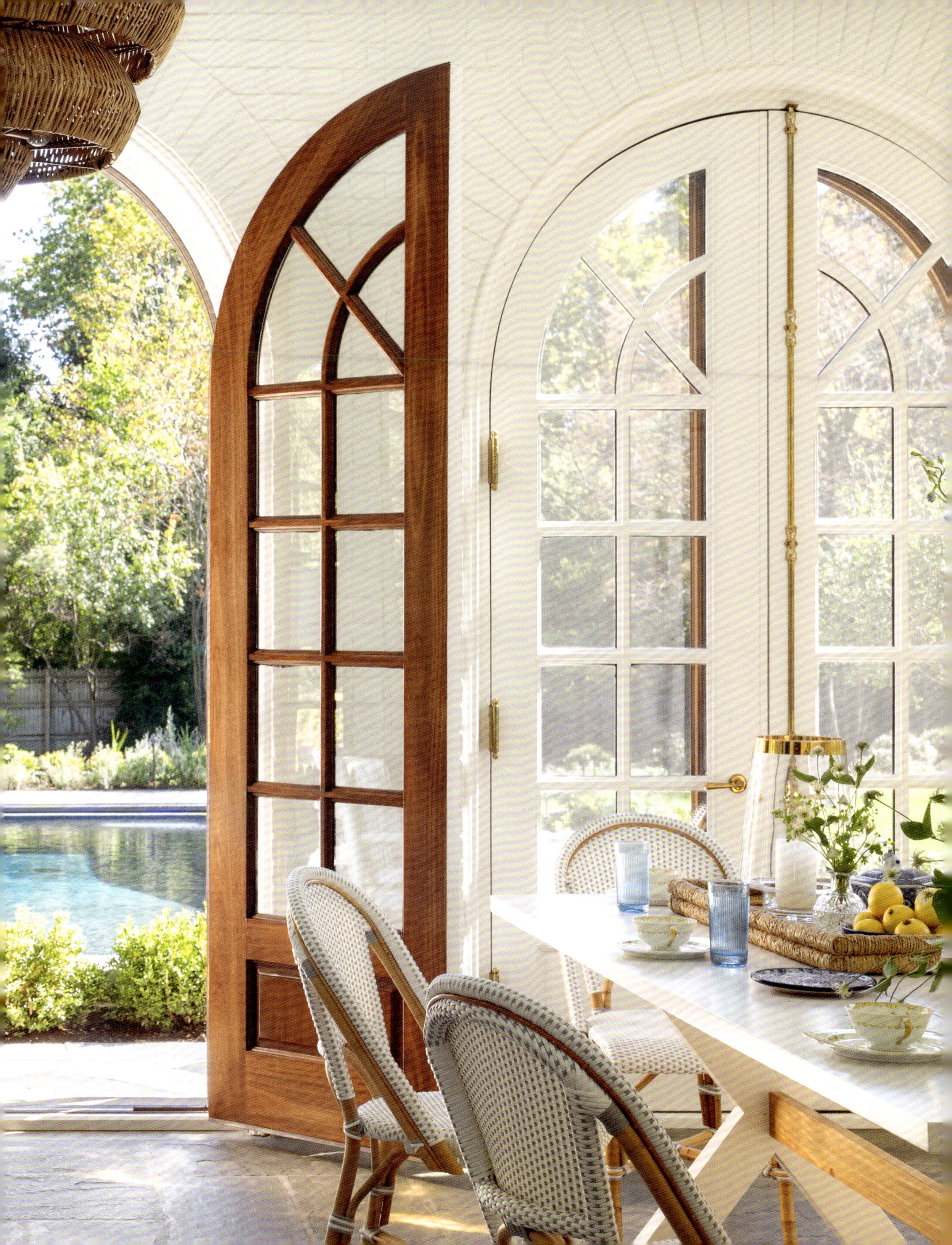

The living room, on the other hand, has undergone much more transformation, which reflects the family's growth: When we first started working together, they had one child, and now they have three kids plus a dog and a bunny. They found as their family expanded that they wanted to use this space less as a formal living room and more as a family room. We added tons of comfortable seating and lots of storage, and ended up putting a TV over the fireplace, which they never thought they would do.

While the living and dining rooms (and the bedrooms, too) are very classic and a bit more formal in style, we took a different approach with the sunroom, which is right off the living room. We wanted to make sure that it didn't feel like we were just repeating the dining room in here, so we went in a much more casual direction to differentiate the two. Although we didn't know it at the time, that space would end up being the perfect transition to the exterior and then the pool house, which the family added most recently.

What's interesting about the pool house is that you have this really historic, significant architecture of the main house, and then this new space, which is being made from scratch, but they need to feel related. We wanted something that complements the main house but without replicating it exactly. The architect incorporated some details drawn from the main house—like wainscoting—to make the two spaces feel connected, but then we went playful and comfortable in our furnishing and finishes so that it didn't feel too serious.

Previous: Since the sunroom opens up to the backyard, we gave it a more casual, airy feel than the more formal rooms in the main house.

Above: We often go bold in a powder room, but we wanted this one to feel elegant and serene, the overall atmosphere of this house.

Opposite: Since the closet is more of a traditional cloakroom, we nodded to its history with a cheeky green Cole & Son wallpaper with a Fornasetti pattern of canes and umbrellas.

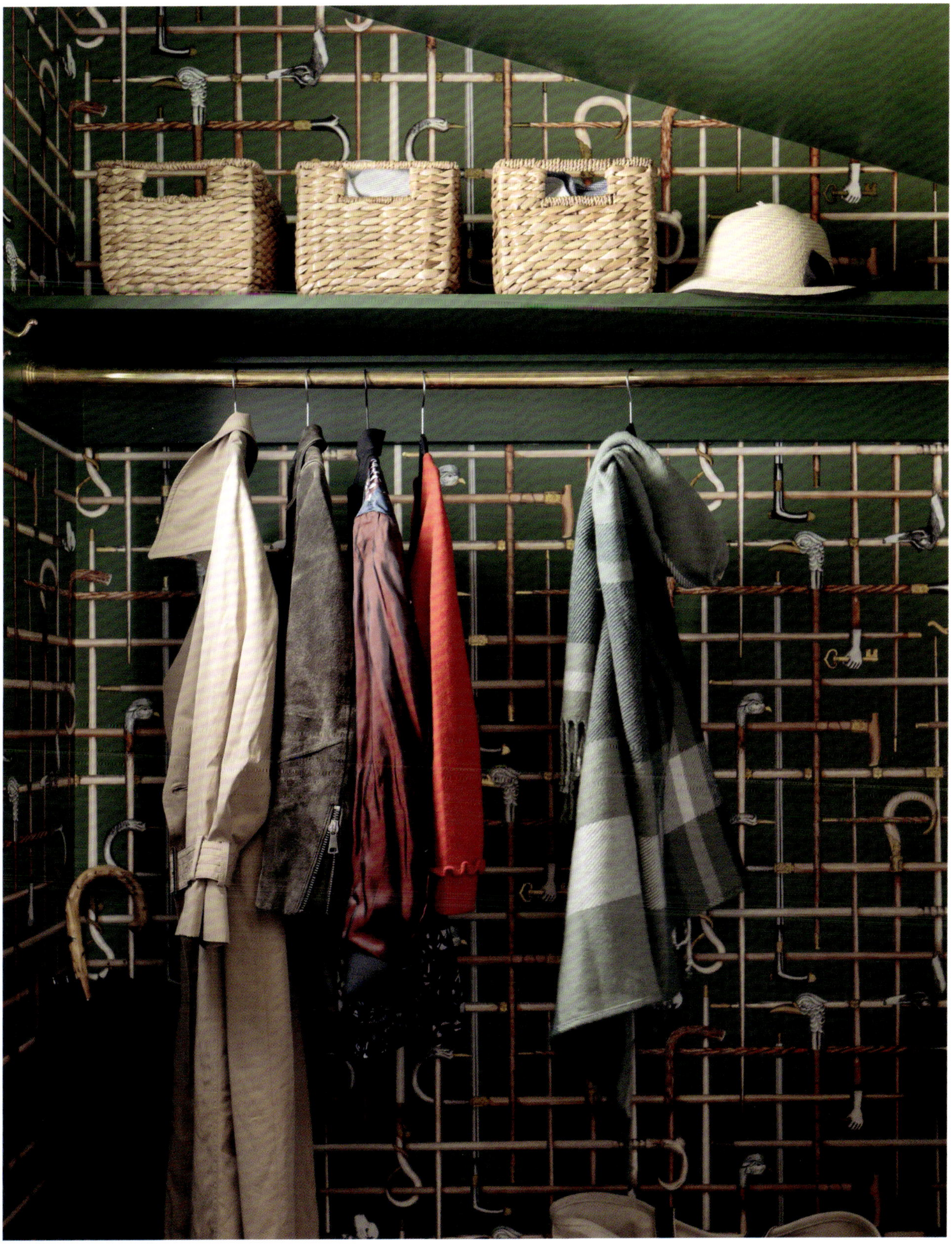

Opposite and overleaf: In the dining room, chairs upholstered in soft blue velvet and a showstopping crystal chandelier draw the eye upward and keep the focus on the house's original doors and exquisite molding.

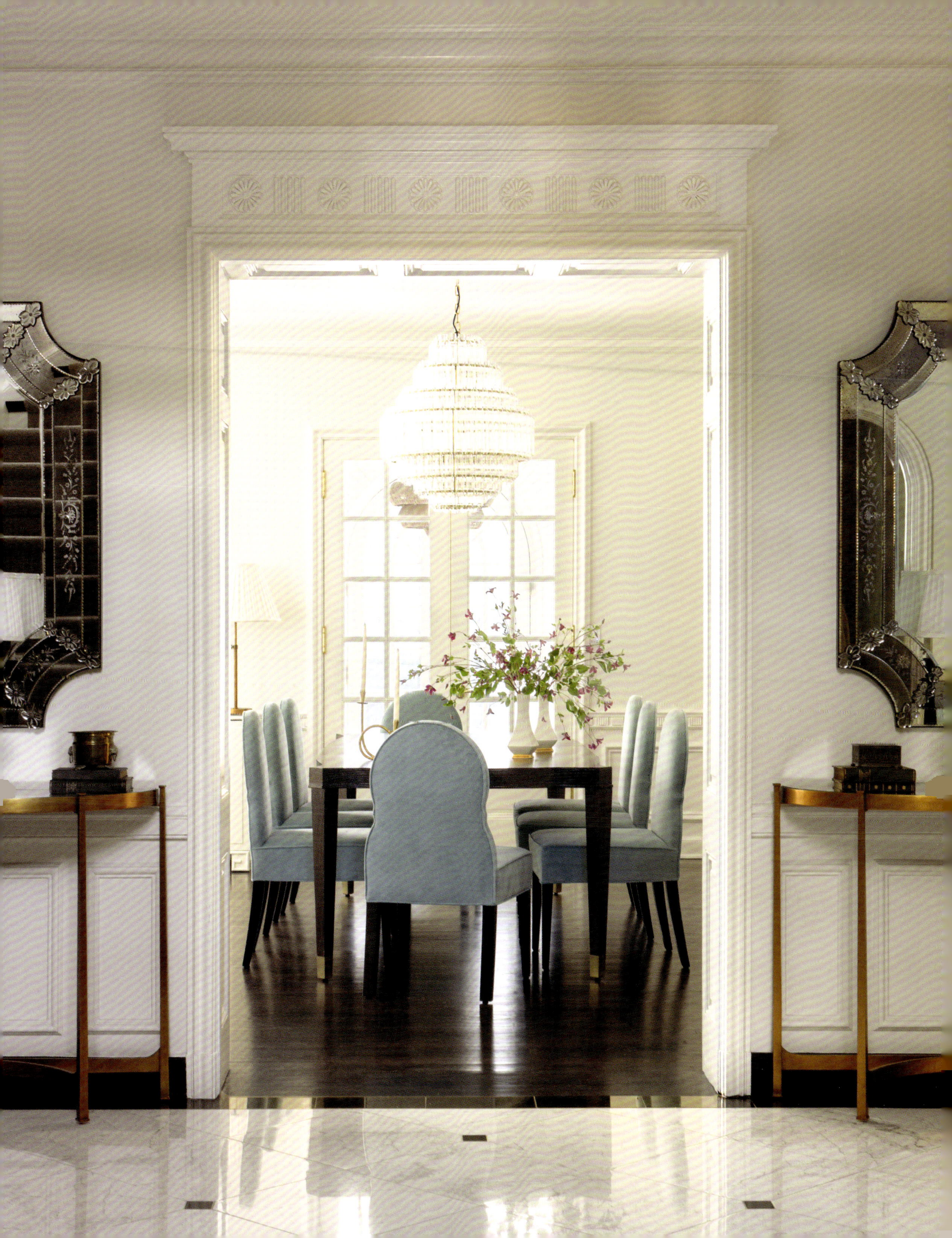

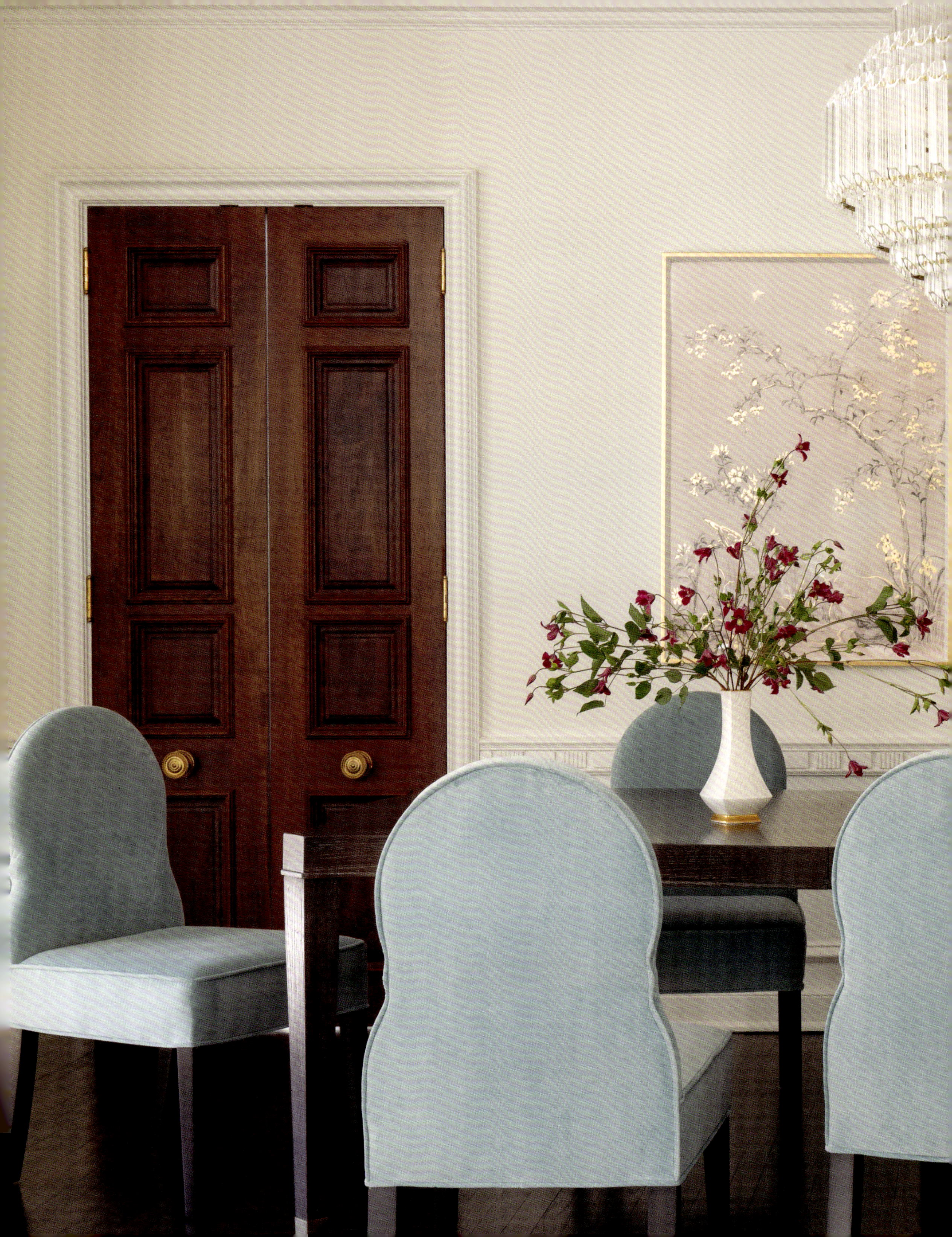

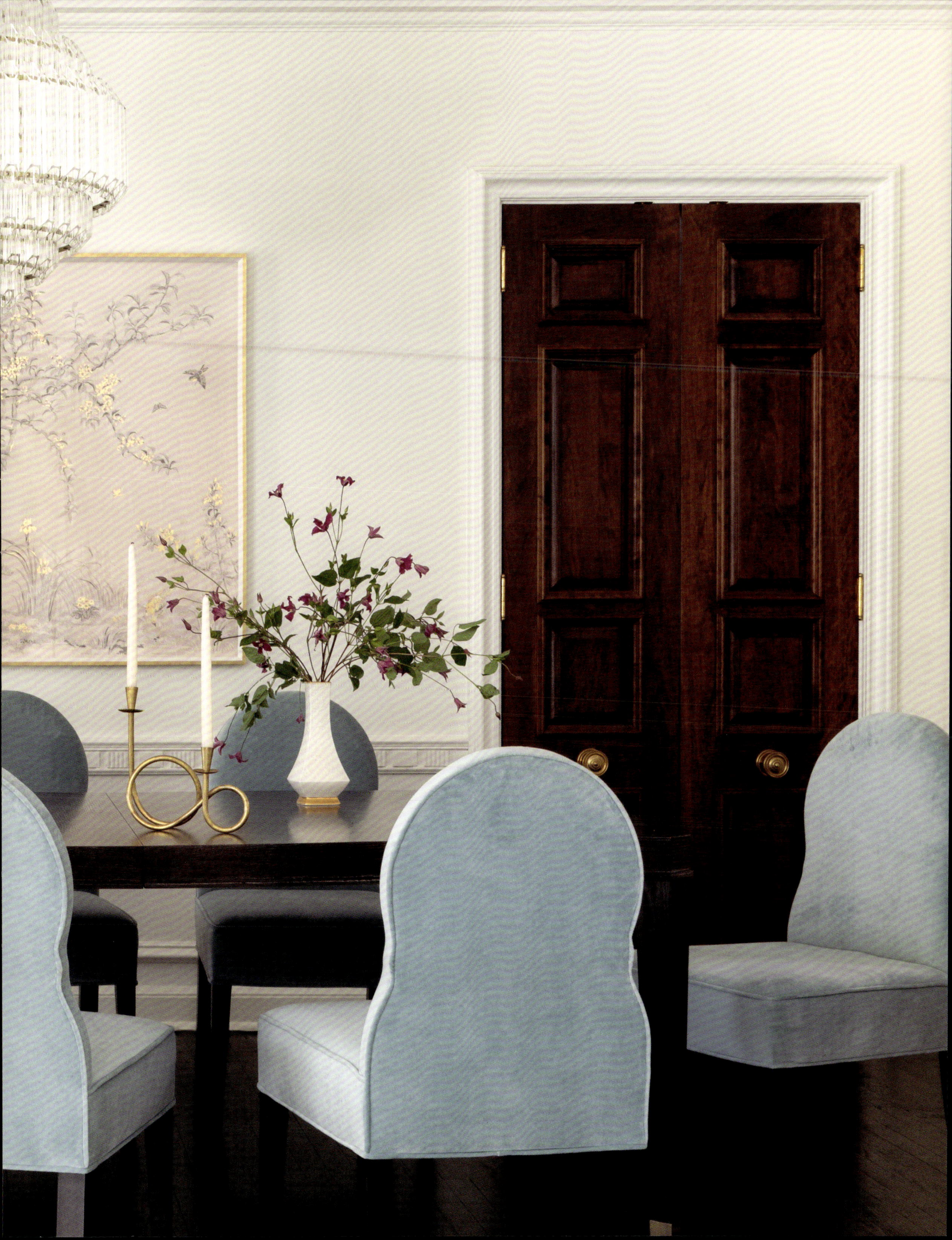

One thing the clients said, though, was that, while they didn't want the pool house to be formal, they still wanted it to feel special. As always, it was the details that helped us accomplish this goal, whether they were the woven texture on the cabinetry, the brass hardware, or the use of wallpaper, even in tiny spaces (like the changing rooms) that might otherwise have been overlooked.

It's no secret that in Chicago pool season isn't very long, so the clients really wanted this to be a year-round space. In addition to the pool, they have a hot tub that they keep open through the fall, winter, and spring, and we developed other elements of the pool house that can be used during all four seasons. The windows over the kitchen counters open to the terrace for indoor-outdoor entertaining in the summer, for example, but there's also a fireplace and a big, cozy sectional for relaxing during colder months.

For a building under one thousand square feet, the pool house holds a lot: There's a kitchen, a laundry room, a bedroom, and it's all very functional with tons of storage. Because of that, it's able to be used in a huge variety of different ways, including for poolside barbecues in the summer or making s'mores in the winter. I love knowing that, no matter the time of the year, my clients have the perfect family getaway right in their backyard.

Right, opposite, and overleaf: The rich wood paneling and original fireplace surround in the den made it easy to go simple and masculine on furnishings.

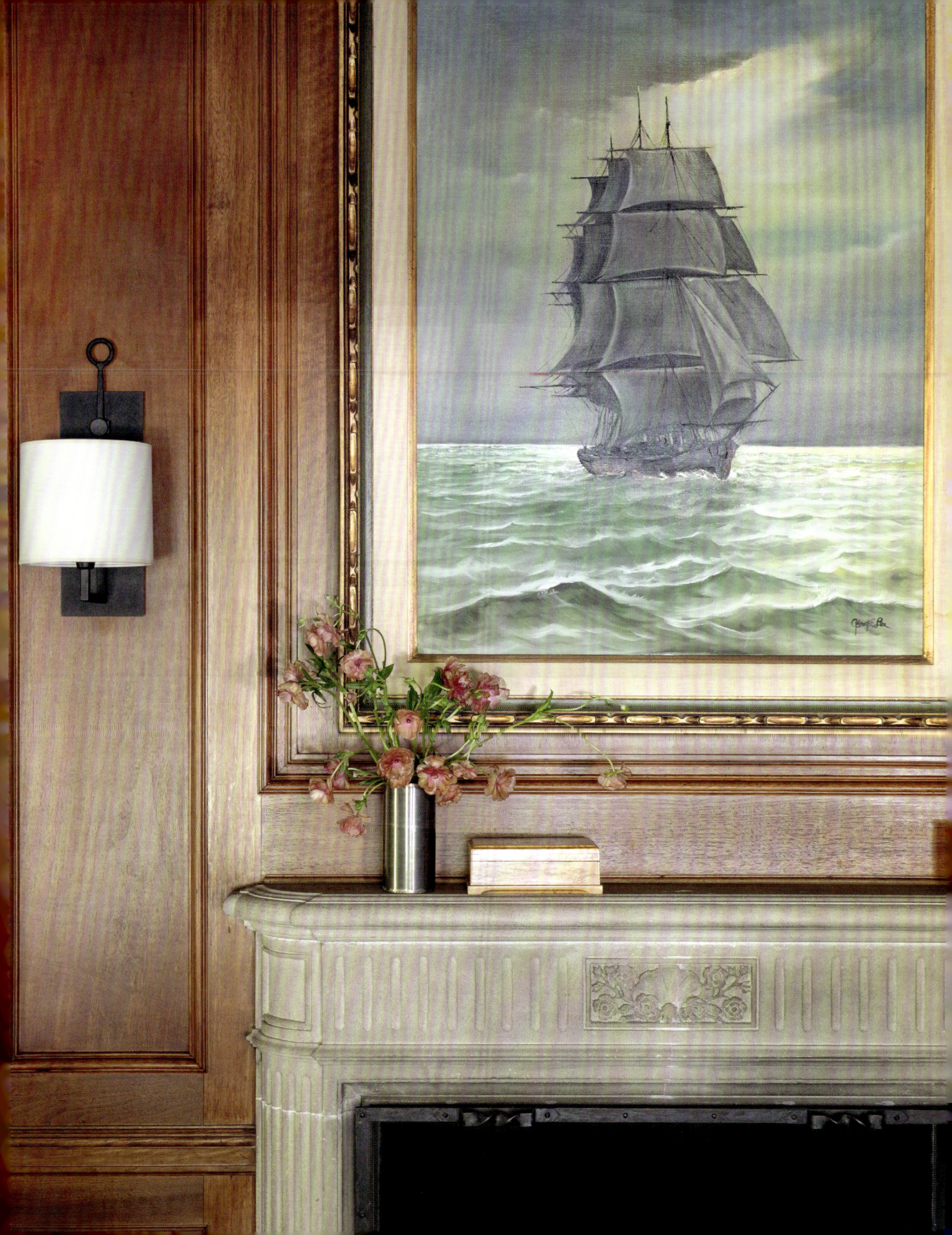

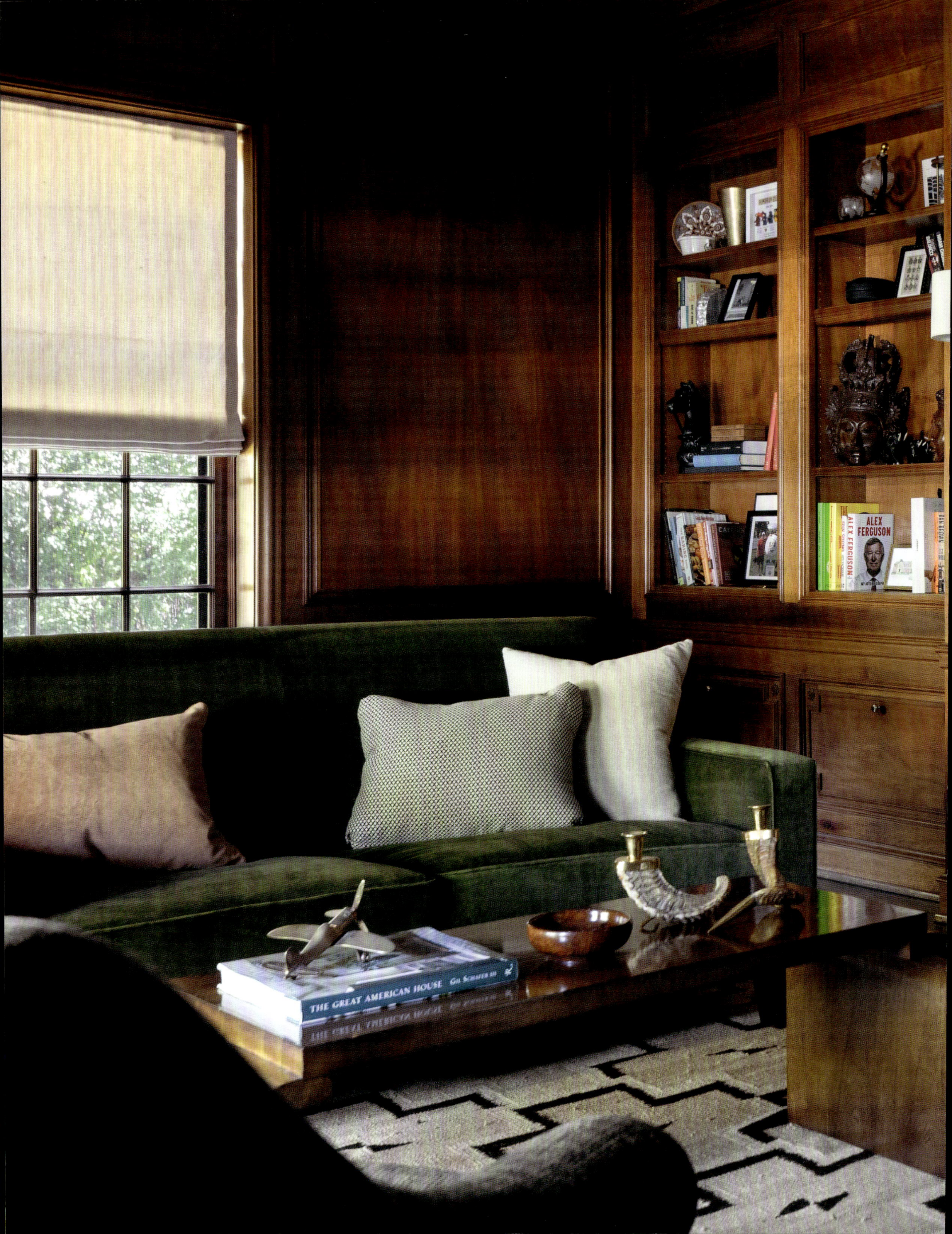
ALEX FERGUSON
THE GREAT AMERICAN HOUSE
GIL SCHAFER III

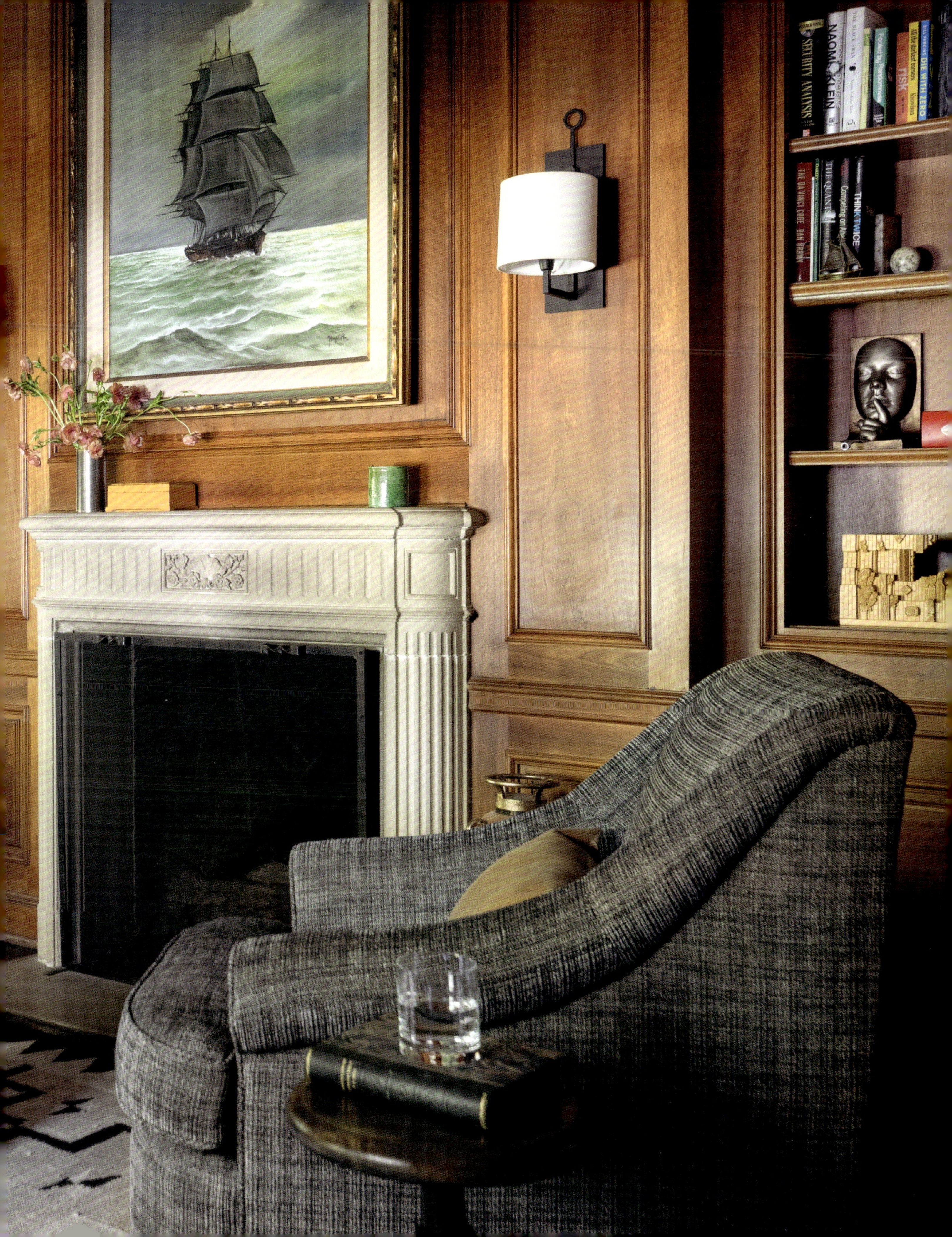

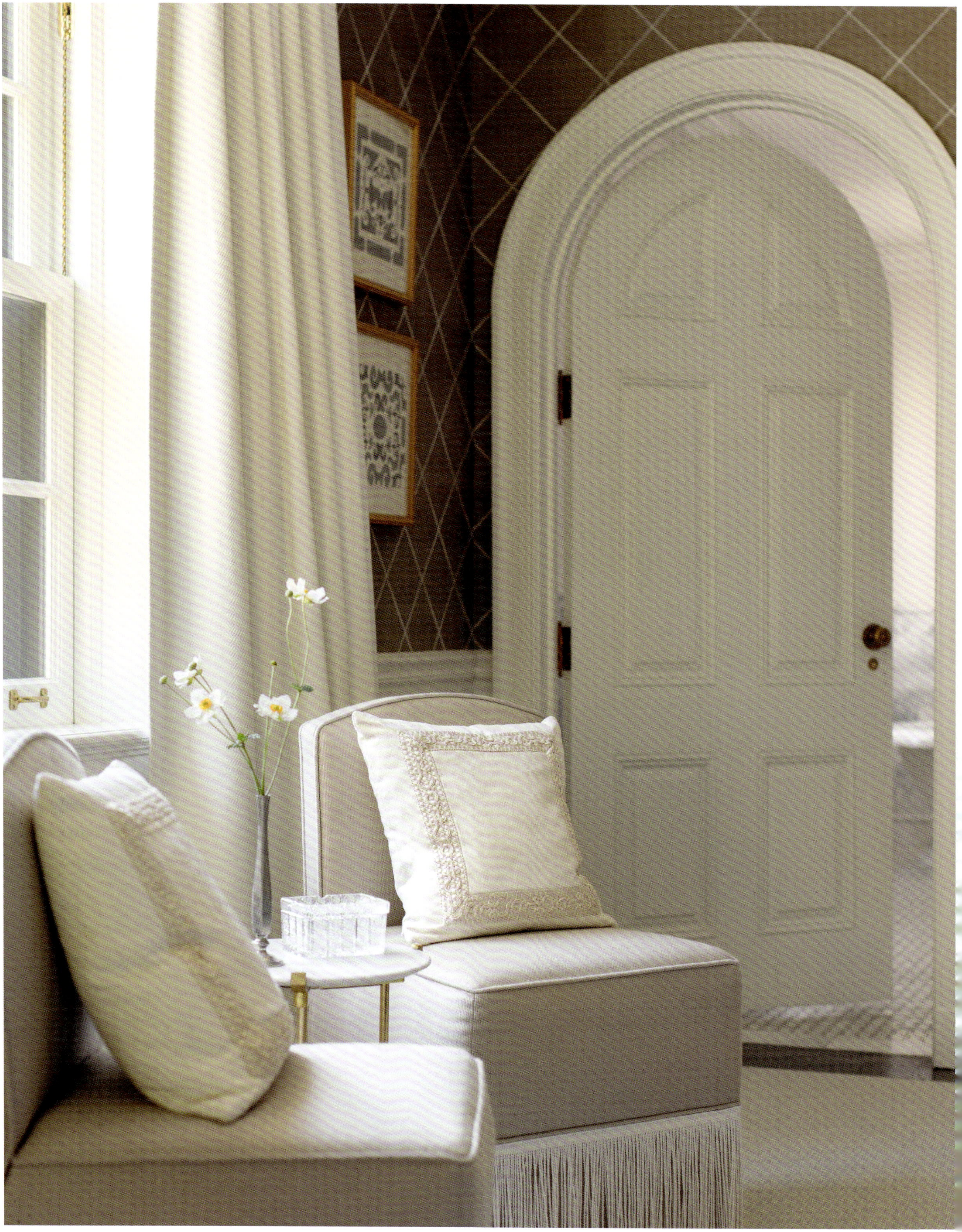

The primary bedroom is classic and tailored, with a defined color palette and a focus on subtle textures.

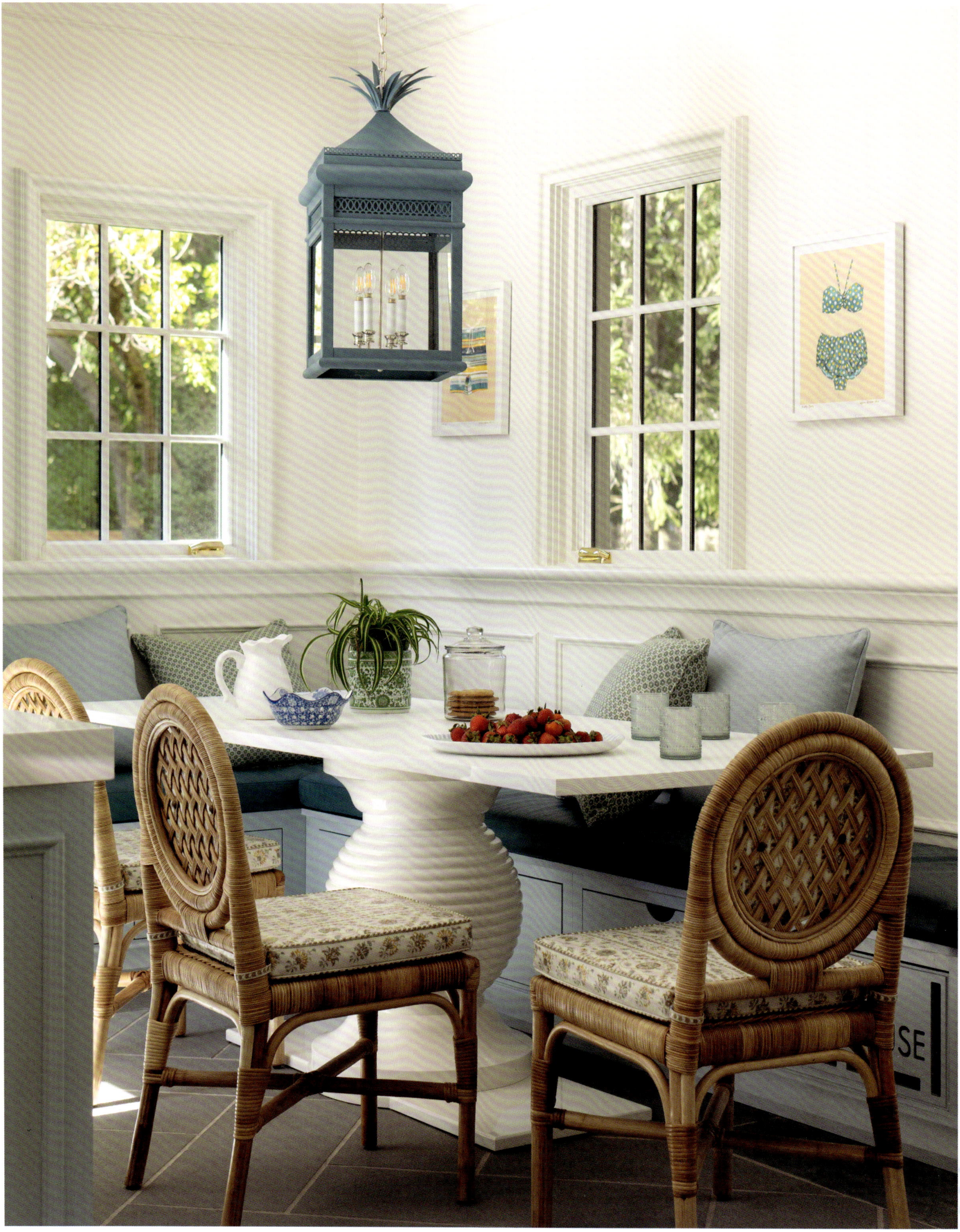

Opposite, right, and overleaf: Since the family didn't do much work on the kitchen in the main house, the pool house presented a fun opportunity to design a more playful, colorful kitchen that's ideal for hosting.

—

Page 220: The pool house's woven cabinetry was a subtle way of tying in a more casual, nautical feel while maintaining a classic look.

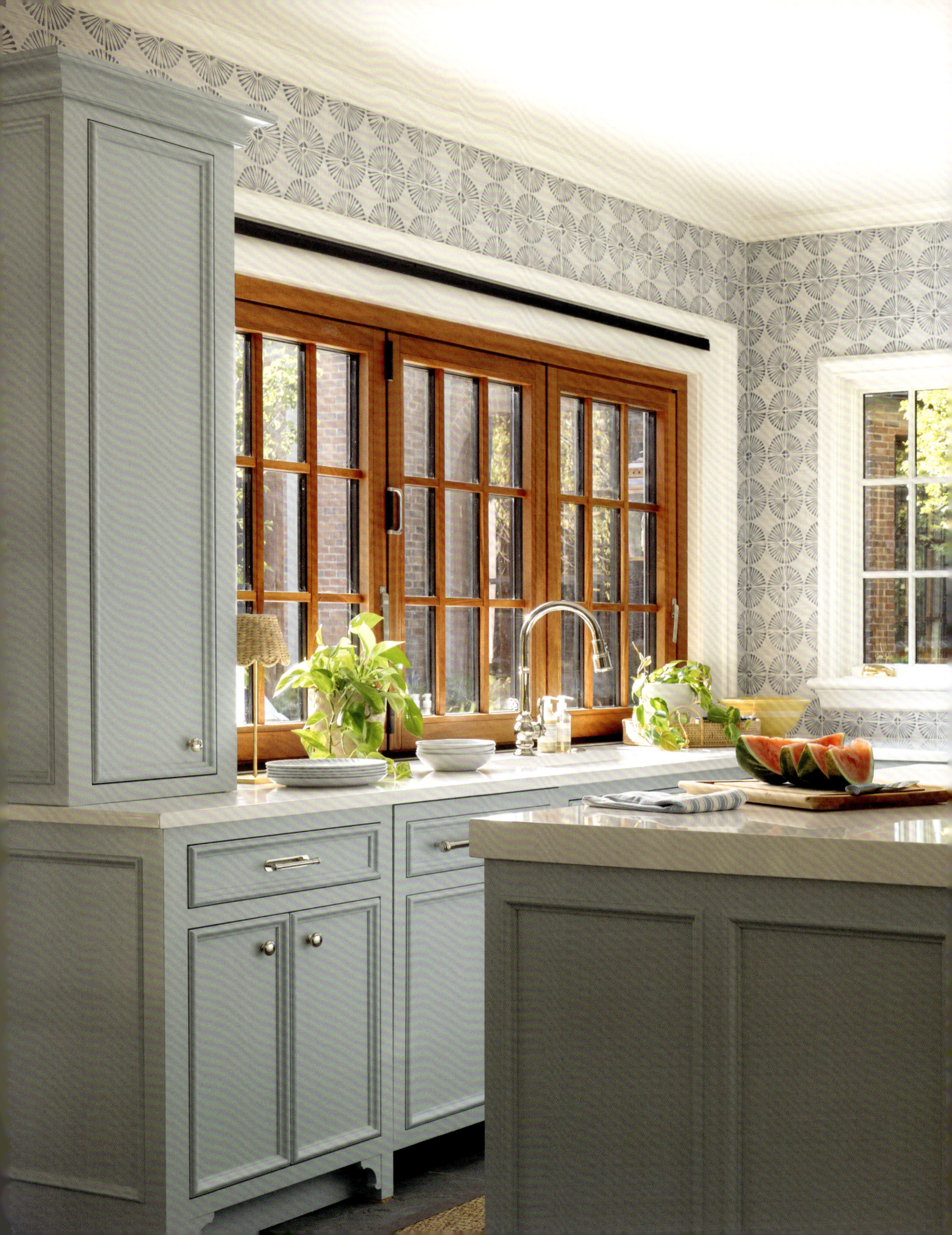

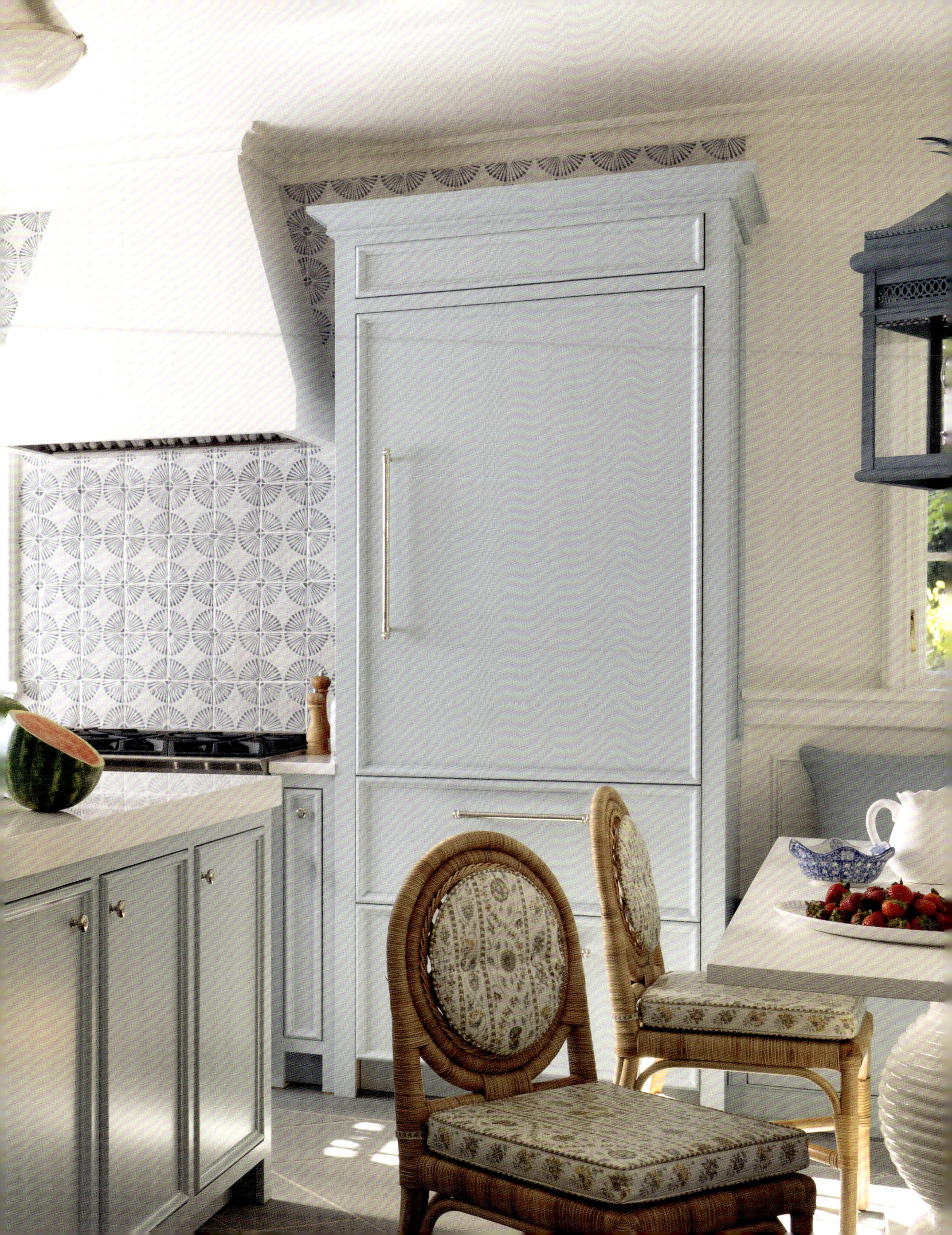

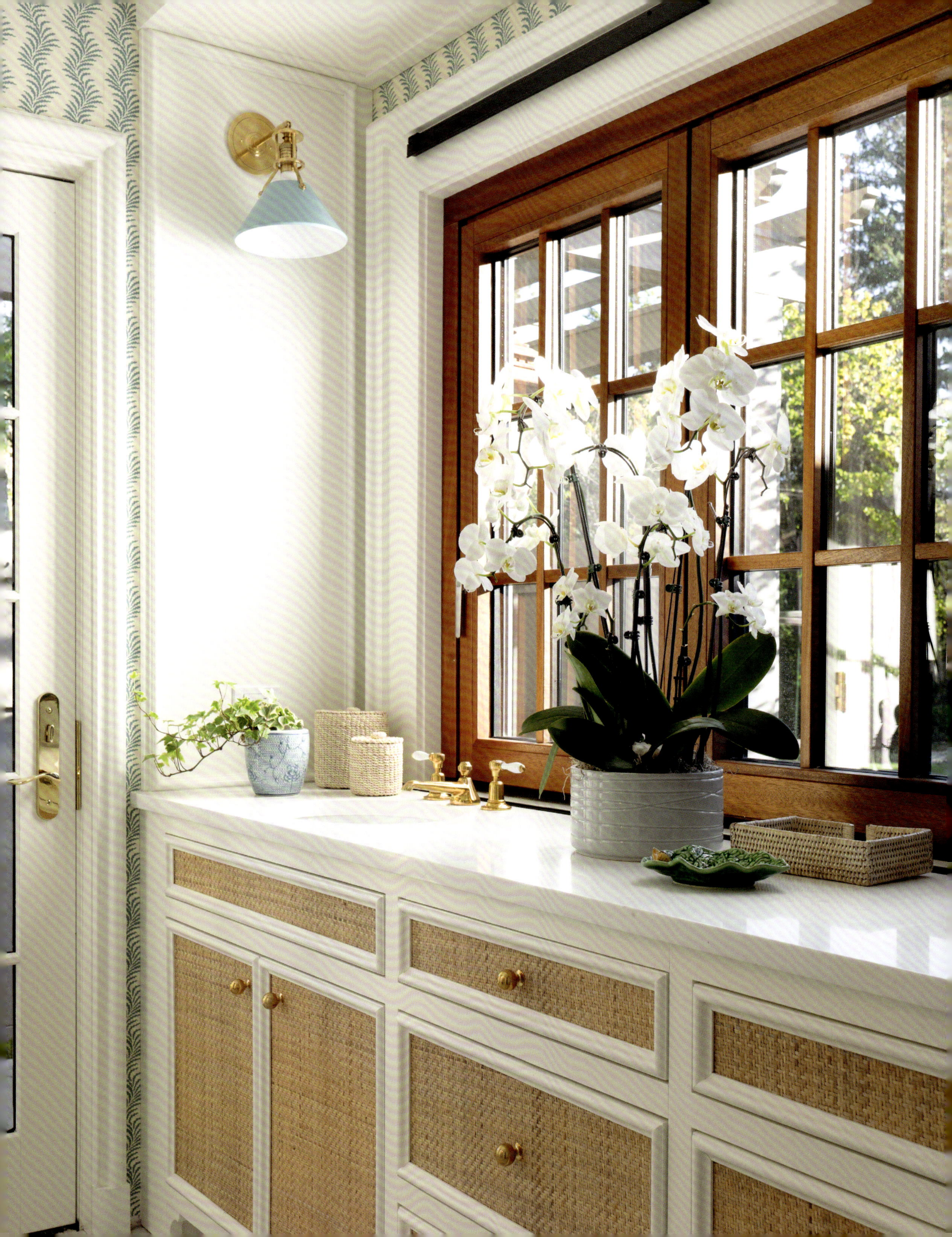

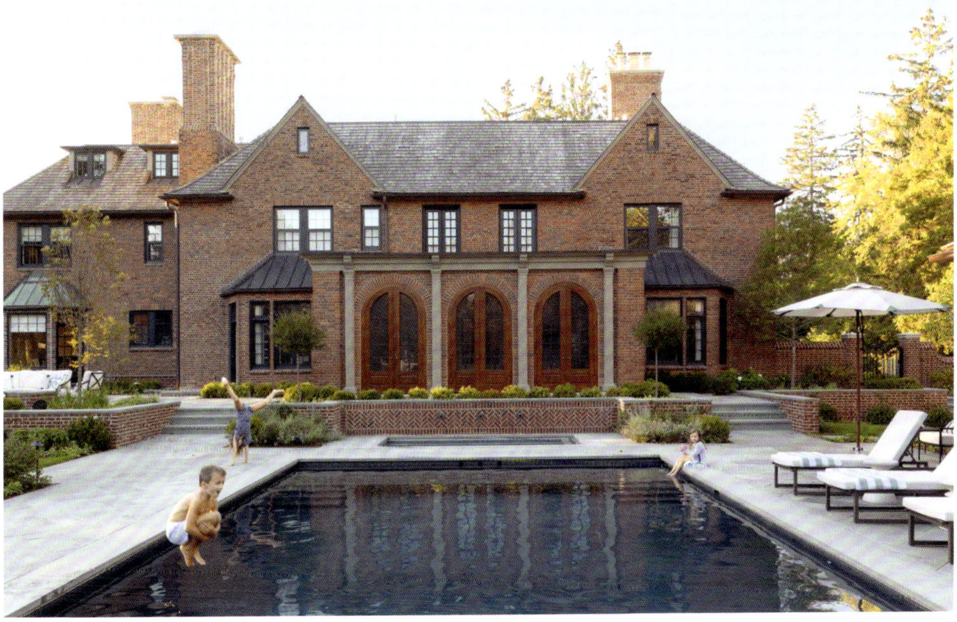

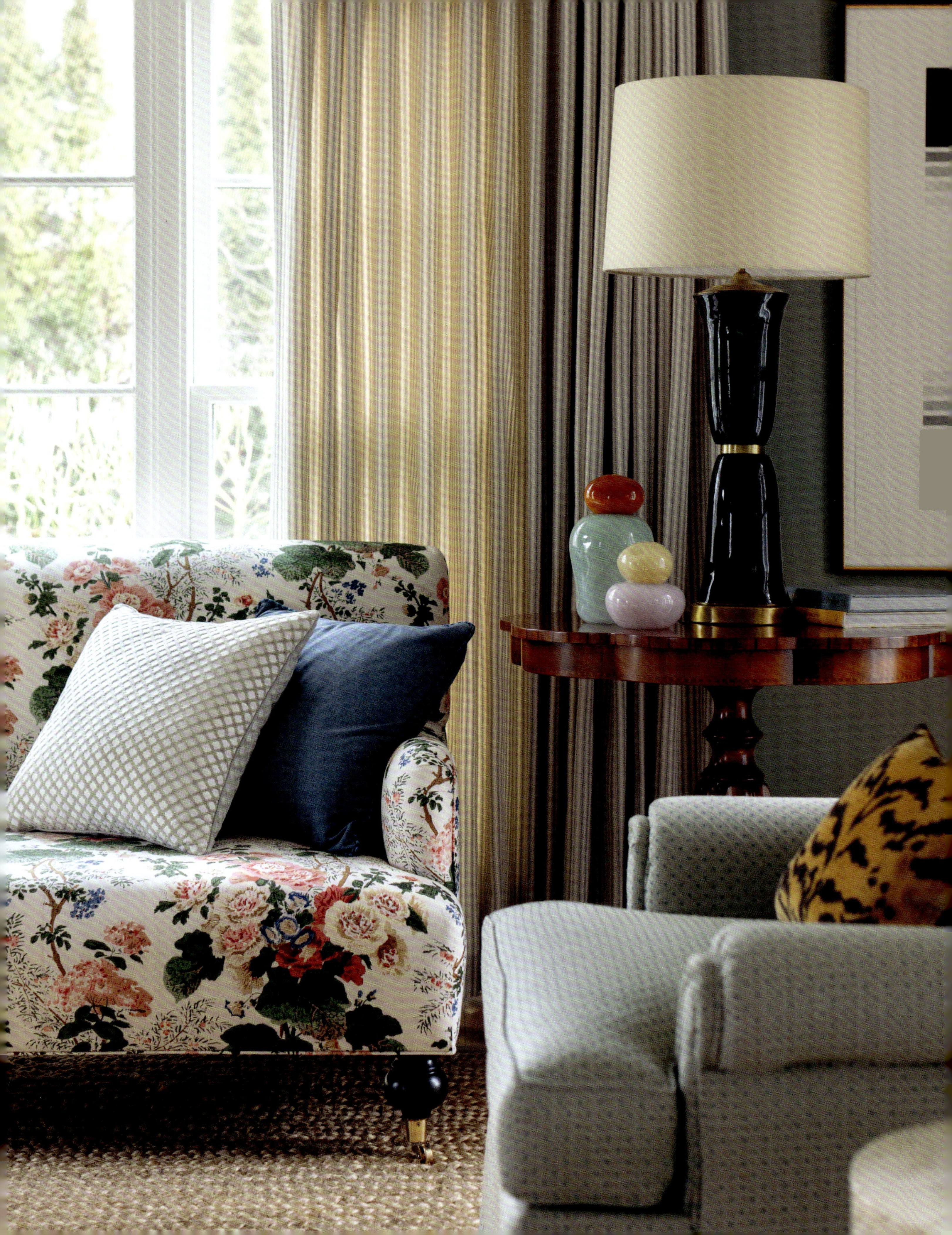

OUR GARDEN HOUSE

My own family's haven for a delightfully chaotic life

(and my blueprint for a livable family home)

Our whole house is an explosion of color, so I thought that using a grayscale pattern in the powder room would make for a strong juxtaposition.

—

Overleaf: It took some trial and error to land on the perfect shade for our formal living room. When we found Card Room Green by Farrow & Ball, we knew we'd gotten it right because it made the whole space feel so cozy.

The year was 2017, and no one wanted to move to the suburbs. Spencer and I were expecting our second child, though, and as both of our families were there, we felt a strong pull. With real estate priced to sell, we went to view a very imperfect house on a very good property. As soon as we saw it, we were struck by the magic of the site and by the home's potential—despite knowing it would likely require a gut renovation.

My mom referred to it as our "garden house," an apt name for a home whose rooms, while not grand by any means, nearly all offer expansive views of the greenery outside through oversized windows and exterior doors. I knew I wanted to embrace that garden feel and bring the foliage and the florals into the house. I'm so drawn to those themes in design, and it felt like the perfect vision for the house.

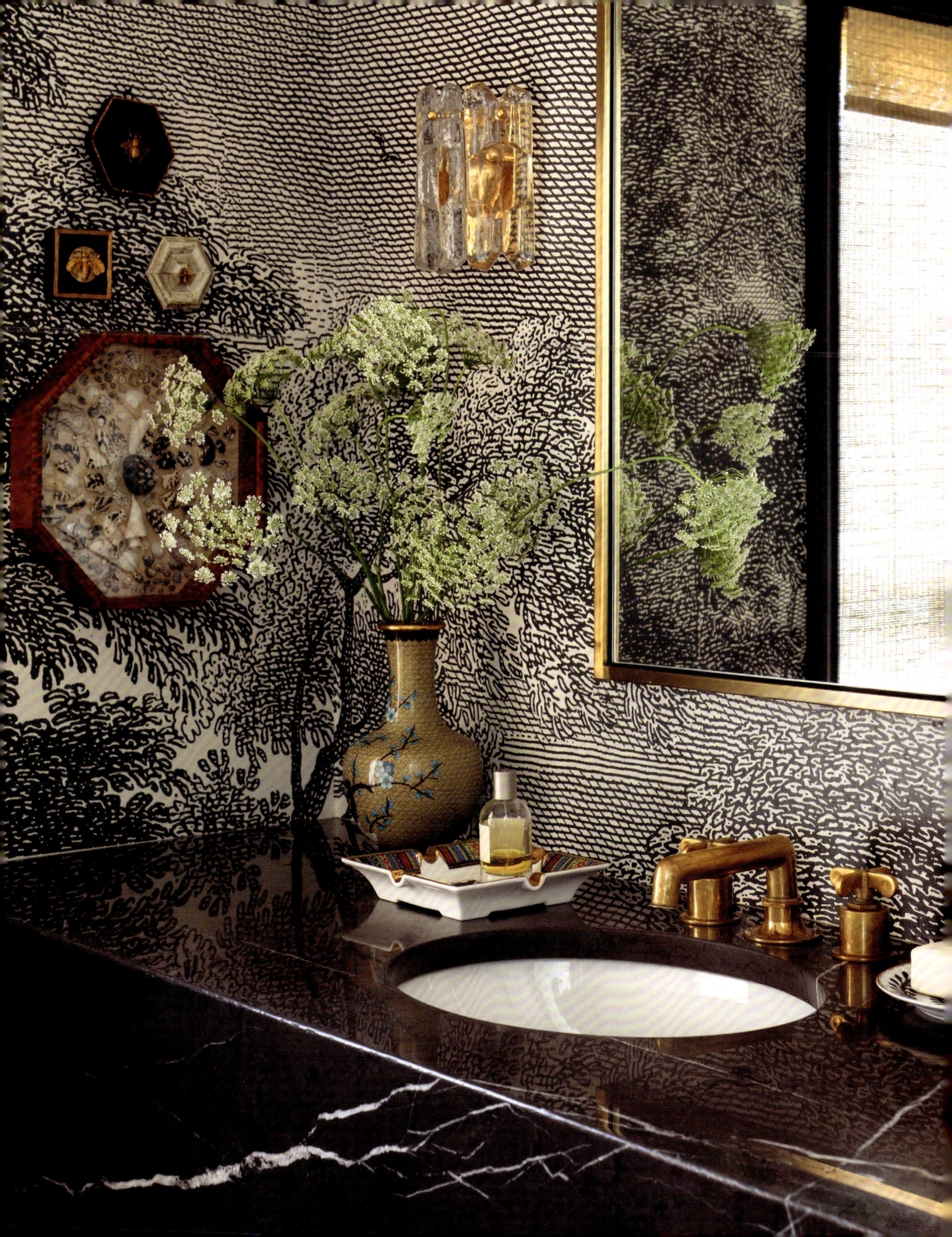

MOMENTS THAT MATTER THE MOST
HIP HOTELS
Interior Design
ABSOLUT BOOK.
EMERALD
LABRADOR RETRIEVER
BARBRA STREISAND My Passion for Design
Mary-Kate Olsen Ashley Olsen
DECORATING

DRESSING THE HOME
PLANT
FORAGED FLORA
ASPEN
TIMELESS
TEXTILES
HIRST
CHANEL
HOUSES

> "I knew I wanted to embrace that garden feel and bring the foliage and the florals into the house."

While we loved the shell, the interior left much to be desired in the way of a practical layout for a busy young family. I was determined to arrange the rooms to squeeze every possible use out of the house's square footage; after all, we are "house people"—I knew we would be thoroughly, lovingly, using this home. From an interior architecture standpoint, I had my work cut out for me when it came to adding character. The house was built in the 1950s in a style that was neither midcentury modern nor traditional. We didn't want to pretend it was something it wasn't (we knew it would never be a prewar home!), but we could create a more classic quality through details like molding, trim, and thoughtful symmetry.

Of course, our new family home wouldn't be complete without nods to each of our own families: adding elements like the dining room table from Spencer's childhood home, a portrait of my grandmother, and framed pages from the issues of *Harper's Weekly* that my grandfather collected really make it feel like a true reflection of where we come from.

We began by reconfiguring the first floor almost completely. When we bought the home, it had a family room at the opposite end of the house from the kitchen, and the kitchen was right next to the dining and living room. We didn't want a huge open floor plan, but knowing how we live as a family, we did want a layout that would lend itself to a more casual way of living. That meant swapping the living and family rooms so that the larger living room was closer to the much-used kitchen. While we kept the kitchen white at my husband's request, I added texture in the form of green grass cloth wallpaper and lots of plants and accessories—then went full drama in the butler's pantry with its rich, high-gloss, hunter green cabinetry; peacock-patterned marbled-paper ceiling; and luminous quartzite backsplash.

Our living room may look formal, but with its furniture upholstered in performance fabric and ample built-ins—the perfect place to corral kids' toys and books—it's also one of the children's favorite spaces. We spend a lot of time there in the winter, especially, when we nearly always have a fire burning in the fireplace. The dining room is a similarly formal-yet-livable space: While I didn't sacrifice style for typical "kid-friendliness," nothing is off-limits. There are a few friends we have over often, and between the three families there are nine kids ranging from one to nine years old. When they come over, it's chaos, but it's happy chaos. My dining chairs are covered in blue slipcovers, and you know what? They still have black pen on them from my kids and that's okay—that's life. I want everyone (kids included!) to enjoy this home and not feel like anything is precious or scary. In fact, when we have friends over, the adults will often eat in the kitchen while the kids sit in the dining room because it seats more, and I love that.

Another thing I love about our home's layout is the screened porch, located on the opposite end of the house from the living room and kitchen. When we entertain, we'll all eat in the kitchen and then the kids will run amok outside while the adults retreat to the porch for a glass of wine.

As an introverted person in a family that lives in the chaos of the kitchen and eats dinner and cooks and spends a lot of time together, I often wonder, When I need to recharge, where do I go? It was important to

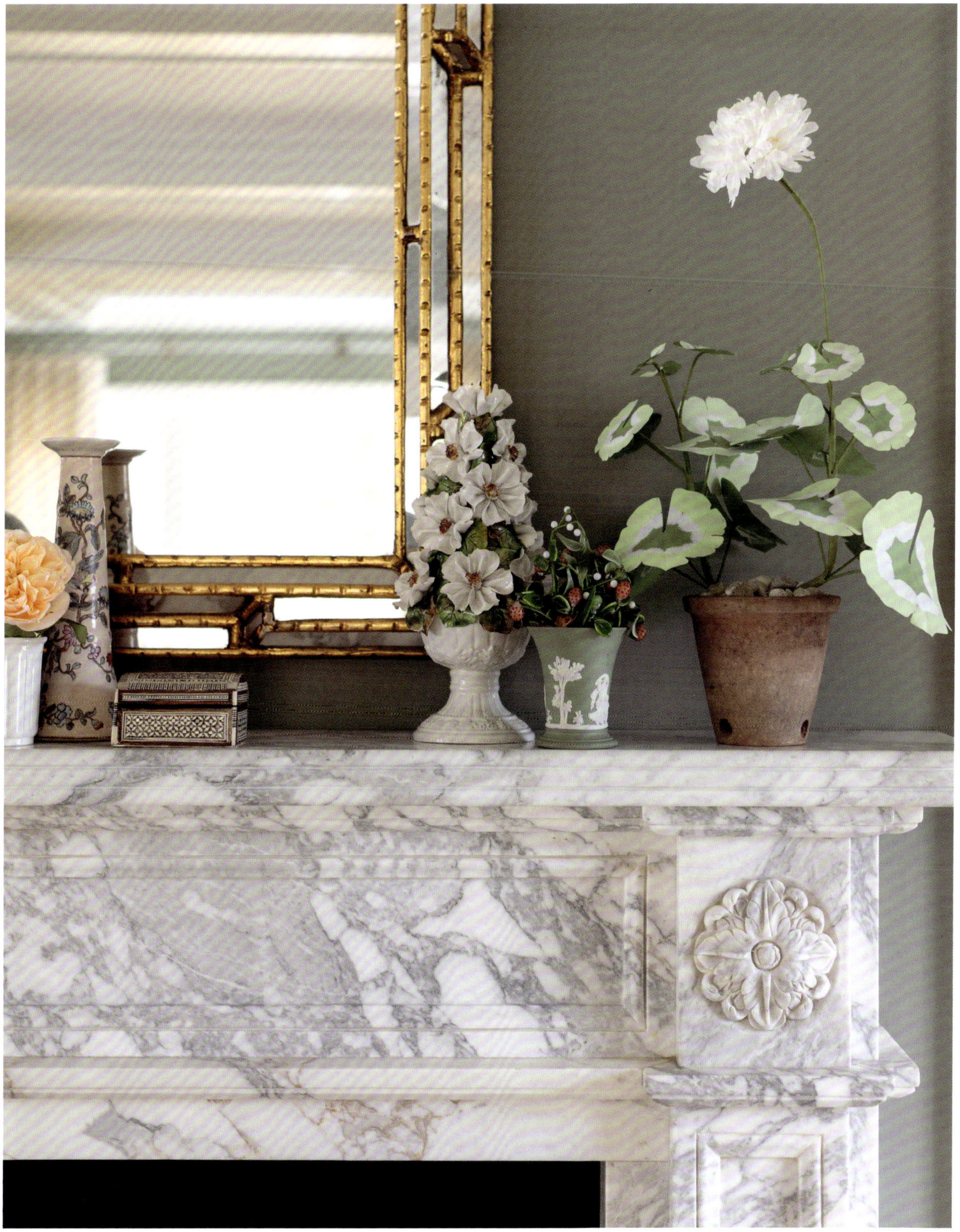

Previous: We designed a custom marble mantel to create character in the house where there wasn't much to begin with.

—

Right: I love the personality that antique chairs bring, and this Regency hall chair is the perfect accent in this room.

—

Opposite: When we bought the house, I asked my mom for this portrait of my grandmother. It was the first thing I thought of for our new home.

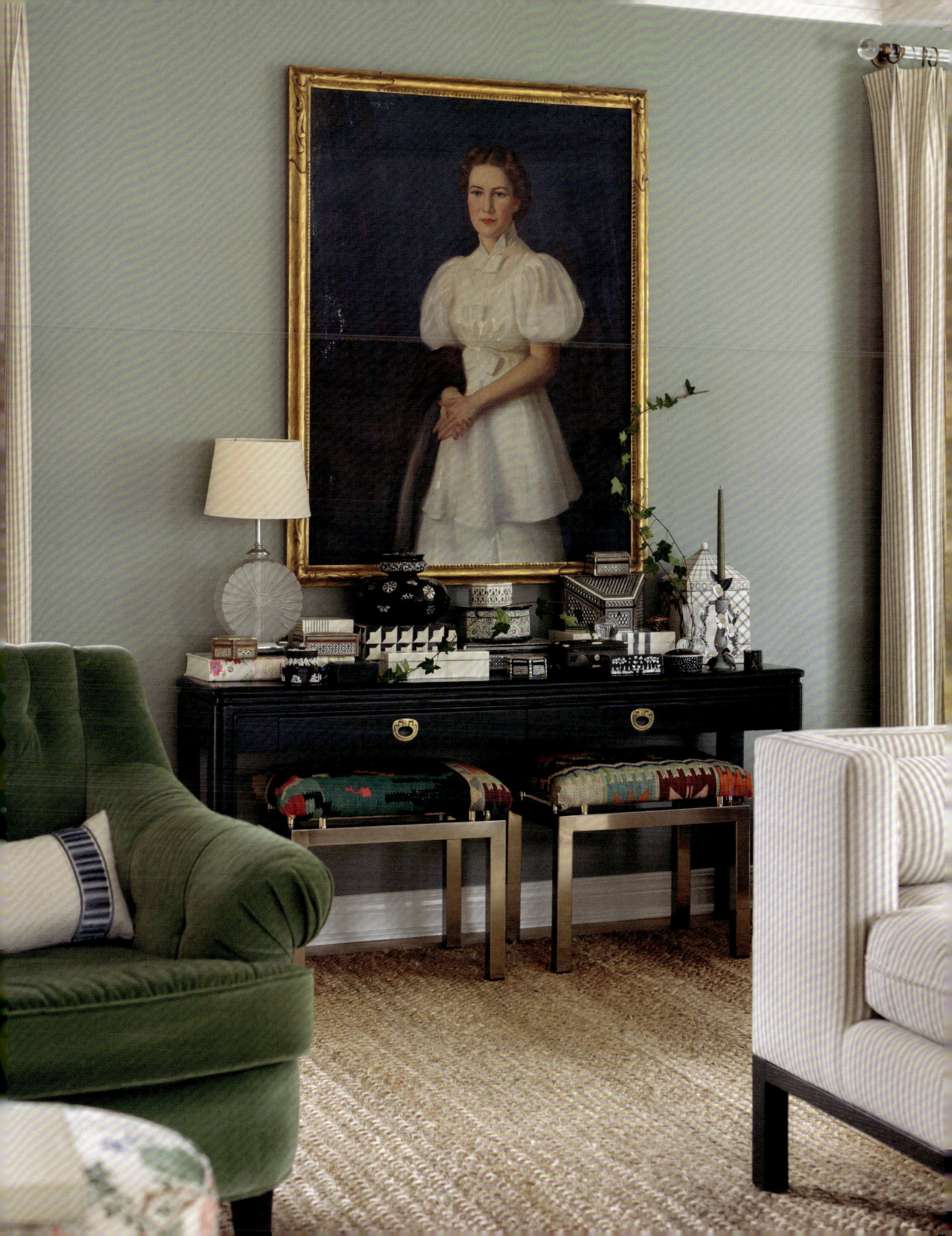

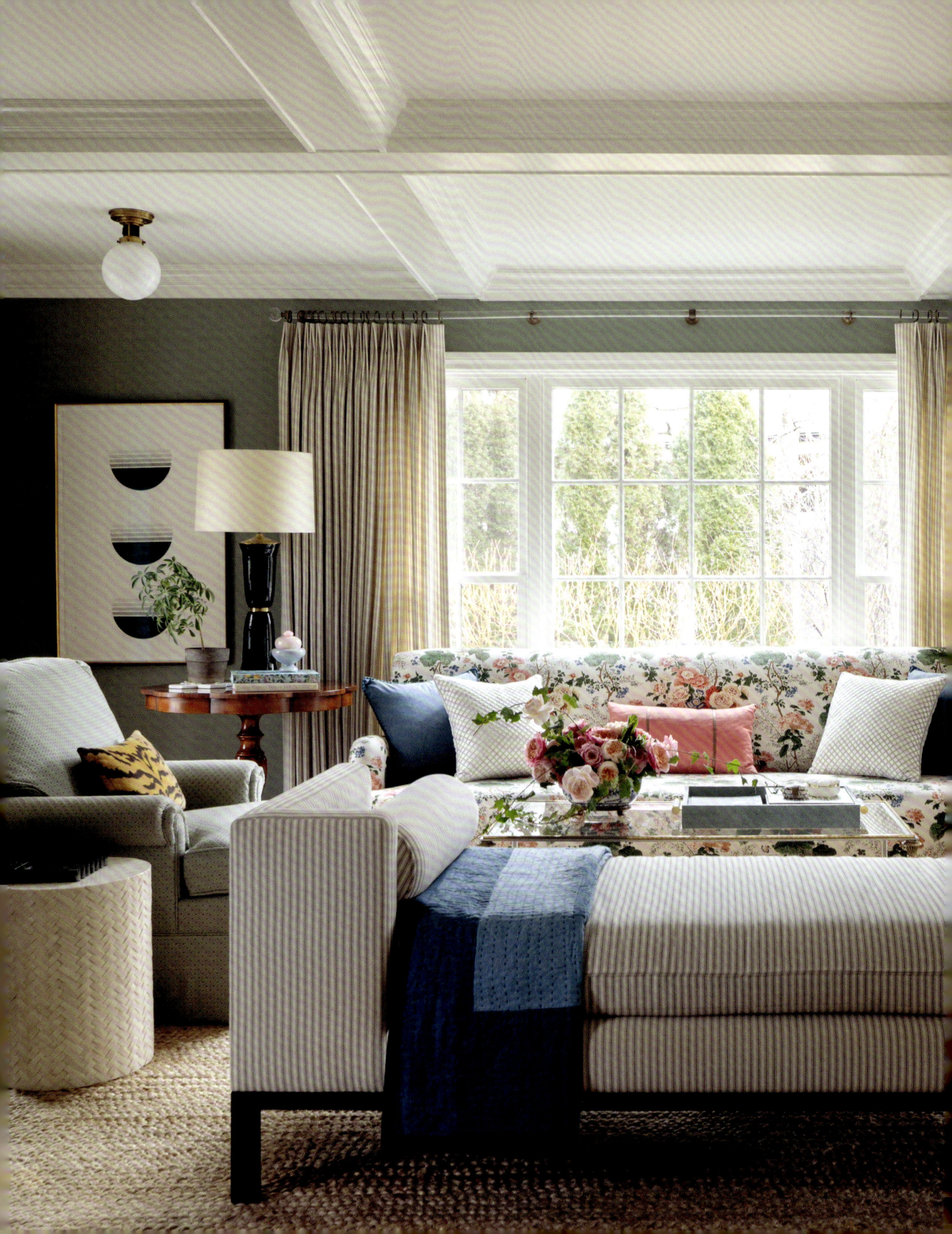

squeeze a chair into the corner of our bedroom. It was a tight fit, and if you looked at the floorplan you might think it wouldn't work, but I forced it. I sometimes need to take a call, and I don't want to do that from the bed, so it's nice to have a spot in my room.

It's magical how this house has developed along with us as our family has grown. When we moved in, I was pregnant with my second. We put our eldest in the biggest room and put the baby next to her, and then we realized that she's the only girl and she's probably going to want her own bathroom. When she got a little older, we moved her into the guest room so that she could have her own en suite.

Now that our kids don't need constant supervision, we have been able to live in our house a bit differently. They'll play in the family room or the basement, and I can sit in the living room and read. We're close by if they need us, but we're not on top of each other. Functionally, as our family evolved, we made changes to the house accordingly. I love the idea that a home doesn't need to be rigidly fixed—it should be a flexible living space that adapts to your family.

As I write this book, we're working on renovating another home, which our family will move into shortly before publication. While leaving our garden house and all of the cherished memories it holds of our children, friends, and family is certainly bittersweet, I have learned so much about how I want to design and live in a truly family-centric house, and I am so excited to see that come to life in our next home—the next chapter of our family's story.

The two graphic artworks flanking the sofa in the living room are by my sister Carly Beck.

Overleaf: It is so meaningful to us that our dining room table is the one that my husband grew up with in his childhood home. We surrounded it with chairs covered in pretty bow-backed, light blue linen slipcovers, so we wouldn't have to worry about the inevitable spills.

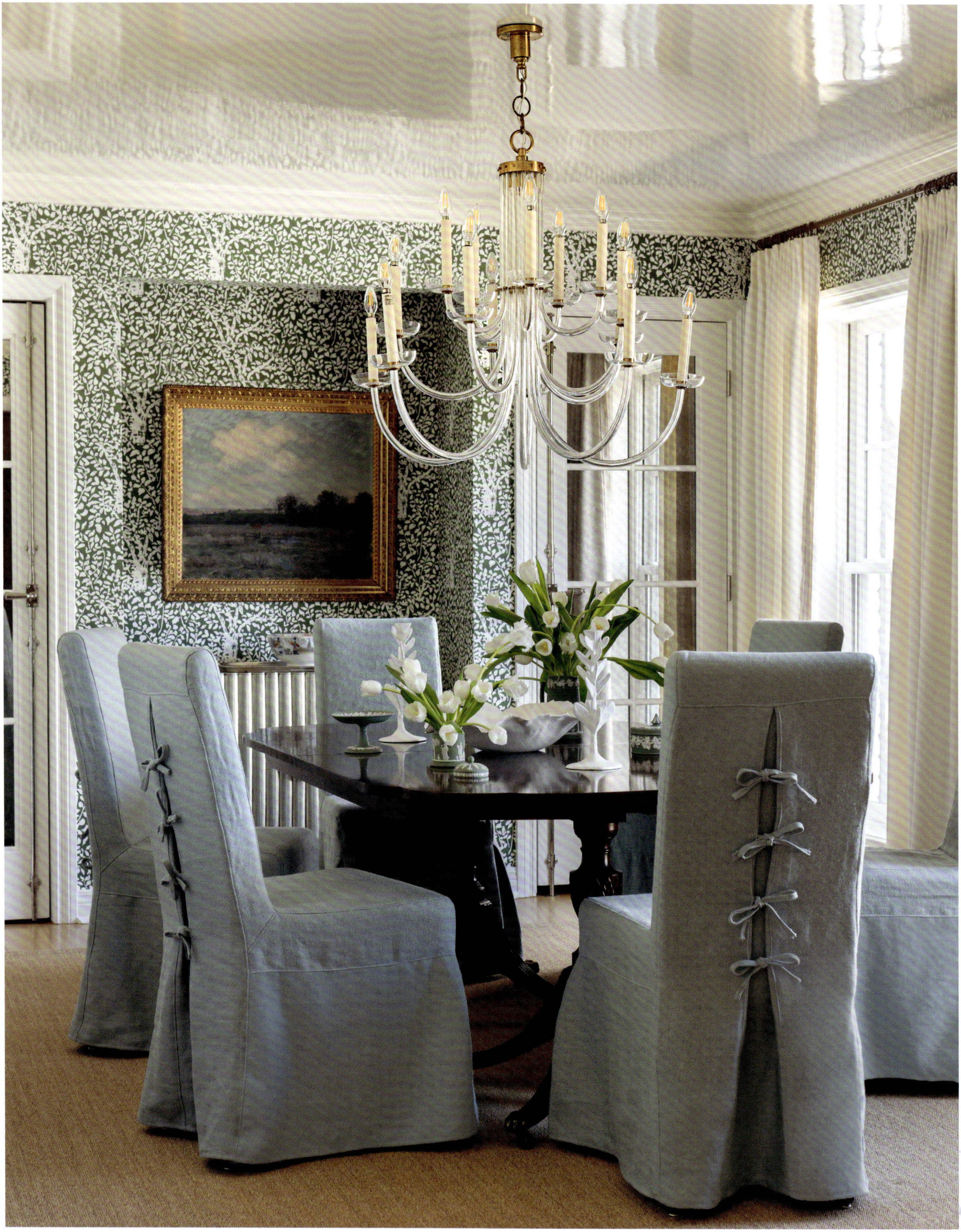

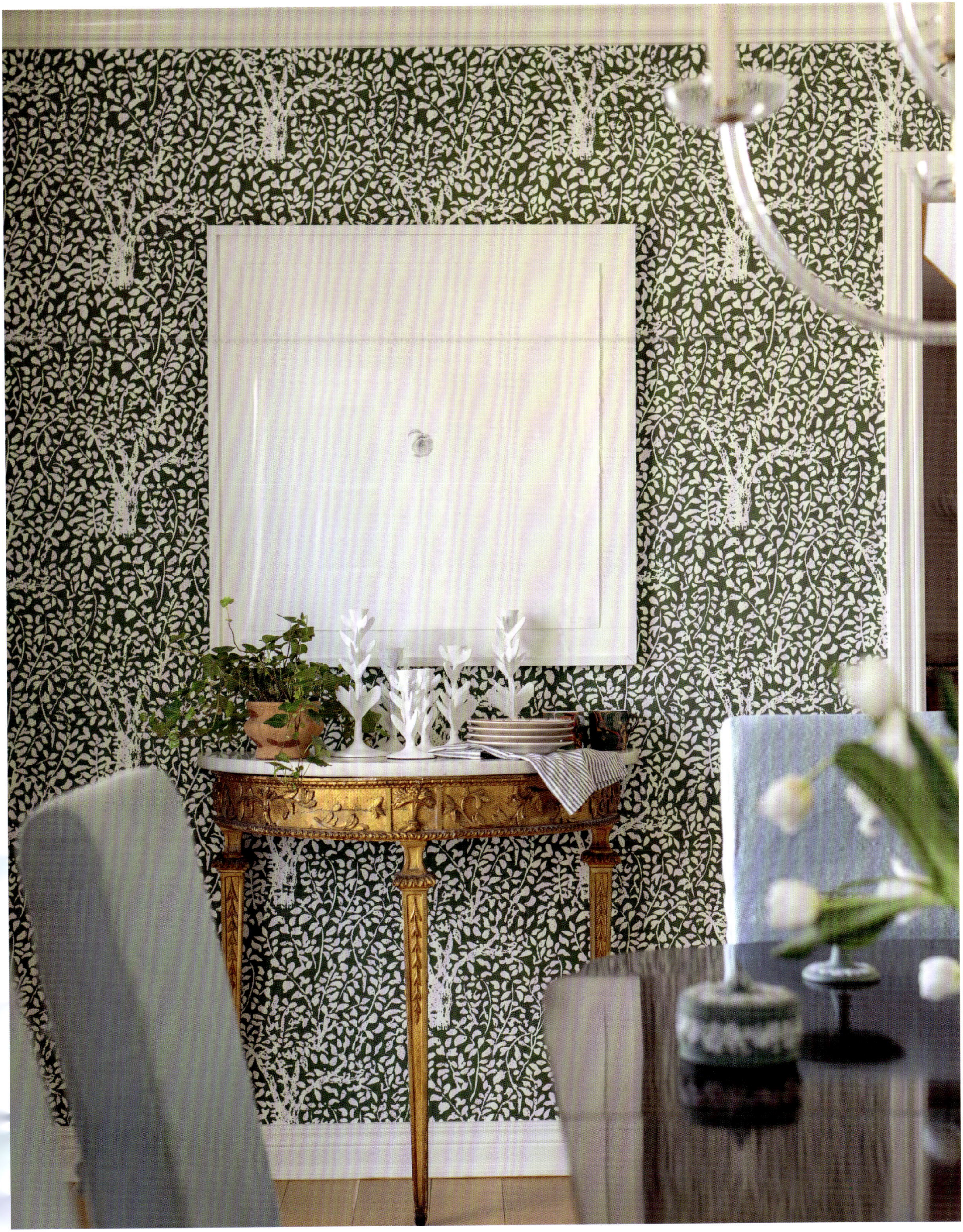

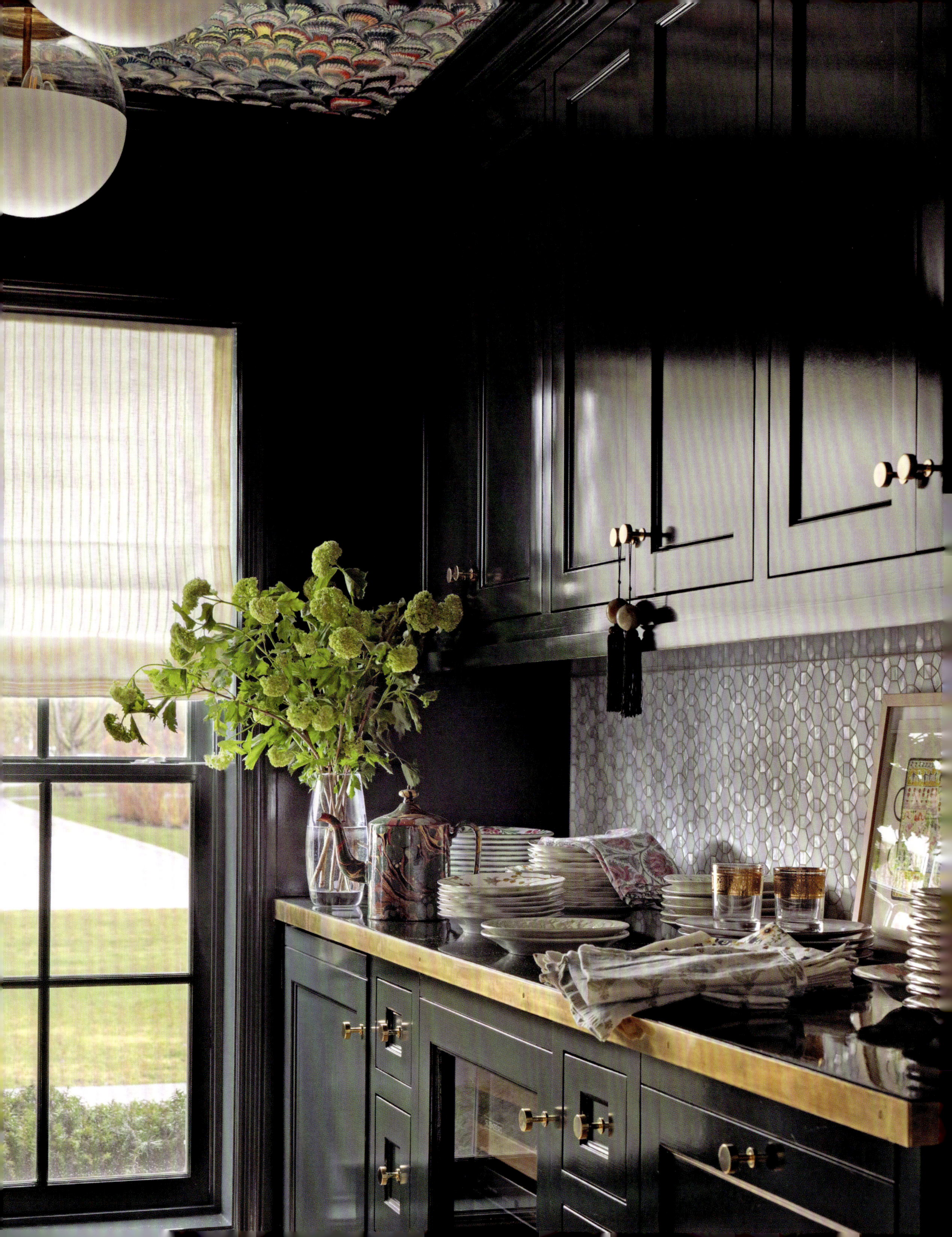

My husband felt strongly about keeping the kitchen white, so as a compromise, we painted the butler's pantry Benjamin Moore's Essex Green, one of my favorite colors (and the paint on the shutters in my childhood home). The backsplash is quartzite.

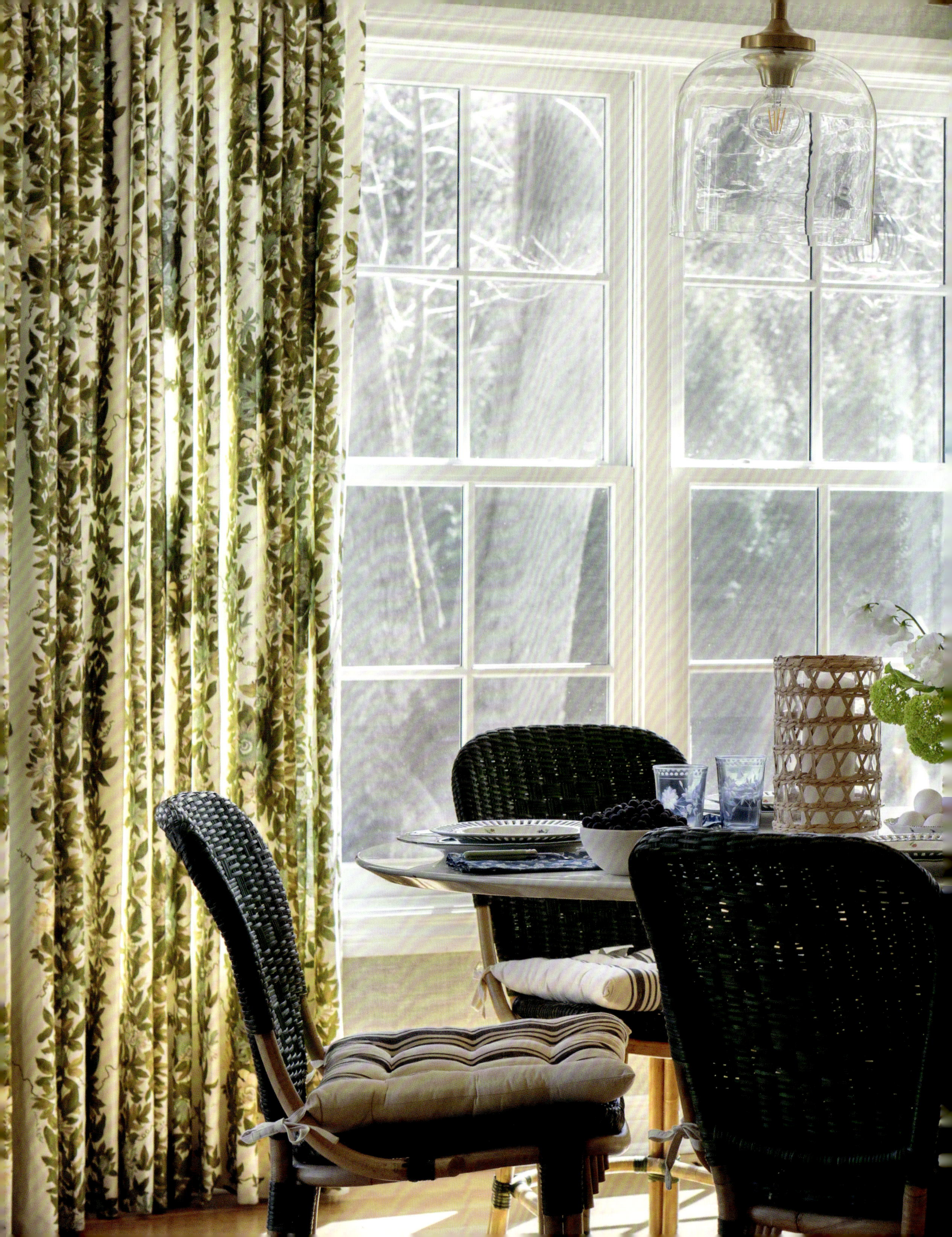

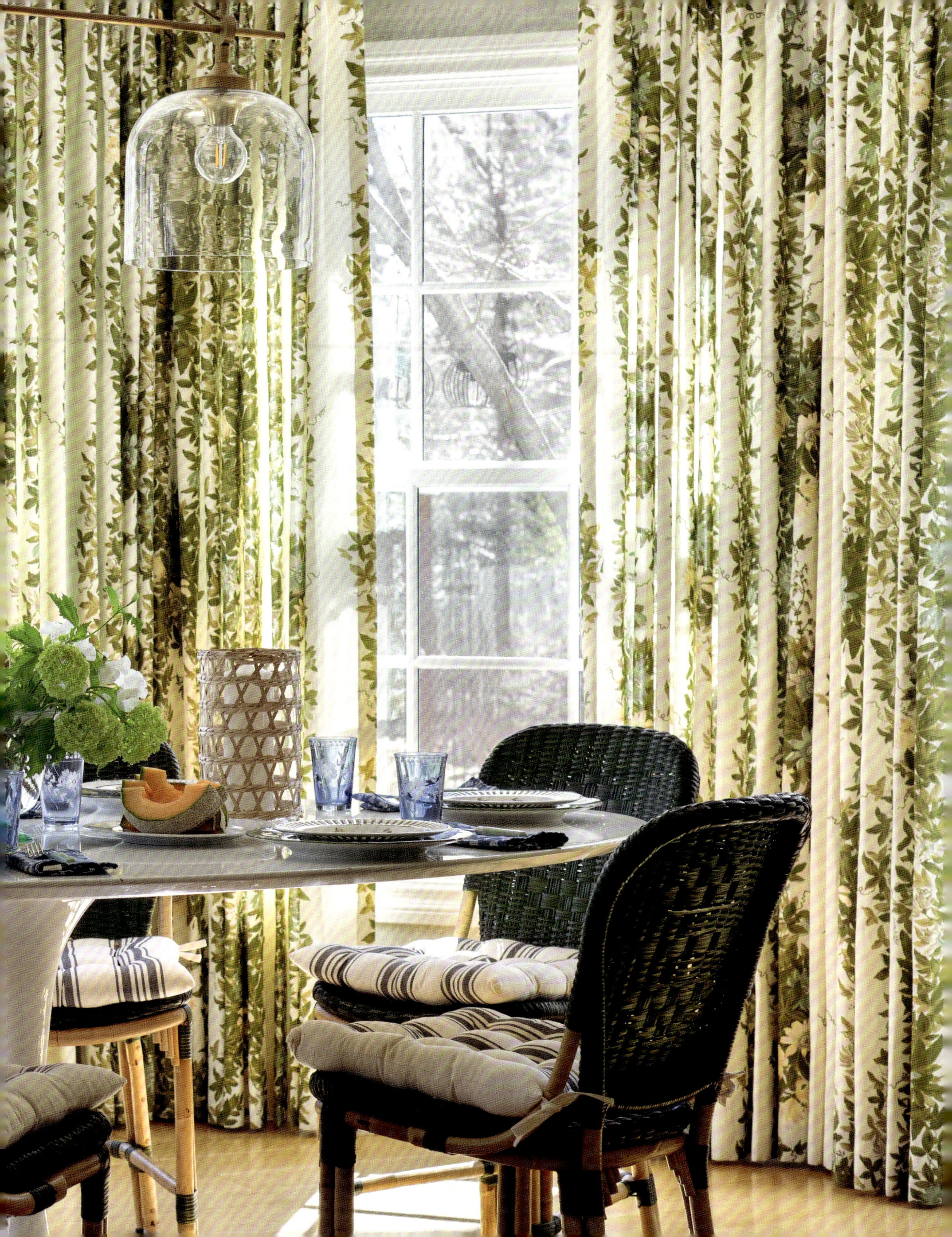

Above left: My grandfather collected *Harper's Weekly*, so I took some pages out of his old issues and framed them for my husband's office.

Opposite: This antique Biedermeier chest was the very first thing I purchased for the house. I bought it at auction without knowing the exact spot for it, but it works perfectly here.

Overleaf: Anyone who knows me knows I love my bed, so this space was important to get right. I wanted to create the feeling of sleeping in a garden.

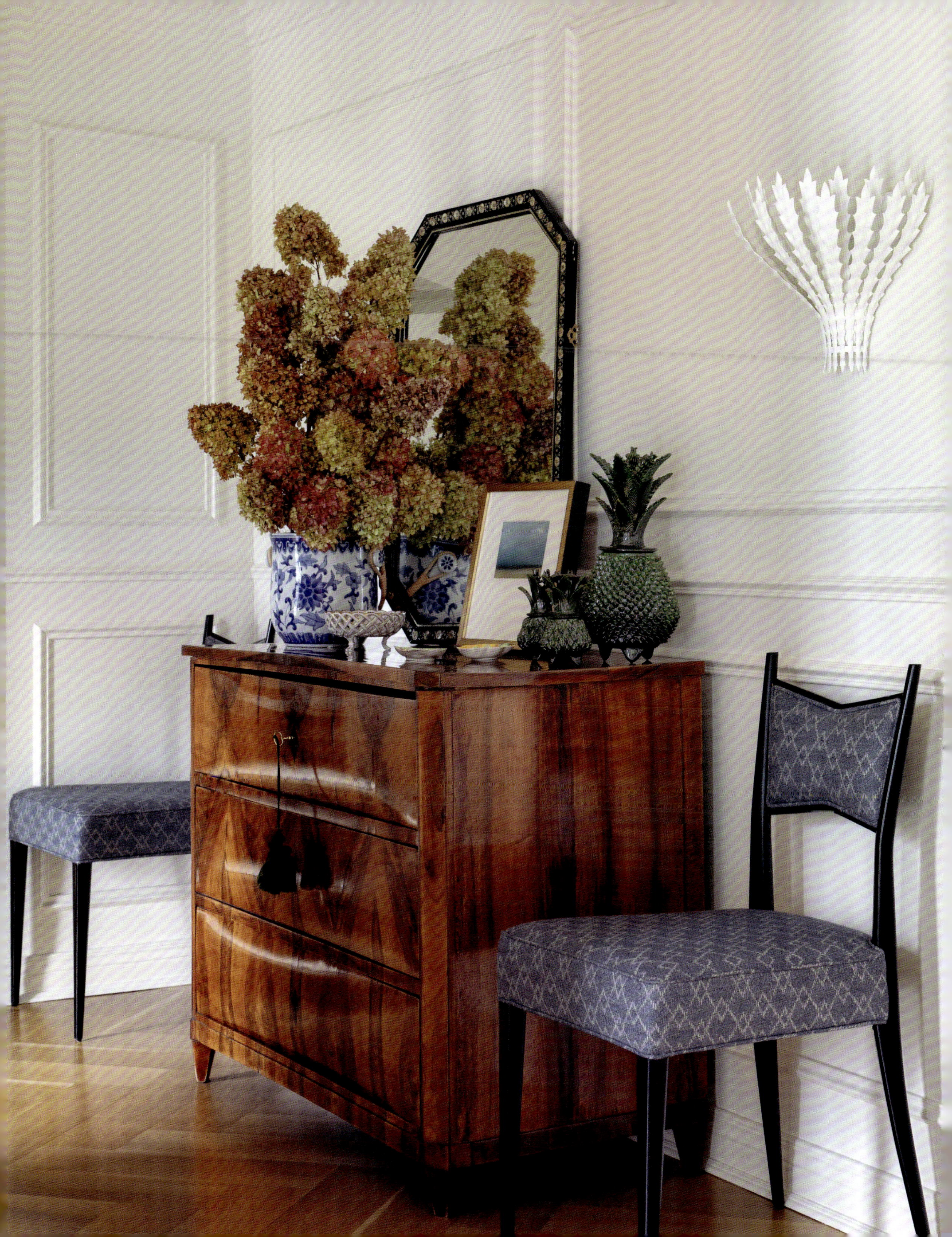

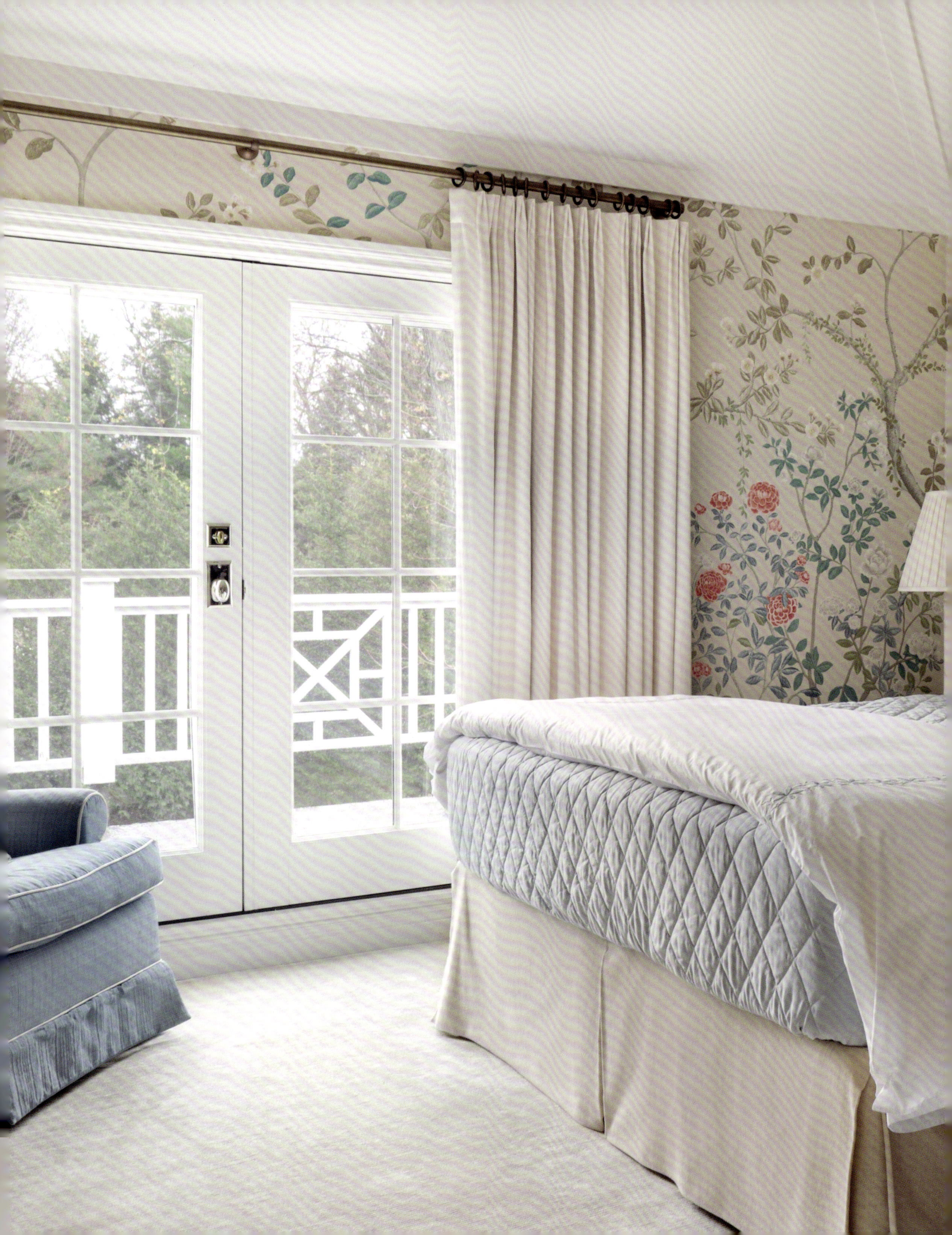

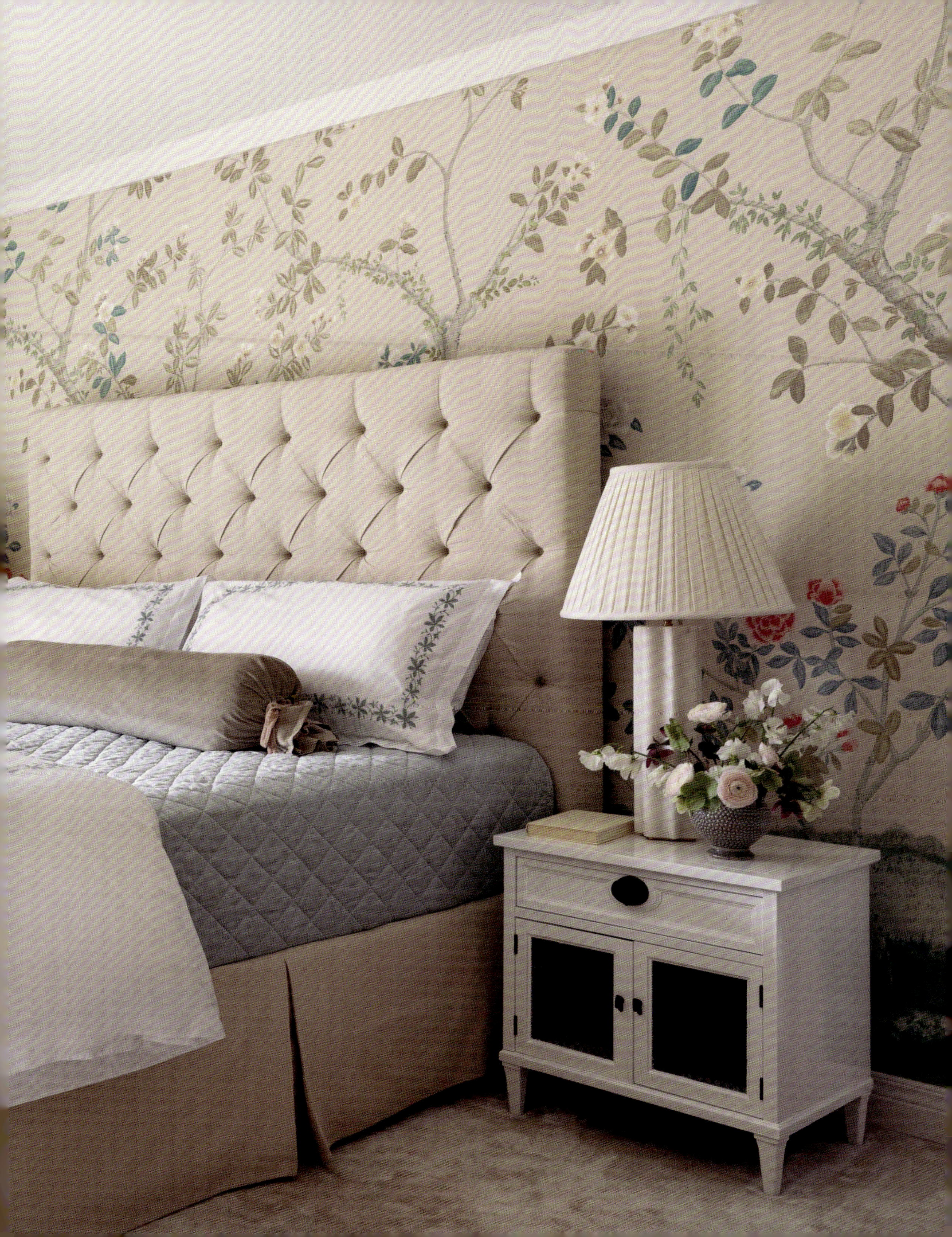

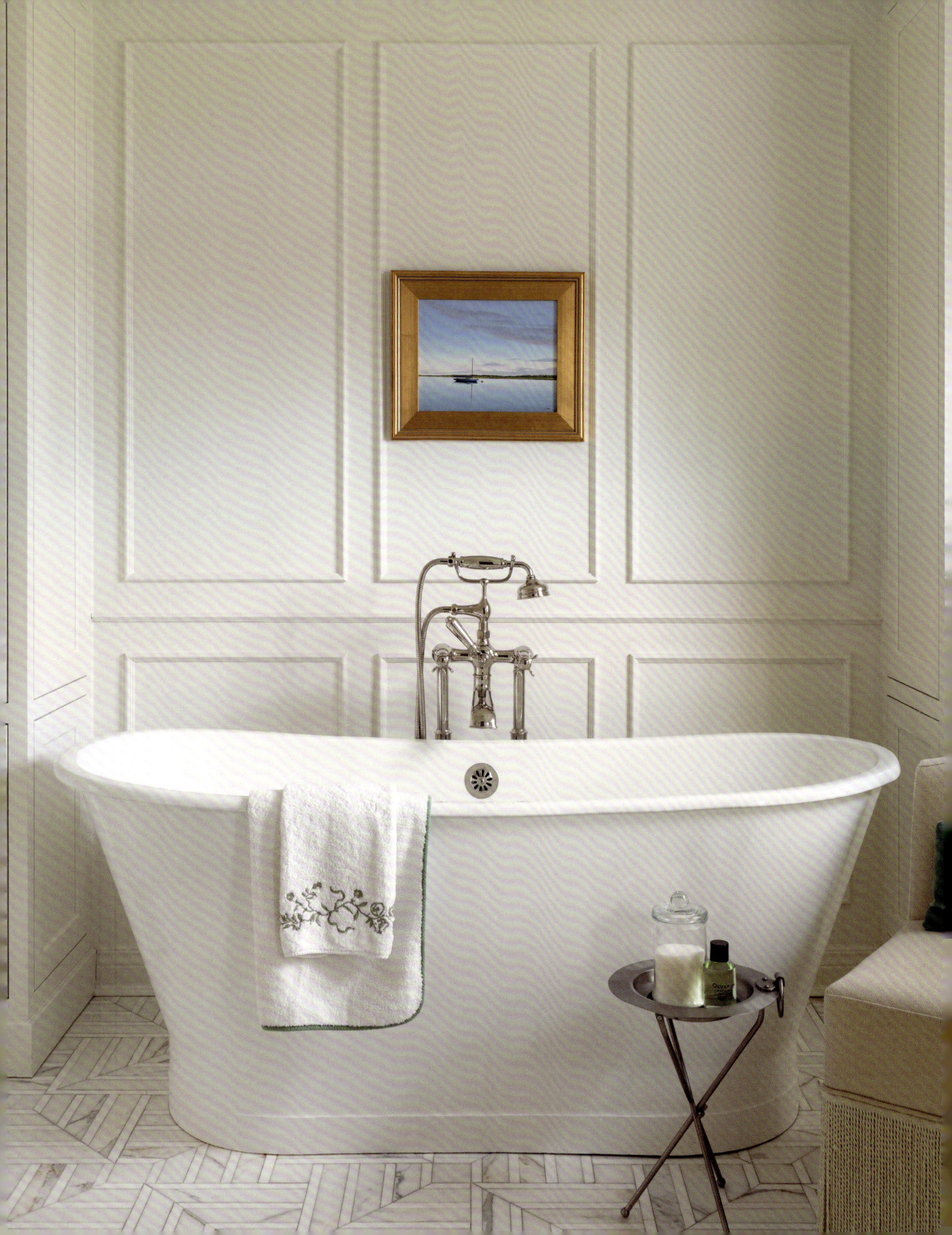

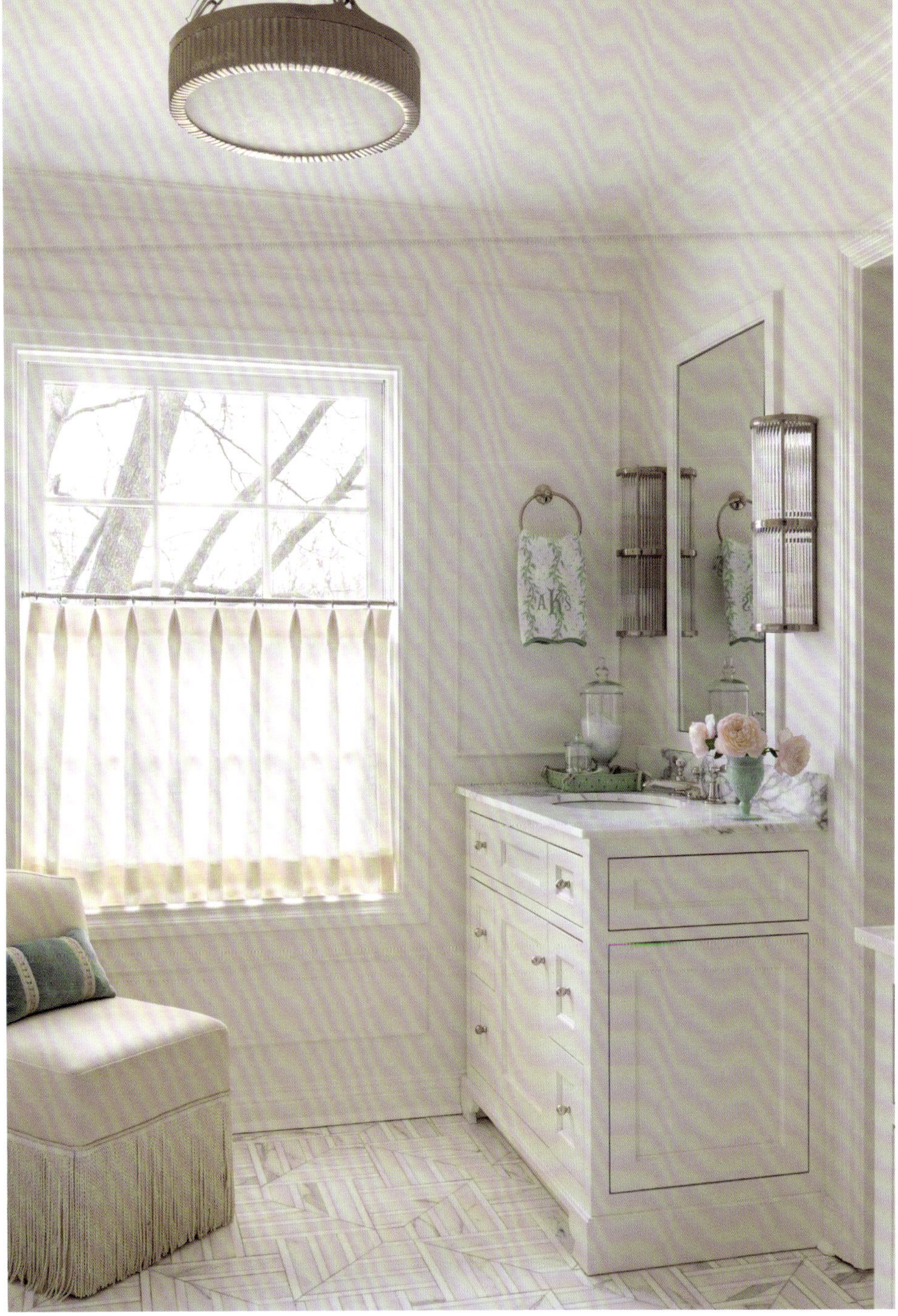

My daughter moved into this room when she was eight and had a lot of opinions. I love that she chose this wallpaper, Hummingbirds by Cole & Son, which is in my grandmother's home, too.

Overleaf: I wanted my youngest son's room to feel sophisticated but still like it was his. Adding elements related to his favorite things—animals, fishing, and the outdoors—created the right balance.

Page 250: My husband and sons are very into fly fishing, so, for my eldest son's room, I designed this rainbow trout wallpaper with artist and textile designer Caitlin McGauley.

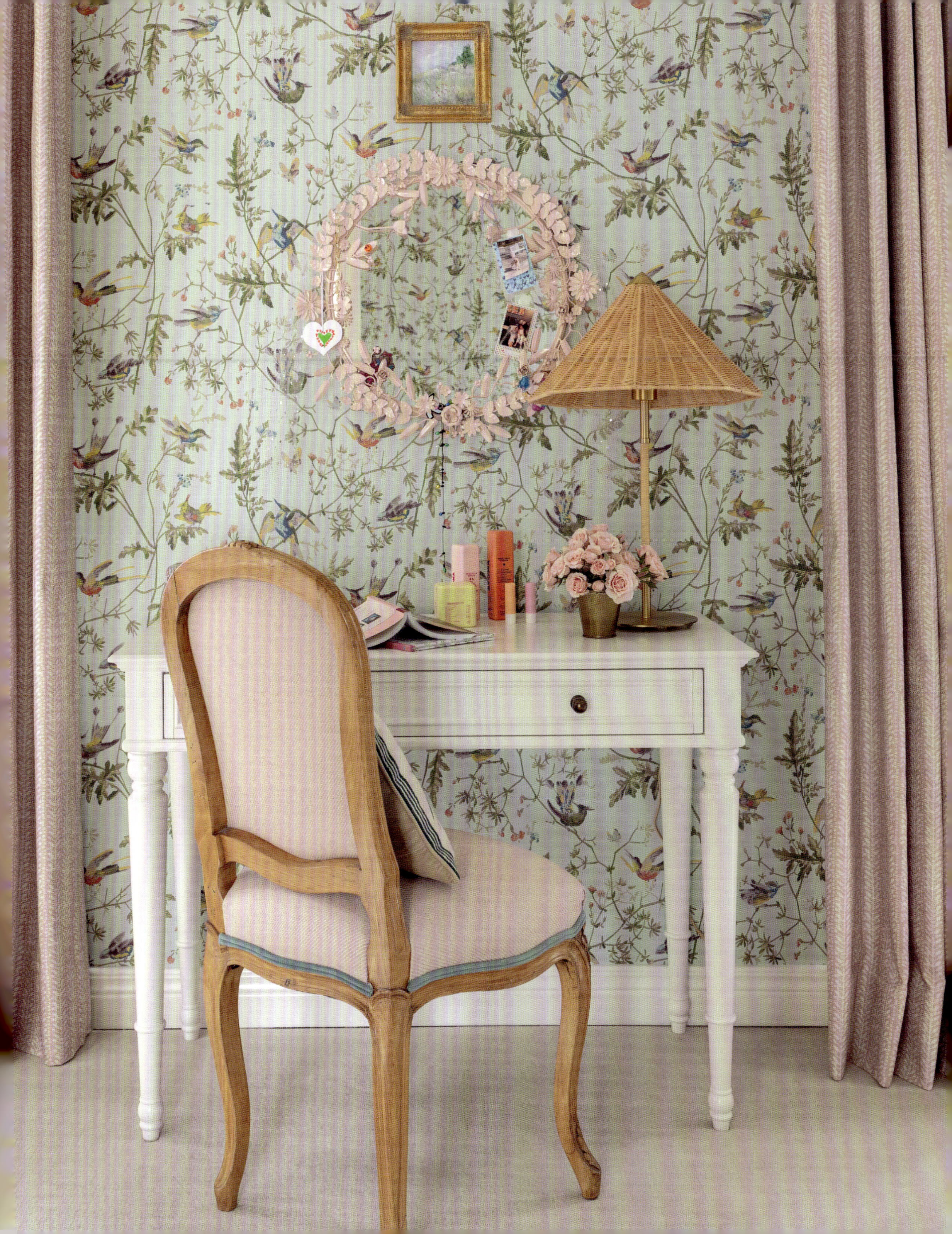

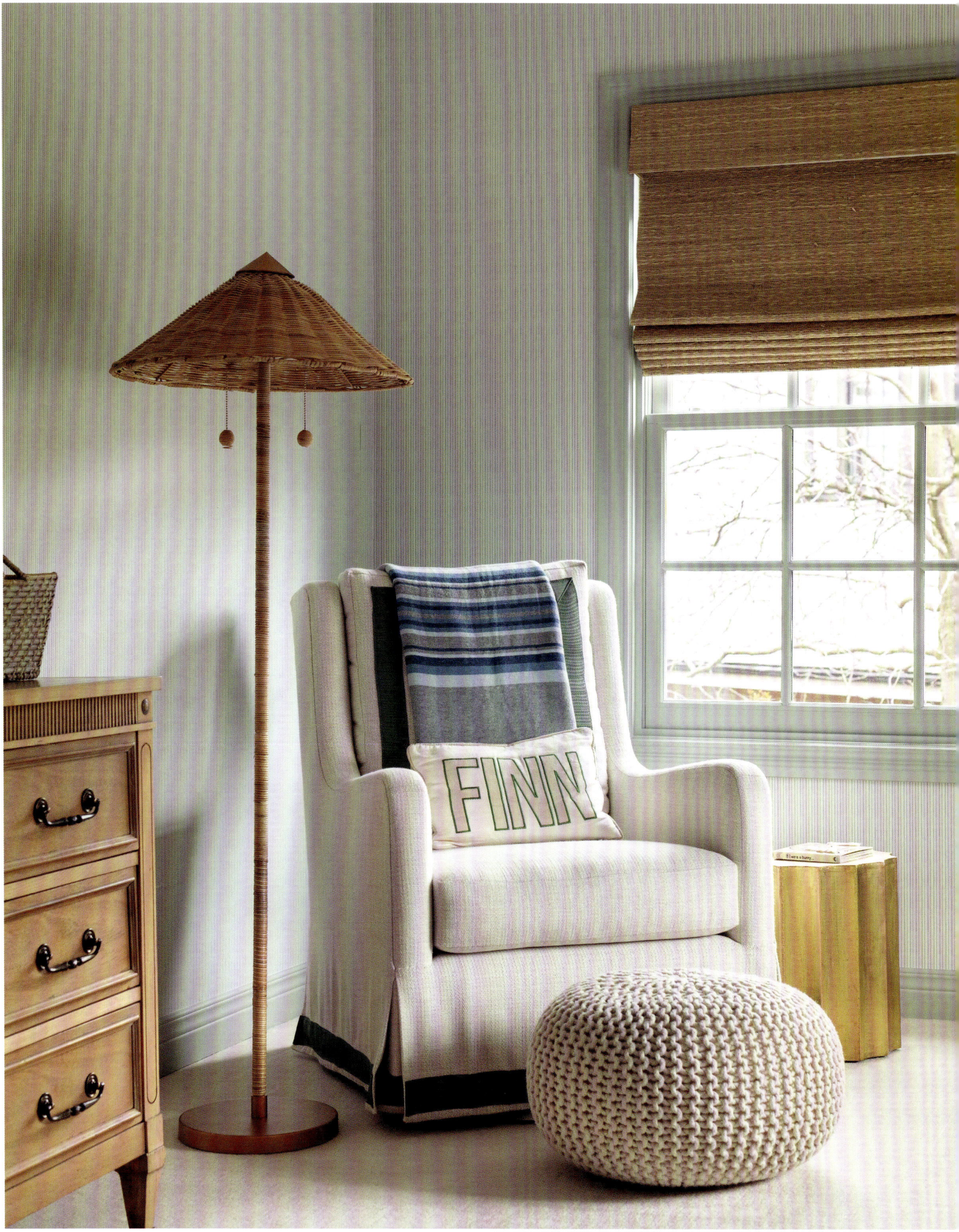
FINN

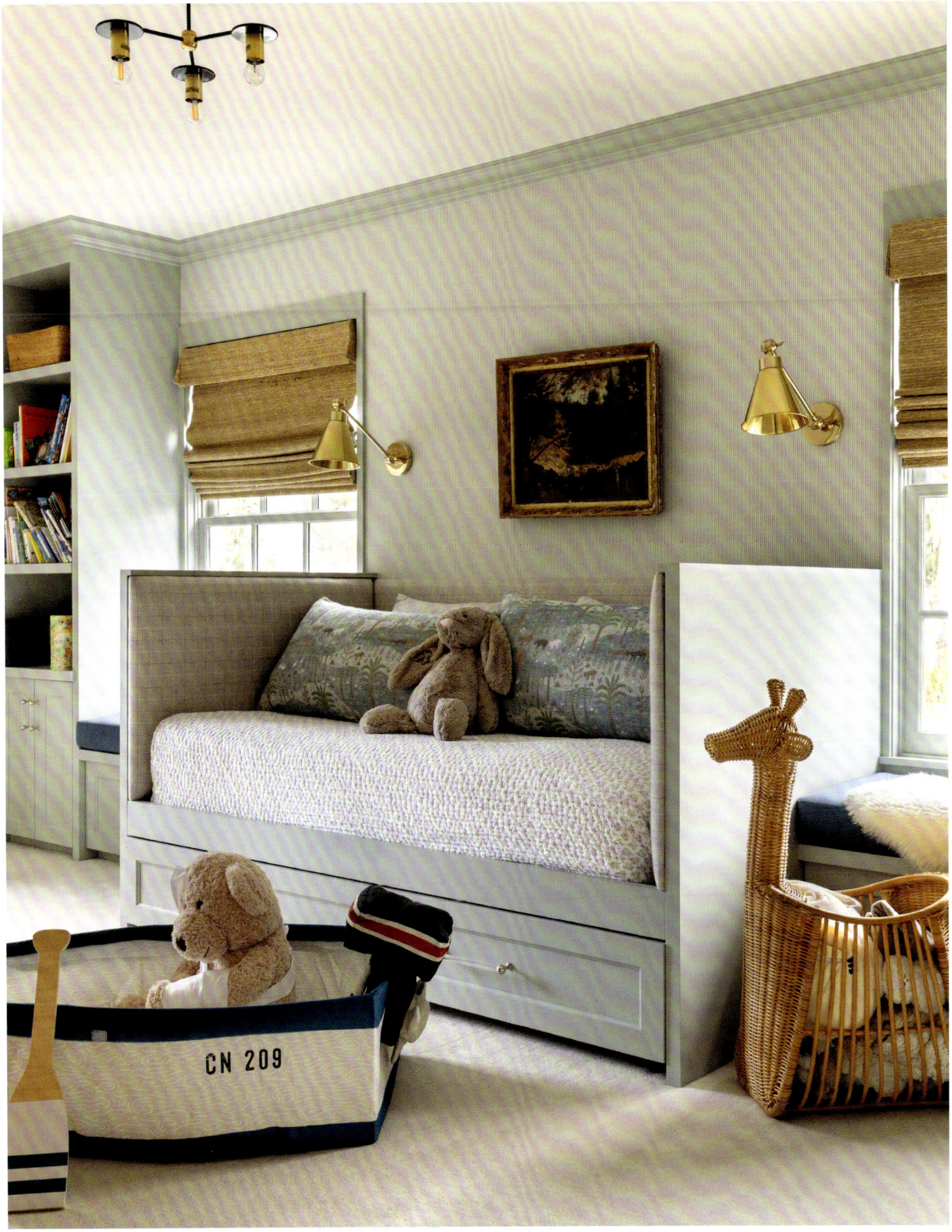
CN 209

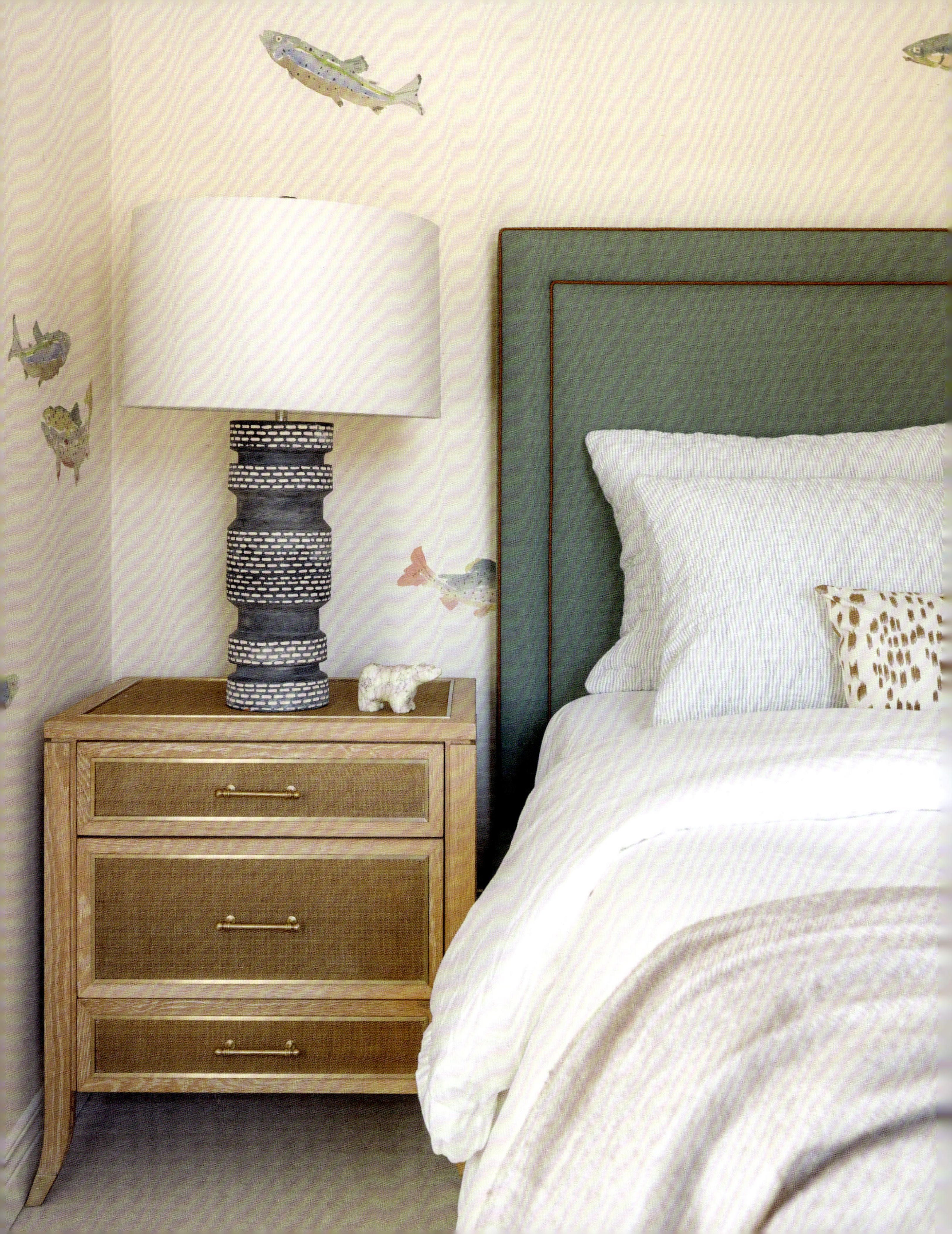

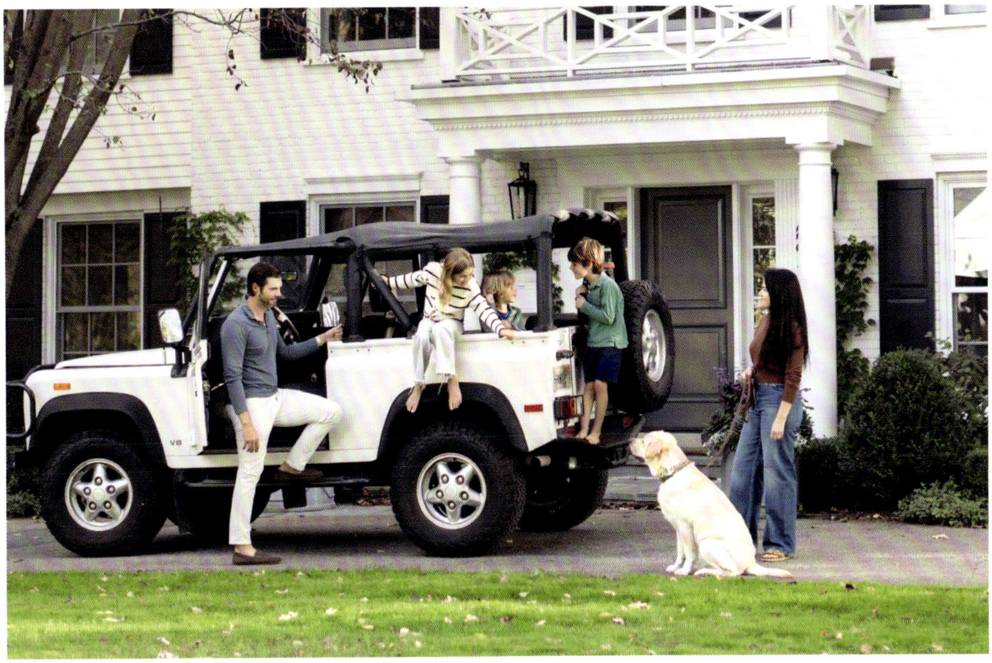

ACKNOWLEDGMENTS

To my clients: You made this possible. You made so many of my dreams come true. Being invited into your homes has been the greatest gift of my life, and I am forever grateful for your trust in me.

Thank you to the incredible team of women I work with: Aimée Mazzenga and Cate Ragan, for bringing my work to life with your photos and teaching me so much, but also just being so much fun to spend time with. Hadley Keller for telling my story with a voice that felt authentic to who I am. Elizabeth Blitzer and Sabrina Hames for being my cheerleaders and encouraging me to get out and talk to the right people to make this dream of a book into a reality. Leigh Eisenman, my agent, and Jenny Florence, my editor, for believing in my book concept and my work. Lucy Sykes-Thompson for designing a beautiful book world for my work to live in.

To the amazing ladies who make up AKD: I am forever indebted to you for your hard work and dedication on these homes, and everything else you worked on alongside me. Not to mention for your patience with me as your leader, no easy feat.

To the fellow designers who allowed me to pick their brains and learn about this process: I am forever in awe of the support within this industry. The openness to share wisdom is something I have never taken for granted.

And now, maybe most importantly, to my family: First, my Spence. You are the calm to my anxiety, the steady to my chaos, the rational to my crazy. I will never not be grateful that you are mine. My kids for making sure I always know what matters. My sisters for being the best friends you could ever, ever ask for. My parents, for supporting me and always showing me unconditional love. To my grandmother for teaching me about style from day one.

None of this work happens without these people, and so, so many more. The wonderful woman who takes care of my children so that I can design homes without the guilt of leaving them. The friends who are sounding boards. The people I've met through Instagram that I now count as true friends. All of you have played a part in making this book to a reality. So, thank you. Thank you. Thank you.

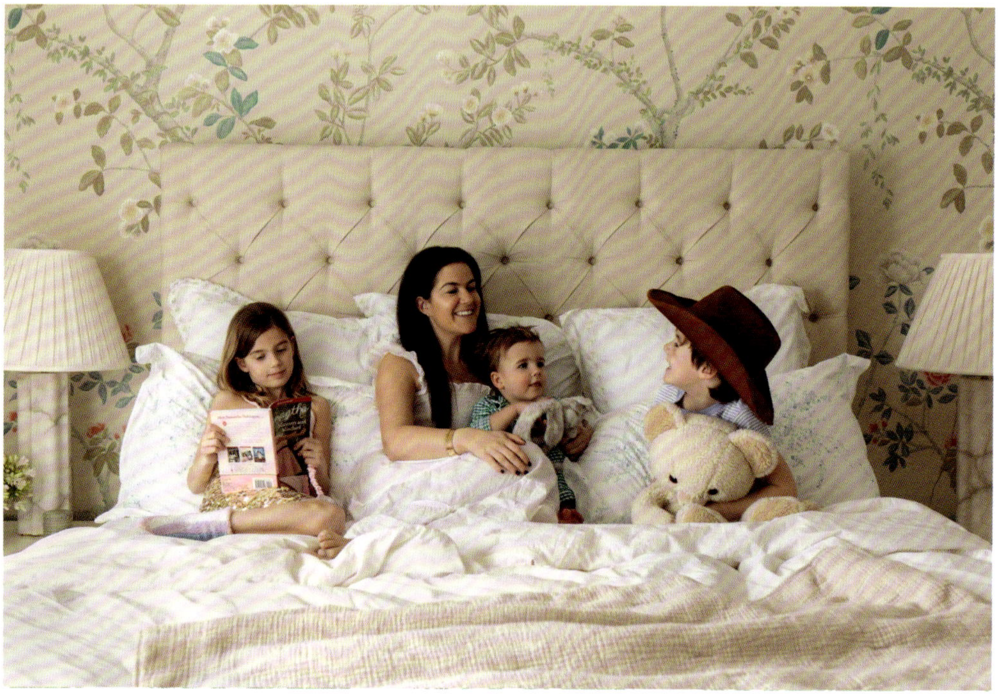

ABOUT THE AUTHOR

Alex grew up in the suburbs of Chicago, where she lives now with her husband and three kids.

In 2009, after she began what she believed at the time to be her dream career in advertising, she started a lifestyle blog and quickly realized that design was her true calling. Alex pivoted to study interior design and went on to open her firm, Alexandra Kaehler Design, in 2011.

Copyright © 2025 Alexandra Kaehler and the Monacelli Press

All photos © Aimée Mazzenga

Calligraphy courtesy of Julia DeRose, kindlydeliverto.com

Spine and back cover: Lee Jofa Captiva Ticking
Endpapers: Lee Jofa Taplow Print
Half title and interior: Kravet Wollerton Leaf
All patterns courtesy of Kravet, kravet.com

All rights reserved. No part of this book may be reproduced, stored in a retrieval system, or transmitted in any form, by any means, including mechanical, electric, photocopying, recording or otherwise, without the prior written permission of the publisher.

Library of Congress Control Number: 2025934601

ISBN 9781580937023

Design by Studio Polka

Printed in China

Monacelli
A Phaidon Company
111 Broadway
New York, New York 10006

Phaidon SARL
55, rue Traversière
75012 Paris

Phaidon.com